PEOPLE OF THE RAINBOW

PEOPLE OF THE

Rainbow

A NOMADIC UTOPIA

Michael I. Niman

The University of Tennessee Press / Knoxville

Frontispiece: Rainbow Gathering, Colorado, 1992. Photo by Gabe Kirchheimer.

This book was printed on recycled, acid-free paper.

Library of Congress Cataloging-in-Publication Data

Niman, Michael I.
People of the rainbow : a nomadic utopia / Michael I. Niman. — 1st ed.
p.   cm.
Includes bibliographical references and index.
ISBN 0-87049-988-2 (cl.: alk. paper). — ISBN 0-87049-989-0 (pbk.: alk. paper)
1. Rainbow Family of Living Light. 2. Utopias—History—20th century.
3. Nonviolence—History—20th century. 4. Social history—1970–   I. Title.
HX806.N555 1997
321'.07—dc21   97-4626

To the memory of Evelyn Niman

Contents

Preface   xi

Acknowledgments   xiii

1. Sunflower's Day: July 3   1

2. Roots, Rock, Rainbow   31

3. "The Way We Make Decisions Is More Important Than the Decisions We Make": The Rainbow Family Council   38

4. The Nuts and Bolts of Making a Rainbow: Rainbow Infrastructure   60

5. People of the Rainbow   99

6. Violence and Peace   114

7. Fakelore   131

8. The Mediated Rainbow: The American Media Look at the Rainbow Family   148

9. Leave Only Smiles: Land Stewardship and Community Relations   170

10. The Rainbow and the U.S. Government   184

Conclusion: Endless Summer   202

Appendixes   217

Notes   229

Glossary   239

References   249

Index   267

Illustrations

Following Page 98

Rainbows Form a Bucket Brigade to Fight a Forest Fire Adjacent to the 1994 Gathering Site in Wyoming

Taco Mike's Oven, 1986 Gathering, Pennsylvania

Baking Bread at the 1989 Northeast Regional Gathering, Vermont

A 3 A.M. Chess Game at "Everybody's Kitchen," 1994 Gathering, Wyoming

One of Many Drum Circles at the 1992 Gathering, Colorado

Serving Lunch at Kids' Village, 1990 Gathering, Minnesota

Cable Car Ride at Moondancer's Meadow, 1986 Gathering, Pennsylvania

New York City Rainbow Family Winter Picnic, Coney Island, 1991

Wedding Ceremony, 1992 Gathering, Colorado

Center for Alternative Living Medicine Apothecary, 1994 Gathering, Wyoming

Welcome Center/Rumor Control, 1992 Gathering, Colorado

Preparing Lunch, 1995 Gathering, New Mexico

Dave (from "Sunflower's Day") Preparing Breakfast at Buffalo Camp, 1990 Gathering, Minnesota

People Milling About, 1990 Gathering, Minnesota

Carrying a Piano into the 1987 Gathering, North Carolina

Rainbows Form a Human Conveyor Belt to Bring Hundreds of Watermelons into the 1991 Gathering, Vermont

Barter Lane, 1991 Gathering, Vermont

Dish-washing Station, 1991 Gathering, Vermont

Mudpeople on the Move, 1990 Northeast Regional Gathering, New York

Chili at Taco Mike's Kitchen, 1990 Gathering, Minnesota

Bicycle Bus, Bus Village, 1990 Gathering, Minnesota

Learning to Drum, 1990 Gathering, Minnesota

United States National Forest Service File Photo, 1978 Gathering, Washington State

Preface

The Rainbow Family of Living Light, also known as the Rainbow Nation and the Rainbow Family, is committed to principles of nonviolence and nonhierarchical egalitarianism. They have been holding large noncommercial Gatherings in remote forests since 1972 to pray for world peace and to demonstrate the viability of a cooperative utopian community living in harmony with the Earth. They govern themselves by a Council whose membership is open to all interested people. All decisions are by consensus. Money is not needed, as all necessities are free at Gatherings. Everyone is welcome.

This book describes different aspects of Rainbow Family life such as how the Rainbow Family Council functions; how the physical infrastructure of the Gatherings work; how members attempt to confront problems nonviolently; who the Rainbow people are; what motivates them to work in a society without money; how they relate to other communities; and how they care for the land on which they gather. It also looks at internal contradictions within the Family and places them within a historical context of North American utopian experiments.

It examines how the mainstream world, "Babylon" to the Rainbows, relates to the Family; how the media see and report the Gatherings and how the U.S. government treats them. It also examines the Family's relationship with Native Americans, from whom they've appropriated much of their culture and spiritual beliefs.

The research methodology involves participant observation, open-ended interviews, content analysis of media reports, and scrutiny of government documents.

The end result is a comprehensive ethnography. Rainbow voices, in the form of interviews and writing excerpts, are present throughout the text.

As an author, I am sympathetic to the Rainbow Family, their goals, and the vision they represent. I am also inspired by their ability to not only survive, but to grow and bring their vision to an ever-widening circle. The Rainbows are torch-bearers for an ideology of hope, one that is all too rare in this age of xenophobia, nationalism, and ethnic strife. I'd like to see the Family persevere; that is my bias. As a scholar, however, it is also my duty to report not only on the successes of the Family, but to examine their faults, shortcomings, and failures as well.

The first chapter, Sunflower's Day, is a piece of ethnographic fiction designed to provide a slice of Rainbow life. It follows Sunflower, an amalgam character, as he navigates through a day at an annual North American Rainbow Gathering. His experiences are real, based both on my field notes and on stories Rainbows have shared with me. The topography of Sunflower's Gathering is also real; it's a combination of the 1990 National Gathering, which took place in Minnesota, spiced with traces of the 1986 National, which took place in Pennsylvania. The goal of Sunflower's Day is to provide an initial description of life at a Rainbow Gathering and, through narration, to bring life to its sights, sounds, and smells.

Acknowledgments

I would like to offer a special note of appreciation to Laura J. McClusky for the unwavering support and inspiration, both intellectually and emotionally, which she provided during the six-year gestation of this book and which she continues to provide today. I would also like to thank Dr. Robert Knox Dentan for the guidance, support, and editorial suggestions that he provided since the inception of this project.

A very special thanks goes to my parents, Hank and Evelyn Niman, for teaching me to respect and appreciate the earth's diverse cultures, for believing in me and giving me emotional support during my many funky projects, and for volunteering for the laborious task of transcribing interviews for this book. Though my mother tragically and unexpectedly died as this book went to press, she lives on both in its pages, and in the memories and deeds of the many people whose lives she touched.

My appreciation goes out to the many Rainbows without whose assistance and cooperation this project would never have gotten off the ground. Foremost among them is Joseph P. C. Wetmore, who spent countless hours reading drafts and sharing his comments and opinions. Also Garrick Beck, who for years has been a Rainbow ambassador without assuming a leadership role; Dianne, and the Ithaca crew; Ilah Davis and the New York squatters crew; NERF; Collector, TC, Felipe and Taco Mike, for showing me how many hours a day a person can work; the D.C. Legaliaison crew; White Raven; Grey Bear; Kaloma Becker; the CALM crew and all those folks who provided interviews, questions, answers, tea, coffee, and food.

I owe a special thanks to the people who made up Buffalo Camp at the 1990 and 1991 Gatherings, especially the tireless cook, Dave Hetherly, José Rodriguez, and Field Horne. A note of appreciation goes to Donna Smith and Michael Schwartz of Discount Natural Foods in Dewitt, New York, who filled my truck with food, supplied the Buffalo Camp kitchen, and fed me for the year I wrote this book. Thanks also to New York City journalist and author Bill Weinberg and to Lisa Rentschler Lavelle, formerly of the Alternative News Collective, for ideas, feedback, and inspiration. Thanks also to Gabe Kirchheimer and Joe Levy for allowing the use of their photographs in this book.

I would also like to offer my appreciation to Vicki and Shawn Perich, Holly Nelson and the friendly open-minded people of Cook County Minnesota, who made me feel welcome in their communities.

I would like to thank Dr. Elwin Powell, who has encouraged me in my work for twenty years, as well as Dr. Charles Keil, Dr. Lawrence Chisolm, Dr. Michael Frisch, and Dr. John Mohawk, who helped guide me through my doctoral studies.

Chapter 8, as well as some of the facts enhancing other sections of this book, would not have been possible had it not been for the authors and supporters of the Freedom of Information Act, an invaluable resource for scholars and journalists.

A special thanks also goes out to supermarket managers across the country who don't lock their dumpsters!

1

Sunflower's Day: July 3

At around 10 A.M. Sunflower looks out of his tent and examines the cold morning mist. He's on Rainbow time. He doesn't really know it's ten. He just knows it's still morning and it feels like time to get up.

He knew it wasn't time to wake up a few hours ago when the mechanical thunder of a police chopper ripped through the forest air. That was something he learned to live with and sleep through. Such rude interruptions are routine at Gatherings. It's just America knocking at the door.

Sunflower, sitting up in his tent, surveys his immediate environment; a dry tent. The green walls make his skin look somewhat yellowish, but a dry tent is still a real luxury, especially since a much-needed rain filled the night air, stopping at sunrise. Life doesn't get much better than a dry tent on a wet morning.

In the distance he could hear drumming, the heartbeat of the Gathering. Drummers had been playing around the clock now for seven days, rain or shine, since June 27. The voice of the drums is reassuring—it means there's family out there. Like the heartbeat of a lover, the drums comfort him each night, lulling him to sleep. Each morning they call him to rise and join the day's activities.

Still, Sunflower longs for the nightly howling of wolves. He hasn't heard them now for over a week. He even misses the regular destructive visits from the bear who rudely demands valuable items—things that a Rainbow anticipating a Gathering can't frivolously feed to wildlife; staples like cooking oil and cigarettes. The absence of the bears and wolves, however, signals the beginning of the Gathering; wilderness is being transformed into city. Still yearning for the lost wilderness,

Sunflower welcomes the city; especially this city, for he knows that by month's end it will revert once again to wilderness.

Sunflower has been at the Rainbow Gathering for three weeks now, having been among the first hundred people on the site. He dug shitters, built kitchens, blazed trails, and welcomed family to the Gathering. It's a labor of love to which he devoted about sixteen hours a day. Now, at the peak of the Gathering, with over ten thousand people around him, Sunflower relaxes, taking it all in, recharging his energies for next week's cleanup. This year he's doing the full ride from setup to cleanup.

From his tent he could hear a crackling fire and hushed voices coming from the "kitchen" two hundred feet away. An occasional loud pop signals that the fire is hot, luring campers out of their warm sleeping bags into the damp morning air. The metallic clanging sounds signal mush, which of course is always preceded and followed by "mud," Rainbow coffee.

But where the hell are his damn shoes? Sunflower took them off they day before when it was hot and he wanted to feel the cool trail under his toes. When the night chill set in later, he couldn't find them. They were spaced out in yesterday's bliss. Today he'd find them. As he crawls out of his tent and stands up, cold squishy mud oozes between his toes. It feels good, but he still wants his shoes. Sunflower surveys Buffalo Camp's twenty-odd tents as he slips his grimy feet into his pants. He spies an orange tent that wasn't there yesterday. Who could it be? An old friend? A friend he hadn't yet met? Space aliens? Walking by, he hears giggles emerge from the orange dome. Definitely space aliens. He wonders about the size of their feet. Do they have extra shoes? Space aliens in Buffalo Camp. Why not?

Hippies and punks surround the breakfast fire. Grey Bear and Plover, dudded out in tie-dyes and sweaters, sit fashioning jewelry from colorful little pellets. Asha and Tony, dressed in black, are engrossed in leatherwork. Dave, his long scraggly blond-gray hair in his face, sits by the fire cooking up a breakfast slop, an oatmealish concoction mixed with leftover rice. Catfoot, a tattered Bugler smoke hanging from his lips, kneels to help him. Sunflower inhales deeply as the damp forest air mingles with smoke, sweat, coffee, and patchouli.

Dave, looking up at Sunflower, exposes his brownish teeth with a smile and motions to a charred coffeepot, "Mud's up." Sunflower adds a splash of cold water, sinking the grounds before unclipping his cup from his belt and filling it.

"Coffee's styling today. Gourmet yuppie coffee." Dave, looking toward the orange tent, explains, "Someone dropped off a big bag of it. Was right next to me here when I woke up this morning. I think it was them." Space aliens came through. Hazelnut at that.

"Zuzus too," Dave mumbles, dishing out a bowl of mush while sprinkling newly found chocolate chips on it. Sunflower eats oatmeal, farina, and other members of the mush family only at Gatherings. Back in Babylon he writes the stuff off as wheat paste, fit only for hanging wallpaper and political posters. Definitely not good eating. At Gatherings, however, the stuff acquires a special taste, approaching delectable. Especially when Dave makes it. Today Dave's mush contains almonds, peanuts, dried apricots, raisins, maple syrup, nutmeg flakes, and ground cinnamon.

Across the fire, hippies are teaching beadwork to punks. The punks, in turn, are giving pointers on leatherwork. Dave, a self-proclaimed Road Dog, starts telling dumpster stories to Paul, a slender schoolteacher from Cleveland, and Tom, a graying house painter from Syracuse, New York. Leila, a Greenpeace canvasser from Georgia, clamors out of the muddy lake. Screaming, she darts over to the fire, water dripping from her goosebumped skin, sizzling as it hits the hot rocks. Collector, the "Donut Man," arrives whistling down the trail carrying a bag of hot garlic and jalapeño doughnuts. Buffalo Camp is waking up.

Dave pours the last drops of mud into Collector's cup. Behind the fallen tree bench are five empty five-gallon plastic water jugs. Plover grabs one and heads down the trail. Asha follows with another. This is a relief for Sunflower, who hauled two full five-gallon containers last night for more than a mile to the Toad Abode tea kitchen. Water's heavy—especially first thing in the morning.

Collector guzzles his coffee. He needs it. He served over twenty-five hundred doughnuts last night. Using a vintage balloon tire bicycle donated by an enthusiastic doughnut patron, ace doughnut delivery envoys dispersed the little garlic and jalapeño sugarcakes to more than thirty kitchens. "They're eating my doughnuts in Bus Village. That's five miles away, and the gravel pit [overflow parking area] eight and a half miles away. They're still warm when they get there," Collector boasts.

"I'll make a few doughnut runs if last night's rain didn't trash the trails too bad," Plover volunteers.

Sunflower also fancied the idea of a bike ride through the woods, but whenever he passed Collector's kitchen, the bike was always out. Collector usually sang out for a runner whenever a bag of doughnuts was ready. There're always volunteers. Why not? What better way to spend a night than giving doughnuts away and collecting thank-you hugs?

Collector's camp is the last on the trail, a five-minute walk past the Taco Hilton. This wasn't an accident. Tacos and doughnuts are as popular at Rainbow as they are in Babylon. The problem is that since everything at Rainbow is free, the price of a taco or bag of doughnuts is the same as for mush or dumpster bread. To ease demand on these two kitchens, Rainbows added the specter of distance to the economic equation. In the case of the Taco Hilton, distance alone did not work to stabilize demand at a manageable level. Therefore the time variable needed tweaking. The Taco Hilton serves their ersatz Mexican delights only at Rainbow Midnight. In practice, this translates into a serene journey through the shadowy dark on a delectable pilgrimage, culminating in a small feast for about 250 Taco Mongers. Dessert is a short hike up the trail.

Collector came to Buffalo Camp this morning after an encounter with a bear. "There are three bears at this Gathering," Collector surmises. "I heard they live with this old hermit in his cabin near here. They just need a little discipline." At the other end of the spectrum of bear theories stood a choral report from a group of teenage squatters from New York: "We seen it, it was a motherfuckin' Grizzly! It was gonna kill us, it's like starving. Ate our cigarettes, the motherfucker!"

Sunflower sips his mud as Collector calmly explains, "I looked out a my tent and saw this li'l bear snatch a backpack out from under the head of this sleeping hippie. I figured this bear went too far, overstepped his boundaries. Guests of the doughnut kitchen deserve more respect than to be rudely awakened by a snorting grunting foul-smelling beast." Collector, in animated fashion, explains how he followed in hot pursuit as the bear tried to drag the pack off into the woods. "The bear stopped and turned around. He reared up and did his ferocious bear act." Collector mimics the bear. "It was cute but not convincing." Collector made a point to remind everyone that he was a sporadic resident of Alaskan grizzly turf. "I kept charging at him. He dropped on his back, paws waving in the air, and started whimpering. I told him not to pull any more shit in the doughnut kitchen."

Had this been a Boy Scout jamboree, Sunflower would immediately dismiss the tale. But this is Rainbow. Rainbows have a strange rapport with their animal neighbors, a rapport like none Sunflower has ever seen. Collector, for instance, has a guard weasel. It lives in a log two feet from his tent, a well-worn North Face brand dome peppered with confectioners' sugar and flour. Twice, the weasel chased away munched-out "hippies" with their fingers in the doughnut filling. Once, it allegedly ran off a bear. It never bothered Collector.

While Collector spins his tales, a new face wanders into camp joining everyone at the fire. Dave fixes him a cup of tea. The newcomer is about forty-five years old, although he looks much older. Sunflower introduces himself, and the two start to talk. The man's name is Paul. After two cups of tea, Sunflower learns that Paul is a former mercenary.

"It started in Vietnam. I was doin' a tour in 'Nam when I married a Laotian woman. A real sweet woman. Communists killed her. I had nothin' else to live for so I spent the next ten years killin' them communists." His steel-gray eyes begin to water. Sunflower notices for the first time that scars cover his face—a gash above his left eye, a deep crease running from the corner of his right eye to his nostrils, another splitting his upper lip in two. He continues, "Least people I thought was communists. Least at the time. I been all over the world. Was a Somocista. Sad time. I kinda knew something was wrong. I fought in Yemen, Rhodesia, Biafra, Namibia." He stares off into the woods, his tone becomes confessional, "I came back to the States, but it hurt too much so I drank. Was drunk for years. One day I wound up at the Rainbow Gathering. Don't know how. . . ." Sunflower listens as Paul goes on, "That's why I'm here now, brother," and with tears forming in his eyes, he goes on, "the killing had to stop. It had to stop." He sits for a moment, smiles, then adds, "I'm home now." Reaching over, he gives Sunflower a hug. Grey Bear, seeing there was hugging to get in on, walks over smiling and joins them.

Dishes start piling up. Sunflower and Paul walk over to the dish-washing station. Their conversation lightens. They talk about hiking trails, swimming holes, and dumpsters as they scrub breakfast dishes.

Buffalo Camp's dish-washing station consists of three five-gallon white food-grade plastic buckets. The retired pickle vessels were given to Sunflower by the folks at Sven and Ollie's Pizzeria while Sunflower was on a supply run in town a few weeks earlier. As Sunflower rinses the cookware, he remembers that the people at the pizzeria promised to visit on the fourth.

Paul scrapes residue from the dishes into the compost pit and then dips them into the first bucket, scrubbing them in a mixture of peppermint castile soap and water. He hands them to Sunflower, who rinses them off in a bucket of fresh water before dipping them in the third and final bucket, a mixture of water and bleach. The clean dishes go on a rack to air-dry, except of course for people's cups, which almost never leave their sides.

"There's always shitter diggin' needs t' get done," Paul bellows as he leaves. "See ya later, brothers," and with a nod, "sisters."

Sunflower gathers spent ashes from the side of the fire and shovels them into an old Nescafé can. The can itself, which mysteriously appeared three days earlier, bothered Sunflower. After studying the can for a moment, he makes a mental note to try to spread the word about the renewed Nestle's boycott. Was that still on? "A workshop on boycotts wouldn't be a bad idea," he announces to no one in particular as he fills the can.

The ashes are for the shitter, which requires a light dusting after each use. Sunflower takes care not to put any live embers in the ash can, lest he start another shitter fire. He did that once. Since he never heard of it happening to anybody else, he felt particularly inept and has been meticulous with shitter ash since.

The Buffalo Camp latrine represents state-of-the-art shitter technology, the product of over two decades of research and development. It consists of a foot-wide, three-and-a-half-foot-deep, five-foot-long slit trench covered by a trash-picked door. Toward one end of the door is a fourteen-by-fourteen-inch hole with a snug-fitting lid. Next to the hole, a pair of footprints were drawn as basic usage instructions. As the area beneath the hole filled in, people would move the door further down the trench, using dirt to seal the trench behind them.

Next to the shitter are two coffee cans. One usually contains toilet paper; the other, ash. Sunflower always checks these cans before dropping his pants. There's also a bucket of bleach water for hand washing and a waterproof bag for reading material, though nobody at Buffalo Camp did much reading at the shitter.

Sunflower always checked the shitter before leaving camp in the morning. The health of everyone who ate at Buffalo Camp depended on the sanitation of that shitter, or more specifically, on the absence of flies and the presence of bleach water. He also usually stomached a peek inside, since, as he often told people, "Fecal consistency is the best indicator of kitchen quality."

Sunflower walks down the shitter trail, reporting, "Shit's lookin' solid, lookin' good." A small chorus answers, "Love ya, Sunflower!" He laughs and pictures himself emerging from the men's room at a New York restaurant, loudly reporting on the general consistency of bowels to the feasting horde.

He shares this vision with Dave, who had asked why he was laughing. Dave smiles, telling Sunflower, "Don't knock them restaurants, there's some styling dumpsters behind 'em." Dave takes another sip of coffee and adds, "I quit my last restaurant job 'cause I thought it just wasn't right to be charging people for food."

Dave looks at the orange tent. There seems to be some movement inside, but the space aliens haven't emerged yet. "You think they got tobacco?" he asks no one in particular, then looking back at Sunflower, he queries, "No word on yer shoes, eh?"

With wet earth still squishing between his toes, Sunflower starts hiking the trail away from Buffalo Camp. While proceeding through a rain-soaked quagmire, he stops for a second, thinking about the Buffalo Camp punks, city kids with nothing but torn sneakers on their feet. He picks up a few downed branches and gathers a few rocks, placing them all in the muck. He then walks over his makeshift bridge, thinking to himself, "That should do." He continues on toward the main trail. He has to make it to Council; he has to announce the loss of his shoes.

When he reaches the main trail, an old snowmobile route, he encounters Plover and Asha sitting next to two full water jugs, talking veganism with Noah, an elderly man in an orange robe. Noah, as it turns out, is a fruitarian with a keen eye for a ripe dumpster. "I been 'ere two days now," he explains, handing Sunflower an apple. "I came 'ere in my Dodge Dart, filled with apples. They're all blems. They're from the dumpster behind an apple-waxing plant in Washington State." With two spare tires lashed to the roof, Noah took the load of cosmetically blemished and rejected apples on a seven-state odyssey culminating at the Gathering. Upon arriving, he turned the contents of the car over to main supply, keeping a few apples to hand out on the trail.

Sunflower examines the apple in his hand. Definitely an ugly apple; core off-center, dull coloration, bruised. It's the kind of apple people pass over at the supermarket in a silent vote for genetically engineered, chemically tainted, waxed, overpackaged corporate agribusiness specimens. He takes another look at the apple in his hand. It tastes great.

"Cut me a piece of apple, Sunflower," comes a raspy little voice. He turns around. It's his five-year-old buddy Tom, on his way to Buffalo Camp for a game of chess. Tom, born and raised on the road by Sunflower's friends, spent a good chunk of his Gathering learning to play chess. For the past three days he routinely made the three-quarter-mile trek through the woods to Buffalo Camp from his mother's tent in Kids' Village.

Despite his young age, Tom was comfortable hiking around on his own. If he got nervous or spooked, the next passerby would take him back to Kiddie Village. Everyone looks out for kids. The danger is not so much the steep trails. Like the world outside the Gathering, the danger is in the people. In recent years "child predators" had come to prey on free-ranging Rainbow kids. Countless Councils and dinner circles have discussed the problem. Discussing it is not a taboo at Rainbow. Children are encouraged to talk about what bothers them. Sunflower, like most other adults at the Gatherings, has learned to keep an eye out for the kids. The solution of collective responsibility is much better than the urban solution of child confinement. Sunflower watches Tom, apple chunk in hand, wander off. Sunflower suddenly is overcome with both joy and sorrow. Joy for all the li'l Rainbows, and sadness for all the kids who will never experience Rainbow's magic.

Tom didn't have any trouble following the Buffalo Camp trail. The first set of directions called for the hiker to follow a deer trail down the hillside, then hang a left on a bear run and follow it into camp. Since then, a people trail wore in, possessing an almost magnetic pull to suck folks along safely through the darkest nights. The biggest advantage of human trails over animal trails is headroom. Since humans have chosen the awkward and aerodynamically stifling habit of walking upright, trees and shrubs must part for a few weeks to allow them passage.

The people at Buffalo Camp learned, however, that just because humans have shaped the terrain to their liking, they shouldn't be fooled into forgetting that it was made up of animal trails. Mario, one of the folks who helped set up Buffalo Camp, learned that lesson the week before when he pitched his tent on a beautiful flat spot that happened to be on a game trail. Recognizing this, he erected a barrier and cleared an area to reroute the trail. Then he stomped back and forth on it, surveyed it, urinated in the appropriate spots, and proudly declared the trail moved. Two days later, he moved his tent. It seems his tent was sideswiped by something he could describe to Sunflower only as "heavy, large, foul-smelling, and snorfully."

Plover and Asha toss their apple cores aside, pick up their water jugs, and head down the trail toward a spring. Sunflower reminds them to mark both jugs "not boiled" to warn folks that they shouldn't fill their canteens or drink the untreated water. "Remember," he shouts as they left, "I want solid shit in that shitter tomorrow."

Noah reaches into his pocket, pulling out two cloves of garlic. Without asking, he knows to hand one over to Sunflower, who immediately starts to peel it. Garlic is the secret drug of the Rainbows. It offers a double-edged sword; fighting off both disease and insects. Rainbow life demands such a miracle remedy. Regular doses of raw garlic thwart colds from perpetually wet tents, obnoxious intestinal parasites, and a multitude of bug bites.

Slowly biting into his garlic, Sunflower thinks, this is just one more thing we do at Rainbow that other folks just won't have any part of in, let's say, the subway. Garlic breath at Rainbow is simply not a problem—most folks don't even notice it. Being outdoors helps. Perhaps garlic dissipates in a natural environment. Garlic reeks in sterile perfumed buildings. Garlic, Sunflower muses, smells especially foul in the vicinity of office furniture, fluorescent lighting, or designer bedding. Perhaps garlic is a more powerful healing agent than previously imagined.

Sunflower, suddenly remembering his missing shoes and the purpose of his day's endeavor, hugs Noah and starts up the trail.

"Hey, is that garlic you're chewing on? Do ya have another piece?" Sunflower looks over to a woman, about twenty years old, sitting among the trees. Sunflower, glad there's no office furniture around, apologizes for not having another piece to share. "Run down the trail until you meet up with an old man who smells like garlic and apples, and ask him." She smiles, says something Sunflower guesses to be "thank you," in some facsimile of a Native American sounding language, and heads off in the direction of the distant orange robe.

Off in the woods to his right, Sunflower hears banjo music. As he walks toward the sound, he sees a sign marking a shitter trail. A musical shitter is a new concept, one worth exploring. At the end of the trail he finds Hobo John, a stocky man in his early forties, knee-deep in a partially dug slit trench, shovel in hand. Two women, Kali, who seems to be in her early twenties, and Sharon, who is about forty-five, are on their knees prying large rocks from the earth with a metal tent pole, while Isaac, a twenty-something skinhead, loosens the dirt ahead of Hobo John with a shovel. Trefoil, a tall, slightly balding college physics instructor, presides over the whole scene performing "It's a Shitter Diggin' Holiday" on his weather-beaten banjo.

Sharon tosses two rocks to Sunflower and asks him to start piling rocks clear of the hole so they could be used later to secure the lid. Lured by song, a small work force gathers, completing the trench in ten minutes. The plan is Hobo John's brainchild: "I decided to spend a day digging latrines since they're filling up quickly. I figured I could dig two or three. With the banjo, on the other hand, we can facilitate the digging of at least a dozen. Work's easy when lotsa hippies are doing it. So this morning I went over to Trefoil's camp and talked him into serenading the next shitter site. I thought the music might attract help. It seems to work."

Sunflower explains to John, "I'd like to help but I got to find my shoes today."

John tells him not to worry, as he looks around, counting about eighteen people milling about. "We got plenty a folks here; should be able to dig five a these styling shit emporiums before knocking off for lunch. Maybe smoke a joint too if I'm lucky."

The sun drifts behind midday clouds, cooling the ground under Sunflower's feet as he approaches a new attraction: the "Trailside Spiritual Happy Foot Massage and Wash Station." For the price of one smile, Sunflower is told, tired muddy feet such as his could be lovingly renewed and his soul "bathed in the spirit of God." The operation is presided over by a middle-aged woman named Star, wearing only a straw hat on her head and a tie-dyed scarf tied around her waist. There are four trays of water. The first is a muddy wash mixture smelling of eucalyptus, the second a fresh water rinse, and the third, a bleach water rinse. "After the rinse, you sit on this stool," Star explains, "while I massage your tired feet." The fourth tray is a fragrant "mineral bath" with what appear to be floating daisies.

Sunflower sits on the stool as Star begins working on his feet. She motions to a small pile of books and tells Sunflower, "You're supposed to pick a book and read it aloud."

"Weird, but harmless," Sunflower surmises, looking down at a well-worn Gideon Bible, three paperback Krishna books, an L. Ron Hubbard sci-fi thriller, and the first half of *The Way of Sufi*. Sunflower chooses the Bible, since a friend had recently told him it contained a few juicy sections and "read like a T.V. soap."

Just what his aching feet needed. "But I say unto you. That whoever looketh on a woman to lust after her has committed adultery with her already in his heart." Toes feel alive. Sunflower flips through the Bible. "And if thy right eye offend thee, pluck it out, and cast it from thee." Sunflower digs the footbath but finds the reading a bit violent.

As Sunflower leaves the foot-wash station he hears the distinctive sounds of a bear; frenzied unending dog barking, frantic hippie wailing, and the banging of pots and pans. It's as instinctive for folks to bang pots and pans at the sight of a bear as it is for dogs to bark. But then again not everyone bangs pots and pans. Sunflower remembers Sam, a talkative nineteen-year-old from Knoxville who yesterday told Sunflower, "Man, I watched a bear trash my camp for twenty minutes. He got all of my food. I just sat there real still and watched." The bears are the great equalizers of the Gathering, policing all the camps, tents, and packs, for private food stashes. Literally dozens of tents were destroyed at this Gathering as they harbored Snickers bars and other zuzus.

With a bear in the area, Sunflower thought it wise to accompany a four-year-old boy and his twelve-year-old sister happening by on their way to Kids' Village. Explaining away the commotion as "a bear dancing with hippies in the woods," he suggests the appropriate behavior for a four-year-old encountering a bear: "Walk around it but don't be frightened." The three of them arrive at Kids' Village just in time for lunch, which is a lucky break for the barefooted Sunflower, as Kids' Village cooks up some of the best chow at the Gathering. Since the kids have all been fed, adults are free to gorge.

Sunflower enjoys visiting Kids' Village. He feels it's a chance to glimpse at the future. As he eats, he watches the kids at play. Adults are welcome, but kids set the rules. At the moment they're Mutant Ninja Turtles from the sewer and they're looking to "fuck someone up." This doesn't sit well with their Rainbow parents and elders. Dan, a slim, balding forty-year-old father of three preteens, explains the dilemma: "If we were to impose nonviolence by force, it would be oxymoronic, but I really don't dig this turtle stuff."

The grown-ups protest the Ninja Turtle game, claiming to be peaceful turtles from a land where all turtles live in harmony. They want to bury their eggs in the dirt and lie basking in the sun. "This is what happy turtles do," Sue, a twenty-two-year-old mother, tells the children. The mutant kids would have none of it, jumping on the rocks the adults said were their eggs.

Stan, a computer programmer from Seattle dressed in Guatemalan coveralls and sandals, is the father of an eight-year-old "turtle." He leans over and tells Sunflower, "The public schools are to blame for this. It takes three weeks of Rainbow to mellow my son out. Then in September, after one week of school, he's back to demanding new weapons for his Power Rangers." The phrase "And if thy right eye offend thee, pluck it out, and cast it from thee" suddenly echoes in Sunflower's head. He turns to the programmer and laments, "It's not the schools, it's the whole fuckin' society. The schools are just a product of the society they serve."

'Sunflower's somber note is drowned out by the noisy arrival of a clown. It's a Rainbow clown with a multicolored face and tie-dyed pants and shirt. The ersatz Bozo astutely intervenes in the turtle drama, telling the children, "You are neither mutant turtles nor bliss turtles. I recognize y'all now. You're hopping rolling turtles." Within seconds the youthful crowd of killer turtles, forgetting the bloodshed at hand, starts alternately hopping and rolling on the ground. The grown-ups, always looking for an excuse to frolic about, happily abandon their eggs and join in.

The clown, Sunflower learns, is a Montessori teacher who had been working on television antidotes to bring to the Gathering. "The secret," she tells Sunflower, "is to be able to always offer the kids an opportunity to have *more* fun. Escaping the confines of clean clothes and concrete playgrounds allows for more freedom. Superheroes," she concludes, "are no match for a good mud puddle." It's no contest. "If you give up on clean clothes, you can skip the toy guns too."

Sunflower likes Kids' Village. Sometimes the future looks hopeful.

"Shoes, got to find my shoes," Sunflower suddenly remembers. On the way out of Kids' Village, he observes a circle of punks sitting with Charlie, one of the nastier drunks from the Alcohol Camp. They're passing around a Dr. Seuss book, taking turns reading it. It's great to have a place to come, when it's time to be a kid again, Sunflower muses as he heads off. It begins to rain.

As he reaches the main trail, Sunflower again hears the clanging of pots and pans. He makes a detour to investigate. About a hundred yards from the trail he comes upon Dozer, a middle-aged, self-proclaimed road tramp and sometime recovering alcoholic. He's accompanied by a 450-pound black bear. Walking through the woods, Dozer lectures the bear about Twelve-Step Programs while complaining about railroad police and Greyhound ticket agents. When they happen upon a camp, Dozer commences banging on cookware in a vain attempt to discourage the bear from its intended rampage. Dozer admits, however, that he has allowed the bear an occasional repast at a few "yuppie" tents where "ol' Smoky" emerged to flaunt Snickers bars and factory-rolled cigarettes to an obviously jealous but sympathetic Dozer.

"Rumor is," Dozer explains, that "this bear ate at least an ounce, maybe more, of prime organic kind bud. It ain't slept since, day or night. That son-of-a-bitch been eat'n for thirty-six hours. We got us one hell of a munched-out bear."

The rain becomes heavy. The ground is once again cold and wet. Sticks and twigs play havoc with Sunflower's toes. "My feet would be doing a lot better if they weren't softened and crippled from wearing shoes for thirty years," he complains to Dozer as they part.

Sunflower, knowing that trees, mushrooms, and the like are having a joyous day, doesn't want to complain, but the rain *is* getting a bit played out. Deep down he knows his discomfort comes not from the rain, but from his conditioned instinct as a building dweller, to avoid the rain. Nonetheless, he decides to seek shelter at the Popcorn Palace.

Coming in from the woods and not from the trail, Sunflower zeros in, not on the colorful trail markers leading up to the Palace, but on the loud laughter of the kernel poppers. In the distance, Sunflower sees a large blue tarp interrupting the dark brown and green forest. As he approaches, he hears the familiar sounds of popcorn—first a metallic shaking sound, then popping accompanied by mumbles of approval. This time, however, the usual sounds are followed by a long loud hiss and a round of disappointed groans as a coffeepot spills into the fire. A steamy white cloud puffs out from under the tarp. From off in the woods, a bird cackles at the whole strange scene.

The Popcorn Palace consists of a cluster of blue tarps surrounding a large cooking fire. The Palace serves around the clock to a steady stream of story-trading, music-making popcorn-munching Rainbows. The presiding cooks sport many a tattoo. An American flag hangs from a tree.

Sunflower pulls his bowl out from his small pack and quickly fills it with the popcorn de jour—organic kernels laced with nutritional yeast, a bit of cayenne, garlic powder, and splashed with tamari. The rain provides an olfactory concert for Sunflower's nose. Hiking in the rain, he often delights to the host of new smells the forest exudes. On the other hand, he's none too fond of the smells that develop while crammed rush-hour subway-style under tarps with soggy hippies.

Today's smell is dog. Definitely dog. A strong dose of dog. The presence of little puppies curled up between two duffel bags provides relief, for at least that means there are dogs to accompany the odor. The smell of dog had been so prevalent around the soggy Gathering during the past week that Sunflower was beginning to worry, thinking perhaps it was the raindrops themselves that reeked.

The popcorn crew, endowed with a large stash of dry firewood, have a sizable bonfire. Taking advantage of the inferno, folks start to take off their wet socks, boots, and shirts, hanging them weinie-roast-style from sticks, holding them over the fire. The soggy specimens start to steam, adding to the rancid stench. More corn pops, this time garlic and tabasco.

People are poking the tarp with sticks, expelling water pockets like giant blue blisters. During the height of the downpour this is mandatory as it keeps the tarp from collapsing under the weight of the water. Karen, a twenty-year-old who recently arrived from a Phish (band) tour, uses a stick to direct water from the tarps into a teapot, thus eliminating a water trip. She says some camps can catch upwards of a hundred gallons of raindrops from a single storm.

The rain lets up about the time the mud's ready for drinking. "This is serious mud," Sunflower comments to no one in particular, sipping from his cup. Having run out of coffee two days prior, the Popcorn Palace is recycling old grounds resourcefully stashed for a moment like this. It's warm and looks somewhat like coffee. Since it meets at least two of the criteria expected of coffee, no one complains. This is, after all, the Popcorn Palace, not the Coffee Palace.

Music starts up across the fire as members of a barbershop quartet take their seats clustered on a wet log. The conductor stands facing them in the drizzling rain. Waving a spatula, he plays them like an instrument as they harmonize with humming sounds devoid of words or meaning. The music inspires the audience to join in, but that's impossible since the music moves too fast and is unpredictable. The tempo increases as the sun appears from behind the passing clouds. Within moments people start cheering wildly. Sunflower looks up from his mud to see a full rainbow appear above the tree line.

Sunflower is counting rainbows. This is the fifth one he's seen this Gathering. While some folks think the appearance of so many rainbows at Rainbow Gatherings is a cosmic signal or divine intervention, Sunflower is more pragmatic. Whenever people marvel at rainbows, Sunflower asks how often they spend time wandering in the rain or sitting around in the rain. The answer is usually, "Only at Rainbow." Those who answer that romping in the rain is a regular part of their lives admit that they are regularly treated to rainbows year-round.

The same, Sunflower found, held true for viewing the Aurora Borealis. Where else but at Rainbow do so many people wander all night without streetlights, flashlights, or automobile headlights to blind them? Foxfire, bioluminescent decaying wood, often found on Rainbow trails, is another prize of these night wanderings. Where else do people get the opportunity to see so much of the nightscape? The rewards are great. He had seen more Northern Lights and foxfire than he ever imagined he'd see in a lifetime. Now if he could only find his shoes.

Pushing on toward the Council meadow, Sunflower looks up to see the clouds release the sky to the sun. Rays of light, neatly carved by tree limbs, are reflecting on the mist rising from the wet ground. His nostrils flare to once again embrace the crisp forest air. The wet ground warms under his feet. It's great to be alive.

The mosquitoes are also happy Sunflower's alive. Mosquitoes love to party after the rain, he observes. Time to splash on some citronella. Garlic, grime, and citronella comprise Sunflower's defense against mosquitoes. He still isn't certain how effective this potpourri really is, but he needs to react in some way to being eaten alive. Besides, he's always looking for an excuse to splash citronella about. Citronella and wood smoke are the two distinct odors Sunflower always brings back from Rainbow. Months after a Gathering, barricaded inside his New York City apartment, he'd unravel his sleeping bag or pull out his poncho and let the fragrances take him back to the woods.

He remembers a man he met at a Gathering years earlier, who had taken to eating mosquitoes. The man would eat every mosquito he killed, until, he postulated, he was sweating mosquito. "They quickly got the message to dine elsewhere," he claimed. Sunflower, however, is not about to eat insects. It took him two years before he built up the courage to eat Rainbow food. Of course this is not to say that the two are related.

Smoky grime works well as insect repellent. He often laughs at the city folks who go to great lengths to scrub themselves daily with sweet-smelling soaps, while at Rainbow making themselves delectable hosts to a menagerie of bugs. This is also one of the great karma checks of the forest. Those who sneak off with their soap and shampoo to pollute the waterways lay the groundwork for their own torture.

The thought of bathing, however, is appealing to Sunflower. It's just turning out to be too nice of an afternoon not to take a quick dip, even if it would put his hard-earned coat of grime in jeopardy. A detour to Tea Time, the teahouse on the lake, is in order. Tea Time is an elaborate operation. There's a community fire, around which people make music and drink tea. It's enclosed by a small fence built from fallen tree branches designed not to keep folks out, but to delineate the boundaries and detour trails away from the fire. The fire and surrounding area are covered by tarps strung over a skeleton made from fallen branches. This alleviated the necessity for constant poking and adjustment of the tarps during rainstorms. At the other end of the tarps is the actual kitchen where cooks prepare tea twenty-four hours a day. Kitchen volunteers pour the hot tea into three urns, where it's dispensed self-service-fashion, a sort of wilderness Automat.

A large American flag emblazoned with a Harley Davidson emblem hangs over the urns. There are many American flags at the Gathering. Some fly upside-down, some right-side-up, some are ritualistically folded by Boy Scouts, some are used as dishtowels, and some are lovingly taken inside tents to protect them from the rain. Some are worn as armbands, others as ass patches; some are decals in car windows, others are burned. Rainbows respect one another's beliefs and their right to carry out their flag rituals as they see fit. This diversity of opinion is what Rainbow is all about—and it's supposed to be what America is all about, Sunflower thinks to himself, still upset about politicians who would burn the Constitution while deifying the flag.

Looking over his shoulder at the Harley roaring across red stripes, Sunflower strips off his clothes and runs into the lake. He doesn't stop running until the water lifts him up, then he throws his momentum forward and dives into the bracing depths. Icy water tingles every inch of his body. A thousand cold fingers clasp onto his head and slide down around his ears and nose, over his neck, back, and chest, chill his belly, tickle his butt, swirl around his testicles, glide down his legs and slap the bottoms of his feet.

Why would anyone would want to wear clothes when swimming? Childhood images of Beaches appear in Sunflower's head. Tens of thousands of itchy bathing suits covering clammy skin. Thoughts of sand-filled jockstraps and sun-seared bikini scars flash across his mind. "Babylon is indeed a sad place," he laments as he reflects on the perversion of turning the human body into a commodity in a libidinous marketplace that has banned its free display. He dives back under the water, feeling his blood circulating.

There is an innocence at a Rainbow beach; an innocence in simple nudity, he thinks. It is refreshing, wet, and free. There are no adolescent boys grinding their genitals into the sand, or women forced to shame over body fat. The anxiety and sexual overtones of beaches where people sheath their bodies to curb supposed uncontrollable instincts are history. Sexuality, Sunflower believes, is something to celebrate, something more than a puerile fascination with nudity. Sexuality is something special. And it doesn't necessarily have anything to do with swimming.

Sunflower takes another dive into the crisp water. He feels sorry for the forest rangers, latent pornographers incessantly photographing naked people; invading private moments with a twisted eye. He feels sorry for the police who ticket and arrest people for sitting in the sun or swimming. He feels pity for the people forced to wear clothes, pity for the people forced to wear ties, pity for the folks who never discover that you can leave Babylon.

He sits on a rock letting the sun dry him while he watches three generations of Rainbows splash, laugh, and bob about in the water. A canoe-load of firewood arrives and Sunflower helps unload and pile it up in the kitchen. Out in the lake a pair of helpless fools canoe in circles. It's a beautiful day.

Sunflower, about to hike on, overhears a woman telling the people at Tea Time, "It's true. The forest rangers are springing for five hundred pounds of watermelon. They're buying 'em as a gift for the fruit feast on the Forth!" Sunflower approaches the woman and casually asks where she heard this, to which she enthusiastically responds, "Oh, I made it up. Why not?" she adds, "For years I spread a rumor that the Krishnas were going to bring an elephant, then in 1987, up the trail it came. An elephant. Sacred elephant poop. The works."

The image of five hundred pounds of watermelon appears in Sunflower's mind. It wouldn't be a surprising sight at a Gathering, he concludes, remembering the story of hundreds of grapefruit floating down river into the 1977 New Mexico Gathering. The river became a massive hydraulic conveyor, with citrus floating right to the kitchens. He can't fathom the Forest Service, as a bureaucracy, buying the melons, but he figures it wouldn't be surprising to hear that some blissed-out ranger spent his paycheck on them. Such things happen.

Sunflower tries pressing on in his journey, heading toward the entropy of the Info Center, but he just has to stop and think about those damn melons. They're the antithesis of freeze-dried backpacking food, which basically is processed nutritional matter minus its liquid weight. Watermelon, on the other hand, is basically a somewhat sweet fibrous water bladder with minimal nutritional value. As such, it is something very few backpackers schlep into the woods. A cold fresh melon in the middle of the forest is a real treat. Actually, Sunflower can't remember a Gathering without watermelon, enough to go around for everyone. Watermelon plants grow out of buried compost pits after Gatherings. Watermelon is a common Gathering smell. Sunflower ranks it right up there with sage, vanilla, citronella, patchouli, pennyroyal, mint, lavender, garlic, tobacco, and wood smoke.

A mandolin-playing minstrel comes down the trail. He stands just shy of six feet tall, with long red hair and a red beard. Like shitter digging, cooking, and hauling water, wandering the trails making music is a respected form of work. A minstrel is a cultural worker, an aesthetic engineer. Rainbow respects its artists.

The trail provides a sensuous multiplicity for Sunflower's bare feet: cool puddles, hot sun-baked rocks, squishy mud, and cracking twigs. Sunflower enjoys the feedback his feet furnish. Wet and muddy feet free him from having to worry about his feet getting wet or muddy. He stomps through puddles that others take great care to avoid, gleefully avenging a childhood of puddle-stomping prohibitions.

With a sensitivity that alerts Sunflower to every rock or leaf on the trail, his feet bring him to the Info Center, the place Rainbows call "Rumor Control." Today it's alive with the pandemonium common of any civic center. Its core is a shelter made of fallen tree trunks. Open on four sides, it has a counter on the front and a pitched roof skinned with a familiar blue tarp, a Rainbow architectural mainstay. A split log about three feet above the ground offers a comfortable seat for Info volunteers. In a small clearing nearby is a steadily growing Drum Circle. Sunflower expects their mellow tune to accelerate into a frenzied celebration by nightfall.

Four large bulletin boards are scattered throughout this area. One is a ride board, integral to Rainbow transit. Every vehicle undoubtedly leaves burdened beyond capacity. Sunflower looks it over. There are rides offered to most major East and West Coast cities. A colorful note with a small feather attached begs a ride to "Belize or vicinity" for Squirrel, who the notice says could be found "beneath a green tarp under the tired pine 50' this side of the elves camp." Directions like these, Sunflower observes, are what set the Rainbow ride board apart from other such boards where people are unceremoniously indexed by phone numbers or post office boxes.

Another board holds personal messages: "Jimmy from Berkeley is camped at Sage Hollow; Woman and two cats looking for rural cooperative community in northeast; Tim at Bus Village needs VW generator; Community forming in Tennessee is looking for people with energy; Herkimer crystal earring found near sweat lodge, inquire at info." Sunflower pokes through the seemingly hundreds of leaves of multicolored paper and finds his message from two weeks ago: "Sunflower at Buffalo Camp." He looks over the day's posted offerings. There's a carburetor, a few avenues for spiritual rebirth, but nothing about his shoes. He borrows a pen from the Info Shelter and scribbles, "Sunflower needs his shoes, brown with orange laces, no feet. Please bring to Buffalo Camp kitchen fire if found." The third board holds announcements for workshops, meetings, circles, spiritual events, and councils. The fourth board bares a map of the Gathering, listing all the major kitchens and camps, of which there are nearly one hundred.

Unlike other maps, which seem to Sunflower to be cast in stone, the Rainbow map is fluid, always changing as new camps and trails are added by the hour. People passing through the Info area use pens and markers to update the map with their conception of where the newly named area should be. The result is a map completely out of scale, bearing no resemblance to the actual geography of the area. Sunflower calls it "participatory cartography." Using the map, people could find their way to most camps. They can't, however, judge just how far, or over what type of terrain, they have to hike to get there.

Sunflower takes the marker and draws a picture of a bear on the map and writes in the words "Bear Range." He then scribbles a quick explanation of bear country etiquette on a piece of cardboard he finds at the info shelter, and attaches it to the map using a stray thumbtack from the bulletin board.

Marker in hand (Sunflower often carries a marker for moments like these), he remembers there was something else he wanted to post. Then it hits him; "Nestle's, Nescafé. Got to let people know about the Nestle's boycott." Meticulously, in large red letters drawn to emulate dripping blood, he scrawled, "There's blood in your chocolate. Boycott Nestle's!" Immediately a man in his twenties, wearing tie-dyed long johns looks at Sunflower and complains, "Brother, like that can really bum someone, like a tripping person, like blood in the chocolate . . . like your words are violent." Sunflower, somewhat taken aback, politely responds, "Brother, buying Nestle's products is a violent act. It's not real blood. It's metaphorical. It's the baby formula thing, man. They're doing it again. That third world thing where they get families hooked on baby formula they can't afford."

Another brother, about twenty years old, with long braided hair and a beard, wearing a lavender skirt and a straw hat, wanders over and adds, "I hear ya, man. Right on. Gotta let people know what's going on." He then adds, "But the slaughter's going on here too every day. There's meat being eaten all over this Gathering. Meat is Murder. We've got to spread that word too."

"And liquid meat. Dairy," adds a teenage woman, standing nearby and listening to the ensuing discussion. "Liquid meat perpetuates the enslavement of animal husbandry," she continues.

"I gotta go, I'd love to hang out here and talk, but I got to find my shoes," Sunflower moans.

"Leather shoes per chance?" the woman queries with a smile.

"I've got to go," Sunflower begs again. The woman reaches over and gives Sunflower a hug. The vegetarian brother joins in. A few other people, Sunflower's not certain how many, see a hug developing and also join in.

As the hug breaks, Sunflower gets the idea to see if anyone has dropped his shoes off at the Info Shelter. There's a bit of a lost-and-found going there, and he figures it's worth a shot.

At the Info Shelter he encounters a television news crew. The reporter is wearing a white shirt, gray tie, and shiny black shoes. Stupid dress for the woods, Sunflower concludes. The camerawoman, while more casually and sensibly dressed, still looks uncomfortable. Both are obviously sweating after the long hike in. He doesn't pay them much mind. He's already quite familiar with this "movie": the same questions basically being asked of the same people followed by a reporter muttering about "the sixties." Sunflower can't relate to the terminology the media often use to describe Rainbow. Being a thirty-year-old, Sunflower doesn't consider himself a "flower child." Since he was barely a year old during the Summer of Love, he doesn't consider himself a throwback to the sixties either.

News reporters, Sunflower feels, aren't malicious in their wording. They're just somewhat inept; trapped by prior notions of what they would be seeing; forced to trivialize something that was too big, too powerful, and too confusing for them to be able to deal with seriously. The only safe way to dispense with it is to lump it with history, the study of dead things, with the sixties, with the "flower children."

Sunflower pictures the newscast. There'd be a roughly edited Rainbow piece immediately before or after the sports and weather. At the end of the broadcast, while credits begin to flash on the screen, the anchors would do their "small-talk-while-shuffling-papers" routine. The weatherman, an overweight jokester with a pockmarked face and shellacked hair, would say something like, "Well Kevin, I hope you're not going to run off and join the Rainbows up there in the forest," at which point they all laugh and wish the viewers a good night. The only clue as to the reality of Rainbow would be the consistent voice of the drums, speaking in the background throughout the segment.

Just out of earshot of the television crew stands Sparrow Hawk, a soft-spoken white-haired women in her early sixties. She's a primary force behind the grandmothers' council. Wearing a Mayan *huipil*, she stands there organizing a sisters' expedition to the parking area. "There's too much male energy there," she cautions. "There's a lot of traffic, a wet slippery road, and a lot of alcohol. The locals are bringing it in. They just don't understand our feelings about alcohol." Pressure is high and tempers are rumored to be growing short. Shanti Sena, the peacekeepers, are needed.

Sunflower gives Sparrow Hawk a hug and thanks her for the work she's doing. He feels sorry for her. Going to the parking area basically means leaving the sanctuary of the Gathering. Sunflower always viewed the parking area, which at this Gathering is five miles away, as the last stop in Babylon before entering Rainbow. As such, it compounds Babylon's problems with Rainbow's. While the Gathering is basically harmonious and alcohol-free, drunks and scam artists infest the parking area. There's a lot of healing to do there, Sunflower surmises. The sisters are bringing sleeping gear and a tarp, planning to spend the night. "A lot of family is still arriving tonight," Sparrow Hawk says, "We want to be there to welcome them home."

"Welcome Home." Magic words. Sunflower hadn't welcomed anyone home for days. It's a civic responsibility to welcome family; sort of like putting in your time on hug patrol or joining in on a chorus of "We love you."

Still barefoot, he wanders over to the trail leading in and out of the Gathering. A steady stream of people are hiking in. A heavyset balding man in his fifties comes up the trail wearing a tattered overcoat and dirty plaid polyester pants. Since he isn't carrying a pack of any kind, Sunflower guesses he already had a camp set up. As he gets closer, however, Sunflower notices a wild apprehensive curiosity in the man's eyes. He quickly realizes, pack or no pack, the man is coming in for his first time.

Sunflower walks over smiling and gives the startled man a hug. "Welcome home brother, Welcome home," Sunflower croons.

With large sad brown eyes, the man looks at Sunflower. He motions to his coat and explains, "This is all I got. I heard a man with my gear would be welcome here." Two passing women overhear him and stop to offer hugs. The man introduces himself as "Sam, Sam the Hobo." He goes on to tell Sunflower and the women how he had been living on city streets when he found a newspaper with a report about the Gathering. "It sounded like a place where I'd be treated like a person again. It's been a few years since I felt like a person. I just need to find a place to sit down and smoke a few cigarettes, talk to folks and try to sort things out."

Sunflower reaches into his pack and hands Sam his bowl. Another one shouldn't be too hard to come by. He points Sam in the general direction of the nearest kitchen, the Road Dog Cafe. "Tell them you're hungry. They'll fix something up for you."

One of the women announces, "There's a tepee in my camp with extra room." Her friend adds, "I think there's an old sleeping bag in the free box." Sunflower smiles as the women accompany Sam off toward the Road Dog Cafe.

The crowd continues flowing in toward the Gathering, some with high-tech backpacks loaded with "styling" camping gear, others with duffel bags of food and dry clothes. Some carry just the bare essentials, a sleeping roll, maybe a piece of plastic to make a shelter. Some have nothing. All are welcome. Everyone stops for a hug.

Supplies were also beginning to pour in. Sunflower watched people carrying fifty-pound sacks of rice, sacks of carrots, onions, potatoes; cases of citrus, broccoli and cauliflower. They brought produce from their own gardens. Locals brought baked goods from their kitchens. The food was finally arriving. Better late than never, Sunflower thought, as he recalled the first days of Seed Camp, with everyone getting by on dumpstered potatoes.

After a few more moments of welcoming people, a short stocky women in her forties beckons Sunflower, "Hey, I got a box of medical supplies for CALM [Center for Alternative Living Medicine], d'ya think ya could give me a hand and take 'em over?" There's always a box of something that needs to go somewhere. Empty hands are always being filled. There's always work to do, everywhere; chop veggies, carry water, haul supplies, cut wood.

The work is often hard. Sometimes Sunflower would stop in the middle of a task and look at his coworkers. Covered with sweat, bathed in dirt, they press on. These people, the hardest workers in the Family, are often the same people Babylon condemns as "bums." Babylon considers them lazy because they can't hold a job, because they refuse to mindlessly accept any order or degradation pressed on them by greedy taskmasters.

Sunflower hikes over to CALM and walks into the pharmacy tent. A woman wearing jeans, a T-shirt, sneakers, and a white canvas hat, is busily engaged in a heated discussion with a naked man as to which homeopathic remedy would most effectively combat a swelling bee sting. They hardly notice Sunflower's delivery. After a few moments, Sunflower breaks into the conversation, asking where to leave the box. They both look at the box and, without saying a word, start unpacking bottles of hydrogen peroxide and alcohol, boxes of Band-Aids, vials of tea-tree oil, and capsules of goldenseal and echinacia. "Where'd this stuff come from?" the naked man inquires. "I dunno, some woman on the trail in," Sunflower replies. "Thanks for bringing it here," the man mumbles without looking up.

As he turns to leave, Sunflower notices an odd sight for CALM, a forest ranger's jacket draped over one of the folding chairs. Next to it is a pair of shoes and a pair of socks. With his curiosity piqued, he starts to look around.

Behind the pharmacy is a body work area with three massage tables. Lisa, a fifty-year-old ranger whom he had met during the previous week, was on one of them. The first time he'd met her, she was taking notes on a small hand-held pad and muttering about "administrative directives." She seemed to be loosening up a little bit more every time Sunflower met up with her.

The last time he saw her she was informing the Rainbows at Main Supply that "the local hardware store is owned by developers responsible for cutting down prime woodlands." She added that "the general store, on the other hand, is owned and operated by a nice couple who make and sell their own crafts." Boycott the forest rapers, buy from the artists.

Today she seems as loose and comfortable as any other Rainbow. She'd come in to CALM for a chiropractic adjustment after spending the morning hiking around the Gathering site answering questions mostly about birds and trees.

Next door in the healing area, a small circus tent, Earl sits receiving his daily acupuncture treatment. It's supposed to help him quit smoking. He's one of many people who use the supporting environment of the Gathering to try to beat drug addiction. Addictions are just one of a host of chronic problems that CALM helps heal.

A brown-eyed pimple-faced nineteen-year-old man who first came to Rainbow last year after running away from an abusive stepfather, walks in needing to get a small cut on his left thumb cleaned and bandaged. The healers not only treat his boo-boo, but seal it with a kiss. Where else would doctors add a finishing kiss to their work? The folks at CALM, it seems to Sunflower, trust the cleanliness of their work and the armor of their bandaging job, enough to complement it with a warm kiss. If a doctor is afraid to kiss a boo-boo, Sunflower surmises, then it's not cleaned right.

Still, the major business of CALM is first aid for the normal cuts and broken bones common to any gathering of this size. Many folks wander into CALM with swollen welts, the handiwork of a myriad of insects. Mike, a forty-year-old carpenter/shaman from Boston walks in and complains, "I could scratch any point on my body and up pops these li'l red bumps." A newcomer, Sunflower concludes, fresh in from the city. "Soon," he assures Mike, "you won't even feel these bites. Give your body time to develop antitoxins."

Fred, a soft-spoken curly haired little man who grew up in the Bronx, but who now hails from the generic West, is helping at CALM. He just arrived at the Gathering yesterday. "It's been a rough year," he explains to Sunflower. "All my money went into a new engine for my truck. But just before I left for Rainbow, my camper unit, you know, where me and my dogs live, fell off on a twisting mountain road near Yosemite. It went all the way down into this steep valley. Now I just got the truck with no back on it—just a frame and the wheels back there. So now we're living, you know, the dogs and me, we live in the cab of the truck. It's like real crowded though." Smiling, he goes on, "But the gas mileage is way better since I lost the camper, and overall, the rig's a lot less sensitive to cross winds and head winds."

A bit further down the trail from CALM is the Jesus Camp. Rumor has it that they have real hot cocoa at Jesus, milk too. Sunflower's bare feet find the turn-off to Jesus' trail just as his ears pick up a shrill scream from the camp. It's unnerving, but it stops quickly. He wanders in and finds that indeed there is cocoa, and two cans of evaporated milk. There's even a bit of sweetened condensed milk left in another can—a real treat.

He fills his cup with cocoa and watches as the last of the sweet goo drips from the condensed milk can into his cup. There's a small fire going, and two guitar players picking. A middle-aged woman with long hair and three necklaces of beads takes out her Swiss army knife and meticulously removes the top of the condensed milk can, tossing it into a bag marked "METAL." Like most kitchens, Jesus has what Rainbows call a "Garbage Yoga Station," where trash is separated for recycling and composting. Sunflower watches as she cleans the can, punches a hole in it using a magic attachment from her knife, and laces a small piece of twine through it. A cup is born. She puts it in the "free" box. Sunflower walks over to the free box, where he looks over the assortment of recycled trash turned dinnerware, and helps himself to a bowl, formerly a margarine tub.

Then the shriek breaks loose again. Startled, Sunflower looks up. He could see only an ordinary campfire with people tending to cocoa, passing bags of trail mix, and strumming guitars.

He puts his new bowl into his pack. Then he notices her, a woman in her twenties with long brown hair, staring at the trail mix and laughing. Suddenly she breaks out into hysterical screams. "No, no, no, not yet, your part is coming up," the guitar player urges. She looks ready to burst again. The guitar player, a young black man with dreadlocks, urges her to "wait wait wait, not yet, I'll cue you when your part comes up." The woman next to her gently hugs her.

The guitar stops, and the guitarist shouts, "Okay, now, now!" The woman lets loose four giant screams. People join her, and everyone applauds. She continues laughing but appears a bit calmer. The scenario repeats itself three more times while Sunflower sits drinking his cocoa, staring suspiciously into his cup. Twice she looks as if she's going to scream off-cue; both times the guitar player politely urges her to wait for her turn in the song. People keep hugging her. The third time her part comes up in the song, Sunflower too joins in with a primal scream.

Sunflower leans over to the woman next to him and asks, "Is everyone here dosed?"

"No way," she answers. "This is a habit-free zone. That sister is having a bad trip. The folks at CALM sent her here for some emotional support. This is a nurturing environment. They think it might ease her through her crisis."

"Habit-free." So no coffee. Every year it seems there are more habit-free spaces at the Gathering. The Jesus Camp is coffee-free, tobacco-free, marijuana-free, acid- and ecstasy-free, and of course alcohol- and narcotic-free. Sunflower sits back and enjoys his cocoa, staring at his cup, wondering if cocoa is a "habit." Maybe they don't know about sugar addiction. Sunflower takes another sip and decides not to tell them. This is drug-free enough, he muses to himself.

To date, Sunflower knows of no opposition to the drug-free areas, maybe because they're also basically judgment-free zones as well, with people neither condemning nor condoning substance use or abuse: no preaching, no one trying to impose their beliefs on other people. However, if someone wants to be away from the temptation or vibes of mood-changing chemicals like caffeine or LSD, here's a haven.

The "drug" issue is sensitive for Rainbows. During his decade-long tenure as a Rainbow, Sunflower never saw the drug trafficking police often claim occurs at Gatherings. The few people he'd seen trying to peddle substances, harmless as Sunflower thought them to be, met with acrimony from everyone they approached. But "drugs" are the shibboleth the police invoke whenever they choose to trample Rainbows' rights. Even today, Sunflower thought, cops twisted on coffee and sugar doughnuts are outside of the Gathering ravaging people's cars and belongings under the pretext of looking for "drugs."

He wanders out of the Jesus Camp dreaming of cops giving up coffee and doughnuts, seeking out drug-free zones and eating healthy Rainbow food. Maybe things would be mellower out there on the road if they would just let the Rainbows feed the cops.

Sunflower looks at the sun. Although many people seem to be just waking up, it's late in the afternoon. He thinks he already heard the conch shell blown earlier, calling Council to begin. By now it must already be in progress. He hurries along the trail. His travel is quickly impeded though, by a ten-minute delay at the joke toll booth. People are backed up in both directions as the makeshift gate opens and closes to let people pass as they share a joke with the assembled audience of about forty.

Soon an exact change lane opens for one-liners. Sunflower quickly gets through with a chicken crossing the trail joke, but not before being talked into helping carry a bucket of fresh dish water to the Soup's Up Kitchen.

Soup's Up is a camp peopled by a mix of white-collar types and hobos. They invariably produce a steady stream of food and serve it around the clock. But this reliable kitchen is also controversial. A dozen muddy dogs of all sizes are sniffing around the kitchen. Every so often a few would disappear, and rumors would fly that they had been cooked up. As one of the few omnivorous kitchens at the Gathering, Soup's Up is an easy target for such gossip. They never seriously tried to maintain their kitchen according to the hygienic standards prescribed by the photocopying Rainbows, those who published *Rap 107* and *Howdy Folks!* Oftentimes their sanitary practices are brought up for discussion at Council. Main Supply had already threatened to cut off rations if they didn't clean up their act. Folks from CALM had put out an advisory warning Rainbows with weak stomachs not to eat there. Soup's Up's sanitation is a sensitive issue, as they are among the hardest-working folks, and their kitchen is one of the first to open and feed the Seed Camp crew. The people from CALM, who denounce their sanitary practices at Council, are still good friends with the Soup's Up crew, and stop there often for coffee or tea.

Sunflower meets up with Speaking Wolf, who is having some orange ginger tea at Soup's Up. Speaking Wolf, a small gray-haired man in his sixties, is often a major player at Council. He didn't see this issue, however, as being worthy of his time. "Soup's Up is cleaning up its act," he explains, "just a bit slower than some folks would like. It's just a matter of patience."

"Maybe a few elders could implore to them the need to clean up their act a bit quicker," Sunflower suggests.

"There's that damn 'E' word again," Speaking Wolf bellows. "We have no elders. We don't automatically respect age. Remember it was old people who fucked up the world and left us all of this plutonium."

Sunflower has a cup of tea with Speaking Wolf and then hikes over to the Council Meadow. Council had been in swing for a while, with Heartsong just about winding up.

Frank, the U.S. Forest Service district ranger, is in attendance. He came to talk about an "operating plan" and to try to encourage Council to consense upon a set of guidelines that his staff wrote up as a proposed agreement between Rainbow and the Forest Service. Before he could speak, however, he has to wait for the feather to work its way around the circle. In front of him is the whole Rainbow movie, running at full naked volume; Heartsongs about visions derived on peyote quests, discussions about shitters, warnings about bad acid on the East Coast, and so on. A large heavyset woman makes an announcement informing people about the High Noon Pre-Council Discussion Circle: "Follow the trail past Krishna, but not quite to Jesus."

A somber note is brought to Council by George, a short-haired man in his late thirties who does legaliaison work. He shares horror stories of state police harassment of Rainbows on the road heading in toward the Gathering. "The state police set up a 'safety check' on the highway in, ten miles from the Gathering," he explains. "The police claim to be checking vehicles for safety violations such as window stickers, fuzzy dice, malfunctioning taillights, and so on. To help spot such infractions, they use drug-sniffing dogs. If the cops want probable cause to search a vehicle," he explains, "they jerk the dog's leash, it barks, and they then have reason to search the car for drugs." The whole situation, so far, turned out to be quite embarrassing for the police, who after searching hundreds of cars, had turned up only trace amounts of marijuana and LSD. George points out that "a random search of a K-mart parking lot would have easily turned up more contraband."

Ranger Frank shifts about nervously as he listens to George explain that "such selective enforcement makes Rainbows many times more likely than average citizens to be arrested on drug charges. The underground press folks who endured the FBI's COINTELPRO program," he continues, "had faced the same problem. Then and now, it's the same story. Government disruption of alternative political and lifestyle groups and movements."

George stops talking for a moment, takes a breath, and passes the feather on to local man in his forties, dressed in jeans, a flannel shirt, and hiking boots. He begins, "I was just sittin' here to see what this Council of yours is all about. Now I have this feather in my hand." He pauses for a moment, looks around, then goes on, "I'll tell you, during my twenty-five years of living here, I never seen a 'safety check' roadblock on any road. Never. Something out there stinks."

A few more people talk about the police situation, then the Council reverts back to Heartsong. The Council is pulling in two different directions. The politicos want to get down to discussing the nitty-gritty mechanics of running the Gathering. This, Sunflower feels, promises a series of long, drawn-out, arduous discussions that, with a little guidance from the Great Spirit, would hopefully yield a consensus or two.

The spiritual element wants to avoid all the difficult nastiness and bickering associated with Council decisions and continue the medicine of Heartsong. They feel that, in time, after everyone's Heartsongs have been heard, lofty problems and disagreements would pale in comparison with folks' love for one another. Only then could they easily be solved.

The politicos started worrying. There are so many issues to be dealt with that if discussion concerning them didn't commence immediately, nothing would get done. Slowly, the feather moves around the Circle. Council hears of a vision involving an eagle, untreated water being served at one of the kitchens, an invocation of the Great Spirit, and runny, drippy fecal matter in two shitters. A woman weeps as she tells of losing her children in a custody battle because of her lifestyle. A young man cries as he explained how happy he is to be here. A "homeless" man tells about life on the streets. A woman asks for sisters to volunteer to work at the parking area. Another woman tells of rude drunks near the gate.

Lisa, the Ranger, now sprinkled with Rainbow-colored glitter, quietly walks up and sits on the outside of the Circle. She has a gleam in her eyes and a dreamy smile. The issue of water comes up. It seems imperative that more water-boiling kitchens be established, as tests indicate a high likelihood of giardia being present in the water. Mickey, a CALM volunteer, asks that the plastic pipe that brought spring water down to the trail be removed. "City folks are conditioned to drink anything that comes out of a pipe despite the posted warnings. We're beginning to see lots of cases of the shits."

Many people, Sunflower observes, are being forced for the first time in their lives to think about their drinking water and where it comes from. Too many Americans take water for granted and don't understand their own vulnerable position in a fragile ecosystem. Understanding water is basic to the survival of the planet. Potable water is omnipresent in America, delivered by government bureaucracies who certify it safe to drink. Drinking tap water equals trusting the government. Water-consciousness is revolutionary. Understanding and respecting water shows just how foolish polluting it is.

In time the feather comes to Sunflower. He describes his missing shoes: "I came here to Council 'cause I need help findin' my shoes. I kinda like spaced them yesterday and I like really need them. Walking in the woods without them is pretty rough, though I don't mean to be disrespectful to the earth or nuttin' like that, and I don't mind the mud cause I like the way it feels, but it's like the little sticks and some of the rocks can be sharp and also I like stepped on some dog shit, which I guess shouldn't of been there. Anyway, like my feet are real wimpy and soft and I need my shoes." The politicos squirm as person after person addresses the feather, telling Sunflower of different shoes they had seen lying around various camps and kitchens.

There was a lone left boot seen near the oven at Taco Mike's that seemed to be a match for a right boot sitting in the free box at Great Lakes Camp, two miles away. There was also an unclaimed set of two right-footed Converse All-Stars found at Doggie Camp. Still, no description matched Sunflower's missing shoes. But many folks promised to look for them.

With the feather still in hand, Sunflower remembers to include his Nestle's rap. His call for Rainbow support of the boycott is met with a resounding "Ho!" He gives some quick thought to asking for a consensus not to use Main Supply funds to buy Nestle's cocoa or Nescafé coffee. Though he doesn't expect any opposition, he thinks it best not to risk raising the controversial issue of whether or not Main Supply should buy coffee at all. Coffee, which has been identified at Council as an addictive drug, had been the topic of many recent Council debates.

In time, the feather makes its way to Ranger Frank, who clutches it as he stands to speak. He explains that he understands that nobody is authorized to sign a document for the Family. Therefore, he has brought copies of the draft of the operating plan for the Council to amend as they see fit, and consense to it. His witnessing the consensus, he claims, will suffice in lieu of a signature.

Sunflower quickly skims over a copy of the plan. It's all pretty basic stuff, just like Rap 107, Rainbow's basic infrastructural operating instructions. It explains how shitters should be dug and maintained, addresses fire-consciousness, cleanup basics, preserving plant life, and so on.

Sky, a sixty-year-old New England carpenter, stands, feather in hand, and tells Ranger Frank, "I think it's rather pretentious that the United States Forest Service, that great whore for the timber industry, with all its clearcuts and taxpayers subsidized logging roads, should be lecturing Rainbows about wilderness preservation." Frank quietly sits there as Sky adds, "It's just ironic, that's all," and passes the feather.

Though the operating plan doesn't contain any points that Rainbows object to, consensus is immediately blocked by Swimmer, a slender, dark-eyed Texan who had been working the parking area. This move unnerves Sunflower, who suspects Swimmer of being some sort of an agent provocateur. He once discussed his suspicions with Grandmother Nova, whom he considers an elder (despite much criticism of the term, Sunflower still believes there are elders). Sunflower admitted to Nova at that time that he was probably just being paranoid. "A little bit of paranoia never hurt anyone," Nova commented, adding, "the Family's example of living in harmony without a governing hierarchy is more of a threat to the government than people realize. What some people view as just a bunch of 'hippies' living in the forest is actually a new reality, very threatening not just to the U.S. government, but to the very concept of government in general." Though it seems a bit lofty in its assumptions, Nova's theory made sense to Sunflower. She went on, "The Family is stronger than the political boundaries drawn on a map. Rainbow Gatherings now take place in countries across the globe, nullifying ethnic and nationalistic conflicts with a common Rainbow bond."

He remembers laughing when Nova told him, "Rainbow, by shattering the concept of enemies, threatens the very existence of war." But he sobered up, when Nova explained, "It is war, and the fear of enemies, that keeps most governments in power."

As for Swimmer, Nova told Sunflower, "It really isn't important whether or not he is some sort of government agent. Since he's at the Gathering, cop or not, he's a brother. If indeed he is an agent provocateur, and indeed wants to sabotage the Gathering, then he's just a brother who needs a bit more healing, a bit more love, and a few more hugs." Incorporating so-called enemies into the circle, Sunflower surmised at the time, is indeed the most effective plan to deal with them.

It would be better to make a point of being nice to Swimmer, rather than denouncing him as a cop. Denouncing him would just initiate an ugly circle of accusations, which would be nothing but detrimental. Besides, maybe he ain't a cop. Still Sunflower doesn't trust him and checked Swimmer's feet for his missing shoes.

The Council unravels as can after can of worms seems to open up. The issue of the operating plan is hopelessly deadlocked. Discussion arises as to whether or not Bus Village is where it belongs, why it is there, and whether or not it can be moved. Could the Council Circle be moved? Are Shanti Sena, the so-called Rainbow peace-keepers, overstepping their bounds? Then the coffee issue comes up again.

Meanwhile, six kitchens have delivered food to the circle. It sits in white five-gallon buckets as Council debates. Three hundred people soon gather to be with each other and feast. Impatient, unwilling to watch their dinner chill and coagu-late, the assembled diners begin to protest the continued Council proceedings: Dinner takes precedence over talk. They circle Council and begin to om, setting up a continuous "Oommmmmmmmmmmmmmmmmm" in an effort to harmonize the scattered energy. Ommmmmmmmmmmmm.

Council, given little choice, breaks for dinner, vowing to reconvene later to discuss the water situation. Everyone pretty much understands that Council, in fact, would not reconvene until the following afternoon. Disappointed, Ranger Frank, rumored to be under orders not to eat Rainbow food, leaves to file his day's report.

The crowd swells to four hundred people who hold hands in silent meditation. Sunflower likes participating in circles. He always seems to sense a small electric tingle in his hands and heart. A voice shouts, "Thanks to the Great Spirit for the food we're about to eat." A few other voices join in a quick "Ho." This is followed by murmurs of thanks to Jesus, Jah, Pan, Yahweh, Krishna, and one or two other deities whose names Sunflower doesn't recognize. A big spiritual smorgasbord, Sunflower muses, as he joins in a resonant "Ommmmmmmmmmmmmm."

People sit in place, pulling out their bowls, to wait for servers from the vari-ous kitchens to make their way around the circle. Dinner consists of five differ-ent kinds of soup, probably due to lack of communication among the different kitchens. This, no doubt, will be discussed at tomorrow's kitchen council.

After a few hugs, not being in the mood for soup, Sunflower slips away in search of a more solid meal—and maybe his shoes. He should be in time to catch the tail end of dinner at the Krishna Camp. Sugar-rich Krishna food would sweeten his flesh for mosquitoes, but, like many other Rainbows, he has a sweet tooth for the stuff. The sugar buzz would be worth the chanting.

Sunflower tries a newly flagged trail that goes in the general direction of Krishna. It seems like a shortcut. After about a hundred yards he meets Rudolf, the trail's engineer, wandering about hopelessly lost. Rudolf, an elderly man with a long flow-ing white beard, had been flagging the trail when he got lost. He blames "sabo-teurs" for allegedly rearranging his markings. Sunflower keeps his doubts to him-self as he guides Rudolf back to the main trail. "If you get lost again," he explains, "just follow the drums. They'll always bring you home."

"I wasn't lost, just disoriented for a minute," Rudolf grumbles.

As Sunflower hikes toward Krishna Kitchen, he passes numerous drummers heading toward main circle, congas and djembes in hand. It promises to be a lively night for drumming.

At Krishna Camp, Sunflower grabs a mixed bowl of tasty Krishna treats, and sits down to eat with friends from Quebec Camp. They all stuff their faces with portion after portion of Krishna junk food while discussing plans for the upcoming Quebec Gathering. Sunflower has many reservations about the Krishnas, who he believes come to Gatherings to proselytize. However, he has always respected them for having the most consistent kitchen, pumping out meals year after year.

Sunflower and his Quebecois comrades devour an entire Frisbee load of sweet gooey "Krishna Balls" before calling it quits. The sun sets to conversations punctuated by the songs of flatulence and belching. Embarrassment is unnecessary. Not at a Rainbow Gathering. People fart, people burp. Big deal. There are many advantages to living outdoors. Again Sunflower's thoughts drift to the New York restaurant he and Dave laughed about over breakfast. What good is a restaurant where you aren't even comfortable enough to pass wind, he ponders. He then raises his cup of lemongrass tea and toasts the Krishnas.

In the distance he hears the drums accelerating. It's nighttime, and his day's quest for his shoes is dimming to failure. Sunflower meanders over to Brew-Ha-Ha, a drug-free tea kitchen known for exotic mixes. Brew-Ha-Ha is also known for its bug-free ambiance, thanks to a former needle junkie who found support from the Brew-Ha-Ha folks years earlier. This year he designed and fabricated an enclosed screen house large enough to seat 150 people. It's in this screen house that Narcotics Anonymous meets every afternoon.

Sam the Hobo, who Sunflower met earlier, is sitting in the screen house jamming away on a battered Hohner harmonica. "I already ate dinner twice," he says. "I'm thinking 'bout eat'n again. This's good food here. Uh-uh. Good food. I'm working at the Joy of Soy Kitchen. Gonna learn how to make tofu."

After listening to a few of Paul's tunes, Sunflower once again starts wandering the trails. It's night now. Sunflower has a small flashlight, but he prefers not to use it. Flashlights only hinder your vision by illuminating the immediate foreground and obliterating all else. Moving on darkened trails is a skill that returns to Sunflower each year after a night of bumbling around in the dark. He feels closer to the earth after he reclaims his night eyes from the bright city lights. His body moves forward as his eyes continuously scan the tree line above, visible only as a pair of shadows eclipsing a blanket of stars. The parting of the trees is like the biblical parting of the Red Sea, opening the forest below for him to pass.

The dark forms of people, some not visible, detectable only by their sounds—the telltale crunching of the trail—pass in the night. Each one croons a warm greeting. There's a mystery in these voices from the dark. They're people without form, yet Sunflower feels closer to them than he does to any of his neighbors back in

Babylon. Sunflower makes friends on the trails with people whose faces he'll never see. He views them as beacons of warmth, who like himself sometimes feel comfortable wearing a dark blanket of anonymity.

Shadows, terrifying in Babylon, take on new meaning. They don't hint at lurking predators but at new friends to offer help when you're lost, confidants to hear your fears, or informative voices to tell you who's serving what kind of tea, food, or music. Yet, in his soul, Sunflower is still a city boy. In his hand he routinely clutches a small flashlight, one that sleeps in his pocket by day. Though he prides himself on not using it often, he still feels more secure with his finger on the trigger, ready to unleash the full force of technological society on a paranoid whim.

The trail leads Sunflower on an enchanted odyssey through a reality more wondrous than any he could dream. The night grows cold, paining his bare feet. He stops often at different camps to soak up the warmth of their fires. At each camp he's offered new culinary delights; pastries, exotic (nonalcoholic) drinks, and a range of music representing the diversity of the Rainbow. He hikes through Zydeco up from the bayou, through a dozen languages of drumming, guitars, sitars, rap, folk, blues, and jazz. Past a cappella singing, violins, fiddles, dulcimers, kazoos, harmonicas, and harps. Past flutes, clarinets, saxophones. The night air is rich with every instrument—none electronically amplified and transformed from itself.

Sunflower's psyche splits. His flashlight-clutching self wanders through a shopping mall of freebies, the ultimate fantasy show without a cover charge. His emerging Rainbow self is spelunking through a future society, sampling a new world harmony. He wanders the trails, his bare feet growing impervious to hazards. At Moondancer's there's a cable car with a swinging trapeze that launches four people at a time speeding and screaming across a starlit meadow; an amusement park where the rides are made of people.

At the SPOT Theater there's a talent show. Early on in the night there had been no performers. Talent recruited from people passing on the trail seeded the show. A twenty-year-old woman with a shaved head performs a vaudeville version of a love song to Moshe Dayan. An old Italian man from Michigan tells of his preparations for dying, blending a serious Heartsong with a keen sense of comedy. He quotes Edward Abbey's last wish to "disregard all state laws regarding burial of the dead." A children's group from Kids' Village does an improv lampooning their dope-smoking parents.

The Faerie Camp, the nocturnal Shangri-la that it is, is alive with hundreds of little bells and oddly illuminated objects. The earth's heart beats loud and fast with the dreads at the Nyabinghe Circle. The Donut Bike flies through the darkness.

A flashing purple light on the trail marks a "safety inspection," a parody of the police harassment going on outside of the Gathering. Sunflower, without footwear, fails. An invisible man squirts him with a water pistol.

Sunflower again passes through the Info Area. New arrivals stream in all night, over forty an hour since midnight. The travel-weary newcomers immediately blend into the magic city. The drums beat untamed and frenzied around a blazing fire. Bathed in sweat and lit by flaming orange reflections, a dozen bodies swirl about the glowing blaze. Putting the delirium of Downtown Rainbow behind him, Sunflower makes his way over to the Lake Trail, for a two-mile hike to Collector's Donut Kitchen. The Lake Trail is more sparsely traveled, the campfires more subdued. As he goes spelunking through the darkness, it feels like wilderness.

His mind filled with little sugar cakes, he presses on toward Collector's. Suddenly, the crunching of the trail turns to squishing; Sunflower feels the cold mud between his toes. One awkward step after the next, the ground grabs at Sunflower's feet. Nervously he hits the trigger, spraying the trail with a blinding light so he could delicately negotiate the mud. Then he extinguishes his light and immediately stumbles, blinded by the aftereffects of the glare. His first instinct is to turn it on again, but he resists; electric stuff is addictive, therefore dangerous.

Sunflower recognizes almost every greeting the passing shadows hail. This is a secluded part of the Gathering. Most are neighbors, camped near Buffalo Camp. One, though, is odd, maybe a short person, but from the sound of footsteps, quite heavyset. As he passed abreast of the stranger, Sunflower instinctively blurts out a "Howdy," but gets no reply. That's not normal. Neither is the stranger's foul, pungent odor. Sunflower freezes. Behind him the beast "snorfels." Sunflower quickly spins around and tries to turn on his flashlight, but it's spent. Damn flashlight. In the darkness he hears the last sounds as the bear wanders off.

He presses on through the night with his senses alert, listening intently to every sound. Another form approaches. Sunflower hails it: "Are you human?"

After a moment Plover answers, "Yeah, I kind of think so, sometimes I ain't too certain. . . . Sunflower, is that you? Did you hear that bear too?" Sunflower momentarily embraces Plover, who is heading over to the Lovin' Ovens. "I heard rumor of a jazz jam there," she explains.

"I heard saxophone music gently oozing down the hill like hot lava when I passed the trail cutoff for the Ovens," Sunflower responds. "Give the bear a hug for me if ya see it again," he implores as he presses on toward Collector's.

After meeting Plover, he meets no one. The dark serenity of the trail makes Sunflower feel close to the forest, as if the woods are embracing him, accepting him, allowing him free passage. He puts his dead flashlight back into his pocket. He no longer fears bears. We're Rainbows, we walk with the earth, not against it. Animals could sense that; they are friends, part of the family.

At Collector's camp, he meets a lone man in his twenties wearing a leather hat and what seems to be a buckskin jacket, quietly tending the small fire. Sunflower blurts out a "Howdy" and sits down for a moment.

The man quietly looks up, smiles, and inquires, "You Sunflower?"

Sunflower nods his head. The man hands him a bag of doughnuts and explains, "Collector said you'd be coming by, he left these for ya."

The faint glow of candlelight illuminates Collector's tent. From inside comes the soft murmuring of voices. Sunflower smiles, bids the man goodnight, and starts back to Buffalo Camp, munching on peanut butter and jelly donuts.

Finally, the Buffalo Camp fire appears glowing below him in the woods. He's thankful that the fire is still going, giving him a mark to zero in on as he feels his way toward camp. Dave is sitting there eating popcorn with Henry, an actor from New York City. Sunflower could hardly see their faces. The fire is growing dim. As Sunflower emerges from the darkness, Dave looks up, inquiring, "Where've you been all day?"

Sunflower, handing over the remaining doughnuts to Dave, gazes around the fire. At least a dozen pairs of shoes, boots, and sneakers lie around it. "People been coming by all afternoon 'n' evening, dropping shoes off for ya," Dave explains. "There's some styling shoes here. What have you been telling people? They just keep coming by saying they hope these'll fit ya. This is better than the shoe dumpster in Santa Monica."

Sunflower quickly looks through the pile. His shoes aren't there. But he acknowledges to Dave, "It's a hell of a pile of shoes."

Sunflower feels bad. Surely someone else needs these more than he does. He fills his bowl with popcorn and moves the tea kettle onto the hot coals. He tells Dave and Henry the story of passing the bear on the trail, taking the liberty to double the bear's size: "It was twelve hundred pounds or so and growling real meanlike."

Dave and Henry listen. Knowing Sunflower, they halve the size of the bear, and convert the growls back to "snorfels." The three men fall silent, taking turns poking at the fire. A flying squirrel sails out of a nearby tree and quickly scurries away. Sunflower pours himself a cup of tea. From the lake he hears the eerie sound of a distant flute reflecting on the water and echoing off of the hills.

His gaze wanders across the fire and locks on Dave's feet, illuminated by the dancing flames. He puts down his tea and casually remarks, "Dave, you're wearing my shoes."

Dave looks down at his feet and starts to laugh. "These are yours? I found them in the free box near the Sweat Lodge."

Henry starts chuckling at the prospect of Sunflower laying his shoes to rest in the free box. "Keep them," Sunflower urges Dave, as he pokes through the pile of shoes, trying them on at random. Sunflower grabs a pair he likes, while mumbling about bringing the rest back to the free box tomorrow. He bids Dave and Henry a goodnight and sets off for his tent.

Outside of his tent, he tosses his clothes aside. The night air chills every inch of his skin. He stands there for a few moments looking at the silhouettes of Dave and Henry against the fire, at the stars shining through openings in the trees, and at the first glowing hints of sunrise. Shivering slightly, he crawls into his tent and zips himself into his sleeping bag. The distant heartbeat of the drums lulls him to sleep as a nearby bird begins its morning song.

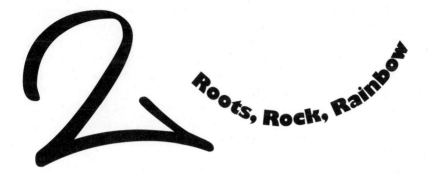

Roots, Rock, Rainbow

We, Sisters and Brothers, children of light, friends of Nature, united by our love for each other and our yearning for peace, do humbly invite Everyone everywhere to join us in expressing our sincere desire, thru prayer, for peace on earth & harmony among all.

—Traditional Invitation to a Rainbow Gathering, 1991

Men, women and children—all of whom together hope to follow the timeless path of love and wisdom, in affectionate company with the sky, winds, clouds, trees, waters, animals and grasses—this is the tribe

—Gary Snyder, *Earth House Hold,* 1969

The Rainbow Family of Living Light is an "intentional group" whose members purposefully gather together to enact a supposedly shared ideology (Erasmus 1981).[1] The Family follows a strong utopian tradition in North America that dates back almost to the time of Western conquest, and it has emerged as the largest utopian community in America. It is a "revitalization movement," a "deliberate, organized, conscious effort by members of a society to construct a more satisfying culture" (Wallace 1956, 265, 279). The self-described purposes of its "Gatherings" are both to further the cause of world peace by prayer and to create a peaceful and cohesive nonhierarchical society that can serve as a model for re-forming "Babylon," the industrialized world.

North American Gatherings, often referred to in the United States as "National Gatherings," are held annually, officially commencing on July 1, and ending on July 7. Including setup and cleanup, the Gatherings actually last about two months, climaxing at noon on July 4 with a silent meditation for world peace: "In that silence, each one of us is left to listen to the wind, feel the earth turn and watch the clouds and sky with our brothers and sisters in the peaceful Cathedral of Nature" (Beck 1991). Rainbows also gather to socialize, communicate, and celebrate life with other Rainbows.

Members call the Rainbow Family "the Family," "the Rainbow Nation," or "the Rainbow Tribe." Anyone can be a member. Indeed, some Rainbows claim *everyone* is, and has always been, a member. All living things are members. The problem, they say, is getting the message to people who have not yet accepted it. It's a doctrine consonant with Sufi and Taoist belief (e.g., Idries 1970; Wong 1990, 17–18). In practice, anyone who attends Gatherings or considers themself a Rainbow, is a Rainbow. While this policy of open membership has, over the years, presented the Family with a host of problems,[2] Rainbows would not have it any other way.

Many of those who convened the first Gathering drew inspiration from the Vortex Festival, a free music festival held near Portland, Oregon, in 1970. While the Rainbow Family's roots certainly are not embedded in a single rock festival, the Vortex festival acted as a catalyst to bring many would-be Rainbows together. The founders envisioned the Gathering as being different, however, from the rock festivals of the late 1960s and early 1970s. Like the Vortex Festival, it was to be noncommercial. The Rainbow Gathering would convene without bands or a central stage. The audience themselves would be the attraction. Unlike San Francisco's 1967 "Be-In," which like the Rainbow Gathering was to be "a gathering of the tribes," the Rainbow Gathering would be in a remote "wilderness" setting. The invitation encouraged people to "join with us in Gathering together for the purpose of expressing our sincere desire that there shall be peace on earth, harmony among all people" (Oracle 1972). The Gathering was to last for four days: On the fourth day there would be a silent meditation for world peace. It was to be a unique event, a great festival of prayer. There were no plans for subsequent Gatherings.

In 1972, more than twenty thousand people attended the first Gathering in Colorado. Initially, Governor John Love ordered them barred from the site. After hundreds of arrests, about four thousand people marched toward the police roadblock, chanting, singing, and blowing bubbles (Hipstory 1990; Jodey, Winter 1988). They were prepared to have their Gathering in jail, if need be. Faced with massive civil disobedience, the authorities let the crowd pass, and the Gathering went on.

The Rainbows, without advance planning, held another Gathering the following year in Wyoming, at which time the participants decided to hold yet another

Gathering the following year in Utah. Hence, the tradition of the annual North American Gathering was born. In 1976, those assembled in Montana agreed to lengthen the Gathering from four to seven days, officially lasting through July 7. In 1978 Hugh Romney, better known as Wavy Gravy, organized a "Kids' Parade," a joyful procession of children to break the meditative silence on July 4. The parade has been a tradition ever since.

At the 1991 Gathering, the children were credited with parting the clouds. A *Time* magazine reporter noted, "An unbeliever must testify that on a cloudy Fourth of July noon, when a parade of children marched to break a morning-long silent vigil at the Circle, the sun came out. And around it was a haze ring that looked a lot like a rainbow" (Skow 1991). Other traditions, like the annual "Peace Pageant," the Faerie Light Show, and the oral "Hipstory" (Rainbow Family oral history) have evolved over the years.

Today's Rainbow Family has grown beyond the confines of the annual North American Gatherings. The Rainbow has proliferated, giving birth to regional Gatherings and projects around the world. The first European Rainbow Family Gathering, for instance, took place in the Italian Alps near the Swiss border in 1983. The organizers, primarily Swiss, drew inspiration from and remained connected to the North American Gatherings, modeling much of their infrastructure, as well as their Council, on the North American model. European Rainbows also draw upon diverse European countercultural activities and groups such as the Greens, Ting[3] (Norway), Systema[4] (Russia), the English Stonehenge festivals, the European peace movements, and squatters' movements. Copenhagen's massive Christiania squat, for instance, regularly provides a kitchen. In 1991, the Family held its first major Gathering in Eastern Europe (Poland).

Meanwhile, in North America, the regional Rainbow movement has continued to grow throughout the conservative Reagan-Bush-Clinton era, with regional Gatherings drawing anywhere from a handful to five thousand people. All are Rainbow Gatherings, yet each is autonomous. They draw from the same inspiration, but develop local flavor. Today at any given time, there is at least one Rainbow Gathering taking place somewhere in the world. Regional Rainbow Gatherings have proliferated, geographically dispersing Rainbow ideas. The idea of a community existing simultaneously in several different locales, however, is not unique to Rainbow. Historic utopian movements such as the Owenites and Fourierists, for example, spread their utopian ideology to satellite communities in the early to mid-nineteenth century.[5]

The Rainbow Family has not yet created, and may never create, a permanent self-sufficient utopia. Gatherings are temporary communities, dependent upon Babylon for material sustenance. While a few Rainbows have dedicated their lives to the Family, for most, Rainbow offers a bargain basement route to "tribal" affiliation without commitment or risk. By bringing its participatory road show around the world, the Rainbow family strengthens and spreads utopian visions while allowing people from various walks of life to sample a radically different lifestyle, even if only for a weekend.

Rainbow Gatherings, interfacing as they do with diverse populations, face many of the same problems of people living in Babylon. The Rainbow Family's approach to solving these problems, however, differs radically from that of Babylon. The successes and failures of this large-scale laboratory should prove instructive to anyone interested in human society and its survival.

Roots

Rainbows attribute the strength of the Rainbow Family to the diversity of its roots. The movement grew from the convergence of two distinctly different and sometimes opposed social categories. One was made up of 1960s peace activists, mostly white, middle-class and educated, who organized the first Gatherings. The other consisted of Vietnam War veterans who came to these Gatherings. While the peaceniks, like many of their utopian predecessors, provided a theoretical framework and belief in nonviolence, the veterans offered an understanding of the realities of war. The peace activists promoted peace, while the veterans were sick of violence. It was a natural union.

The veterans, using skills learned in Vietnam, created much of the Gatherings' infrastructure, from "MASH/CALM" medical facilities to field kitchens and latrines. The confluence of these two groups working, living, and loving together, was part of a national healing process when American involvement in the Vietnam war ended. Where "hippies" and construction workers squared off in the 1960s, peace activists and veteran warriors started building a new society in the 1970s and 1980s. The combination gives the Family a strength that many Rainbows feel it would never have had otherwise.

The Rainbow Family also united diverse peace, pacifist, "alternative-lifestyle," and spiritual groups (including Christian, "Pagan," Sufi, Hindu, Taoist, Jewish, Buddhist, and New Age groups) who otherwise had little contact with one another. The Hipstory, the Rainbow Family's oral history, recalls how in the 1960s the American counterculture was fragmented with people divided among competing political or spiritual camps:

> The Viet Nam war was raging on. There were a lot of us out there who saw the need for people to come together. A few of us met. . . . We spoke amongst ourselves. Wouldn't it be nice, we said, to hear that bell ringing as it were, for everyone to come together. We should do this! Lets invite everybody to come . . . and really go do it. Do it outside of [the confines of individual] nations and religions. OK, you want to be from a particular nation, you have a

particular tribal heritage, you have a particular way of doing your
religious worship—great. Join us. We love you. Welcome home.
(Hipstory July 3, 1990)

In the years since the first Gathering, a wide array of people accepted the invitation to join the Family. A group of Rainbows writing for the Rainbow Family
newspaper, *All Ways Free,* explains: "A diverse and decentralized social fabric began to weave itself from the threads of hippie culture, back-to-the-landers, american
indian [sic] spiritual teachings, pacifist-anarchist traditions, eastern mysticism, and
the legacy of the depression-era hobo street wisdom" (Legaliaison Network 1990).
Other mutually incongruous cultures converge to give rise to the Family. One
embarrassing reality that haunts the supposedly egalitarian Rainbows, for example,
is a class schism between Rainbows who are professionally employed in the corporate sphere, and Rainbows who are "homeless" and jobless. Rainbows credit
this convergence with making the Family strong.

Garrick Beck, who was involved in organizing the first Gathering in 1972 and
who has been an active Rainbow ever since, sees today's growing Rainbow Family as having complex roots:

> Oftentimes the photographer or the newspaper reporter
> comes in, sees three tepees and people walking [around] in loin
> cloths and taking sweats, and concludes that we are basically a
> modern day imitation of Native American life. That's not really
> accurate. There are a lot of people who are way deep into Tibetan
> Buddhism. . . . I think there is a whole root of the Gathering scene
> that comes out of the Beatnik philosophy. . . . One of the key roots
> is in the Sufi movement. There are roots in the Hasidic, and
> Kabbalistic movements. There are roots in the midwestern Ameri-
> can born-again Christian movement. I'm not talking about Tammy
> Bakker TV evangelism nuts. I'm talking about people who have
> religious experiences out on the prairies, and the prairie preach-
> ers; they were teachers during the Depression and they preached
> during World War II and Korea—Pacifism. There are roots in our
> movement that came out of the Korean War. These aren't iso-
> lated cases. These are streams that have come in here, roots in
> our movement through the Sierra Club, the Audubon Society and
> those kind of professional-style ecological movements. There are
> roots in the movement certainly from Jamaica and the Rasta[farian]
> scene. There are roots in our movement out of the freedom that
> occurred during the Allende years in Chile. There are roots in the
> movement from the Spanish anarchists in the nineteen thirties. . . .
> There are people involved in the Rainbow who lived for years with

the aborigines and then drifted back into western civilization and found us and said *YEAH!* There are roots in our movement from Viet Nam Special Forces. There are roots in our movement from Naval Intelligence. There are roots in our movement from people who were working with the CIA and who bailed out of that because they felt those guys were just bastards. People who were working with the CIA because they believed there was a conflict going on in the world between Good and Evil, between Communism and Capitalism, and who worked for the CIA, and the more they found out the more disgusted they got and they jumped ship. . . . When they jumped ship they were looking for who is out there who is really trying to do something in this situation who is not just candy assing up to somebody else for a dollar or a bone. And, you know that is the real strength of the whole Rainbow is that it's *way* more diverse than you would think by a quick glance. (Beck interview 1990)

Garrick Beck drew inspiration from his own roots, growing up amongst the players of *The Living Theater,* a spectator interactive radical theater troupe founded by his parents, Judith Malina and the late Julian Beck.

Many Rainbows argue that the Family's roots predate the first Rainbow Gatherings or even the North American utopian experience by thousands of years, much as Sufis argue that Sufism is more ancient than Islam (Idries 1970). Like Sufis, Taoists, and Buddhists (Cleary 1987, xi–xii), Rainbows claim their Family in some form is ancient, perhaps as old as the species: "The Rainbow Family of Living Light didn't really begin at any specific time, and has never really existed as a formal organization. In many ways, it is a fundamental human expression, the tendency of people to gather together in a natural place and express themselves in ways that come naturally to them, to live and let live, to do unto others as we would have them do unto us" (Legaliaison Network 1990).

The inspiration for many Rainbow values comes from groups with whom there is little obvious connection. For example, much of what was considered new during the 1960s communal renaissance or the utopian movements of the nineteenth century, two periods with a profound influence on the Family, has actually been successfully practiced by the Hutterites since the sixteenth century. The Hutterites, a German Anabaptist movement dating back to 1528, have over four centuries of experience in communal living and pacifism. In the 1870s, the entire Hutterite population migrated to the United States, to escape oppression resulting from their strict adherence to pacifism. Most fled to Canada during World War I when they were again persecuted because of their pacifist beliefs. The current Hutterite population in the United States and Canada numbers over thirty-three thousand people (Oved 1988, 357). Rainbow Gatherings, with their hedonism, are clearly not in the Hutterite tradition, nor is there currently any discernible interaction between the two groups. Most Rainbows are unaware of the Hutterite history of communal pioneering or that their radical new economic ideas have been time-tested and proven sustainable by the conservative Hutterites.

If you ask Rainbows about the Family's roots, you are more likely to hear about Grateful Dead tour,[6] known simply as "Tour," at Gatherings, than about the Hutterites. Tour's roots, like Rainbow's, however, clearly predate the so-called Woodstock generation, having a foundation in American Bohemian traditions. The vagabonding spirit, seen so clearly at Rainbow Gatherings and on Grateful Dead Tour, has long been a utopian tradition (Fogarty 1990, 26). Rainbow and Tour journeying is also an American tradition with firm roots in cultural phenomena such as automobile "gypsying," for example, which developed in America between 1910 and 1920 (Belasco 1979, 11).

The Family also has conscious roots in the revival of primitivism and paganism. Michael John, a professional flight instructor active in the early Gatherings, explains: "Our roots are in the pagan festivals of the Middle Ages, and the Dark Ages, and the time after Christ, when the way we celebrate the summer and our union was common practice for people . . . by being here, something has called us to that memory, to give us the chance to re-experience that. I think that the Rainbow Gathering is just the re-surfacing of the ancient festivals" (interview 1990). Rainbow Family rituals often self-consciously reproduce "pagan" rites the Wicca ("white witch") movement has reconstructed. On a deeper level, however, Rainbow ideology replicates ancient European peasant revolutionary traditions, both in its commitment to absolute equality and its celebration of a past egalitarian Golden Age (e.g., Berger 1979; Blickle 1981; Cohn 1970); its pacifism recalls that of the defeated peasant revolutionaries (e.g., Dentan 1994).

The idea of a utopian model that will reform "Babylon" is an old American tradition, beginning with John Winthrop's "City on a Hill" speech to the Puritan colonists going to Massachusetts (Miller 1956, 78–84), continuing throughout American history (e.g., Holloway 1951). By the late twentieth century, the American "antimodern" revulsion against nineteenth-century industrial capitalism had taken the form of idealizing the "primitives" celebrated by Mormonism and anthropology (e.g., Coates 1987, Dentan 1983). Recasting the medieval Golden Age as a Native American idyll fits this tradition.

Rainbow ideology syncretizes these Euro-American traditions with Thoreauvian pacifism, simplified "New Left" politics, and the "Eastern" religious ideas that flooded America in the years just prior to the first Gathering (cf. Mehta 1979). The resulting mix is so rich and continuously in flux that any description of the Rainbow Family's roots must be inadequate. Since Rainbow ideology holds that all living things are part of the Family, all roots must eventually lead to the Family.

"The Way We Make Decisions Is More Important Than the Decisions We Make": The Rainbow Family Council

3

The Rainbow Nation is the blossoming of the people . . . the togethercoming of all persons who recognize the essential Oneness of humankind and all creation. The Rainbow chooses organization through cooperation, . . . pursuing a path of harmony for life.

—*All Ways Free*, Summer 1990

WE GOVERN BY CONSENSUS AND PEACEFUL RESPECT. Our council meets daily and provides [a] forum open for everyone to attend. The [G]athering is a participatory workshop in self-government

—North East Rainbow Family, 1991

The Rainbow Family's governing body is a "Council" (with a capital C) whose membership is open to all interested persons. It strives toward being nonexclusionary and nonhierarchical. In Rainbow jargon, when two or more people meet for discussion, they are "counciling." Hence, the Rainbow Family has numerous Councils, each with authority to make decisions only when all people affected by the decision have the opportunity to join the Council. Two people can council to decide how they will spend their evening, or a kitchen's Council may convene to decide the day's menu.

Decisions that affect the entire North American Rainbow Family are made by a large main Council, often referred to simply as "Council," which consists of anyone who wants to participate. This Council meets annually, "on the land" (at the North American Gathering), from the first through the seventh of July.

Arriving at a decision requires consensus by the entire Council. When Council reaches a decision, Rainbows say they have "consensed." Unlike majoritarian democracies, Rainbow Family Council participants never vote. The fact that the smallest minorities have effective veto power prevents majorities from ignoring their concerns. No Rainbow Family Council makes any decisions until those participating reach a compromise acceptable to *everyone* concerned. The process demands creativity, perseverance, and an extraordinary amount of patience. When it is functioning properly, it eliminates the trimmings of electoral democracy: the perpetual campaigns of competing ideological camps, each firmly entrenched in its own philosophies and unwilling to compromise, forever battling for hegemony. The result is not a fractured society, but a large family, whose members argue that it is strengthened by unanimity and untainted by authoritarianism.

Sky Bear, a Rainbow brother from Pennsylvania, describes how Council works:

> Consensus groups do not vote. To vote is like admitting failure because consensus is not happening. There is usually a long discussion before a group reaches a consensus. This drives newcomers up a wall. But consensus groups believe that at least one solution that satisfies everyone is out there. We just have to find it. We listen to whoever is talking, believing that the answer might come from anyone in the circle. It is a good idea to pass the speaking energy around the circle in a sun-wise [clockwise] direction giving in turn each person the opportunity to speak or be silent. All of us need the practice to be quiet and listen. We might have our idea that seems to want to jump out now, being impatient, as our past experiences have led us to believe in contradicting others, and picking apart their ideas, [we] need to wait until our time comes back around. How surprised [we are] to learn that another has expressed our very own idea before us, and maybe in a clearer fashion. Or another idea has changed ours. So we listen to the GROUP mind, and try to quiet our own. Consensus groups take care of two things, Task, and Maintenance. Task is the problem that the group is working on. Maintenance means that the group pays attention to people's feelings so that everyone can feel good about the consensus. (Sky Bear 1991)

The Rainbow Family is rare, among utopian communities, in its strict adherence to governance by consensus of the *entire* group. Only a handful of groups have followed Quaker and Native American traditions in developing consensus governments. Among them are the Philadelphia Life Center, an urban community started in 1971, consisting of about eighteen cooperative homes affiliated with the Movement for a New Society (M.N.S.); the Alpha Farm, an Oregon cooperative also founded in 1971; and New Mexico's Lama Community, founded in 1967.

The Lama Community insisted on consensus of the entire membership after experiencing a failed attempt by a group of members to take control of the community (McLaughlin and Davidson 1985, 77). Their full group consensus process, which began as a reaction to a bad event, was eventually abandoned after members tired of "day-long meetings" (McLaughlin and Davidson 1985, 77). The Movement for a New Society, however, like the Rainbow Family, has maintained a strong commitment to consensus government. The Movement has prepared training manuals aimed at teaching other groups how to practice consensus government, which they view as a powerful tool for raising consciousness.

What is noteworthy about the Rainbow model is the scale on which it has been applied. The Rainbow Family, with over one hundred thousand participants worldwide,[1] has governed Gatherings of up to thirty thousand people successfully, by consensus, since 1972. The Alpha Farm, by comparison, also has a successful track record with consensus, yet they have only twenty members. Rainbows view large Councils as being potentially rich with diverse ideas. Joseph Wetmore, a longtime Rainbow and student of consensus government, observed, "Large numbers of people at Council is a strength, not a weakness. The more people at Council, the more likely that a person with an innovative solution to a problem or a person who sees a fatal flaw in a suggested plan of action will be in attendance" (1990a).

The Rainbow example testifies to the viability of consensus government and its potential application on a large scale. Still, most participants at the large North American Gatherings forgo attending Council. Their apathy leaves the Gatherings governed by an activist minority. This minority often consists of "elders" who have attended many Gatherings, a ruling class whose existence Family members often deny. Full participation by thousands of Gatherers would make the Council unwieldy and chaotic. Rainbows aim for a middle ground with most camps or kitchens, and all ideological viewpoints, represented at Council. Ironically, it is the apathy of the masses, expressed in their absence from Council, that allows for a cohesive governing body. Smaller Gatherings, however, like those held in Quebec, have nearly full participation at Councils. Many Rainbows, in the utopian tradition of creating a model for reforming the larger society, view creating and maintaining a working example of consensus government as a primary motivation for holding the Gatherings.

While the Council discusses the logistical business of the day, as well as the future of the Rainbow Family, the Council circle also serves as a forum for the personal passions and poetics of individual participants. Some people come to the Council to make announcements, others to solicit help for a project or a personal problem; some come to share their thoughts, desires, fears, and emotions; others come simply to smile, giggle or listen. Garrick Beck explains: "Maybe 500 people or more sit in a big circle and each person gets to speak and everyone who attends is a member of the Council. People speak whatever is on their mind, and the Council goes on all day, and sometimes it is fascinating, and sometimes it is comic, and sometimes it is frustrating, and sometimes it is boring, but it is!" (Weinberg 1989b, 9–10A).

One thing that it is not, however, is predictable. Heated arguments may momentarily halt for group hugs, after which the arguments resume, usually more productively. Long-winded diatribes may be followed by jumping jacks, tearful stories by prayer, and consensuses by jubilant singing. A typical Council may include a mother crying about the state's seizure of her children, a man talking about the consistency of a recent bowel movement, and announcements about the loss of a "sacred" rattle or a favorite pair of sneakers. The same Council might listen to a poem, debate turning a mentally disturbed person over to the authorities, and discuss where the next day's food will come from or how to respond to a police roadblock. Beck writes:

> We feel this is an advanced and subtle process that puts the benefit of everyone at its heart, that recognizes the innate intelligence of the human character, that keeps poetry music and lightness in the midst of our debate and that awakens us to the experience of direct personal participation in the process of our association.
>
> It is so sweet, so tasty this process—even when it is bogged down, it is full of compassion and commitment. We have . . . found it to be an effective means of self-organization and found it to be an effective aid in the prevention of political decay. (Beck 1986, 16)

Rainbow Council has taken many forms over the years, using differing methods interchangeably at various regional and North American Gatherings. There are, however, distinct features that are supposed to be common to all Rainbow Family Councils. Foremost is respect: respect for the person speaking, respect for everyone's right to speak about whatever concerns them, respect for all views and opinions, and respect for the Council itself. Council pays respect to the person speaking, regardless of what their class status would be outside in Babylon. Gathering economics are vital to the functioning of Council. Gatherings take place on public land,[2] thus there are no landlords who can stand up in Council and threaten an eviction if they don't get their way. Kitchens feed everybody, whether or not they work; people can find clothing in free boxes, and community shelters protect people from the rain. The workers are their own taskmasters; there is no supervisory class. Thus, anyone can take time off from a "job" to attend Council. Anyone can speak up without fear of losing their means of sustenance.

The Feather

Another common feature of Rainbow Councils is passing an object, usually a feather, from speaker to speaker within the Council circle.[3] The function of this object is to focus the Council's attention and respect onto whoever has the floor at any given time. This focus keeps the Council orderly and centered. The Rainbow family currently employs various "processes" to determine how to pass focal objects.

Although a feather, sometimes attached to a staff, is the traditional "focal object," more and more Rainbow Councils are substituting randomly chosen objects so as to refocus attention on the speaker rather than the object itself. Arguments over whose feather to pass, and people's possessiveness about their feathers, have caused problems in the past, inducing various Rainbow Councils to pass bowls, stones, or shoes instead. Bowls, which many Rainbows claim represent "female energy," are often passed to balance the excessive "male energy" allegedly represented by staffs.

A Council's becoming attached to a given focal object is not unique to Rainbow. Some, however, see such an attachment as advantageous. Jack Zimmerman and Virginia Coyle write and teach about the Council process. They argue that a consistently used focal object is beneficial: "Many councils that meet regularly use the same object over a period of months or even years, so that it becomes a symbol of the group's integrity and its capacity for spirited communication" (1991, 80).

The Family worries, however, that "sacred" feathers and staffs might lead to a hierarchy. Council newcomers might view the person who owned or cared for the focal object as a leader. Rainbow Councils, on various occasions, could not begin until the person with the proper feather arrived. Free of "sacred" props, the Council stands on its own merit. People admonish someone who interrupts a speaker to "respect the feather," although it is acceptable to shout "ho!" when one agrees with the speaker. Friendly and sometimes not so friendly shouts of "Respect the feather" punctuate arguments even when a bowl or shoe, for instance, is the focal object. A forest ranger, having picked up the habit after participating in a number of Rainbow Councils, chided a disorderly participant in a town meeting in Tofte, Minnesota,[4] to "respect the feath . . . er . . . person speaking" (Nelson Video 1990).

Interrupting a speaker is taboo, for focused listening is key to all Council procedures. Zimmerman and Coyle write: "Not too long ago, before our ears became accustomed to an increasing barrage of stimulation, many people knew how to listen attentively, while tracking an animal or hearing the approach of rain—or sitting in council with a group of their peers. When we are graced with that kind of listening and devoted to its practice, our ability to be empathic grows and we enter a world in which decisions are made by discovery and recognition rather than argument and voting" (1991, 80–81).

The ranger who implored his audience to respect the speaker is just one of many U.S. Forest Service representatives who have participated in Rainbow Councils over the years. For many, it was an eye-opening experience. The Okanogan National Forest report on the Rainbow Family describes Rainbow Council as "a loosely-knit group where anyone is welcome and anyone can speak." The report concluded, "Their organization is quite democratic in nature; no perceived chain of command exists, and no one person is going to give orders" (Okanogan N.F. 1981, B2).

Forest Service interest in the Rainbow Council grows out of more than simple curiosity. Although the Family has an unwavering policy of not signing permits, the Rainbow Family Council sometimes engages in informal treatylike verbal agreements with the U.S. Forest Service, the National Park Service, and a host of local governmental agencies and law enforcement organizations with jurisdiction over the areas where Gatherings occur. Forest Service people, operating in conventional bureaucratic modes, often find Council baffling. One Forest Service official writes: "The frustration level at these councils is high; with no pre-set agenda, quite often trivia rules as the major topic. In addition, interruptions are frequent and moving from one subject to the next without full discussion or decisions of the topics at hand is also common. Thus, to get down to those areas of real priority requires a great deal of time and just plain tenacity" (Quintanar 1981, 2).

When the Heart Sings

Unlike Forest Service officials who come to Rainbow Councils with an agenda to cover, most Rainbows view the Council as an open forum for all concerns, be they business or what Rainbows refer to as "Heartsong." The smiles and giggles mentioned earlier are an integral part of the Council. Sharing emotions and feelings creates a bond that strengthens people's ability to cooperate in creating consensus. For this reason, large Rainbow Councils usually start with Heartsongs before business. During Heartsong, participants pass a focal object clockwise/sunwise around the Council circle through each person's hands, giving everyone an opportunity to speak. The speaker entertains no questions, but passes the object on when done. This is especially true of the first Councils at any Rainbow get-together. It is a way for people to say hello, introduce themselves, and share their basic concerns.

Heartsongs are often compelling stories or tormenting problems, coaxed out into the open by the supportive environment nurtured in the Council circle. At one Gathering, for example, a man revealed he had recently learned that he was infected with the AIDS virus. A woman told of being gang-raped by fifteen men. Little children used the forum to bounce their ideas off of adults. The Council invited introverts to express themselves and encouraged listeners to take the opportunity to share the wisdom of their observations. Councils are sometimes convened solely for Heartsong. Meetings specifically held for such "confessions" have been acknowledged by sociologists as important ingredients for success in many different groups, ranging from the Shakers (Holloway 1951, 226) to Alcoholics Anonymous[5] (Dentan 1994, 69–108). The Council is thus more than a simple decision-making body. For Rainbow People it is a sacred, healing space. People talk as if Council decisions are divinely inspired; in any case, some magic is necessary for hundreds of people to be of one mind.

On the other hand, failure to reach consensus on an issue is not necessarily a problem for Rainbows. They point out that coming up with two solutions, or a composite formulated by synthesizing parts of different solutions, is often superior to the more conventional approach of adopting one idea outright and abandoning another entirely. On occasion, the Council is unable to consense to any solution to the problem at hand, yet Rainbows still see the meeting as productive. Long, seemingly inconclusive, meetings, a common feature of non-Western societies, are useful for airing problems. Karan Brison, an ethnographer who lived with the Kwanda, observed that the airing of grievances in such meetings has a therapeutic effect: "Public discussions provide a forum where people can persuade others through skillful oratory, and display their right to be 'considered wise'" (Brison 1989, 97).

A Difficult Vision Evolves

Some decisions, however, must be made. One such decision is up to the Vision Council, which meets on the last day of the Gathering to choose the locale for the following year's Gathering. At the 1987 Gathering in North Carolina, the Vision Council, in which all Rainbows are welcome to participate, took three days of around-the-clock discussions to choose Texas as the site for the 1988 Gathering. People still debate whether this decision was divinely inspired or resulted from persistent lobbying by a small group. Consensus encourages people to work together, but it also permits them to abuse it for their own purposes.

About the 1987 Vision Council, Learner Harmony, a longtime Rainbow, wrote:

> The last VISION Council turned into an endurance contest, to put it mildly, 3 $^1/_2$ days with only one break. This was caused by 10 to 20 people, mostly brothers, with egos bigger than themselves, pulling power trips on the Council. First they tried to railroad Nevada as a site for the Gathering. Then after the break, they all changed their minds simultaneously and railroaded Texas.
>
> Finally in weariness the people left at the Council exhausted their will to struggle, and the Council gave up to a form of con-

sensus, but in reality, the consensus was not there. There is no substance of consensus.

We are on the cutting edge of a new form of government. If this experiment is going to work, we are going to have to develop rules (guidelines) by which the problems that arise are resolved.

Consensus by attrition is one of those problems that must be resolved. It is not, in fact, true consensus, and it is not going to work. If attrition is allowed to pervert the consensus process, I do not see any advantage in it over the republican system by which this country is currently governed and probably a disadvantage to a democratic system which makes laws by majority vote. (Harmony 1989, 28)

A similar situation arose during the 1988 Vision Council in Texas. Again decision was by attrition. This time a handful of tired rain-soaked people made their decision shortly before sunrise. Truthhawk, a participant, describes the scene:

One guy was asleep, one woman couldn't even talk she was so zoned out, and the general feeling was, we weren't really the vision council anyhow. As I walked towards my tent, I heard Phil again asking for consensus for Nevada.

The next day I heard about the "decision" the vision council had made the night before. (Truthhawk 1989, 28)

The chaos of these two Vision Councils highlighted a procedural weakness in the Rainbow Council. The Council at the Nevada Gathering eventually consensed a policy that no Rainbow Family Vision Council consensus could be reached after sundown. While the Council could continue into the night, the full Council would have to ratify all decisions in the light of day.

While addressing the problem of consensus by attrition, the edict did not address another weakness of the Rainbow Council: its vulnerability to obstructionism. Since a single member of Council may block consensus indefinitely, consensus councils work only when *all* participants are genuinely committed to finding mutually equitable solutions to questions at hand. Blocking consensus, Rainbows point out, should be a means of last resort when compromise is impossible. A block, they say, means, "I cannot live with this decision; if this decision is final, I can no longer be a part of this group."

A Coup in Minnesota

In 1990 the Council process was threatened again, not by endless Councils, but an absence of Council altogether during the critical three-week Seed Camp stage of the Gathering. The problems associated with the 1990 North American Gathering's Council exemplify how Rainbows deal with Counciling problems.

Key decisions during the 1990 Seed Camp were made not by Council but by a small group claiming to "represent" the Rainbow Family Council. This group negotiated road closures and logistical concerns with local Forest Service officials. For the sake of brevity, I will call them "the Gate Crew." Armed with the minutes of a "Council" most people were not aware occurred, the Gate Crew erected a gate controlling traffic on the road leading to the Gathering area. Their most controversial action was to relocate Bus Village[6] to an isolated area some distance from the Gathering, as the Forest Service preferred in past years[7] (Marshall May 15, 1980). The Forest Service recognized the Gate Crew as being "in charge" of the Gathering by virtue of the Crew's control of the access road. The arrangement suited the Forest Service, since it gave them a definite "leadership" with whom to negotiate, a convenience they had wanted for years.

The scouts[8] who selected the Gathering site, however, had planned to locate Bus Village much closer to the main Gathering. This change in plan left new arrivals confused and angry. The Gate became a focus of discontent, with daily confrontations as live-in vehicles attempted to drive past it to where they thought Bus Village would be located. There was no forum, however, to rectify these concerns since regular Council meetings involving all concerned parties—and thus having decision-making authority—had not begun.

People discussed the Gate during the informal Heartsong circle that was meeting daily, but this circle lacked the governing authority of a Main Council. A number of small Councils were operating, dealing with the concerns of various groups within the Gathering, such as the Banking Council and the Kitchen Council. None, however, won universal recognition as the Main Council. With more Rainbows arriving daily, and the actual Gathering getting closer, Council clearly needed a jump-start.

The established and recognized process for initiating a formal Rainbow Family Seed Camp Main Council is simple. The first step is for an initiator to announce in the main circle area that he or she is calling a Council to deal with an agenda that that person then describes. Rainbow participatory principles enable anyone to convene a Council; all voices should be heard. At the 1990 Gathering, the Council was called by José Many Paths, who was incensed by the chaos at the front gate and by what he viewed as subversion of the collective process (Many Paths interview 1990).

The Council convener must set a time. Then the task of notifying everyone at the Gathering begins. José allowed himself and others a full day to travel about and make certain that word of the impending Council reached the far corners of the Gathering. José was soon joined by others who wanted to see a Council begin. Together they spent the rest of the day, evening, and night hiking from camp to camp, from fire to fire, spreading the word of the upcoming Council. They made the announcement at dinner circles that evening as well as at breakfast circles the following morning. In the course of spreading the word of the forthcoming Council, José met many people, ate well, and had an opportunity to visit new camps.

For a Council to win recognition, it must represent, as well as possible, the interests of everyone affected by its decisions. If key people, like the members of the Gate Crew, have no opportunity to attend, Council's decisions will be illegitimate. A new Council would have to convene to include them so that all people concerned could participate in making the decision and understand how the Council came to its decision. If it is clear, however, that people are avoiding Council so as not to be held accountable for their actions, Council will, as a last resort, proceed without them. That Council would also discuss how to best deal with people who are dodging Council.

Seed Camp Councils like the one described here have authority only to solve problems at hand, not to make or change Rainbow Family policy. Rainbow Family policy decisions for the North American Rainbow Family can be made only on-the-land at the Gathering at Councils on the first through the seventh of July,[9] when the North American Rainbow Family officially meets as an entity.

The Council that José initiated met at Rainbow noon, roughly the time when the sun is high in the sky, on June 30, and began in a traditional fashion. A participant sounded a conch, blowing it while facing each of the four directions, to announce the beginning of Council. Everyone joined hands, forming a circle. There was a moment of silence, followed by a collectively uttered "Om." José, as the initiator, explained why he called the Council and then passed the feather to the person sitting next to him in the circle. The Council began with Heartsong and evolved into "business."

For most people who arrived on-site during the latter half of June, this was their first Council. As such, it provided a forum for long-overdue discussions about infrastructure problems such as where to locate water systems and latrines, even though this was not the specific subject José convened Council to address. The subject of drinking water turned out to be the most consequential topic, because laboratory reports indicated that none of the water on-site was potable. There was talk, for instance, of water-boiling kitchens, which in the end never came to be. The Council did, however, authorize a "Magic Hat Dance" to go from camp to camp, raising money to combat the water problem. The money was eventually used to buy truckloads of drinking water from the local fire department and from commercial dairy haulers.

The Gate Crew was, of course, a major topic. People were less concerned with their closing the road than with the way in which it was closed, the way the Crew operated. Council, with three hundred people present, affirmed the scouts' "vision" for a closer Bus Village. Without debate they agreed to abolish the gate and open the road.[10] The decision had more of a moral than a practical effect. The Gate was an established fact. People had set up camps near the closed road.[11]

Logistically, opening the road would have caused chaos, allowing vehicles into what had already become a central area of the Gathering.

Thus, despite Council's veto of the gate, it still stood, and despite Council's declaring the road open, it was still closed. People from the Gate Crew were neither attending Council or respecting edicts of Council consensed to in their absence. Thus, it was not a full Council. Council could decide only how to interact with the Gate Crew or how to bring them to Council. It could not make decisions that would affect the Gate Crew. A delegation from Council went to the gate area to explain Council's decision to the Gate Crew. A member of that delegation recalls how a Gate Crew leader told him he "didn't care what Council wanted," explaining he had "been with Rainbow for 19 years." These "new people," he went on, "were too new to Rainbow to make any decisions." He also said he didn't recognize any Council other than the one that would meet July 1–7 (Wetmore 1990).

The Council decision turned out to be a success, not in opening the road, but in forcing a disturbing issue to the surface. The Gate Crew's response seemed to indicate contempt for the Council process. Many Rainbows present at the time started suspecting the existence of a shadow Rainbow Family government operating free from the democratic constraints of Council. Bureaucratic organizations that deal with the Rainbow Family have seldom accepted consensus government, often looking for Rainbows they could recognize as leaders.[12] Ranger Bob Burton's widely distributed description of the Rainbow Family accurately alludes to an ad hoc hierarchy: "There is no easily defined leadership group or formal organization in the Rainbow Family. Members will tell you that none exists, that decisions are made by consensus, that all have an equal say in decision making and that the power is equally shared. As a Gathering develops it becomes apparent, however that some shares are more equal than others" (Burton 1990).

Left unchecked, there is a tendency for a de facto hierarchy to form, especially among people who negotiate with the Forest Service. In the case of the Gate Crew, this emerging hierarchy was easily checked once its existence became public knowledge. The ease with which any Rainbow can initiate a Council, or participate in one, works against power plays. José, for instance, was relatively unknown within the Family, and had never actively participated in Council proceedings before initiating the Seed Camp Council. Since Rainbows generally reject authority and leaders, an exposed hierarchy will perish through ostracism. Rainbows who resist such a hierarchy will easily win support.

Under protest, key players in the Gate Crew yielded to peer pressure and attended what turned out to be a loud and lively Council meeting on the following day, July 1. Although the road was still closed and the Gate stood in place, both became subjects of debate in what, for the Family, was the proper forum—Council. The discussion made it clear that opening the road would cause chaos. The popular face-saving option was for Council to order the closed road closed. This consensus, however, eluded Council. In the end, although the road stayed closed without a consensus, most participants were satisfied because they had called the Gate Crew to account for their actions.

The July I Council had a full agenda and elicited lively discussion on all issues. It was cut short, however, at about 6:30 P.M., when various kitchens brought dinner to the Council Meadow. Council could not withstand the presence of warm food. A growing crowd of would-be diners entered the Council circle and demanded Council break so they could eat. Despite unfinished business, Council closed for dinner. The circle filled with music afterwards, and Council did not reconvene until the following day. Anticipating lively entertainment, a good-sized crowd turned out for this Council and later spread the word of Council activities throughout the Gathering. The Council, chaotic as it seemed, was firmly back in operation.

A New Way to Council

While the Council "process" is slowly evolving on the North American level, smaller regional Rainbow Councils are developing more rapidly, experimenting with innovations to improve the way they council. These smaller regional Councils are finding answers to many of the problems plaguing the larger North American Councils. The North East Rainbow Family (formerly the New England Rainbow Family), known in Rainbow circles as "NERF," is one of the larger and more active regional groups. A look at NERF's development illuminates how a regional Rainbow "organization" coalesces.

NERF began in 1987 as the New England Rainbow Family. New Englanders, camped in the Scuzzy Womp[13] Camp at the 1987 North American Gathering in North Carolina, first discussed the idea of forming a New England regional Council (Mariann interview 1990). They later called a Council at that Gathering to discuss ideas for, and plan, a New England regional Gathering. Held the following month on private land in Wendell, Massachusetts, the Gathering drew about five hundred people. There NERF, as a Gathering entity, was born. As the New England Rainbow Family, NERF held Gatherings of about fifteen hundred people in Vermont's Green Mountains National Forest in 1988 and 1989. In 1989, NERF became the North East Rainbow Family, representing a region that, in addition to the New England states, included New York, New Jersey, Quebec, and Canada's Atlantic provinces. NERF's largest Gathering attracted over four thousand people in 1990 near Ithaca, New York.

The 1990 North American Vision Council in Minnesota, impressed with NERF's track record for relatively problem-free Gatherings, consensed to have NERF choose a site for, and organize, the 1991 North American Rainbow Gathering. It took place in Vermont. NERF dutifully accepted this unwanted burden, planning for the Gathering during Fall, Winter, and Spring Councils. While planning the Gathering that they were to host, NERF began analyzing its own "Council process," feeling that it was beginning to buckle under the weight of larger Councils associated with planning the North American Gathering. The 1990 North American Thanksgiving Council hosted by NERF in Wendell, Massachusetts, thus exemplifies how Council procedures develop and how regional Families plan a North American Gathering.

A Rainbow Thanksgiving

The facilities in Wendell were ideal for the Council. The Rainbow Family occupied the town hall for meals and music and the town meetinghouse for counciling and sleeping. Between the two buildings was the town common, ideally suited for running, jumping, throwing Frisbee, and circling to chant "Om." The ground rules agreed upon by both NERF and the town of Wendell were simple: no fires in buildings—not even sacred fires—and no loud outdoor noise at night. The Rainbows took care not to disturb the handful of neighbors in the isolated hamlet.

About three hundred Rainbows, mostly from the northeastern states and provinces, but with representatives from as far away as California, arrived at Wendell. A hundred or so arrived early on Thursday evening to share a Thanksgiving feast. On Friday morning, a well-fed scout Council met to discuss potential sites for the upcoming Gathering. The sites that nobody had actually seen, they agreed, sounded the most promising.

Friday evening, the Thanksgiving Council officially began, with an opening circle, food, music, dance, and celebration. Friday night was playtime, strictly a social event. Work could wait. The actual business at hand was to begin on Saturday and continue on Sunday, commencing both days at Rainbow noon and running until sunset. NERF, having learned from the Vision Council fiascos in North Carolina and Texas, had already consensed to a rule barring decisions after sunset. The rule prevented stubborn caucuses from subverting, through sheer endurance, the intent of government by consensus. However, it had drawbacks. While it worked well at midsummer Gatherings, when the sun set around 9 P.M., the rule put a serious time constraint on November Councils, when the sun set at 4:30 P.M. The situation was especially troublesome since Rainbow noon rarely occurs before 1 P.M. Therefore the NERF Council had to spend most of Saturday's precious little counciling time in heated debate as to how the time should best be spent.

The Council began smoothly, using a four-stone rotation. At the start of Council, someone places four stones in the middle of the circle of people, forming a smaller circle. Two opposite stones are "male," the other two are "female." Would-be speakers queue up according to gender behind one of the stones. The feather or object of focus, in this case a bowl, is then passed sunwise, or clockwise, by the speakers around this inner circle from stone to stone. The stones assure that a man or boy speaker will be followed by a woman or girl, thus counteracting any tendency for "male energy" to dominate Councils. After speaking, participants step back into the outer circle, allowing others to queue up to speak. Speakers can reenter the inner circle by queuing up to speak again, if "the spirit" has so driven them.

Initially as a joke, one person put down his conch shell, proclaiming, "I'll just leave my marker here." The idea caught on. The room was crowded, and it was physically difficult for people to line up behind the stones. Soon people had lined up cups, bowls, hats, hairbrushes, and other personal belongings behind the different stones, much as bar patrons line up quarters on a pool table.

To help the Council run smoothly, participants agreed to have four vibeswatchers and two gatekeepers help with the proceedings. Vibeswatchers monitor the tenor of the Council, intervening to keep it calm, while discouraging anger, aggression, or other manifestations of "bad vibes." The vibeswatchers, selected by Council consensus for their levelheadedness, interrupt Council, no matter who has the feather, if they feel the "vibes" are getting out of hand. Upon stopping the proceedings, the vibeswatcher will usually recommend a moment of silence, a group "Om," a stretching exercise, or a group hug. Once the "vibes" have "mellowed," Council can resume. The concept is not unique to Rainbow. The Movement for a New Society, for example, also recommends vibeswatchers in its councils.

Gatekeepers brief late arrivals about which Council procedures are in use, what is presently being discussed, who has said what, what has already happened, and so forth. Their purpose is to keep late arrivals from wasting Council time by bringing up points already discussed and raising irrelevancies. Once briefed, newcomers can participate fully in the Council without having to guess what is actually going on at the moment.

With vibeswatchers and gatekeepers in place, the Thanksgiving Council launched into Heartsong. An old woman spoke of retiring into a proposed Rainbow Peace Village,[14] as opposed to an "old folks home." "I'm counting on you folks to take care of me," she implored. She also said she wanted to be buried under a hazelnut tree. She felt this arrangement would be more environmentally sound than a cemetery. Greg from California, on his first trip east, discussed his fear of winter. Others talked about empowering children by involving them in the planning for Kids' Village. People worried that the "war" on drugs could be a smokescreen for a war on Rainbows. The American obsession with child molesting, someone else noted, could rationalize a war on parenting in alternative communities. A brother who had been living on the road warned the Family not to let the middle class dominate Councils. "Middle-class people," he implored, were "brought up knowing their voices would be heard" and were therefore more "articulate" than poorer Rainbows.

An hour into Heartsong, someone suggested that the Council move to dealing with the concerns of organizing the North American Gathering. Practical logistical problems loomed, not the least of which was the lack of a workable Gathering site.

Nevertheless, many people objected to truncating Heartsong. An emotionally charged procedural discussion ensued, as the Council attempted to identify a precise time for the move to occur. On one side, people were concerned that Heartsong be respected as an intrinsic part of Council, not to be slighted or in any way rushed. Heartsong had to lead off Councils, they asserted, because it brought people together psychologically and spiritually. Other people argued that sisters and brothers had traveled great distances to participate collectively, hashing out serious and complex logistical issues in a short period of time. Since Heartsong did not fall under the new rule against consensus after sunset, it could take place then, they insisted.

The argument about how to ration the limited time became long and drawn out, with numerous short breaks imposed by the vibeswatchers for hugs, om circles, and so forth. After sixty-three minutes, the Council decided to continue Heartsong. Opponents realized that the quickest way to get to the topics of Gathering planning logistics was to yield and let Heartsong run its course. Two Heartsongs later, however, the Council renewed the debate, which lasted for another twenty-two minutes, before moving on to planning the North American Gathering.

Once discussion of the upcoming Gathering began, Council decided to break up into four committees, which hashed out specific issues and then returned to make recommendations to the whole Council. Smaller groups, people argued, facilitated better discussion. The four subgroups concentrated on spiritual affairs, site selection, political realities, and material concerns such as fund-raising and banking, kitchens, and supply procurement. The consensuses of these smaller circles came to the full Council on Sunday for discussion.

Sunday's Council revolved around the reports from the four sub-Councils. Each group had selected a reporter to convey to the Council the recommendations of the group. The reporters focused discussion, entertained questions, and clarified the group's recommendations. The site sub-Council's report posed no problems, as it required no action. Not having any acceptable sites to evaluate, they suggested criteria for selecting a site, but recommended postponing the choice of a site until Spring Council. The Political sub-Council recommended that Quebec Hydro's James Bay II project, slated at the time to flood major portions of Cree land in Northern Quebec (e.g., Anon. 1991; Weinberg 1990b; LaDuke 1990; Linden 1991; McCutcheon, 1991; Cultural Survival [Canada], 1991a), be a focal topic of the Gathering. The sub-Council recommended organizing a protest of the project, to take place after the Gathering. The Council consensed a sub-Council proposal to create a Political Information Center at the Gathering; this center would serve as a networking area for political activists.

The spiritual concerns sub-Council addressed the physical layout of the Gathering, concurring with the site selection sub-Council that finding a site with a central meadow should be the main priority. The lack of a central meadow at the 1990

North American Gathering, they felt, caused the Gathering to be "scattered" and contributed to many of Council's problems. The site, they said, should be laid out with four main spurs "heading in the four directions," emanating from the central meadow. Based on recommendations from the Material sub-Council, the Council consensed to appointing a Banking Council of ten people to manage money raised for the Gathering.

The Council could not agree upon an exact list of items that "Magic Hat" (a communal collection) money could be used to buy. While nobody felt that Magic Hat money should pay for alcohol, some people thought it should cover meat and coffee expenses for the Seed Camp crew. Many Rainbows who come a month early for Seed Camp and construct most of the Gathering's infrastructure, they said, are "serious" coffee drinkers or habitual meat eaters who had a right to their coffee or meat—especially in light of their monumental effort for the Gathering. The issue involved more than the politics of eating. It became a class issue. The people who controlled the money, the argument went on, had no right to use their economic clout to dictate a diet for the moneyless. People still objected on political, vegetarian, spiritual, and health grounds. A debate followed about the use of the Magic Hat funds. When the discussion segued to dairy products and issues of animal husbandry and "enslavement," Council tabled the whole question to be discussed by Spring Council. If the Spring Council couldn't reach a decision, eventually a Supply Council would take up the discussion. Participation in any of these subsequent Councils, of course, would be open to all interested parties.

Also on Sunday, the Council identified numerous aspects of the planned Gathering that needed further examination, including some political concerns. Volunteers formed fifty "focalizing" committees to take responsibility for discussing a list of topics pertaining to the upcoming Gathering (see Appendix).

The committees were responsible for facilitating spaces and activities at the Gathering, and organizing politically around issues that affect Rainbows, like working to protect free speech and preserve the First Amendment. The largest committee was that formed to discuss the Council itself. The weekend concluded with people promising to stay in touch and work together throughout the winter and spring. The vast majority of these committees, however, never met again.

Although the North American planning Council would not reconvene until spring, NERF organized a smaller regional Mid-Winter Council, which took place in Ithaca, New York, during January of that year. At the top of the agenda for NERF's Winter Council was how to run a Council. Many people within NERF wanted to refine and specify Council procedures so as to offer revamped Council procedures to the North American Rainbow Family's Spring Council, which NERF was to host.

On the second day, after protracted discussion, the Mid-Winter Council consensed to the following procedures to be used for the rest of the day and offered to other Councils in the future:

1. The Council opens with a group Om.
2. The facilitator and cofacilitator introduce themselves,[15] the previously prepared agenda, and Council procedures.
3. The Council chooses at least two vibeswatchers, at least two gate keepers, a timekeeper (optional) to make periodic announcements regarding what time it is, how much is left until dark, etc., and scribe(s) who act as recording secretaries.
4. The Council checks for consensus on the people chosen.
5. Brainstorm agenda list.
6. Heartsong
7. Agenda Review (prioritize list and set time frames for different subjects)
8. Check for consensus on agenda.
9. Post agenda where Council participants can easily see it.
10. Follow agenda as set by Council consensus—one issue at a time.
11. Pass the chosen object sun-wise to allow each person to speak in Heartsong or on business related to the issue.
12. The speaker will not be interrupted except for "process points;" interruptions which are used to point out when Council procedures are not being followed.[16]
13. The speaker can choose whether or not to accept questions.
14. If the speaker chooses to accept questions, they will be accepted in sun-wise order around the circle.
15. After the feather/chosen object makes its first pass around the circle, the group can continue to go sun-wise around the circle, with or without the object until the topic comes to completion or consensus.
16. Everyone is responsible to help facilitate the process by being aware of topic, time, vibes, feelings and clarity.

NERF members felt that their Rainbow equivalent of Robert's *Rules of Order* would do for Rainbow meetings what the *Rules of Order* did for parliamentary procedures: rationalize them by providing an authoritative way to solve disputes about how to carry on discussions. The Ithaca Council also addressed the problem of mixing Council time with meal time, but did not come up with a firm resolution. Despite enthusiastic lobbying, NERF's structured Council process was never adopted by the larger on-the-land Councils at the North American Gatherings. Elements of the NERF Council model, however, have been used periodically by the larger Council.

Rainbows continually make suggestions like Sky Bear's or NERF's to perfect evolving Council procedures. Slowly and sometimes painfully, different Rainbow Councils incorporate some of these suggestions. The best of these ideas will withstand the test of time, becoming part of most Rainbow Councils. Specific Councils also adapt to their own unique needs. At the European Gatherings, for instance, where translators repeat everything in five languages, "They use a talking stick rather than a feather, and do not formally call for consensus as we do, but simply keep going around until no one says anything further on a subject, whereupon it is declared consensus" (Endicott 1990).

Rainbows hope that as the Family matures and strengthens its still-young traditions, Council will continue to evolve. As one Rainbow said, "The way we make decisions is more important than the decisions we make."

A Persistent Democracy

A surprising reality of the Rainbow Family's egalitarian approach to an inclusive consensual democracy is how unique it is in the history of North American utopian communities. None of the groups[17] chosen by Dolores Hayden for her study *Seven American Utopias: The Architecture of Communitarian Socialism, 1790–1975*, for example, practiced consensus government (Hayden 1976, 360–61). In fact, only three of the groups practiced electoral democracy. Yet Hayden identified these groups, four of which were religious and three nonsectarian, as together providing "a fair representation of the ideological and geographical spread of the communitarian movement, between 1730 and 1938" (Hayden 1976, 5). Yacoov Oved, in his study *Two Hundred Years of American Communes,* concurred, pointing out that "an examination of the administrative procedures in communal settlements points to conspicuous elements of authoritarian leadership" (Oved 1988, 379).

One of the communities chosen by Hayden, the Amana colony, revered by historians as one of the most successful nineteenth-century utopian communities, saw participatory democracy as limited by human nature. William Rufus Perkins and Barthinius L. Wick, writing a colony-sanctioned Amana history in 1891, described the Amana government, as "one of an oligarchical nature," where "the interests of all are entrusted to the wisdom of a few" (Perkins and Wick 1891, 68). Such an "oligarchy" did not, according to the authors, "endeavor to make human beings more perfect than humanity is capable of being" (67). This supposed oligarchy did, however, have certain trimmings of democracy. Trustees were elected, but only men could vote, and only middle-aged men could stand for office (Holloway 1951, 171; Perkins and Wick 1891, 68). Once chosen, trustees were generally reelected, as the colony shunned changes in government (Perkins and Wick 1891, 68). Interestingly enough, within the elite circle of trustees, consensus was practiced (68), with "the few" demonstrating respect at least for each other. Amana was not unique among nineteenth-century utopias in its disenfranchisement of women from government. Even when communities revolted against dictatorial control and instituted democratic reforms, those reforms often limited women's roles and power.[18]

Male dominance can also be found in the Rainbow Family Council where male voices often dominate proceedings, even if just by sheer might of volume. Despite some denial, most Rainbows now admit that Babylon's male-dominated culture has polluted their Council process and are consciously addressing the problem with awkward innovations such as those practiced in Ithaca. The fact that women and men have to line up separately behind stones to ensure that women's voices are heard attests to the persistence of the problem.

The Rainbow Family's ability to maintain an open and inclusive form of government, continuously striving to be more inclusive, for a quarter of a century, defies accepted communal theory. Rosabeth Moss Kanter, in her landmark study *Commitment and Community: Communes and Utopias in Sociological Perspective,* observes that "the most enduring communes were also the most centralized and the most tightly controlled" (Kanter 1972, 129). The only other long-lasting large nonhierarchical group operating under consensus rule is Alcoholics Anonymous, which, like the Family, is an "occasional group" (Dentan 1994, 70–71; cf. Pospisil 1964, 404–96).

While some communities shed charismatic leadership for a more democratic model (McLaughlin and Davidson 1985, 153), shifts away from democracy prove more common. Oftentimes the more participatory and Rainbow-like the government, the more likely the community would forgo it for an authoritarian model. Corinne McLaughlin and Gordon Davidson, communitarian scholars[19] and cofounders of the Sirius Community in Massachusetts, express sympathy with this trend. They see communities who shed decentralized governance as "developing clearer lines of authority as they learn from experience to be realistic about what works and what doesn't" (McLaughlin and Davidson 1985, 154).

McLaughlin and Davidson, in their book *Builders of the Dawn; Community Lifestyles in a Changing World,* cite the experiences of the late spiritual huckster Sun Bear[20] (Vincent LaDuke) as he experimented both with democracy and authoritarianism at his Bear Tribe Community. Sun Bear, echoing sentiments similar to those expressed by the Amana a century before him, concluded, "People are at different levels of ability to take responsibility, and so authority and power should reflect that" (McLaughlin and Davidson 1985, 155). Sun Bear, in an oxymoronic lament, recalled how he "tried for a long time to *make* people equal," but failed (McLaughlin and Davidson 1985, 154 [emphasis mine]).

Leaders like Sun Bear, in this paradigm, seem to be divinely anointed with leadership abilities. McLaughlin and Davidson write, "Ultimately, power is not something that can be given to someone. Someone is powerful because of their personal qualities: vision, confidence, creativity, good judgement, enthusiasm, consistency, strength, etc." Rainbows, on the other hand, believe that such qualities develop with nurturing. They often cite lack of confidence, for example, as having its roots in class or sexist oppression; with a little bit of respect, it can be overcome. Rainbows are adamant that all people, regardless of their perceived handicaps, have the right to represent themselves in Council.

The Rainbow Family, over the years, has also experienced reactionary backlashes against adherence to total consensus. They have, however, thus far maintained at least a rhetorical commitment to consensus. For example, a handful of dissenters blocked consensus at the 1991 Vision Council, which sought a site for the 1992 North American Gathering. Responding to the failure to achieve consensus, several Rainbows proclaimed "total" consensus was not necessary. They argued that the Gathering would take place in the Four Corners (Colorado, New Mexico, Arizona, Utah) region, as favored by the majority. After this proclamation, most folks left the Council and went home. The remaining hangers-on, after seven days of counciling, reached a consensus by attrition to gather in South Dakota.

The end result was two North American Gatherings in 1992, one in Colorado and one in South Dakota. The Colorado Gathering was backed by the "old guard" of Family elders, who were well placed within the Focalizers communication network (see next chapter). The South Dakota Gathering was primarily promoted by one Family dissident, a brother named Zeus. The Colorado Gathering drew nearly twenty-five thousand people (Foster 1994), while the South Dakota Gathering drew fewer than five hundred. While a true *consensus* was never reached, Rainbows *voted* with their feet, following the advice of a supposedly nonexistent leadership, and heading for Colorado. The South Dakota Gathering has since been forgotten, with Rainbow history placing the 1992 Gathering firmly in Colorado.

The Vision Council in Colorado that year consensed to hold the following year's Gathering in the southeastern United States. In a conciliatory move, the small South Dakota faction consensed to also gather in the Southeast. It was the scouts this time who couldn't reach consensus as to where in the Southeast the Gathering would be. Hence, the North American Gathering was split again, with two Gatherings, each drawing about five thousand people, one in Kentucky and one in Alabama. A tiny group from the previous year's South Dakota Gathering met in Tennessee. The Kentucky and Alabama Gatherings stayed in close contact and rescued the consensus process by both consensing on a Wyoming Gathering for 1994. Fed up with all the confusion and frustrated with the disruptive powers accorded to dissenters by the consensus requirement, some Rainbows started talking about modifying their procedures. While not completely abandoning consensus, they sought majoritarian alternatives.

The facilitators who created the 1993 Rainbow Guide published their thoughts on consensus. They began by praising consensus as giving "every person a chance to be heard and their input considered equally, giving the smallest minority the strongest chance to change the collective mind" (Guide Crew 1993). They continued, however, that "consensus can include the fact that someone objected. Look for the big picture. No single voice whether relevant or not can squash the common will.

Any system that persists in absolute consensus cannot long endure" (Guide Crew 1993). They suggest that lone dissenters leave the Council circle with three people of their own choosing and discuss their point of view. If the dissenter fails to convert at least one person to his or her opinion, then that person should yield or withdraw from Council with the protest noted. Rainbows often refer to this and similar suggested Council modifications as "consensus minus one," the predecessor, possibly, of "consensus minus two" and so on.

Universal participation in government, and the resulting long and sometimes chaotic meetings, have led to authoritarian backlashes throughout North American utopian history. Even communities founded upon democratic ideals, with democratic foundations in their constitutions or bylaws, tended toward authoritarianism. Yacoov Oved observes, "After a period of direct democracy with endless debates to the point of prohibiting efficient management because the decisions could not be made, the pendulum would swing to a period in which a power-hungry dynamic personality took over" (Oved 1988, 381).

The "endless debates" cited by Oved are similar to the Rainbow Family's long inconclusive meetings. While Rainbows find the meetings, which often fail to accomplish their initial goals, valuable (albeit frustrating), other groups have fallen to pieces around such meetings. McLaughlin and Davidson write of a "widespread community disease called 'meeting-itis,' known to afflict especially those communities where there is a strong emphasis on including everyone's input on every issue, and everything is decided in lengthy group meetings" (McLaughlin and Davidson 1988, 77).

McLaughlin and Davidson favor decentralizing the decision making process with "smaller decisions decentralized to specialized groups," saving time for "real conflicts" (McLaughlin and Davidson 1985, 77) to be aired before larger groups. Rainbows practice decentralization, relegating micromanagement decisions such as kitchen administration to sub-Councils. All problems, however, can still be brought up for full Council discussion, as Rainbows feel that *all* conflicts, no matter how petty most folks may perceive them to be, are potentially serious and divisive. Anyone can bring any issue before the Council for discussion.

Central to the Rainbow Council is its respect for individuals, their voices, and their rights. Since any individual can block consensus and force protracted discussion, consensus places individual concerns on an equal footing with group concerns. This power of the individual stands in direct contrast to commonly accepted communal theories that place individualism in conflict with collectivism. Kanter writes, "Full commitment and unequivocal belief, central to the viability of a utopia, involve the individual in giving up some of his differentiated privileges and attributes, at the same time that he gains belonging and meaning" (1972, 57). Rainbows, however, prefer to have their cake and eat it too. They see themselves as carrying the banners both for the conservative American libertarian tradition of rugged individualism and for the sometimes opposed utopian communal tradition in America.

Despite the Rainbow Family's rise against a historic tide of centralized control in utopian communities, it has persevered. Rainbow government is self-consciously egalitarian and participatory with long inconclusive meetings. It holds individual rights and concerns to be paramount, even to the point of letting one dissenting voice block consensus at a Gathering of thirty thousand people. By all historical indications it should have been short-lived or have failed. Yet as it celebrates its twenty-fifth birthday, the point, for instance, at which Kanter declares a community to be a "success" (Kanter 1972, 245), it is still growing and still true to its original form of consensus government.

4
The Nuts and Bolts of Making a Rainbow: Rainbow Infrastructure

Everyone knows that theorizing or describing, and actually doing are often worlds apart.

So it is in the doing of these things that one discovers the non-hierarchical methods of working together—the exact methods that we humans will need to know, use and teach in the future.

—Garrick Beck, Basic Rainbow, 1986

Rainbow Gatherings represent an effort to realize a utopian libertarian-anarchist vision. They serve as trial runs for a new society based on cooperation and nonhierarchical organization rather than on competition and hegemony. An examination of the nuts and bolts of Rainbow infrastructure offers insights into how this vision works in actual practice.

From Seed . . .

White Raven, mother of five adult children, is a former U.S. Information Agency officer and the ex-wife of a U.S. Foreign Service officer. Today she is an independent video maker and social activist. She is also one of the primary "focalizers" responsible for "facilitating" the 1990 North American Rainbow Gathering in Minnesota. The story of the Minnesota Gathering, according to White Raven, began a year earlier at the Vision Council of the 1989 North American

Gathering in Nevada. The Council had met for three days without coming close to a consensus. On the eve of the third day, White Raven explained, a group of Minnesota residents met by chance at one of the kitchens and started to discuss whether or not they felt they had the strength to host a Gathering. After some discussion, the group, some of whom had just met, decided they could do it. The next day, Vision Council discussed Minnesota. White Raven took the feather and proclaimed, "Minnesota is the land of Gitche Gumee, Shining Big Sea Water, and it's the home of Hiawatha, and his mother Nokomis. And in the woods are Walking the Bear, and the moose and the wolves and the fox and the beavers and the looons." A consensus followed shortly (White Raven interview 1990).

After celebrating the consensus, the Minnesota Rainbow Family faced the sobering realization that they had volunteered for a yearlong effort. Learner Harmony, who was living in Minneapolis at the time, responded to the challenge immediately: "[I was] telling folks to get ready and start to get potlucks together. . . . The Gathering's gonna come here whether we're ready or not. . . . I came directly back and started getting folks together to get ready for the Thanksgiving Council" (Harmony interview 1990). The immense work of preparing for the Gathering was a labor of love: difficult, but feasible as a cooperative effort. White Raven described the group of Minnesotans that coalesced around the task as "the mellowest, easiest, most wonderful group of people I've ever worked with."

Throughout the winter they raised funds, educated local forest service officials about the Family, planned logistics, and scouted for a site. In the North, it is common to scout in the winter to establish a list of possible sites and then reassess them after the spring thaw. Failure to reassess sites may lead to surprises. For example, the site for the 1990 Quebec Gathering appeared pristine when covered with snow (Louie interview 1990), but by Gathering time the spring thaw revealed a local dump strewn with debris. Site selection is a tricky business for Rainbow Family scouts. Rainbows demand a site that is both remote and accessible, with a physical layout suitable for a smooth-working, spiritually focused Gathering. Responsibility for finding the perfect site falls on the shoulders of the scouts, who will later be blamed for any site imperfections that may arise.

The following wish list of site attributes, established by the 1991 Thanksgiving Council, describes the perfect Rainbow Gathering Site.

Meadow	The first priority for the site is a sizable, centrally located and environmentally hospitable meadow for the main circle/Council.
Water	The site should have adequate potable or easily treated water for drinking.
Environmental Impact	The site must be able to sustain a Gathering of the magnitude expected, without any long lasting adverse environmental effects.

Parking	Designated parking areas should be able to accommodate all vehicles expected. Areas with highly flammable ground cover, poor drainage, or poor accessibility should be avoided. The parking area should be within hiking or reasonable shuttle distance to the central Gathering site.
Access	The site should be accessible to handicapped persons, but not to ordinary vehicles.
Private Land	Sites with private land either on the site or nearby should be avoided.
Swimming	The site should include an area where people can swim.
Toxics	Scouts should carefully evaluate the potential sites for toxic pollutants such as defoliants used on roads and power line right of ways [polluted sites should be avoided].
Terrain	The site should have good drainage for trails, camping areas and meadows. Factors such as slope should be evaluated.
Impact on Local Community	Adverse impacts on the local community or their infrastructure should be avoided.
Auxiliary Meadows	The site should provide meadows, other than the central meadow, for a variety of special interest camps and purposes.
Isolation	The site should be isolated from nearby population and tourist centers.
Local Political Climate	Although an unfriendly political climate should not eliminate a good site, other factors being equal, the local political climate should be taken into consideration, to minimize harassment by officials.
Local Forest Service Attitude	Again, other factors being equal, a cooperative stance on the part of the Forest Service is a plus.
Firewood	The accessibility of fallen wood for fires should be taken into consideration.
Insects	Areas with nasty bugs should be avoided whenever practical.
Police Logistics	Since various police agencies have "harassled" [the standard harassing hassle] Rainbows en-route to Gatherings, a site with several approach roads would be preferable.

Selection of a site that is remote yet able to sustain community activities has been a common goal throughout North American utopian history. The Amana, for example, an eighteenth-century German pietist communist group, moved their eight-hundred-family community from Erie County in New York to then-remote Iowa to get away from the urban influence of nearby Buffalo. According to early Amana chroniclers, "They preferred some secluded, quiet place in the West, where they could practice the doctrines of their creed undisturbed, and carry on communism without coming in contact with the rest of mankind" (Perkins and Wick 1975 [1891], 54). Hutterites are also among the many groups who sought secluded sites for their communities, trying to limit contact with the outside world (Oved 1988, 354).

Rainbow Gatherings are usually accessible only after an extended hike on a forest trail or closed road.[1] The surrounding woodlands form a natural barrier, separating Rainbows from Babylon. The Rainbow entrance "gate," usually a welcome station on an approaching road or trail, forms a distinct boundary, demarcating entry to Rainbow's experimental world. Such boundaries and approaches are common to utopian communities (Hayden 1976, 42–43).

The Minnesota Rainbow scouts, in their quest for a perfect Rainbow site, gained a new familiarity with their state's wild lands. During the first week of April, the Scouting Council met to discuss the sites under consideration (Harmony interview 1990). Having not yet decided where the Gathering would occur, a group of scouts paid a return visit to one of the sites being considered, Barker Lake, in early June. That evening a spectacular display of Northern Lights filled the sky, followed in the morning by a rainbow. The group took these events as omens (White Raven interview 1990; Grey Bear interview 1990a). Although they had not found a reliable source of potable drinking water, the scouts felt "the spirit" had guided them to the proper site. They returned to the camp at nearby Pine Mountain and recounted the omens. The scout council consensed to the site choice less than a month before the Gathering was to begin. With time working against them, they could not afford to be too finicky.

Having selected a site, the Minnesota Family quickly sent out a traditional *Howdy Folks!* invitation to Rainbow Focalizers across North America, Mexico, and Europe. Bearing a map to the site on the cover, the four-page mailing admonished Rainbows to "be prepared for cold and wet weather" as well as "mosquitoes, flies and ticks."

The invitation included a suggested list of items to bring and not to bring to the Gathering. On the not-to-bring side were alcohol, weapons, hard dangerous drugs, pets, nonrecyclable trash, and nonpeaceful attitudes. The list of things to bring included bulk food, water, tents, sleeping bags, warm clothes, rain gear, a bowl, eating utensils, a cup that could be hung from your belt, drums, guitars, and other musical instruments, buckets, mosquito netting, water safety items, and a "childlike, open sense of wonder, anticipation and fun."

Previous years' invitations, as well as other Rainbow publications, contain more extensive checklists, reminding readers to bring sleeping bags, tents or tarps, flashlights, toiletries, menstrual necessities, condoms and other contraceptives, first aid supplies, books, and bubbles (Pennsylvania Rainbow 1986; Anon. n.d.). Despite these lists, many people, short on cash, arrive at the Gathering lacking basic essentials. With them in mind the 1986 *Howdy Folks!*, for example, encouraged people to bring extra items to share with those less prepared.

With the invitations sent out, the work of fulfilling its promises falls in the lap of the Seed Camp volunteers.

Seed Camp

Strapped for resources and often subsisting on dumpstered food, the Seed Camp is made up of committed volunteers who lay the infrastructure for the Gathering. They must be craftspeople, engineers, sanitarians, hydrologists, diplomats, economists, ecologists, urban planners, and ditchdiggers. The water and waste systems they construct will determine the health of thousands of people. The trail system they lay out will determine where camps will cluster. They are responsible for both building a city and safeguarding the environment. The relations they establish with the local community and government agencies set the tenor for the Gathering to come.

Participants get a chance to follow ideas from conception to realization. The Gathering offers students of peace a chance to witness conflict resolution in practice: pacifying hostile law enforcement officials and dissipating community fears. City-planning students can, in four or five weeks, watch a vision become a city as the core group of one hundred people grows to ten or twenty thousand. Thousands of feet, thousands of tents, and thousands of pounds of human feces will test Seed Camp decisions about layout and space utilization.

Diane Zimmerman, a public health nurse who helped organize the 1990 NERF Gathering, says the Seed Camp sets the tone for the Gathering. The final outcome of the Gathering, however, she points out, rests with the masses who follow. She warned the Seed Camp crew at the NERF Gathering that while "planning is fine," they shouldn't expect the Gathering to unfold exactly as they envisioned it (interview 1990).

Seed Camp participants are often challenged by a chronic lack of resources, since wealthier Rainbows bearing supplies to donate don't usually arrive until the official start of the Gathering. Most Rainbows who arrive at the peak of the Gathering see a horn of plenty—not the scarcity that characterizes early Seed Camp, where volunteers have had to survive, for example, on a diet of "nothing but whole wheat noodles and pickle." Taco Mike recalls that particular Seed Camp: "We didn't even have any salt to put on the stuff for days and days on end. . . . It was bad." In the end, however, a local turkey farmer came through, providing a late spring version of Thanksgiving (Taco Mike interview 1990).

To experience a Gathering from the very beginning and to see the Seed Camp in action is, according to Garrick Beck, one of the most astounding parts of the Rainbow experience. Especially interesting, he explains, is the mix of people:

> [Among the] hardest parts [of the Gathering] are the beginning phases of Seed Camp when those people who know what they are doing and have a lot on the ball and have tools and equipment and ideas and visions are vastly outnumbered by people who don't know what they're doing, who don't have anywhere else to go, who don't have any tools, who don't have any oatmeal, who don't have any pots and pans and who are there because the Rainbow is a place where they have received love and affection and care. And there you are wanting to build a visionary utopia and what you have to do instead is to keep a kitchen clean for hungry people who barely know how to take care of themselves. (Beck interview 1990)

Seed Camp is often composed primarily of people who live "on the road." Although it only takes about a week to set up most Gatherings, Seed Camp usually commences a month early, allowing people who are otherwise on the road or "homeless," to extend their Gatherings. Seed Camp workers often stay for cleanup as well. Thus, the poor contribute a disproportionate amount of work assembling and disassembling Gatherings, which are primarily attended by the middle class.

With many participants lacking basic outdoor skills, the Rainbow Seed Camp also functions as a training facility. Skills, like food, are to be shared. The difference is that, while skills can be multiplied by teaching and sharing, limited food stocks can only be divided. Many Rainbow Seed Camps survive, however, on the wastes of America, subsisting on "expired" or cosmetically blemished discarded food from supermarket dumpsters. "Dumpstering" is humbling and enlightening for middle-class Rainbows, slumming as they accompany their hobo brethren on dumpster runs. While dumpstering is in itself harmless, mainline American communities and their press, witnessing these dumpster forays, often react with fear, contempt, or hostility.

As peak Gathering time nears, more affluent Rainbows arrive, bringing food, tools, and money. While this influx relieves the financial crunch often felt during Seed Camp, it adds new problems. Every day the population of the new city increases exponentially. The health of the Gathering, the cohesiveness of Council, and the preservation of the environment all depend on the Seed Camp crew's ability to spread "Gathering consciousness" to scores of newcomers.

Volunteers must disseminate this information quickly. People accustomed to the conveniences of "modern life"—instant hot wash water, plumbing that whisks away bodily and soapy wastes, and rubbish-swallowing garbage trucks—can rapidly contaminate a Gathering. An ignorant person can, for example, sabotage the water table or jeopardize the health of a nearby kitchen through careless and irresponsible defecation.

A "Rap 107" crew shares the message of Gathering etiquette at the main entrance ("the Gate") to the Gathering. They welcome the newcomers "home" and give them the "rap," explaining how to live in harmony with the woods. Rainbows view the rap, although basic, as slightly more advanced than an academic introductory course, such as English 101; hence the name "Rap 107" (Hipstory 1990). A typical Rap 107 (see Appendix), oral or printed, admonishes Rainbows to walk softly, respecting plants and animals; protect water sources and use latrines; share communal fires; recycle wastes and pack out trash; and not bring alcohol or weapons into the Gathering.

Gatherings also have a central area for disseminating information: the "information area" or "rumor control." It usually consists of a shelter staffed around the clock with informed volunteers often in two-way radio contact with critical areas of the Gathering such as CALM and the Gate. The radio system is frequently powered by solar energy. The information area also contains a series of bulletin boards and a constantly evolving map of the Gathering. Separate boards carry personal messages, information about rides offered or needed, information about regional Gatherings, announcements of upcoming political events, information on issues such as water treatment, ticks, and police harassment, and announcements of workshops. Workshops and activities posted on a bulletin board at a NERF regional Gathering, for example, ranged from "Harmonic Breathing," "Dances of Universal Peace," and a "People with Addictive Personalities Meeting," to a "Forest Service Talk on the Finger Lakes Area," "Cultural and Biological Insecticide Alternatives Workshop," and a meeting to "Facilitate a Network for People Interested in Finding Communities."

How to Poop in the Woods

Rainbow bulletin boards traditionally carry postings stressing lavatory skills. A Gathering's high population density combined with its primitive conditions forces people to come to terms with the toxicity of their own excrement, something most people would rather not think about. According to a Cornell University study of bathroom design, "Urine and feces are regarded as dirt and filth, so much so that the individual not only wants to dispose of them as thoroughly and quickly as possible but also wishes to be completely disassociated from the act of producing them" (Kira 1967, 98). In this aspect of life, people are much like cats.

Americans normally flush their bodily wastes away to a sewage bureaucracy for disposal. Faceless technicians concentrate New York City's fecal wastes, for example, into a sludge that tanker ships, until recently, dumped in the Atlantic Ocean only a few miles offshore of New York's beaches. New York's waste, a porridge of feces and solvents, is now dehydrated and spread on farmlands in Arkansas and Texas (Stauber and Rampton 1995, 99–122). Most New Yorkers are neither aware of, nor concerned about, this befouling. Rainbows, on the other hand, are left, after defecating, contemplating their own impact on the environment as their stool steams beneath them. To have defecated irresponsibly in a watershed or to leave one's feces exposed for flies to carry to kitchens is, Rainbows say, "terrorism." The consequences are well known among Rainbows. Diarrhea, the "Rainbow Runs," is a recurring problem.

Rainbow publications therefore refer to the "Shit-Fly-Food-You" connection (Secret Rainbow Press n.d.; NERF 1991). An article in the Rainbow newspaper, *All Ways Free,* for instance, quotes an imaginary fly to get the point across, "'Well, guess I fly over to Main Kitchen and dance on some food,' said the fly, picking up a wad of shit in its proboscis" (Wood Winter 1989). A proper Rainbow latrine (called a "shitter"[2] at Gatherings) usually consists of a deep, narrow slit trench, covered by a plywood sheet with a small hole in the middle and a tightly sealing cover. Latrine users sprinkle cool ash or lime over their feces, then wash their hands with a chlorinated rinse at a nearby wash station. Rainbows argue that their latrines (minus the chlorinated rinse), when properly used and maintained, are environmentally friendly. In 1990 the Forest Service, in conjunction with Rainbow Family members, devised the following guidelines for Rainbow latrines:

> Latrines will consist of a dug hole at least 30 inches by 30 inches and 36 inches deep or comparable slit trenches. Latrines will be rodent and fly proof. Latrines will be located at least 200 feet from streams and lakes, be covered with plywood or similar material and be sealed at the edges with earth. User access will be by trap door through the cover. Latrines will be shut down and filled when their contents are within 15 inches of the surface. Buckets of lime and/or wood ash will be provided for use at all latrine locations. A hand washing bleach water station will be at each latrine. (Superior N.F. 1990[d])

Few latrines in the developing world, by comparison, come up to these standards. Lime, which is used to make tortillas, and ash, which is used to repair cooking hearths and pave floors, are too valuable to dump into outhouses.

The Rainbow Family's obsession with latrines has paid off. Latrine-consciousness has grown to the point that by 1990, Leroy Oliver, a Cook County (Minnesota) health official observing the Rainbow Family in Minnesota, noted: "They've been at it for a number of years. . . . They're putting those latrines farther away from their kitchens than I expected by more than double" (Nelson 1990). Asked by a County Supervisor how close Rainbow latrines were to Barker Lake, Oliver pointed out that a Minnesota Department of Natural Resources outhouse was much closer to the water than any Rainbow latrine. Latrine-consciousness, however, has side effects. Returning to city life after a summer in the woods, some Rainbows find the idea of defecating indoors disgusting. An apartment with a bathroom ten or twenty feet from the kitchen stove is hard to accept after "Fly-Shit-Food-You" indoctrination.

Rainbows' willingness to discuss how people defecate, a subject that makes most Americans cringe, illustrates the pervasiveness of the Rainbow critique of American society. The *Rainbow Oracle*, a primer for the first Gathering in 1972, includes an attack on "the dangers of the modern toilet seat." According to the *Oracle*, "The unnatural position which the modern toilet forces us to take may be responsible for gas, constipation, damage to the colon resulting in hemorrhoids and other problems" (*Rainbow Oracle* 1972, 100).[3] The solution, according to the *Oracle*, "is to simply get a small pan and when you must move the bowels, squat over the pan."

A Land without Money

Rainbow "shitters" fit with Rainbow's alternative economic organization. At a commercial event people pay admission to a promoter, who then provides a basic infrastructure, renting fiberglass chemical toilets, selling food, and paying entertainers to perform and servants to clean up after the event. The Woodstock festivals, in 1969 and in 1994, exemplify such commercial ventures. At Rainbow Gatherings, however, the participants *are* the event; they dig their own latrines, provide for their own needs, and clean up after themselves without monetary incentives. Rainbow Gatherings, as a matter of principle, are free and noncommercial. Using money to buy or sell *anything* at Rainbow Gatherings is taboo.

At the peak of the Gathering, Rainbow kitchens produce savory treats that are often on a par with the finest vegetarian restaurants; yet all food is free. Likewise, coffee, herbal tea, theater, music, and medical care are all free. Penniless people may enjoy the Gathering to its fullest, without being barred by poverty from any activities. Unlike a concert or sporting event, there are no prime seats and there are no cheap seats. The key to the Rainbow economy is sharing. People bring what they can to share, often depositing surplus items in "Free Boxes." While some people arrive destitute and hungry, others show up with a truckload of produce, a hundred feet of hose, a box of medical supplies, or a pocket of cash for the "Magic Hat."

Such alternative economic organization has traditionally been central to utopian movements. Many nineteenth-century "Bible communists" were guided by New Testament tales of the Apostles who "sold their possessions and goods and distributed them to all as any had need" (Oved 1988, 371, citing Acts 2:4). According to the New Testament, "Those who believed were of one heart and soul and no one said that any of the things which he possessed was his own but they had everything in common" (Oved 1988, 371, citing Acts 4:32). Many nonsectarian utopian communities also practiced communism. Rosabeth Moss Kanter writes, "Shared ownership of property helped to create a we-feeling and to implement those ideals of brotherhood central to the forming of utopian communities" (Kanter 1972, 94).

Contemporary utopian communities like Twin Oaks, a Virginia commune with about seventy-five members, practice communism as part of their quest for "equality and justice" (Kanter 1972, 23; McLaughlin and Davidson 1985, 117). At Twin Oaks, all money, even that earned away from the commune, goes into the collective treasury. Even clothing is community-owned. Such communism calls for more commitment than typical Rainbows, who leave their wealth locked up in the parking lot, are prepared to make. Even committed land-based communities such as the Farm in Tennessee, however, were forced to abandon communism in the face of financial hardship (Bates 1993; Traugot 1994, 55–64; Gaskin interview 1994a).

While the economy at Twin Oaks is essentially cashless, labor is monitored and workers are paid with labor credits based on how much work they do and how onerous or undesirable the work may be (Fogarty 1980, 170; Goldenberg 1993, 258). Such a system of labor credits resembles experiments such as Josiah Warren's mid-nineteenth-century Equity Store (also dubbed the Time Store) in Cincinnati. At the Equity store, people exchanged notes representing hours of labor for goods or services offered by others (Webber 1959, 167; Holloway 1951, 118–19). Warren's system is being mimicked today by diverse groups ranging from the Ithaca, New York, cooperative community, establishing "Ithaca Hours" as a standard of exchange, to fundamentalist Christian tax resisters, using barter credits. Historically, systems involving labor credits were also used by several short-lived communities (Kanter 1972, 95).

The Rainbow Family, however, rejects all forms of money, including alternative currencies like time credits or barter notes. Rainbows are volunteers, working without any regulatory mechanism to monitor their commitment. For Rainbows, like many successful communities studied by Kanter, "participation in the great communal enterprise . . . was its own reward and generated its own motivation" (Kanter 1972: 96; cf. Amish). Likewise, contributions to the collective coffers are truly voluntary, since there is no system for taxing or tithing wealth. In fact, many Rainbows are lazy or stingy, a reality that compels others to work more diligently or be more generous.

Rainbows say that money, like guns, doesn't belong in "the church," that is, within the Gathering. They accept money, however, by necessity, for the Magic Hat. "[Its] magic lies in the miracles sharing can do" (Rainbow Family Tribal Council, n.d.). This money goes for purchases of commodities from vendors in Babylon. The Supply Council is responsible for arranging such purchases. The Banking Council is responsible for Magic Hat collections, maintaining balance sheets and records of expenditures for public perusal. Regarding money, also known among Rainbows as "Green Energy," *All Ways Free* (summer 1989) notes: "Caesar's image has no place among us except as our individual gift to the whole."

Magic Hat bulk food and supply purchases, as well as donations of bulk food and supplies not destined for a specific kitchen or camp, go to Main Supply. The Supply Council coordinates Main Supply, which serves as a warehouse/distribution facility, outfitting camps and kitchens according to need. Supplying Kid's Village, whose kitchen serves children, mothers, and expectant mothers, is a top priority. At the end of the Gathering, after cleanup, the Supply Council distributes surplus food and supplies, sent with travelers to other Gatherings or stored by volunteers for future Gatherings. For example, Supply Council sent some surpluses from the 1990 NERF regional near Ithaca, New York, to the Quebec Rainbow Gathering held the following week, where NERF expected food would be in short supply.

It is important to note that while Rainbows shun monetary transactions and sharing is common, there is no consensus among Family members that the Rainbow economy is, even temporarily, communist. Many Rainbows, even those who freely share their time and resources at Gatherings, view themselves as anarchists, libertarians, or conservative individualists; not communalists, communards, or communists. Their actions, however, are often no different from those Rainbows who see themselves as Marxist, socialist, or communist. It is the tendency of individuals to act communally that gives the Rainbow Family its unique character, as a cooperative community of individualists.

For the 1989 European Rainbow Gathering in Norway, focalizers asked people to bring food instead of money. Since food, and almost anything else needed at a Gathering, is expensive in Norway, the *Howdy Folks!* suggested buying staples before entering the country. Facilitators volunteered to coordinate food purchases in various European countries, assuring both diversity and abundance of foodstuffs. Focalizers asked people to bring whatever was both "cheap and good" in their area, hoping that "with thinking and good planning we can make a good, cheap worry-free Rainbow, with a magically-happy hat in the most expensive land in Europe" (Norway Rainbow 1989).

People donated most of the food, for example, at the 1990 North American Gathering in Minnesota as they arrived. The Magic Hat nonetheless collected approximately four thousand dollars during the Gathering (Harmony interview 1990). Hence, the organizational overhead for the Gathering was only twenty-five to thirty cents per participant. The U.S. National Forest Service, in contrast, playing a minor and arguably unnecessary role at that Gathering, spent about $310,000 (Joens July 9, 1990; Tofte July 9, 1990).

The Gathering's modest budget does not, however, reflect the true value of goods and services at the Gathering. Gatherers do not need money. Aside from putting money into the Magic Hat, the people who attend Gatherings don't have much to do with it. By standard economic indicators, the Gathering, with little "economic activity," appears impoverished. The following observation about precapitalist Poland in the 1980s also applies to Rainbow Gatherings:

There are no billboards, no neon, no carry-out; the shops are marked only by nondescript signs. . . .

To a Western economist, though, such things look like poverty and underdevelopment; when people sit around the family dinner table instead of going to McDonald's and a movie, there is no cash transaction, little for the GNP. Yet the family dinner table represents a kind of cohesion that Americans are groping to recover. (Rowe 1990, 21)

Rainbow has simply expanded that family dinner table atmosphere to the magnitude of a McDonald's.

Ironically, it was in 1990s "postcommunist" Poland that commercialism polluted the Rainbow economy, albeit marginally. At the 1992 European Rainbow Gathering in Poland's Bieszczady Mountains, local entrepreneurs set up camp in a parking area two kilometers from the main Gathering. There they sold bread, snacks, kielbasa, beer, and cigarettes to the assembled Rainbows and local spectators (Mrozowski 1992).

Trade Circle

While money is taboo at Gatherings, barter is acceptable. A "Trade Circle" or "Barter Lane," where Rainbows exchange handmade items such as jewelry, clothes, bags, and such, along with crystals,[4] books, and other items, is a standard feature at Gatherings. Trading items that should be shared, like food or drink, is taboo. Rainbows do trade freely, however, in "zuzus," slang for sweet treats such candy bars. Snickers bars are a perennial favorite. "Rainbows don't trade things people *need,* they give those away. They trade things people *want,* but can easily do without" (Wetmore interview 1990).

In past years, Snickers trading threatened to get out of hand, with people trading jewelry and clothing for the gooey zuzus. Some Rainbows saw the Snickers trade as undermining the Family's commitment to money-free Gatherings. At many Gatherings in the 1980s, Candy bars became a medium of exchange with a somewhat standardized value. At the 1984 Gathering in California, for instance, a Snickers bar had become the value equivalent of a Walkman in the Trade Circle, since music was abundant and candy and batteries were in short supply. Unlike general-purpose money, however, candy bars can't store value, since they depreciate in the sun. They also tend to be eaten.

Many people who were trading and eating Snickers bars at Gatherings, never considered buying them when not at Gatherings. In the land of free healthy food, the Snickers bar had come to represent a special frivolous treat, much like buying a sporty car in Babylon. Opponents of Rainbow Snickers commerce arrived at the

1984 Gathering, and later Gatherings, with bags of Snickers bars, which they handed out for free in the trade area. Abundance destroyed their value. In the 1990s Snickers commerce declined, but traffic in crystals is on the rise, with crystals taking on many characteristics of general-purpose money.

Some Rainbows find the trading area, with its constant haggling, alien to the spirit of the Gathering. One suggestion, published in *All Ways Free,* called for laying out the Gathering with the Trading Circle far removed from the "spiritual areas" (*All Ways Free* Winter 1988). Quebec Rainbows boast that their Gatherings don't have trade circles, seeing their absence as making for a better, more spiritual Gathering. Other Rainbows view the trade area as a key component in a Rainbow Village, with barter vital to an alternative economy.

Either way, Rainbows usually agree that money has no place at the Gathering, including the trade area. Rainbow Councils and Rainbow literature stress that the Gathering is not commercial. Rainbow Family opposition to commerce at the Gatherings goes beyond ideology; the Family's First Amendment right to gather applies only to noncommercial events. The Rainbow Family's purism about commerce is a luxury allowed by the fact that they are a nonterritorial occasional group (Dentan 1994, 70–71; cf. Pospisil 1964, 404–6). As such, they face no persistent economic pressures. Permanent utopian communities throughout history, by contrast, have been forced by mortgage payments and building maintenance to confront the economic realities inherent in a landbase.

Historically, communal groups try to establish economically self-sufficient settlements (Hayden 1976, 15). Economic success, however, while paying the bills, does not guarantee spiritual success. In some cases, commerce is all that is left of these communities. The nineteenth-century Oneida and Amana communities, for example, evolved (or devolved) into corporations that have survived to the present day, manufacturing cookware and kitchen appliances, respectively.

Contemporary permanent communities face the same economic realities as their nineteenth-century forebears. To pay the bills, Twin Oaks (Virginia) manufactures hammocks and provides clerical services (Goldenberg 1993, 259); businesses associated with the Farm (Tennessee) have engaged in a wide variety of activities ranging from landscaping Nashville's Opryland to manufacturing electronic components for the Federal Emergency Management Agency (FEMA) (Black 1993).

By contrast, Rainbows as a group produce nothing other than what is consumed on-site.

Kitchens

The most noticeable components of Rainbow Gatherings are the kitchens. Word of Rainbow kitchens reaches newcomers quickly: bring a bowl and you'll eat, bring a cup and you'll drink. Local curiosity seekers who hike into the Gathering "just to take a look," often wind up making utensils for themselves out of available materials, after smelling food or exotic teas. Frisbees, for example, make good plates, as do large leaves, flat rocks, and pieces of fallen bark. North American Rainbow Gatherings, often with over forty kitchens, offer a variety of foods seldom available in isolated rural communities near the Gatherings. Rainbows often take this abundance of "free food" for granted, although in Babylon good food is usually an extravagance. The Rainbow kitchen, however, is more than a place to go for food or music. Whole neighborhoods develop in clusters around kitchens, which act as twenty-four-hour community centers, serving as churches, schools, or shelters from the rain.

Taco Mike, one of the Rainbow Family's most popular cooks, describes a good kitchen as providing "good food and a nice home." According to Mike, "Every kitchen develops its own community within the actual town . . . and within that town you have a store on every corner. That's what the kitchens are . . . a store on the corner of the Gathering site" (interview 1990). Kitchens provide much of a Gathering's character. Elaborate kitchens, whose construction requires both sweat and creativity, spring up throughout the Gathering, often complete with wood-fired ovens made from fifty-five-gallon drums.

At the National Gathering in Minnesota, the Rock Soup kitchen served a mélange of soup twenty-four hours a day for two weeks. The following excerpt from an interview with Greg and Abram of Rock Soup typifies how a kitchen gets started:

> Q: The name, "Rock Soup," Where did that name come from?
>
> Greg: It comes partly from the stone soup legend. The story I first heard from my grandma was: There were two soldiers and they were traveling on foot and they had a big pot, and no other food, so they stopped on the side of the road and got a rock and a pot and filled the pot with water and started to boil the rock. Soon people were coming back from the market in the village with armloads of stuff and stopped when they saw the fire going and asked, "What you got?"
>
> "We got stone soup." And they talked it up and the people would want some soup and started chipping in some celery, another guy had some potatoes. Soon they had stone soup. This is rock soup cause we play a lot of music, stay up late.
>
> Q: So you sort of started the same way, coming here with a pot?
>
> Greg: Yeah. Well I got here a little before Richard did. I was camped across the way. When I met Richard, there was like that

fire pit there and one pot of split pea soup sitting on the ground. . . . He made a pot of soup and we decided we'd make some coffee; find some salt; put up a prep counter. When people started coming in we got this rail and the fire pit; more food started coming in; then this big half barrel soup pot; a bunch of rocks; this oven. Yesterday we fed about 1,000 people soup. That's just about a week after we dumpstered [our first] vegetables and stuff. . . .

That's just the way it works out here. Like right now we built an oven and we don't have anything to bake in it, but it will show up. It will be here tomorrow. Everything just sort of takes care of itself; everyone takes care of each other. . . .

I heard today there's a real kind baker from Colorado; and he heard about the oven from one of the sisters who's living here and he wants to come 'n do some baking; and he's a real fancy shmansy baker. That's great. (Rock Soup interview 1990)

No two kitchens are alike. The Joy of Soy, for instance, traditionally prepares tofu for other kitchens to cook with, while the Sprout Kitchen specializes in live bean sprouts. The Kids' Village Kitchen is geared to meeting the dietary needs of infants, children, nursing mothers, and expectant mothers. Other kitchens such as Sage Hollow, Sunrise, Lotus, and Quebec prepare a wide variety of foods ranging from tea to dessert. Most major kitchens send food to the main circle at dinnertime. Representatives from different kitchens meet at Kitchen Council in the morning to plan the evening's meal.

Some kitchens have pioneered their own Rainbow cuisine: food found only at Gatherings. Collector's Donut Kitchen is an example. Collector recalls,

We've made all kinds of jelly donuts; any kind of preserves you could bring us. We do pizza, which has cheese in it; we have all kinds of nut butters and stuff; almond; we did do one time marijuana donuts, but they didn't work out too well. . . .

We do garlic, onion, peppers. We do spaghetti, avocado donuts, kiwi donuts, pickle donuts. That's an interesting donut in itself. We do ice cream donuts when we get hard frozen ice cream. I've even done split pea donuts this year. I hate split peas so they got fat donuts. Refried beans, chili, sweet and sour pork, government issue pork, tuna fish: 135 donuts to one can of tuna. You got to have cheese though too. What's nice about a donut is that you can do so much with so little, and everyone likes it. The only complaint that people have is that I use too much sugar. . . .

Towards the end of the Gatherings we're usually trying new

experimental recipes using different fillings. We've used everything from escargots to carrion. (Collector interview 1990)

Collector transgresses mainstream definitions for doughnuts and expands doughnutdom into the realm of the Chinese Pork Bun. To enjoy many of Collector's "wahwahs," one simply has to stop thinking about them in terms of doughnuts.

In 1990 Collector hitchhiked to the Gathering. Hitchhiking, the most popular mode of transport during the early and final stages of the Gathering, limits the amount of material many Seed Camp and cleanup workers can bring to or take from the Gathering. Collector arrived with only a backpack and the two key components for Donut Kitchen; a cast-iron fry kettle and a large smile. Everything else materialized, enabling the Donut Kitchen to pump out doughnuts eighteen hours a day for three and a half weeks. In the end, after each of the fifteen thousand or so Gathering participants got all the doughnuts they wanted, Collector packed up and thumbed on.

Taco Mike's kitchen, often acknowledged by Rainbows and Rainbow watchers as the Family's most impressive architectural achievement, works in much the same way. In 1986 and 1990, Mike's crew constructed two-story structures, using only fallen timber, rope, and an occasional nail. Both buildings included lofts, ovens, and ample work counters. The 1990 Taco kitchen even had sporadic running water, with a nearby spring tapped and piped to a spigot in the food preparation area. Mike's kitchen, like Collector's kitchen, starts every year simply as a "vision," lacking material and supplies. Mike, like Collector, hitchhiked to the Gathering in Minnesota.

> All of it [the kitchen] just comes together at the Gathering. I can't haul nothing with me because I live by my back-pack. . . . So I got to give [it] away every year and every year I show up and I only have me and my back-pack and maybe a crew. Then we scrounge everything. . . .
>
> [This year] we got three big grates, one griddle, and one oven in now, and we'll put the other one in tomorrow. The guys're burning out my other oven now.[5] (Taco Mike interview 1990)

Mike's kitchen is the foremost meat kitchen at the overwhelmingly vegetarian Gatherings. Its omnivory menu is upsetting to many vegetarian and vegan (dairy-free vegetarian) Gatherers. Even though Mike's kitchen usually serves a vegetarian option, Rainbow rumors[6] often transform its omnivory into carnivory. People eye the Taco Kitchen with suspicion whenever, for instance, a dog is missing. Mike's crew—primarily seasoned travelers, hobos,[7] and rail tramps—often tease cringing vegetarians, boasting how theirs is the only kitchen not plagued by free-roaming dogs. On the subject of meat, Mike explains: "I won't discriminate against my food—or people. A lot of the crew that works here and around the site year after year—they smoke tobacco, they drink coffee and they eat meat. That's just a basic truthful fact. . . . If I got it, I'll cook it. Again, I don't discriminate against food. Food is food. If it's healthy for you, I'll cook it" (interview 1990).

The meat argument was further aggravated in Minnesota by the presence in Mike's kitchen of two live goats named Chili and Bar-B-Que. A local man donated them early in the Gathering, expressly stating that they were food. The goats survived Seed Camp, but vegetarians and animal lovers found their presence in Taco Mike's kitchen worrisome. On two occasions they were "rescued" and brought to Kids' Village, where a ride was arranged to take them to California where they would live happily ever after with a community of vegetarians. On both occasions, however, the shortsighted goats made their way back to Taco Kitchen, a mile away, where the remnants of Taco Mike's crew eventually ate them two days after the official end of the Gathering.

While chowing down on goat stew at Mike's kitchen in Minnesota, a seasoned rail tramp shared his recipes for "pond duck" with me as horrified vegetarians looked on. Pond duck, or more specifically, ducks found in municipal parks around the country, make "good eating in a pinch." However, he adds, "the damned things are so hard to catch, what with all them people screaming at you." My foolish query as to why he couldn't just put out a bit of bread as bait and then easily grab a duck was met with immediate laughter from the assembled hobos and road dogs. "If we had some bread," he loudly explained, "we wouldn't be eatin' pond duck!"

In Taco Mike's kitchen/restaurant/neighborhood, class boundaries that are ubiquitous in American society temporarily vanish. While the environment is especially comfortable for hobos and road dogs, all types of Rainbows frequent Mike's.

Other kitchens provide different environments. The Hare Krishna kitchen, Rainbow's oldest and most consistent kitchen, has a strong religious theme. Bhakti Steve, who identifies himself as both a Krishna disciple and a Rainbow, explains: "We don't feel like we're just feeding people food. We're feeding them *prasadam*. *Prasadam* means the Lord's mercy. . . . When we're making [food] we're making it with love for God. That's why home cooking is the best. . . . because it's made with love. You go to some restaurant—these people with so much anxiety, thinking about so many different sinful things. . . . They're cooking your food, that's why you get upset stomachs" (Bhakti Steve interview 1990).

Dinner at the Krishna kitchen is usually followed by chanting. Some Rainbows question the motives of the Krishna Camp, accusing them of coming to the Gathering to proselytize. The Krishna Kitchen environment, they point out, is conducive to recruiting. The food usually contains large amounts of sugar, giving diners a sugar "high." While on a "sugar rush," they hear or chant the Krishna chants. When they leave Krishna camp, the sugar wears off, causing depression. The cycle repeats when they return to Krishna to eat again. Visit Krishna: feel good—leave Krishna: feel bad. Ben & Jerry's Ice Cream, of course, has the same effect.

Another criticism some Rainbows level at both Krishna Kitchen and Taco Mike's is that they serve two American staples: Taco Mike serves meat, the Krishnas, sugar. Eating, like counciling, is an area where the Rainbow Family is continuously introspective and contentious. Among Rainbows, as among other utopian communities, diet is not just "a matter of personal preference," but also a "matter of philosophy and belief," so that "agreeing on a diet can be a political issue, a power struggle over what is the 'Correct' system" (McLaughlin and Davidson 1985, 80).[8]

Indeed, dietary issues sometimes lead people to create special communities, like specialized Rainbow kitchens. The short-lived vegetarian Kansas Emigration Society, for instance, created a community in 1856 for vegetarians who otherwise would be "solitary and alone in their vegetarian practice," and "might sink into flesh eating habits" (Fogarty 1990, 32).

The Farm community in Tennessee embraced a similar vegetarian ethic a century later, seeing vegetarianism as a more efficient, healthier, and cheaper way to feed people. Farm families view themselves as running a demonstration project on "how to raise healthy children on a non-animal diet." Vegetarianism is easy, they point out, since "vegetables don't try to run away" (Traugot 1994, 39). Their experiments with nontraditional foodstuffs such as soybeans and wheat gluten led to both their discovery of Ice Bean and their prominence in the Vegan epicure movement. Successful Farm food and publications businesses center around promoting vegan diets.

Other communities, like Rainbow, embrace vegetarianism as a popular principle, but its practice isn't universal. Brook Farm (Massachusetts 1841–1847) communalists felt that "humanitarian principles . . . extended to the protection of their animal brothers" (Webber 1959, 184); however, these principles were riddled with loopholes. "They were against eating meat—although of course that did not mean they weren't to have some slabs of pork in the Sunday beans" (Webber 1959, 184). They were also against hunting, making an exception, however, for rabbits. Rabbits "were suspected of nibbling the crops and were forthwith executed and consumed at [the] table" (Webber 1959, 184). Rainbows, likewise, occasionally serve up a possum or a slab of beef, but most kitchens are vegetarian. Some, however, aren't. It's as simple as that.

Drug use, like meat eating, is problematic for Rainbows. Discussions about substance abuse have given birth to kitchens free of suspect substances. The Brew-Ha-Ha teahouse, for example, is drug-free. Unlike some drug-free events held elsewhere in the United States,[9] Brew-Ha-Ha is free of almost all drugs,[10] including the two drugs Rainbows use most, caffeine and tobacco.

Marilyn Dream Peace, the director of a California mental health clinic, facilitates Brew-Ha-Ha from year to year. She founded the Kitchen at the National Gathering in Pennsylvania in 1986. That year, she attended the Gathering with a shy friend who was new to Rainbow. Facilitating a kitchen seemed like a natural way to help the friend plug in. Dream Peace also ran into another friend who had kicked cocaine at the previous year's Gathering after a fifteen-year addiction. He was now active in Narcotics Anonymous. "And so," she recalls, "the three of us had this idea of doing a drug-free environment" (Dream Peace interview 1990).

Brew-Ha-Ha became a popular Gathering fixture as well as a haven for people trying to give up coffee, cigarettes, or marijuana. In 1990, Brew-Ha-Ha also became insect-free, with the addition of a massive screen pavilion made from parachutes and mosquito netting. The pavilion was the gift of a recovering addict, who had sewn the entire structure together by hand. Marilyn Dream Peace and her husband, Shalom Compost, make it clear that, although drug-free, Brew-Ha-Ha is not necessarily antidrug. Some drugs, used responsibly, they argue, can be mind-expanding; but they have no place at Brew-Ha-Ha (Dream Peace interview 1990).

The difficulties of making a building are dwarfed by the challenges of keeping one operating. For the frail structures to survive use and the elements, they require constant maintenance. Cooking grates and oven drums, for instance, are usually used around the clock, yet they are held in place by clay. Hence, they require daily rebuilding. Likewise, restaurants held together by twine, that serve a thousand meals a day, also require similar maintenance to keep from collapsing.

Compared to other North American communities, the Rainbow infrastructure, with its pit toilets and oil drum ovens seems primitive. Similarly, early visitors to the Farm in Tennessee often described the community, with its ancient vehicles and unpainted buildings, as having a third world feeling (Popeonoe 1984, 91). During the Farm's early heyday in the late 1970s, the per capita annual cash income was only approximately four hundred dollars (Popeonoe 1984, 95). It was in many ways a third world community nestled in the American heartland. For a poor third world community, however, the infrastructure was pretty splendid.

Likewise for the Rainbow Gatherings. With the Magic Hat usually collecting and spending only between twenty-five cents and five dollars per person, Rainbow Gatherings are also cash-poor communities, despite the abundance of middle-class guests. By world standards, however, the Rainbow infrastructure is impressive, adequately meeting all basic needs and maintaining healthy conditions for thousands of residents—albeit without microwave ovens or bread machines.

Hydraulics

Operating a kitchen requires a regular supply of water. Kitchens need three grades of water: (1) potable water, for drinking and preparing food that does not reach a high enough temperature long enough to kill bacteria; (2) cooking water, easily made potable by boiling or filtering, for use in thorough cooking; (3) wash water that, when treated with bleach, is usable for washing dishes and cookware. While the need for water remains a constant, water delivery systems differ radically at Gatherings from year to year. At the 1991 North American Gathering in Vermont, volunteers laid four miles of plastic pipe, bringing water close to most major kitchens. At the previous year's Gathering, on the other hand, most kitchen workers had to carry buckets of water from distant sources.

At the height of the 1990 Gathering, Taco Mike estimated his kitchen used about 1,000 gallons a day (interview 1990). On most days the spring piped into his kitchen met this demand, providing raw water for his crew to treat. Rock Soup, using 275 gallons a day, and Brew-Ha-Ha, needing 500,[11] on the other hand, were both a half mile to a mile from the nearest source of raw water (Rock Soup interview 1990; Dream Peace interview 1990).

Hauling water to kitchens is a major task. Using five-gallon containers, Brew-Ha-Ha, for example, required one hundred arduous trips per day: "I carried one bucket from that creek and it was when things were real wet and boggy. . . . I fell and spilled the whole thing, went back and got another one and got it back here. It was a two-hour trip. . . . For five gallons of water. . . . [Then] this guy Bam Bam came along and saw my five-gallon bucket of water and washed his muddy hands in [it]. He thought it was for hand washing" (Dream Peace Interview 1990). Bam Bam, realizing his mistake, volunteered to get another bucket of water. Four and a half hours later he returned with it. For Brew-Ha-Ha, recruiting volunteers for the onerous water runs was a major concern. Sometimes they suspended operations for lack of water, but usually things ran smoothly with passersby on the trail volunteering to haul water.

Brew-Ha-Ha's water source in 1990 was a hose next to a fast-moving creek. The hose carried creek water to a spigot adjacent to a trail. The spigot was removed by Rainbow sanitarians who viewed it as a health threat, since many city dwellers would fill their canteens with water from a spigot and drink it without treating it. Removing the spigot forced people to venture into the mud, see the creek, understand where the water was coming from, and remember that treatment was necessary to make it potable.

Rainbows also work to protect the watersheds from pollution at the Gatherings. Simply telling everyone not to use soap in or near the water is not a hundred percent effective. A better solution is to provide warm showers away from watershed areas. At the 1991 Gathering, for instance, a hand pump powered a shower system. Shower users each brought a piece of firewood to help heat the water and pumped for the person ahead of them in line. Like a car wash on a sunny winter day, the shower usually had customers queuing up to use it. Under such conditions, water gains value and respect. At Gatherings, water represents labor and is therefore not to be wasted. Rainbows handle water gently and treat it carefully. A container of clear clean water, especially on a hot day, has an undeniable beauty.

Water controllers have built societies, concentrating power and capital, and shaping governments (Wittfogel 1957; Worster 1985). Water at Rainbow Gatherings, by contrast, is not under central control. Water is not a mystery, and no one covets the secrets of hydraulics. Unlike "hydraulic societies," egalitarian Rainbows share an understanding of basic water supply technology, much like the primitive agricultural economies described by environmental sociologists: "Where everyone in the community knows roughly as much as anyone else about the process of irrigation, where the work is within everyone's sphere of competence, and where the ends of water use are elemental human nutrition, there is no compelling reason for much hierarchy or discrimination. Power is diffused, elites are inchoate" (Worster 1985, 32). Sharing the responsibility for infrastructure maintenance undercuts the tendency to centralize power. Potable water is often not readily available at Gatherings, but information on how to tap springs and how to purify, store, and handle water *is* available. Much of this information and expertise comes from military veterans and back-to-the-landers.

CALM

Another vital area of the Gathering, open to everyone, is the Center of/ for Alternative Living Medicine (CALM). Some Rainbows say the acronym CALM also stands for "Creative Alternative Living Medicine." Either way, the key phrase is "Alternative Medicine." Rainbows sometimes refer to CALM by the military acronym "MASH," or mobile army surgical hospital, named by the Vietnam veterans who set up the Family's initial first aid facilities. CALM practitioners now prefer "CALM" to "MASH," however, since they view the facility as having evolved into more than a field hospital. CALM has become a comprehensive health care facility, tackling everyday health problems as well as "chronic" and "terminal" diseases.[12] It is a place where Rainbow doctors and healers offer their services to their fellow Family members.

For many Rainbows, CALM provides their annual trip to the doctor. The medics treat patients, rich or poor, not as inferiors, as in many urban clinics, but as equals. A healer talks about working with an alcoholic with severe impetigo: "[He] had blistering oozing wounds all over his body. He was a drunk. Rather I should say he liked to drink alcohol—because I think that his heart was really quite sober. He came here really at the bottom and we took him in to CALM and we taught him how to tend each one of those wounds with the attitude that a mother would treat a wound on her baby's butt" (Jimbo interview 1990).

CALM functions like a conventional Western health clinic, inasmuch as it is a place where sick and injured people go for treatment. That is where most similarities end. CALM's Boulder Bob, who works between Gatherings with an alternative health care clinic in Boulder, Colorado, says that most Western medical praxes "take care of only the symptoms and don't deal with the base of what's causing the problems." CALM, however, works to "make the whole person feel good; make the whole person feel happy and well" (Boulder Bob interview 1990).

Just as the Gathering's hydraulic system is demystified, so is its medical system. CALM stresses self-healing. Boulder Bob says CALM is "all about taking people who have abilities to deal with other people and having those people show other people how to take care of themselves, heal themselves" (interview 1990). Captain Crunch, a chiropractor who has been working with CALM for more than two decades, adds, "Healing comes from within. In society they don't want to deal with the healing. They just want to remove the symptoms and get back to what they were doing" (Frederick 1990d).

Water Singing on the Rocks (Water), a CALM healer, explains: "People in this country have been so mystified by doctors and lawyers, [they] don't know how to take responsibility for themselves. Your body is your temple, and you are going to live in your temple all your life—until it's time to change temples. You have to take care of it. You have to know who you are and what you're doing" (Water interview 1990).

Rainbows see this demystification of healing as a primary difference between alternative "living" medicine and traditional Western "dead" or "allopathic" medicine, in which "people are poisoned in attempts to make them well." Medicine Tools, another CALM healer, adds:

> [In] the world we grew up in we weren't informed of our medical options and our possibilities for self care. We were told you go to the doctor—that's it. The man in the white jacket you can tell more secrets to than your priest. [They are] the priests of our day; with their chapels of our day; with their nuns of our day; with their sacraments of our day; with their consecrated knife of our day; with their alter where they lay the sacrifices of our day; with mind numbing drugs for the recipients of such activities; with the exchange of coin; the whole thing. In [my] personal opinion, what they call medicine, what they call magic, is black magic. It's magic because it's not understood by the common man. Black, because the intent is to make profit. (Medicine Tools interview 1990)

The term *allopathic* is a clue to the history of the Rainbow tradition of healing. It originated around 1830 as a term of abuse for mainstream medicine, intended to contrast with "homeopathic." Homeopathy, which originated in Germany in 1810, treats diseases with tiny doses of remedies that in larger doses make healthy people exhibit symptoms similar to the symptoms of the disease under treatment. It also stresses exercise, proper diet, and pure air, as do most Rainbow healers (Dwork 1981).

At the 1991 North American Gathering, I visited CALM with my leg badly swollen from a mysterious sting. They treated it with "apis" (Latin for "bee") homeopathically, in other words, with a tiny amount of the pathogenic organism. The swelling, which had persisted for half a day, disappeared within two hours. The use of the Latin term, however, suggests that homeopaths are not above a little mystification themselves.

Most CALM healers, like nineteenth-century naturopaths, reject "artificial" cures (e.g., drugs) in favor of "natural" ones (Bynum 1981; Warner 1977–78). Two other nineteenth-century alternative medical movements, osteopathic and chiropractic, have moved close to mainstream medicine, but their rejection of drugs keeps them attuned to Rainbow, and Hippocratic, thinking.[13]

CALM healers interact with patients more than mainstream American doctors do. CALM practitioners stress talking with patients, both to get a comprehensive symptom picture and also to establish trust by showing that the healer cares about the patient (Semmes 1991, 458–59). Trust is essential, since many healing methods employed by CALM practitioners require active patient participation. CALM tries to provide a comfortable nurturing environment where patients can, as one healer put it, "feel like they could lay their head down and get fed and get suckled like our moms used to do when we were sick" (Jimbo interview 1990). Taking time to work with patients lets the CALM staff find what they feel is the most effective technique for dealing with specific physical problems.

CALM does not limit healing by following a single theory or approach: "At CALM, all these different ways of healing that in the outside world are in competition with each other—all work synergistically. Nothing gets fixed by just one modality—it's all synergistic—they all work together and help each other" (Water interview 1990).

Jimbo, a medical doctor by trade, has worked with CALM at North American Gatherings since 1984. Born into a family of doctors, he rebelled against what he viewed as a "disgusting, heartless profession" (interview 1990). Trained and certified to practice what he refers to as "straight medicine," Jimbo complements his private practice with a healthy dose of "Chinese medicine, traditional Chinese acupuncture, acupressure and herbal medicines" (interview 1990). At Gatherings and in private practice he now spends hours with his patients, learning their medical histories and "listening to their heartsongs" (interview 1990). His medical training helps with diagnosis, his specialty at CALM: "One thing I have, that a lot of these people don't have, is diagnostic skills. . . . Someone comes in here and they say, 'I have an earache.' They go to an alternative healer and he'll say, 'Here put this garlic in your ear, here take this, uh, echinacia, here do this, do that.' They never look in the ear. I know what an infected ear looks like on the inside. I know the toxicity that can come in the natural course of an infected ear. . . . I learned the natural course of diseases" (Interview June 28, 1990).

Based on his diagnosis, Jimbo attempts to connect each patient with an appropriate healer.

> What I try to do is to try to understand the energies of a particular patient, the energies of a particular healer and try to gravi-

tate those two together. . . . One of the greatest virtues of a good healer is that radiance that is dispelled from a good magnetic attraction to a patient. You know you radiate out energy and patients come to you. . . . Most people just go to the doctor because he's the guy around the corner. Here at Rainbow you end up seeing the healer that you need to see because your energies are entwined together; because there is a true attraction. And I just try to facilitate that. . . . I make sure that any serious case is seriously taken care of. And I make sure that mature healers are involved in it. All of us. We're a team; there are no individuals here. There are some really mature skilled healers here. There's no need for one person to take a case [alone] here. I mean we're all here to share and love. One person can crack the back; one person can rub the back; one person can soak the feet; one person can talk heart to heart. (interview June 28, 1990)

At every step the healer explains the curing procedures. Healers respect patients' ability to understand what is happening to them.

Healers share their art. Anyone interested can get involved with CALM. Marianna from Mexico City, for example, who has no academic medical training, relies on her experiences as a mother to help other mothers: "Here is where I am able to do what I like to do. Here I take care of babies. I have experience with my kids—and they seem to be very healthy—so I tell the other ladies what I have done to have healthy kids; and it seems to work. I teach pregnant women to have birth without pain" (interview 1990).

Novices begin with simple tasks like washing feet, cleaning wounds, and dressing minor injuries. Apprentices work with various healers, observing and learning their different methods and helping them administer treatment. In time, they consult or take on their own cases, starting with simple minor injuries. This way, healers pass on their skills, assuring an ample supply of future healers, thus sparing Rainbow the burden of an elite shamanic class. Healers say this aspect of CALM threatens the "medical establishment" the most, because it undermines the scarcities common to commercial Western medicine.

Medicine Tools says he's "kind of an eternal medical student" at CALM, adding that "there's not a university in the world that can make available the number of masters . . . or selection of various [healing] arts: I've seen psychic healing—which for many years I thought was pure bullshit. I've seen and participated in it. . . . I've seen the chiropractic art taken to new and higher places. . . . I've seen acupuncture prove its worth. . . . Basically, we'll be whatever kind of medicine man they need. If they need somebody dressed in a wizard's robe to come out of the darkness and fix their boo boo—and it *will* fix it—we'll manifest a wizard. If they need a doctor in a white coat, we got one of those too" (interview June 23, 1990).

At first glance, CALM's hodgepodge of battered tents is unimpressive, but its healers claim to have cured cancer and to have freed diagnosed "psychotics" from their medications (Water interview 1990; Tools interview 1990). A more typical case would be that of Holly, a thirty-five-year-old chemist who spends her annual vacations at Rainbow Gatherings. In 1991 she was determined to attend the North American Gathering in Vermont despite a painful back ailment that defied medical care for two months. Her back was injured further while traveling to the Gathering, leaving her in pain and nearly paralyzed when she reached Vermont. After a day at a local hotel, a friend arranged for an emergency vehicle to transport her to the CALM unit at the Gathering, where she was treated with acupuncture and massage. Two hours later she was hiking. A month later, the pain still had not returned (Holly interviews 1991a, 1991b).

Many people come to the Rainbow Gatherings seeking freedom from alcohol and narcotics addictions. Like Alcoholics Anonymous, the healers at CALM classify addiction as a "disease," without stigmatizing sufferers. Addicts are patients who need healing. Jimbo recalls, "One guy was really a serious junkie, shot up and everything, and he came to us to detox. We did ear acupuncture and herbal remedies. He's been free now for five years and he runs rehab centers" (Jimbo interview 1990). CALM claims many similar successes in helping patients recovering from common American addictions like tobacco, "bad foods," and "bad relationships" (Jimbo interview 1990).

The American Medical Association has lobbied successfully to outlaw many forms of medicine practiced at CALM (Weiner 1989, 248–49). CALM's healers contend that they're just treating family; it's a private matter. The feeling is that family won't testify against family. In Minnesota (1990), "just treating family" involved about 150 people a day during the peak of the Gathering (*Cook County News Herald* 1990b). In West Virginia, in 1980, an Appalachian community accepted CALM's offer of free medical services. Rainbow healers don't fear prosecution because, despite the large numbers of patients they treat, complaints about treatments are few. Of those who complain, few appeal to outside authorities about CALM care.

CALM, however, is not problem-free. The quality of treatment is spotty. An ideal CALM has reasonably competent healers and a large supply of remedies. At small regional Gatherings, however, CALM may be less than ideal. One of the worst CALM facilities in recent years was at the 1990 Quebec Gathering. The Gathering, which endured a chronic lack of adequate food supplies, was also without sufficient medical supplies or qualified healers. The suggested treatment for an infected foot laceration, for instance, was to "walk around barefoot and let the earth heal your foot, brother." The Gathering was located on a garbage dump.

Even well-equipped CALM units have their problems. At the 1987 Gathering in North Carolina, a man approached the CALM unit with a bee sting. A woman with a similar sting was already receiving treatment from a male healer—a cup of herb tea and a full body massage "to get the blood flowing and dilute the venom." When the man requested treatment from the same healer, the healer responded, "What did you do to make that bee want to sting you?" Then, without examining the sting, he handed the sting victim a leaf of tobacco and told him to chew it up and make a poultice with it. The healer then returned to the body rub. At the 1991 Gathering, a woman newspaper reporter was receiving a body rub from a male "healer" when he began to probe her vagina. CALM Council dismissed the healer, but similar problems recur at CALM, just as they do at mainstream medical facilities.

CALM focuses not only on healing, but on preventing disease as well. In this capacity, CALM volunteers monitor hygiene at kitchens, water sources, and latrines during Gatherings. Lacking coercive power, CALM alleviates most kitchen health problems with friendly advice. When, even after contact by CALM volunteers, a particular kitchen still doesn't clean up its act, the CALM Council recommends that the Supply Council cut off food supplies until sanitation improves. During the 1990 North American Gathering, the CALM staff went one step further. Several people reported having diarrhea after eating at the Sage Hollow Kitchen. CALM threatened to surround the kitchen with a circle of Omming (see chapter 6) Rainbows, unless they closed down for twenty-four hours to assess hygiene. Sage Hollow ceased operations; its offended chefs packed up and left the Gathering.[14]

The CALM Council also raises funds for water purification equipment. The widespread use of such equipment, CALM anticipates, will prevent many of the intestinal disorders common among city Rainbows exposed to living water.[15]

For many CALM volunteers, healing work is not limited to the Gatherings. Some also work in clinics, while others travel the country in converted school buses and vans, setting up shop at music festivals, political events, soup kitchens, and so on.

Working at the Gathering: The Mojo of Drudgery

This is a story about four people named Everybody, Anybody, Somebody and Nobody. There was an important job to be done and Everybody was sure that Somebody would do it. Anybody could have done it, but Nobody did it. Somebody got angry about that because it was Everybody's job. Everybody thought Anybody could do it, but Nobody realized that Everybody wouldn't do it. It ended up that Everybody blamed Somebody when Nobody did what Anybody could have done.

—*All Ways Free,* February 1986

Rainbows, in describing how Gatherings "come together," often use the term *magic*. Magic, in this case, refers to hard work done by a dedicated corps of volunteers. Work at the Gatherings is a labor of love. To many seasoned Rainbows, it would be inconceivable to come to a Gathering and not work. Collector explains that he couldn't simply come to a Gathering and not make doughnuts: "I haven't been able to do that yet. I show up on the site and the first thing somebody asks me is where's my doughnut factory going to be? I can show up here dead empty with nothing with me, just a bowl and a spoon, and within being here for four hours, somebody will hand me a pot and grease" (Collector interview 1990).

Taco Mike concurred: "I can't go to a Gathering and not do something. I can't do it" (interview 1990). Marilyn Dream Peace views the Gatherings as a chance to provide service: "It's my once a year church. . . . It's a very spiritual experience for me. It's a service, you know, like the Christmas giving and [sharing] service (interview 1990).

Service to the Rainbow Family is, for many people, a celebration. Dianne Zimmerman, active in organizing NERF Gatherings, explains:

> I look at this like my work as a nurse, [providing] a service. I look at my whole life as trying to do service, and, by serving others, I get an incredible amount of juice. . . .
>
> It becomes this dance and there's nowhere in the world that I know of that I can go and really see that, and have it be so clear to me that everything's sacred, everything's real special. And that's what keeps me able to do the work. I get real high from it. I feel really blessed by it. (Zimmerman interview 1990)

News photographers often come to a Gathering and shoot many pictures of people dancing, but few of people digging latrines, washing dishes or sorting trash for recycling. Rainbow workaholics hardly defy common mediated portrayal of Gatherers as lazy slackers—they are the backbone of the event. "How people arrange to do the work that the community needs to survive as a group" is a primary issue communities must tackle in order to survive and prosper (Kanter 1972, 64).

The question, according to Rainbow Garrick Beck, is,

> How do we motivate men and women to do the work that needs to be done without monetary incentive and without one person lording over the next lower echelon that lords it over the next lower echelon? These are the real questions that The Rainbow is answering. . . .
>
> At New Age festivals and fairs the vegetarian food is terrific and everybody's got beds within the cabins. There's nothing wrong or

bad about it. But for all that the lecturers may [say] at the 10:00 A.M. and the noon and the 2:00 P.M. classes, the fact is that some servant is being paid to make that bed, cook that food, sweep that floor and polish that door knob. And that's not very New Age to have an educated class that sits there and is so holy and beautiful; and a servant class that really empties the garbage, and really fixes the roof and so. . . .

Rainbow is a society where rich and poor disappear, where the notions of rich and poor disappear because everybody's living in lean-tos and huts and all you have is what you carry in. . . .

Take a look at how [Rainbow] accomplishes the basic needs of society without punitive justice. Because that's revolutionary. The fact that we dance under the moon, the fact that we believe in love as an idea and peace as a goal doesn't make us special from hundreds and hundreds and hundreds of other groups. We're all in that together. But, the fact that we motivate the hard work of human society without money, that's revolutionary. (Beck interview 1990)

The ability to motivate people to work has traditionally been the hallmark of a successful community. Historically, however, many so-called utopian communities, such as the Oneida community (Klee-Hartzell 1993, 183), exempted leading citizens or charismatic figures from the more mundane forms of day-to-day drudgery (Fogarty 1990, 47). The well-to-do gentry who settled the Union Colony in Colorado (1869) were even encouraged by community organizers to bring "servant girls and other hired help" (Fogarty 1990, 57) lest they have to do their own chores. Within three years the Union Colony, servants and all, dissolved as a utopian experiment, becoming the town of Greeley, Colorado.

Rainbows work for the love of community. Sociologist Rosabeth Moss Kanter writes, "Communal labor emphasizes joint effort, with all members, as far as possible, performing all tasks for equal reward. The important thing for the community is not who does how much of what work but that the job gets done" (1972, 95).

All Rainbows are expected to work, regardless of their status within the Family. However, in reality, there are "Drainbows" who don't pull their weight, and don't have to, since the Family does not *require* anyone to work. Their laziness is more than compensated for by Rainbow workers pumped up with spiritual mojo. An Irish journalist observed of the 1993 European Gathering, "Nobody has to do anything, yet an amazing amount of work has been done" (O'Halloran 1993).

Rainbows *do* realize that some people work harder than others and are therefore worth more to the community than others. Because of their commitment to "egalitarianism," they don't, however, institutionalize the distinction between willingness/ability and unwillingness/disability into holders of power and subjects of power, dominators and dominated (cf. Clastres 1994, 96).

Collecting firewood or hauling water for a kitchen are two of the simplest ways to "plug in" and taste Rainbow drudgery. Rainbow kitchens *always* need fresh water and firewood. Taco Mike, for instance, began his kitchen work by hauling water and wood for the Hobo Hilton Kitchen. Doing so, he got a chance to see firsthand how a Rainbow kitchen operated under "primitive" conditions, far from running water.

Mark Starwatcher, the CALM Kitchen facilitator at the 1990 North American Gathering, usually puts in seventy- to eighty-hour work weeks without bosses or timeclocks while at Gatherings. For him, the work is a "high":

> There is a certain high you get from service. . . . [It's] not in your average paycheck. It's like, "We're paying you money. We can treat you like shit." I would much rather have a compliment than the money, but the money of course is nice. The money is the nuts and bolts. A compliment is the spiritual side of it. That's what I like about Gatherings. A Gathering is a blend of the highest spiritual stuff you'll ever see, and the most gritty nuts and bolts you'll ever see, and mixed in a way there's no dichotomy. . . .
>
> We're all here together and have a common goal, a common purpose. You get people who are on both ends of that spectrum. You get road dogs who drink too much and work their butts off, and then you get bliss ninnies who are real high and spreading light and love but they never pick up a stick of wood to feed a fire. And then you got this vast mass in the middle that does them both and does them well. It's a dance. You need all three aspects. (Starwatcher interview 1990)

Seasoned Rainbows regularly tell newcomers: "If you see something that needs to be done, do it!" Tasks should be done, not discussed. Many Rainbows start working at Gatherings because they stumbled onto a job that wasn't getting done or a job that needed more people. A sister, on finding a fallen tree blocking a path at the North American Gathering in Minnesota, began unsuccessfully trying to move it. Passersby joined her, and soon the path was clear. Water Singing on the Rocks began working full-time at CALM after witnessing epidemic diarrhea at the 1987 North American Gathering. More health work was obviously needed. Water volunteered to fill that need (Water interview 1990).

While not required to work, most people eventually succumb to the spirit of the event. John, manager of a large suburban shopping mall, was visiting family in the vicinity of the 1990 NERF Gathering. Curiosity led him to the Gathering. He immediately joined in the work, carrying food for a kitchen.

> As I was walking in the very first day, a guy at the top of the trail said, "Are you going down to the kitchens?" and I said, "I don't

know, buddy. It's my first time here." And he said, "Well, are you going to follow the main trail?" and I said "Yeah," and he said, "Then you'll pass a kitchen. Can you drop this off?" It was a box of muffins for the kids. And he had gotten it from somebody from the outside, somebody baked them and took time to wrap them and put them in a box and gave them to him. He didn't know me from Adam or Eve. He just hands me this and trusts me to do that. I accepted that task willingly. . . . I think if he asked the person in front of me or behind me, they would have gladly done it also. I think there's no real pressure that you *have* to do anything. I think that's the real Rainbow concept that you don't *have* to do anything. . . . It's effective. (John [mall manager] interview 1990)

Abram of the Rock Soup kitchen is a chef by profession and a cook at Gatherings. While happy to cook all day and all night at the Gathering, he isn't satisfied cooking and baking on his paid job in Babylon. He explains: "I don't like to *have* to cook. I like doing it cause I want to; feeding my brothers and sisters. Doing it for somebody else to get rich off it isn't the idea" (Rock Soup interview 1990).

Rainbows complain that, in Babylon, jobs require uncomfortable and often counterproductive behavior. Mother Nature, of Rainbow's J.E.S.U.S. camp and kitchen, won't work at a standard job: "I work all the time, but I don't work for money. I found that the institutions won't let me work the way I feel I have to work, as a teacher, as a social worker, as the many things I've done. They won't let me do it with love. And I won't work with any institution that doesn't make love its first obligation" (Mother Nature interview 1990). She works constantly, however, at Gatherings "but nobody tells me how to do it, just the spirit of God" (interview 1990).

Rainbows appreciate and respect the labor that makes Gatherings function. Digging a hole is rewarding when those around the hole digger appreciate the hole. Imagine a laborer working for Consolidated Edison, digging up a New York City street. Cars whiz by, belching exhaust in her face as they miss killing her by inches. People on the bus stare blankly but never smile—the shiny shoes of busy professionals click by on their way to grab a splotch of frozen yogurt. The faces above are detached and expressionless, not acknowledging her existence. Children in school are warned to study, or they too will be ditchdiggers, plunging into a Dantesque inferno, condemned to a subterranean class.

Contrast digging a latrine at a Rainbow Gathering. Musicians and birds serenade. Passersby smile and say hello. They share food, drink, and hugs. Maybe they even grab a shovel and take a turn digging. Children with little shovels might play by the side of the half dug hole, their parents promising that they too can dig their own shitters in a few years. The fragrances of the forest, of fresh soil being turned, surround the digger. At the end of the day someone may hand her a "Rainbow Shitter Digger" T-shirt, to commemorate her latrine-digging accomplishment.[16] She drops her pants, if she's wearing any, getting the long-awaited honor of being the first to poop in the fresh new hole. At first reading, this description may seem to be sickeningly over-romanticized. Yet both the descriptions of the Rainbow worker and the New York City ditchdigger *are* accurate. It is the contrast that makes them seem surreal.

To come to a Gathering and not work, to be a Drainbow, is to miss the point of the Gathering. Yet many visitors come to the Gathering and "kick back," without contributing. John, the mall manager, observed that Rainbows respect those who work the hardest. When they speak in Council, he noted, everyone listens. No one is too good to work. Garrick Beck once cautioned me not to waste time interviewing anyone "sitting there scratching their belly under the tree trying to get you to turn on the tape recorder so they can talk, they're full of baloney" (Beck interview 1990). He suggested, instead, interviewing people digging latrines, hauling water, and working in the kitchens.

Rainbows, like their utopian cousins, collectivize their efforts, forming large work groups to take on major tasks (Kanter 1973, 226; Kanter 1972, 97). At the 1995 regional Gathering in Ithaca, for instance, a well-organized work party repaired a washed-out access road leading to the Gathering site. At the 1994 National Gathering in Wyoming, over a thousand Rainbows spontaneously joined together to fight a nearby forest fire.

Anyone, however unskilled, can work in whatever area of the Gathering they find interesting. People learn their tasks on the job, with coworkers as teachers. If bored with the task at hand, a Rainbow can choose another and start out fresh. This Rainbow version of career mobility undermines the development of entrenched hierarchies in any one area of the Gathering. It also lets workers escape boring, monotonous, or aggravating jobs, while still allowing community service. Sharing skills also builds workplace democracy. Since most workers understand all aspects of the task at which they are working, they can contribute both managerial and production skills. After a few Gatherings, a Rainbow can do most of the jobs necessary to make the Gathering work. Hardly a new Rainbow idea, the principle of job rotation has firm roots in utopian history, practiced by diverse groups such as the nineteenth-century Shakers and Fourierist Phalanxes[17] (Oved 1988, 439; Kanter 1972, 96) and by most contemporary communes[18] (Oved 1988, 439; Goldenberg 1993, 259).

Rainbow Communications

CALM's hints for a healthy Gathering, like other pieces of necessary Rainbow news, currently spread through a decentralized horizontal web (Bey 1991, 110) of rumors, publications, Internet Usenet groups, and "focalizers." Within a day of site selection, Rainbows disseminate vital site information through a network of friends calling friends, telling people in food co-ops, posting notices on bulletin boards, posting on Internet Usenet groups, and so on.

Rainbow Family information travels primarily through a network of "regional Rainbow focalizers." A regional focalizer is a local contact for an area who is in touch with other Rainbow Family members in that area by phone, by personal contact, or through a local newsletter. "A focalizer is a wealth of information—a valuable resource—someone who is in tune" (Varkonyi 1990).

An international listing of focalizers makes it possible to send information to thousands of Rainbows throughout the world in telephone tree or chain letter fashion without sending a mailing directly to everyone. The focalizers' network funnels information with a personal touch, so that it comes not from a stranger but from a friend, who heard from a friend, to tell you. . . . People pay more attention to a letter or call from a local focalizer than to a mass mailing. Reciprocally, the focalizer not only brings information to local Rainbows, but also publicizes local Councils, fund-raisers, and other special events, through other focalizers, to the Family as a whole.

To improve communication among local Rainbow groups, a Focalizers' Council convenes at major Gatherings. The North American Council often appoints a "focalizers' focalizer" to update and maintain a list of active focalizers.

> Being a focalizer is a delicate task. No individual can speak for the Rainbow Family, yet each of us volunteers our energy to share the Rainbow vision in our region. At our councils in Nevada, we conceived this forum with a hope that each person on this focalizers list would take the time to share heartsongs and ideas about future Rainbow [Gatherings] within their local circles. The local circles would share this info amongst regional and national circles. When many diverse perspectives flow, the many colors dance in harmony. What can your circle contribute to the Gatherings, what could you do without? What will make the Rainbow shine brighter? (Wirtshafter 1989)

This network lets all Rainbows participate in Council, including people who don't attend Gatherings. It permits year-round organizing around such issues as fighting Forest Service regulations that limit the right to hold a Gathering. Focalizers also organize fund-raising and planning for upcoming events. The 1989 Focalizers' Council institutionalized special-interest focalizers to complement regional ones and to facilitate communication between people working on specific issues. For many people this network of focalizers transforms Rainbow from a once-a-year activity to a year-round part of their lives. The focalizers' network also provides local Rainbows with a contact whom they can ask about Gathering specifics. If the focalizer doesn't have the answer, at least she would know who to ask and how to reach that person.

Often, exact directions to a Gathering site are not widely available. Rumors of a Gathering lead people to a given area, where they search for clues to zero in on the site. Neil Collins's experience on his way to the 1990 European Gathering in Austria is typical: "I was hitching from Horn to Zwettl, hoping to find it from there. My ride passed a trio of longhairs hangin' out under a tree having a picnic near a dirt road turnoff, [I] told the driver it was my spot. He thought it strange, I'm sure, but let me out. Cops had taken down all the signs, so it was a good thing people set up this little post on the 'main' road or I woulda missed it for sure" (Collins 1990).

Another Rainbow had similar problems finding Seed Camp before the 1989 Quebec Gathering:

> A really wonderful man who drives the school bus for the vil-
> lage helped me find that Squatec is also the name of a lake. Que-
> bec Gathering would be held there. The town where the people
> working for the Gathering lived was about 20 miles back up the
> road. It was the little town I had just passed where a kid on a bike
> had tried to speak to me in French. I hadn't understood a word. I
> smiled, nodded, and kept on the road.
>
> He might have been trying to give me the secret message that
> I was standing in a town called Lejeune and my travels were over.
> Anyway, the kind driver took me back to Lejeune in his school bus.
> (Kyla 1989)

Rainbows regularly wander into gas stations, convenience stores, and the like asking for directions. Locals usually know where the Rainbows are camped, how many there are, and how to find them. A stop at the local forest service ranger's station or call to the local police will also usually net directions. The state of Minnesota published directions to the 1990 Rainbow site, which highway tourist information stops handed out across the state. The tourism office in Sept Iles, Quebec, also handed out maps with handwritten directions to the Gathering site. Once close to the Gathering, one need only look for plastic whirligigs, ribbons, rock sculptures, and so on to find the site.

Lacking any clues whatsoever, Rainbows post queries just about anywhere, hoping another Rainbow will happen by and respond. Author Herbert Gold notes, "In cafes in far corners of the world, in Boulder (Colorado) or Athens (Greece). I sometimes read the notice asking RAINBOW FAMILY! WHERE ARE WE MEETING? and the answer, telling in which forest and what date. Once I came upon the news on the cork board of a laundromat near a boat basin in Pointe du Bout, Martinique" (Gold 1993, 67).

Rainbow Publications

Rainbows also stay connected, like most utopians before them (Barkun 1986, 90), via publications. The most popular is *All Ways Free.* Founded in 1985, *All Ways Free* has no permanent office or staff. *All Ways Free* does not accept advertising, sell subscriptions, or peddle individual papers. Like other Rainbow Family projects, it bills itself as "free and noncommercial" and relies on the same principles of giving and sharing as the Gatherings. The summer 1989 staff stated, "Nobody pays for a *Free*; each donation is a free gift to the next brother or sister who gets one." The *All Ways Free* collective raises money in ways traditional to the alternative press, by fund-raising parties and concerts.

Copy often comes in faster than money, forcing the collective to make hard decisions about what to print and what to cut. In the Fall of 1987, for example, the *All Ways Free* collective had a full paper's worth of copy in hand, but no money for publication. In place of *All Ways Free,* they published a two-sheet (four-page) newsletter, *All Most Broke.* Regional focalizers photocopied and distributed it. In a plea for donations, Stephen Wing, writing for *All Most Broke,* described *All Ways Free:*

> Its purpose is to gather the words & images you'd like to share with your Family, and circulate them—not only to keep our circle strong, but to extend the circle by offering the Rainbow heartsong to the rest of our human relations. It's an extension of our Giveaway to the human family of the planet. For Rainbow People who've never heard of us, for those who can't get to a Gathering, our words can be the reaching, maybe the touch, eventually even the clasp of hands that welcomes a brother or sister home.
>
> Think of those winter evenings when you've kindled your fire with the daily news of wars and conquest. Wouldn't it balance things a bit to lean back and open your fresh copy of All Ways Free for news of the Rainbow Family, pictures & poetry from the Gatherings, info about regional happenings, links to your kinfolk in all parts of the world? (All Most Broke Fall 1987)

Like other Rainbow projects, the *All Ways Free* volunteers reach decisions by consensus.

Ideally, a consensus publication should function like a council, publishing voices and ideas that a traditional hierarchical publication would squelch. Such openness prevents entrenchment of a hierarchy or a predictable editorial slant. Potentially, however, the *All Ways Free* collective could become a seat of power since it controls a key tool in the Family's communications web. Therefore, Rainbows say *All Ways Free* should be published from a new location,[19] with a new staff each year.

Council, meeting "on the land" during the Gathering, decides which volunteers will take *All Ways Free* home for the year.

Publishing experience is not a prerequisite for facilitating an edition of *All Ways Free*. The winter 1988 issue begins its "Dear Family" column: "Here it is—sorry it's late, we never made a newspaper before—but here it is." Although late, the collective did master the basics of publishing and eventually produced a forty-page half-tabloid newspaper.[20]

The lack of newspaper publishing experience makes the paper unpredictable. Unconstrained by style guides, each page is a montage, and each article possesses a different flavor. The winter 1988 edition challenges the problematic issue of article placement and exemplifies editorial freedom. Traditional editors place articles according to their importance, with the "most important" stories toward the front. This issue has two front pages, both folded on the left, and no back page. The unpaginated pages read toward the center from both ends, coming together in a circular centerfold laid out to be read while rotating either the paper or the reader. Readers cannot discern which text is upside-down and which right-side-up, nor which front page is more legitimately a "front page." An attitude of collective irreverence toward journalistic form and pagination eliminated the politics of placement.

Rainbow Peace Projects International Newsletter is another widely circulated Rainbow publication. Ostensibly a networking organ for "Rainbow Peace Projects," a loose alliance of cooperative communities working for peace and environmental goals, the newsletter expanded to discuss other Rainbow issues. At its height in 1990 it had over fifty contributors and subjected *All Ways Free* to amicable critique, publishing, for instance, complaints about "censorship" by *All Ways Free* (Jeri 1990). But in the Rainbow spirit, it also printed pleas for money and copy for *All Ways Free*.

The Rainbow Family also supports growing numbers of regional Rainbow publications like *Ho!*, which serves Rainbows in the southeastern United States. *Ho!*, like *All Ways Free*, relies on donations for funding, distributing the paper free of charge. The collective points out that Rainbow is a "Do-nation," meaning a nation of doers or workers (*Ho!* spring 1991). The *Ho!* collective also organizes fundraising concerts and parties, with profits split between *Ho!* and *All Ways Free*. Run by a consensus council, *Ho!* serves four Rainbow Family bioregions: Katuah ("the mountains"), the Cumberland plateau ("west of the mountains"), the Piedmont ("east and south of the mountains"), and Florida.

All four regions hold annual Gatherings (*Ho!* spring 1990). *Ho!* serves as a networking tool to help plan and publicize them, not just in the Southeast, but also among people planning to travel to the region. Such regional Family publications help Rainbows from other areas plan their travels around Gatherings. The Quebec Rainbow Family publishes the *Journal de L'Arc-en-Ciel* ("Rainbow Daily"), a predominantly French-language magazine. Mirroring the priorities of the Quebec Rainbow Family, the *Journal* stresses "spiritual" topics, primarily about supposed Native American teachings.

Rainbow publications, like the utopian publications of a century earlier, strive not only to keep Rainbows in contact with each other, but to act as a public relations device, explaining the Family to curious seekers much as utopian publications heralded and explained their communities (Armstrong 1981, 35). Unlike the Rainbow press, however, the utopian press sometimes took a more activist role in outreach and organizing. The *Coming Nation,* for example, a paper started by utopian writer Julius Wayland in 1893, evolved into the largest-circulation radical newspaper in the country (Fogarty 1990, 154–55). Wayland and his followers used profits from the paper to buy land and start the Ruskin Cooperative (1894–1899) in central Tennessee (Egerton 1977, 67). At its peak Ruskin included thirty-two homes, a hotel, a communal dining hall, and a theater (Fogarty 1980, 161), all supported by profits from The *Coming Nation* and an active canning business (Egerton 1977, 70).

Spinning Webs: The Guide and the Internet

The Rainbow Guide, first published in 1977, is a worldwide directory of Rainbows. Originally titled *The Rainbow Nation Cooperative Community Guide,* it is the brainchild of longtime Rainbow Michael John. *The Rainbow Guide* lists not only names, addresses, and phone numbers, but also people's skills, resources, and Heartsongs. It describes what people have to offer and what they feel they need. Resources offered range from "Wanderers welcome to camp in our field" to the use of a recording studio (Rainbow Family Net 1988). Using the *Guide,* people can contact natural practitioners and healers; mental patients find organizations fighting for their rights; computer professionals can share ideas; homeless people and travelers can find a welcome place to spend a few days; Pagans and Christians alike connect with spiritual communities; environmentalists and anarchists network internationally.

Needs are just as important in the *Guide* as offerings. A Rainbow brother in Elizabeth, New Jersey, writes: "I have no services to offer but I would like Contact and Friendship with Brothers and Sisters all over" (Rainbow Family Net 1988, 11). A brother in Brooklyn states simply that he needs "Love" (Rainbow Family Net 1988, 13).

The Rainbow Guide is also a resource for government agents attempting to disrupt Rainbow Gatherings (U.S.F.S. Texas May 11, 1988).[21] Rainbow Guides now carry "copyright" notices such as this one carried in 1988: "Use of the contents herein by the U.S. Federal Government, or its agents, Law Enforcement Agencies of any State, or their agents, or by anyone NOT a self-declared MEMBER of the Rainbow Family is *expressly prohibited*" (*Rainbow Guide* 1988).

U.S. Forest Service Special Agent Billy S. Ball ignored this notice, using the *Guide* in May of 1988 as he spread false rumors proclaiming that the 1988 North American Gathering would not take place. Ball's staff, at government expense, tried to telephone all U.S.-based Rainbow Family members in the *Guide,* advising them not to come to Texas (U.S.F.S. Texas May 11, 1988). Many Rainbows, however, explained to the callers that they "no longer lived there" or that there was "no one there by this name," information the Rangers dutifully recorded (U.S.F.S. Texas May 11, 1988). The Gathering went on as scheduled. For years invitations advised Rainbows to "ignore all rumors of cancellation," for the Family has encountered disinformation before.

Both information and disinformation about Gatherings now travel electronically through the Internet. Rainbows with access to the four ingredients for cybergabbing: electricity, a telephone line, a computer with a modem, and an active account with an Internet service provider, can both post and read messages on the Rainbow Family's news server, alt.gathering.rainbow.

World Wide Web wanderers can surf to a Rainbow Family "page," containing electronic copies of Rainbow publications, *Howdy Folks!* for different Gatherings, Rap 107, photographs, newspaper clippings, and bibliographies of Rainbowesque publications. Rob Savoye, a self-proclaimed hacker living on the outskirts of Boulder, Colorado, maintains the page as a volunteer project. He includes this disclaimer: "This is Not an official document of any kind by the Rainbow Family. This Home Page is my own creation, and as such only represents my own ideas."[22]

The advent and growth of the Internet, seen by many Americans as revolutionizing communications, has not radically affected Rainbow Family communications. The Family's own non-electronic web of photocopied notices, letters, rumors, ribbons, and plastic whirligigs was in place and functioning years before the advent of the Internet. The Rainbow system of communication, with information eluding central control by simultaneously flowing through varied media, is theoretically akin to the Internet; it's just sometimes a bit slower.

On occasion, however, old-fashioned Rainbow communications channels put the electronic net to shame. The *Howdy Folks!* notices for the 1995 NERF regional Gathering, for example, were mailed out on May 3. Most focalizers received them by May 5. By May 6, second-generation copies were posted in food co-ops, laundromats, and so on. By May 8, third-generation *Howdy Folks!* were being mailed to friends, making their way around college campuses. On May 10, someone posted a transcription on the Internet.

For Rainbows, electronic communication has many shortcomings. The most obvious problem is accessibility. Many Rainbows lack knowledge or materials needed to get on-line. Rainbow resources on the Internet are only available to middle-class and wealthier Family members. Electronic "discussions" exclude too many Rainbows to be in any way indicative of consensus on any issue. The Internet has, however, created a global forum, allowing *some* Rainbows in North America to communicate with fellow Rainbows around the planet. This intercontinental sharing of ideas may prove pivotal as the Rainbow Family evolves into the twenty-first century.

The Rainbow TAZ—Creating a Momentary Utopia

Rainbows are proud of their ability to create an environmentally sound infrastructure on demand in the "wilderness," and to manage it by consensus. More than just a spiritual or a political body, Rainbows see their Gatherings as small-scale actualization of a utopian vision of sharing: "Whenever I hear about somebody's visionary religion or political ideology, I don't care one bit. I don't care one bit about the ceremonies. . . . I don't care whether they dance in circles naked or they sit in rows with jackets on listening to one person from the pulpit. Doesn't make a difference to me. The question I have is what is their social program? Who are they feeding? Who are they housing? How are they cleaning up the earth? . . . That's what I care about" (Beck interview 1990). On this level, Rainbow Gatherings are successful. Everybody is welcome—regardless of wealth, mental or physical health, background, religion, or origin. The Family will, to the best of its ability, heal the sick, feed the hungry, clothe the poor, befriend the lonely, and house the wanderer.

These infrastructural accomplishments set the Family apart from the "Movement" groups of the 1960s with which the mainstream press identifies them. For example: "Woodstock Nation was simply lacking in the essential ingredients necessary to create a truly alternate society. The counterculture did not control its own communications and never developed a meaningful infrastructure. As a result, there was always a great deal of talk about creating a sense of community, but the community never went much beyond pitched tents, makeshift campsites, good dope, electric rock and mellow memories" (Rifkin 1979, 103). While the Rainbow Family controls its own communications and has developed a substantial infrastructure, some argue that it is still no more than the makeshift community of pitched tents described above. Gypsies[23] and vagabonds in every culture have endured similar criticism.

Throughout this chapter, I have linked the infrastructure of Rainbow Gatherings to the Family's utopian predecessors. Like many utopian groups, Rainbows prefer to Gather in a remote site; diet plays a central role in the life of the community; they share skills; they rotate jobs and have a communal economy. In essence, nothing the Rainbow Family does to construct their Gatherings is new or unique.

What is unique is how the Family has woven these traits together to form a gypsy city, continually appearing, disappearing, and reappearing. This same city was the sixth-largest municipality in the state of Wyoming in 1994 and the third-largest in Vermont in 1991. It remains essentially unchanged, whether it congeals in Montana, Alabama, Texas, California, Pennsylvania, Quebec, Poland, Spain, Ireland or Russia. Rainbows regard friendly or hostile receptions much like stationary cities regard the changes of season.

The Rainbow Gathering is an actualization of what anarchist theorist Hakim

Bey calls the Temporary Autonomous Zone (TAZ). Revolutions seek permanent change and, in doing so, lead to violence and martyrdom (Bey 1991, 100–101). Revolutionaries aim to hold territory. The TAZ, by contrast, does not directly engage the state, but instead "liberates an area (of land, of time, of imagination) and then dissolves itself to reform elsewhere" (100-101). TAZ theory maintains that a "free enclave" can be maintained by regularly "moving the entire tribe" (102). Unlike immigration, however, the "tribe" moves by dissolving into the larger society (Babylon) and reconstituting in another time and space. Demographers refer to this practice as "fission-fusion" (cf. Dentan 1992; Dentan 1994; Fix 1975; Neel et al. 1964).

Historians and science-fiction novelists write of utopias past and future. Bey asks, "Are we who live in the present doomed never to experience autonomy, never to stand for one moment on a bit of land ruled only by freedom?" The Rainbow Family, in realizing a TAZ that dances the globe, answers with a resounding NO!

Rainbows form a bucket brigade to fight a forest fire adjacent to the 1994 Gathering site in Wyoming. Photo by Gabe Kirchheimer.

Taco Mike's oven, 1986 Gathering, Pennsylvania. Photo by author.

Baking bread at the 1989 Northeast Regional Gathering, Vermont. Photo by Gabe Kirchheimer.

A 3:00 A.M. chess game at "Everybody's Kitchen," 1994 Gathering, Wyoming. Photo by Gabe Kirchheimer.

One of many drum circles at the 1992 Gathering, Colorado. Photo by Gabe Kirchheimer.

Serving lunch at Kids' Village, 1990 Gathering, Minnesota. Photo by Gabe Kirchheimer.

Cablecar ride at Moondancer's Meadow, 1986 Gathering, Pennsylvania. Photo by Gabe Kirchheimer.

New York City Rainbow Family Winter Picnic, Coney Island, 1991. Photo by Gabe Kirchheimer.

Wedding ceremony, 1992 Gathering, Colorado. Photo by Gabe Kirchheimer.

Center for Alternative Living Medicine (C.A.L.M.) apothecary, 1994 Gathering, Wyoming. Photo by Gabe Kirchheimer.

Welcome Center/Rumor Control, 1992 Gathering, Colorado. Photo by Gabe Kirchheimer.

Preparing lunch, 1995 Gathering, New Mexico. Photo by Gabe Kirchheimer.

Dave (from "Sunflower's Day") preparing breakfast at Buffalo Camp, 1990 Gathering, Minnesota (author's feet at right). Photo by Joseph Levy.

People milling about, 1990 Gathering, Minnesota. Photo by Joseph Levy.

Carrying a piano into the 1987 Gathering, North Carolina. Photo by author.

Rainbows form human conveyor belt to bring hundreds of watermelons into the 1991 Gathering in Vermont. Photo by author.

Barter Lane, 1991 Gathering, Vermont. Photo by author.

Dish-washing station, 1991 Gathering, Vermont. Photo by author.

Mudpeople on the move, 1990 Northeast Regional Gathering, New York. Photo by author.

"Chili" at Taco Mike's kitchen, 1990 Gathering, Minnesota. Photo by author.

Bicycle bus, Bus Village, 1990 Gathering, Minnesota. Photo by author.

Learning to drum, 1990 Gathering, Minnesota. Photo by author.

U.S. National Forest Service file photo released in compliance with the Freedom of Information Act, 1978 Rainbow Gathering, Washington. Photo courtesy of the U.S.N.F.S.

5 People of the Rainbow

I yam what I yam and that's all that I yam.

—Popeye the Sailor Man

Who Are These Rainbows?

It takes all sorts of folks to create a Rainbow. Members see themselves as forming "a tapestry of humanity cutting across lines of class, race, religion, ethnicity and gender." They see the Family as "a working model of multiculturalism; a society where differences are celebrated and unity achieved" (Wetmore interview 1990).

The definition of a Rainbow Family member is broad. In principle, "everyone is a Rainbow; some people just don't know it yet." Rainbows regard all visitors to the Gatherings, whether they are there for an hour or for a month, as Rainbows. Hence, they view reporters who come to observe Gatherings as Rainbows, and treat them as sisters and brothers. They treat locals who stop in for an afternoon to satisfy their curiosity the same way. Forest rangers patrolling Gatherings sometimes resist incorporation, but Rainbows view them as fellow Rainbows, albeit oddly dressed. Rainbows treat even police officers and undercover law enforcement agents who come to monitor, control, or disrupt[1] the Gatherings, as Rainbows, albeit misguided. They just need a bit more love and healing than most Rainbows do.

The prescriptive unconditionality of Rainbow love and acceptance, and the

Family's refusal to limit it to deserving members of the in-group, set it apart from other groups that promote or have promoted alternative lifestyles. Indeed, most long-lived utopian groups throughout history differ from the Rainbow Family in that they were, and still are, restrictive in admitting new members (Dentan 1995; Oved 1988, 385; Kanter 1972, 127). Utopians have traditionally hand-picked members, accepting only people who would blend easily into the community, the way many private schools select their students, taking the brightest and easiest to educate, and leaving emotionally disturbed or learning-disabled students for the public schools. Most communities also established bottom-line requirements for commitment, demanding that new members commit money or property to the group.

The Amana Community, for instance, seldom admitted new members (Perkins and Wick 1891, 70), and then only after two years' probation (Holloway 1951, 172). The North American Phalanx also put new members on probation. Hutterites, despite their extraordinary population growth, have only admitted approximately a hundred members who were not born Hutterite since arriving in North America (Oved 1988, 361).[2]

The Society of Separatists of Zoar, Ohio (1817–1898), widely recognized as one of the most successful cooperative communities, selected new members only if a need existed in the community for their particular trade or craft. Such applicants, after selection by the trustees, were subject to a year's probation, after which they could become full members only upon ratification of their application by the full community. Zoar even preferred to hire workers rather than admit new members. Even members' children did not receive automatic membership, but were subject to the same scrutiny as new applicants (Nixon 1973, 89). Similarly, members' children at the Farm in Summertown, Tennessee, must be approved for membership after their eighteenth birthday.

Rainbow membership, by contrast, is open not only to those with skills or resources the Family needs, but also to those who need the Family. The Rainbow Family requires new members only to "bring their belly buttons," and will waive this requirement under extenuating circumstances. Some members live under bridges, some in condominiums. For most, the Gatherings are a vacation from Babylon, but for a dedicated minority, Rainbow is a way of life. Rainbows call themselves "Hobos," "Rail Tramps," or "Road Dogs," as well as "teachers," "social workers," and "computer programmers." Road Dogs call the road home, perpetually traveling, usually hitchhiking. A Hobo is a dedicated Road Dog, with no plans or desires to settle down. Rail Tramps are similar to Hobos and 'Dogs, but prefer hopping trains. It is rare for a 'Dog, Hobo, or Tramp to own a vehicle.

Hobos, 'Dogs, and Tramps tend to come from poor white rural backgrounds and often speak with a southern drawl. Most Rainbows hail from the middle class, however, being either "drop-outs" or "weekend Rainbows." The Magic Hat fills with both pennies and crumpled wads of fifty- and hundred-dollar bills. Rainbows come in all ages. Contrary to the media depiction of Rainbows as "aging hippies," the Family currently draws much of its strength from neophytes between the ages of eighteen and twenty-five.

Rainbows often take unique names, which they call "spirit names" and which mark a major transition in their lives. Some use their *nom-de-arc en ciel* (Rainbow name) only at Gatherings, while others use the new names year-round. A quick glance through any Rainbow Guide reveals a diverse array of such names. Mark Starwatcher, for example, took his name in 1986 to celebrate a radical change in his lifestyle. Starwatcher quit paying rent and moved "into the woods," where he slept under the stars, eventually buying a star chart so he could learn more about his new home—hence, the name "Starwatcher" (interview 1990).

Mother Nature recalls getting her new name in 1975 when a Russian friend visited her farm in northern Michigan and explained that her maiden name, in Russian, means "nature." Her initials also spell out the first three letters of the word "nature," and she is the mother of twelve children, hence she adopted the name "Mother Nature" (Mother Nature interview 1990). Mother Nature, a talk-ative middle-aged women with rural charm, first encountered the Rainbow Fam-ily eight years later in 1983, when the North American Gathering was held thirty miles from her remote Michigan farm. She heard that Rainbow People have "spirit names," so she introduced herself as Mother Nature. The first person she met "smiled real big and said, 'It's about time you got here'" (Mother Nature inter-view 1990). She's been "Mother Nature" ever since.

Felipé, a friendly soft-spoken fifty-five-year-old Yaqui Indian, is also a familiar face at Gatherings. He "facilitates" a kitchen, famous among Rainbows, which feeds thousands of people at each Gathering. At the 1990 North American Gathering, Felipé, with the help of Hawk, a bald man in his late forties with a faded marijuana leaf tattooed on his scalp, erected and operated the Kids' Village kitchen. Felipé also got married at that Gathering. His life changed when he found the Rainbow Family: "I'd been drinking. [I] Found myself on the way to New Mexico in a car, passed out drunk. When I woke up, I was on top of this mountain. I looked down and saw all these tepees and children playing. I broke into tears. People came and sat around me. Pretty soon, the tears were tears of joy. It was a purification" (Hager 1990, 51).

Since the 1977 New Mexico Gathering, Felipé has been living a life of giving and sharing, taking his kitchen and its Rainbow spirit around the country, often feeding the "homeless." With a few pots and pans, a lot of love and Rainbow Magic, his kitchen survives on the road, attracting support wherever he sets it up.

Snake Mountain Bear ("Bear" for short) is a tall heavyset man in his mid-for-ties. Usually clad in jeans, he is an imposing Vermonter whose face comes to life with a smile that lets you know you've met a friend. Bear describes first encoun-tering Rainbow Family members during the 1970s at Earth People's Park in Norton, Vermont:

They impressed me at that time. They stood out from the hippies. Looked like them but they seemed different. They seemed more aware of the human family. . . . I always was interested in families. I came from a broken family and I always wanted to be in a family that was intact. So much of my focus in life was family life. I had my own children and I wanted to go to an alternative lifestyle where I could rear my children in what I perceived to be a godly way. In line with the will of the Great Spirit. Wanted to educate [them] myself because I felt that there were poor role models in public schools and that their values were poor, ministered a lot of confusion to kids. . . . Meeting a few [Rainbows] created within me a real hunger to meet more Rainbow characters. I was wondering are these few representative of the group. (Bear interview 1990)

Crow arrived at the 1990 North American and NERF Gatherings with what was then his home, a 1951 Ford school bus. The bus, two stories tall, with a skylight, loft, and natural wood interior, fit right in at Rainbow's Bus Village. Bus Village, a regular facet at Rainbow Gatherings, hosts a large community of vehicle-based North American "gypsies." "Bus people," even though they usually live on the road, seldom refer to themselves as "Road Dogs," "Tramps," or "Hobos." They prefer to be called "gypsies," a title shared by more well-to-do Rainbow travelers. The distinction is based mostly on class. The bus people consider themselves as having their "trips more together," since they sleep in beds (as opposed to bed rolls), own buses, and thus are propertied. They tend to be better at making and managing money and often have middle-class family roots. Crow, who lived on the road in buses from 1986 to 1992, explains the lifestyle: "It's Rainbow living. But it's only *one* way a Rainbow can live. I mean some Rainbows can live in their backpack or a tent or a car. . . . It definitely fits the Rainbow life. You can jump into your house and go anywhere. You can go to a Rainbow picnic, or to a Rainbow Gathering and you have everything there—so you can pump out food for a lot of people—or have a good hangout spot and you're always totally at home. Like . . . right now, [I] can make coffee, or give you a sandwich" (interview 1990).

Alita, who lived in buses for four years, finds the bus lifestyle compatible with her life as a migrant worker. With the bus, she is at home in any part of the country: "I used to do migrant work, or even get a job somewhere, or work for three months and then travel for six or seven months until I was broke, and then travel again. Now I'm living in a bus, so when I sit down to work, I don't have to pay rent" (interview 1990). Alita first encountered Rainbows as college dorm mates: "We had a big family shampoo [bottle], and a big family toothpaste [tube], and we just shared everything, co-opped dinner etc. . . . I loved it. So I went to the [1982 Idaho] Gathering with them" (interview 1990). After the Idaho Gathering, Alita returned to college and her friends all dropped out. Eventually, they returned to school and finished their degrees, while Alita opted for a more nomadic life.

Joseph Schwartzbaum is an elderly Jewish Holocaust survivor from Chicago who survived five years in a Nazi concentration camp. He has been coming to Gatherings since 1980.

> When I came to America everyone used to say, "Oh, the bad Germans." I say [the Holocaust] had nothing to do with Germans. It happened to many civilizations in the past centuries. . . . At the beginning the people don't notice it, it doesn't start right away with killing. It starts only slightly . . . you know. "We are superior than the others." Slowly but surely it gets to a point that [allows] murder or rape or anything without the slightest conscience; and then it's too late. So I say it has nothing to do with that they were Germans. It happens in any country. (Interview 1990)

The Gatherings are his vacation from urban violence and fear.

> I'm enjoying [the fact] that people are not at each other's throat like they are in the cities. In the big cities, or smaller cities, or in business, [they are] constantly trying to attack each other; constantly afraid of each other; constantly on defense. Matter of fact I talked with the Ranger today again about it. And I [asked], "Would you dare, or your wife dare to go in Chicago at dusk?" People are scared: rape, killings. I say, "Would you do it?" And he says, "no." And I say, "Here it's thousands of people, five, ten thousand people. Potentially there can be twenty, fifty rapists in potential. Or robbers." And I say, "Yet everyone behaves. Strange people walk in the dark, they are not afraid, without fear. This alone," I says, "shows that the people want to live like humans." (Schwartzbaum interview 1990)

Gary Thomas, an outgoing man in his early forties, studied to be an art teacher. His first Gathering was the 1983 North American Gathering in Michigan, where he spent most of his waking hours drumming. He returned in 1985, to the North American Gathering in Missouri, where he started blowing automobile-sized bubbles: "And from there a career was born. . . . And now there's no difference between the Gathering and the outside world to me. I'm known as the Bubbleman wherever I go. The supermarket—driving down the road—schools; just Bubbleman. People call me Bubbleman. And now I've made a business out of trying to share lighter being and consciousness with, um, bubbles. That's what my card says: *See Ya Lighter*" (Bubbleman interview 1990). His "Bubbleosophy":

People are just like bubbles. We're all different sizes, just like bubbles, and we're all different shapes, just like bubbles, and we're all different colors, just like bubbles, and some of us last longer than others, just like bubbles, but we all come from the same source. Bubbles come from Joy, and we come from love; and when we don't realize we come from love, we fall in love. When we do realize we come from love, we rise in love; just like a bubble. Then we'll have more bubbles, less troubles, then you can let your kid come out and play some more. (Interview 1990)

The Bubbleman finds bubbles healing. Between Gatherings and Bubble Gigs, he brings his bubble show to hospitals and nursing homes: "What heals me, is the joy and laughter of children playing and chasing after the bubbles, or just standing there astounded, watching me. Or going to a nursing home where people are really sick, and watching them smile, and that becomes *my* healing therapy" (interview 1990).

Remi, a Caribbean Rastafarian[3] man in his mid-thirties, comes to the Gathering to contribute to the Nyabinge drumbeat that drifts through the night.

I came to the Rainbow Gathering to focus my energy on being grateful to my brothers and sisters and to be free and play drum in a Root Mon style, and at this Gathering I've enjoyed myself a lot because people have been for the most part very receptive. The tradition that we use as Rastas is called Nyabinge. It's an ancient African tradition and we use Nyabinge to bring forth our forefathers and our roots and our peoples, and it's a heartbeat rhythm that we use because it symbolizes the heartbeat of life to bring all I and I together. . . . We come forward to the Gathering to mash it and to mash it in Nyabinge tradition. . . . The drum is a very powerful tool . . . because drum is a language, it's a form of expression. Like when we do certain rhythms we communicate with each other. . . . And also we have lots of family that we've established over the years. . . . So we come forth to a Gathering for two reasons mainly. One: To have a little bit of oneness and unity with my drum like a prayer. To come forth together and to pray with this drum here. And second: to unify with my brothers and sisters. Like certain brothers I haven't seen in a few months. (Interview 1990)

The Nyabinge drumming at the Gathering, according to Remi, reaches out beyond the Gathering to call people "Home."

We use drum as I and I weapons. We mash down the walls of oppression, through the Nyabinge tradition. And that is I and I main purpose for coming forth. To free up all the people out there that are driving fancy cars, and making major payments, that haven't come out to this, that don't even know this exists. For our rhythms to reach those far and few between. That is I and I purpose in coming to the Gathering. . . . And to call them forth so they can realize their place, and call them home. And maybe it won't call them to the Gathering, but maybe it will call them to find their individual purpose. Maybe as an artist, a great painter. Maybe as a musician. Maybe as a sculptor. So our drum rhythms are designed to call souls that [have], been slightly misguided or led astray by the false preachers. (Interview 1990)

John, the shopping mall manager, compares Rainbows with his customers who drive "fancy cars" and make "major payments."

[Mall shoppers] got more clothes on, yes, but there's not a whole lot of difference. Pretty much, you've got your Rainbow people here, you've got outside people here. I've seen people today in really good pants and clothes; you can tell that they are just here to look around. And that's kind of the reverse spectrum at a mall. Usually you have nicer clothing on as a general rule. Then there's people who come in, transients, who don't. So it's pretty much the same . . . the ratio's different, that's all. . . .

At a mall situation, people are coming there for a service. To an extent people are coming here for a service. They're trying to get in touch with their feelings; they're trying to kick back—become the person that they know that they are—without the outside pressures. So in that respect I think Rainbow provides a service like a mall would. If you need a new pair of sneakers you would go to a mall to get them. (Interview 1990)

Sexism, Racism, and Homophobia

At the peak of a Gathering, the number of men and women seems about equal. But men outnumber women by about three to two[4] in the *Rainbow Guide*. Men also visibly outnumber women during the Seed Camp stage of the Gathering. On June 16, two weeks before the 1990 North American Gathering was officially to begin, for example, there were about five times as many men as women on-site. This is typical. A primary reason for this imbalance is that Hobos, Rail Tramps, and Road Dogs, the majority of the early Seed Camp work crews, are usually men. "Male energy" is therefore disproportionately represented in many crucial infrastructural decisions. The gender imbalance is the same during the final stages of cleanup, where Hobos, Rail Tramps, and Road Dogs again predominate.

Rainbows idealize egalitarianism, but for years men have dominated Rainbow meetings. The Family was born at a time when men dominated the counterculture; when authorship in the alternative press was overwhelmingly male; and when women were still commonly referred to as "chicks" (Miller 1991, 16). Most principals in the first Gatherings were men. Consequently, most of the old guard now are men. During the first three hours of the four-hour 1990 Hipstory, a collective Rainbow Family oral history recited at each year's North American Gathering, no women's voices were heard. Eventually, two women spoke, but only after one of them pointed out that it was time for "female energy."

Men have also, over the years, dominated Council and facilitated most kitchens and camps. Only now, as the Rainbow Family is in its third decade, are women's voices respected alongside men's. The emergence of the regional Rainbow movement and of Regional Gatherings, in which women play a major role, drives the new Rainbow gender equality. North American Gatherings now offer a "Sisters' Space" or "Sisters' Meadow," a place set aside exclusively for women. "Sisters' Circle," a daily women's council, serves both as a support group and as a forum for discussing sexism in the Family. The "Brothers' and Sisters' Circle" provides a forum for men and women to address gender relations together.

Almost all Rainbows condemn sexist attitudes in the abstract, but male "locker room" conversation still surfaces at Gatherings. This type of talk, often including comments about a particular woman's body, rarely goes far, as newly sensitized Rainbows often police their own conversation. The reasons for restraining from sexist talk are twofold: first, the raised consciousness of men, and second, the empowerment of women. As an act of conscious self-censorship, sexist speakers sometimes will pause and say, "Let's just stop talking this shit." Other conversations, however, simply end defensively: "We'd better shut up before the sisters hear us." Misogynist attitudes and activities run unchecked, however, at the Alcohol Camp (see chapter 6).

While some Rainbow men argue that the Family has transcended sexism, most admit that the Family, as a microcosm of the greater society, has imported at least some sexist baggage from Babylon. Rainbows gladly discuss sexism, sometimes ad nauseam, but ironically, men often try to dominate these meetings, maneuvering to outdo each other in a contest to prove who "respects sisters" the most. The atmosphere is sometimes paternalistic as men jockey to explain how highly they "value sisters' input." Women who talk openly about sexism within the Family are sometimes met with hostility. A woman who asked, "What about sexism?" on the Family's Internet news group, for instance, was accused by fellow Rainbows of being a provocateur (a "flamer," to cybernauts).

However, Rainbow women often acknowledge that Gatherings provide a less sexist atmosphere than Babylon. The Gatherings, according to one sister, are different. Sexism at the Gatherings, she feels, is less of a problem, "because there's more support from sisters here. I can always find sisters who are hooked into feminism and will support me." This contrasts with Babylon: "[At] a couple of different places where I worked there were no other women that I could connect with. . . . There was a support group of women who I would see maybe once a week. Around here it's like, if something weird is happening, I know I could find a sister close by" (Alita Interview 1990).

Unlike the outside world, where sexist attitudes are reinforced by friends, coworkers, and Rush Limbaugh[5] wannabes on talk radio, sexist men at Rainbow Gatherings are in an environment where overt sexism is clearly condemned. In this regard, the Family has made inroads in trying to combat sexism. Sexual equality has long been a concern of many utopians as they challenged the traditional sex roles of their time. The Shakers, for instance, were early advocates of "sexual equality" in their communes (Nickless and Nickless 1993, 119; Holloway 1951, 78), where women held half of the positions on boards of trustees. Amanans preached that "the ministry of the gospel depends on Inspiration and is not limited by class or sex" (Perkins and Wick 1891, 62). They promoted women's rights to teach and "exhort in public meetings" (Perkins and Wick 1891, 62). Tennessee's Nashoba Community (1825–1830), a multiracial commune dedicated to religious emancipation, sexual emancipation, and the emancipation of slaves, was organized by Francis Wright, who continued on as a leader in the women's rights movement (Fogarty 1980, 121–22, 153).

Virginia's Twin Oaks Community is a leader among contemporary utopias in its fight for equality of the sexes, which members see as central to their mission (Goldenberg 1993, 258). Anthropologist Jon Wagner observed that Twin Oaks "may be among the most non-sexist social system in human history" (Wagner 1982, 37–38). They even developed and use an awkward nonsexist language, which replaces all gendered pronouns such as "he" or "she" with "co" and "cos" (Goldenberg 1993, 264).

Most utopian communities mirror the Rainbow Family, however, and not Twin Oaks, with sexism alive and well in the supposed nonsexist utopia. While promoting "gender equality," Shakers maintained a celibate society with a strict division between man's work and woman's work (Nickless and Nickless 1993, 120). Central New York's Oneida Community (1848–1880) practiced a revolutionary form of "free love," which supposedly freed women from the shackles of marriage. In reality, according to letters written by Oneida women, "community women simply exchanged one smaller, patriarchal family structure for a larger, collective one" (Klee-Hartzell 1993, 184). Even toys and children's books at Oneida were separated for use by one sex or the other (Klee-Hartzell 1993, 193).

Women in Owenite communities such as New Harmony (Indiana, 1825–1827) suffered oppression, despite founder Robert Owen's liberating rhetoric. Owen believed that "women would not be economically dependent upon men if they had livelihoods themselves," hence the Owenites provided female members with "regular employment." In reality, however, "women who worked in Owenite communities had to spend their 'free' time doing traditional female work" while men and children lounged and played (Kolmerten 1993, 41). One reason for the endemic sexism at Owenite communities is that despite Owen's call to create a "new moral world" based on egalitarianism, most people joined an Owenite community for a "new start in life" (Kolmerten 1993, 39; Holloway 1951, 106). The Owenites, in their willingness accept *anyone* as a member, were similar to the Rainbow Family. It is therefore understandable why the Owenites, like the Rainbows, experienced the sexism of the outside world in their utopia. Rainbows are combating sexism with some success. The Owenite communities didn't last long enough to truly examine their gender roles.

There were also utopian groups that made no claims to be antisexist; challenging sex roles was not on their agenda. Hutterites for example, while maintaining a pacifist, communistic society for four centuries, maintained a strict patriarchy, with most women spending an extraordinary portion of their adult lives pregnant (Lambach 1993, 242). In fact, most cenobites cite Pauline Christian tradition as a rational for their patriarchal attitudes (Dentan 1994, 84).

The Twin Oaks Community, cited earlier for its successful strides toward sexual egalitarianism, has gone one step further than most utopians, including equal rights for gay people in their egalitarian doctrine and actions. They even made a point of actively recruiting overt homosexuals to round out their diverse membership (Kern 1993, 205). Other like-minded contemporary groups, such as the Farm, encouraged tolerance for gays, but stopped short of encouraging gay pride among their homosexual membership. For most liberal utopias, homosexuality was all right, but gays still belonged in the closet.

Rainbows both celebrate and shun homosexuality, depending on which neighborhood of the Gathering one visits. Gay bashing, verbal or otherwise, in principle, is unacceptable at Rainbow Gatherings, although, like drunkenness and drug abuse, it occasionally surfaces. The Common Loaf Bakery at the 1991 North American Gathering, for instance, was run by members of the "Christian" Island Pond Community who disseminated hate-filled antigay literature with their fresh bread. Many Rainbows unsuccessfully tried to explain to the bakers that homophobia had no place at a Gathering. Some were more militant and picketed the bakery. Many others, by their apathy, were complicitous with the homophobes. Few, however, sympathized with their homophobia.

At Gatherings heterosexual men often wear skirts for comfort or show each other affection, both physical and emotional. Such an accepting environment allows gay men, "faeries" in Rainbow language, to be openly gay without much fear of ostracism. Even avidly heterosexual bikers and Hobos, people who tend toward homophobia in Babylon, usually interact peaceably with their faerie brothers, whom they respect for living the Rainbow ideal of "being themselves." Many faeries have found the comfortable nurturing environment of the Gathering a good place to experiment with "coming out of the closet." In the same respect, lesbians say they find Gatherings comfortable and nonoppressive. While the Family is a step ahead of mainstream society in its acceptance of homosexuality and its fight toward equality of the sexes, it is *not* cutting-edge. Like the nineteenth-century Shakers, the Rainbow family offers a reflection of contemporary feminist thought, but is not taking a leading role in developing a feminist doctrine. Likewise, the Family's respect for an emerging gay culture is certainly praiseworthy, but not pioneering.

Rainbows also regularly condemn racism, and overt bigotry is rare at Rainbow events. African Americans, however, are still underrepresented at Gatherings. A primary reason is that African Americans are also underrepresented in the middle class, from which the Rainbow Family draws many of its members. Road Dogs, Hobos, and Tramps are also disproportionately white, because of the added difficulties African Americans face in trying to hitchhike or ride the rails through predominantly white America. Compared to the rural locales where they are held, however, Gatherings seem well integrated. But many Rainbows still feel the Gatherings need to be more of a Rainbow. Garrick Beck, for instance, thinks it would be a good idea to send Seed Camp workers out to nearby cities to post Gathering invitations in inner-city neighborhoods traditionally missed by the Rainbow information web (interview 1990).

People at the 1990 Thanksgiving Council expressed similar sentiments. Everyone agreed that "something should be done" to attract African Americans to the Gathering, but nobody suggested actually doing anything and, in the end, nothing happened. Of the fifty committees the Thanksgiving Council formed, none dealt with questions of race or associated class issues. The prognosis for inner-city outreach during Seed Camp is poor. Rainbow apologists give two reasons: first, there is usually more work to be done on-site than there are people to do it, hence there is no time for new off-site projects; second, people go to Gatherings to get away from cities, not to return to them. Once on-site, most people would rather remain on-site. The Seed Camp crew, predominantly poor rural whites, is also not well equipped socially to do outreach in African American communities. Rainbows often recruit on a personal friend-to-friend basis. The lack of racial diversity, in this light, suggests that the predominantly white Rainbows associate primarily with other white people, leaving African Americans out of the loop.

Despite the Family's failure to integrate Gatherings, segregation is often a forgotten issue among Rainbows. Rainbow "prophecies," for instance, speak of "ancient" Indian "spirits" influencing "white people of all different nations" (Weinberg 1990a; Hipstory July 3, 1990), effectively ignoring other peoples.

One popular New Age myth concerning "the Legend of the Rainbow Warriors," goes a step further, patronizing Native Americans while belittling Asians and blacks: "The Legend of the Rainbow Warriors suggests that the true destiny of the nation is to synthesize for posterity the cultural heritage of the various races: the *intellect* and *will* of the light-skinned people, the *intuition* and *spiritual awareness* so highly developed in the red-skinned people, and the *gifts* of the yellow and black skinned people as well" (McFadden 1992, 28–29 [emphasis mine]). The Rainbow Family, despite the feebleness of its efforts toward racial inclusion, still provides a breath of fresh air when compared to New Age groups. Media reports, however, often identify the Rainbow Family as a New Age group, perhaps further adding to their difficulties in attracting blacks.

The Family's whiteness is not by design, but reflects a segregated Babylon, both in the United States and in other countries that host Gatherings. Historically, integrated utopian communities were few and far between, and even then, most were integrated with only token nonwhite representation. Nashoba, possibly the best-known nineteenth-century interracial utopia, was integrated only because the white leadership *purchased* their black members to "emancipate" them (Egerton 1977, 20). More indentured servants than equals, the "former" slaves were expected to earn back for the colony the cost of their purchase. Other supposed utopias were, much like the greater society that enveloped them, segregated. The Fairhope Colony, established in Alabama in 1895, for example, was widely hailed as a successful socialist experiment, yet blacks were institutionally denied membership. In fine liberal tradition, colony leaders often talked of establishing a separate black colony (Fogarty 1990, 172).

As discussions of race and multiculturalism become more prevalent in society, Rainbows are becoming more aware of their own de facto segregation. A few Rainbows continue to push for discussing the issue, but most would rather ignore it—waiting for the day integration magically occurs. Others are in denial; in response to an ongoing electronic discussion on racism, one Rainbow wrote, "I have to be blunt at this point. Racism at Rainbow is a perpetrated LIE." Urban Rainbow events, such picnics, do draw from somewhat more diverse racial communities. The Rainbow Gatherings are slowly starting to integrate more fully as more urban Rainbows start attending Gatherings.

Another underrepresented group at Gatherings consists of disabled people. The Rainbow Family has, over the years, tried to make Gatherings more accessible. CALM's facilities have grown, providing health care for elderly and chronically ill Rainbows who could not otherwise attend Gatherings. Able-bodied Rainbows sometimes help disabled Rainbows get around the Gatherings. Moving wheelchair-bound Rainbows over steep muddy trails sometimes becomes a festive chore, usually attracting a small crowd for the arduous task. Seeing Rainbows take similar care to help blind Rainbows navigate around Gatherings.

Due to their "wilderness" locations, however, Gatherings will likely continue to be difficult and sometimes treacherous for disabled people, who usually wind up camping and spending most of their time in Bus Village. Easy accessibility, an essential ingredient for allowing full participation of disabled people, is often elusive in the remote locations cherished by Rainbows. Unfortunately, many disabled people are often left outside of the physical boundaries that Rainbows establish to separate their utopia from Babylon.

Spiritual or Political?

The Rainbow Family has a vision that is both spiritual and political. The fundamental schism in the Family stems not from racial or class conflict, but from the confrontation between "politics" and "spirituality." Political/environmental activists appreciate the networking and organizing potential of the Family and the Gatherings. Many spiritually centered Rainbows, however, would rather keep politics out of "the church." They view Gatherings as tranquil sanctuaries in which to escape the world's problems.

In Rainbow speech "politics" also refers to internal Rainbow Family politics, ranging from Council policy to Gathering logistics. Mere discussion of these matters is also controversial, with some spiritually centered Rainbows demanding that more Council time go to Heartsongs and less to business. Politics dominated much of the 1984 North American Gathering in California. Political Rainbows organized a peace caravan, leaving the Gathering to join protests at the Democratic National Convention in San Francisco, the Olympics in Los Angeles, and the Republican National Convention in Dallas. Greenpeace, Earth First! and other environmental organizations or movements[6] were also prominent at the Gathering. Many apolitical Rainbows at the time feared that the political activity would bring the wrath of Babylon, causing the U.S. government to challenge future Gatherings. U.S. government documents show the government did indeed take note of political organizing at the 1984 North American Gathering, especially in reference to the demonstrations planned for the upcoming Republican National Convention (Modoc N.F. 1984a: 9).

Political organizing has been a prominent facet of North American Gatherings ever since. A delegation of American Indian Movement (A.I.M.) members came to the following year's North American Gathering in Missouri to organize support for a vigil in St. Louis during the trial of Leonard Peltier, an A.I.M. member charged with murdering an F.B.I. agent during a shootout at the Pine Ridge Reservation in South Dakota. More recently, Rainbow Councils have consensed to having a separate information booth for political networking, built next to the main information booth.

Political awareness at Gatherings has been born of necessity, says Joanne, a veteran political organizer and longtime Rainbow: "It's the instinct of survival. You've got to care about the water and your support system or you're not going to survive as a species. . . . Our survival is in jeopardy, we've got to do something if we really want to survive" (interview 1990). United States Forest Service efforts to outlaw the Gatherings have also served to politicize Rainbows who would otherwise have been content to "bliss out" in the woods.

Utopian groups have often faced the difficulty of balancing their political aspects with their more serene spiritual aspects. Some religious groups, like many political Rainbows, however, saw political activism as the fulfillment of religious doctrine. Shortly after the turn of the century, for example, radical Shakers rejected the group's traditional isolationism, and became active in a pre–World War movement for global disarmament. Activist Shakers also fought against the domination of agrarian monopolies, fought for women's suffrage, worked to assist poor peoples, fought against alcoholism, and were involved in other controversial philanthropic causes (Oved 1988, 60–61).

The Hopedale Community (Massachusetts, 1842–1887) practiced their Christian doctrine by carrying on an uncompromising fight against slavery and for women's rights, and by expanding educational opportunities for all (Holloway 1951, 121). The short-lived Skaneateles Community (1843–1846), a Fourierist Phalanx located in Central New York, like the Hopedale Community, practiced a type of political activism. That activism, by contrast, precluded any spirituality, as Skaneateles residents had "no use for religion," which they viewed as divisive, producing "strife and contention rather than love and peace" (Holloway 1951, 124).

The Rainbow Family is divided among members whose political activism is based in spirituality, whose political activism precludes spirituality, and whose spirituality precludes political activism. All are united, however, in their rhetorical support for a nonviolent, nonhierarchical cooperative society.

A Nomadic Utopia

Rainbows see strength in their diversity. Their willingness to accept any living being as a member sets them apart from the vast majority of utopian experiments both historically and in the present time. The Rainbow Family open-admissions policy, however, is not unique. Other groups have subscribed to the same inclusive ideal. What is unique about the Family is that it stands practically alone among utopian communities that have survived the quarter-century mark intact, despite its universal membership. Alcoholics Anonymous, which like the Rainbow Family, is an occasional group and an intentional community (Dentan 1994), interestingly enough, has also survived despite being nonrestrictive in its recruiting.[7]

The utopian landscape, however, is littered with the remains of groups, who according to historians, fell apart *because* of their broad-minded admissions policies. The Owenite communities would accept anyone, but such an open-admissions policy both fueled the paternalistic attitudes described earlier, and eventually led to the dissolution of the short-lived colonies. Scholars blame the class mix, in particular, at the Owenite communities for their downfall; the better-educated members did not mix with the working-class members and resented having to perform manual labor. The class schism formed a seam upon which the colonies ripped apart (Holloway 1951, 111).

Sociologist Rosabeth Moss Kanter observed that "a general lack of selectivity in recruitment" was common to many of the short-lived communities she studied. "For example," she writes, "[short-lived communities] tended to welcome individuals of all ideological persuasions and to recruit by impersonal means, such as advertising, rather than by personal contact" (Kanter 1972, 122). Members of more successful groups, by contrast, "had a common religious background, similar social or educational status, or a common national or ethnic origin" (Kanter 1972, 93).

Successful utopian groups also tried to mold their new recruits to fit their communal model. Members were often expected to renounce ties or relationships that were potentially threatening to group cohesion and to replace their identity as an individual with a cult-like identification with the group. The Rainbow Family, by contrast, values individual expression and does not demand any type of renunciation. Police officers showing interest in Gatherings, for example, despite their conflicting role, are readily accepted as Rainbows.

Many late-twentieth-century communes, formed at about the same time as the Rainbow Family, ended their idealistic "open door" policies after experiencing "too many visitors, too little responsibility, or too much turnover" (Kanter 1973, 22). The Rainbows, on the other hand, have for a quarter century accepted all who came to participate or be healed, as Rainbow Family members. While the Family is still overwhelmingly white, an embarrassment to a group named "Rainbow," such exclusion is not by design, but is largely inherited from the greater society.

All historical indications show that the Rainbow Family, like Alcoholics Anonymous, with their idealistically inclusive admissions policies, should have failed years ago. Their saving grace, however, lies in their temporal nomadic nature, which sets them apart from permanent land-based utopian experiments. Since Gatherings, like AA meetings, regularly break down and re-form, long-term social problems have a chance to dissipate. Difficulties developed at one Gathering can be solved by new camping or living arrangements at the next Gathering. The Family is large enough, with many subgroups, to absorb diverse backgrounds and views and still provide a supportive environment for everybody involved. It might take a few Gatherings, however, for someone to find that niche.

6

Violence and Peace

"Welcome Home" should be a hug and a bowl, not beer breath and begging. The Gate [should be] a smile and rap 107/701, not commands and condescension. [A Gathering should be about] Pulling together and sharing, not separation and hoarding.

—Greg Sherrill in Bushwah 1991

Rainbow Gatherings are seldom the cohesive respectful utopian societies many Rainbows envision. They are rife with contradictions and conflicts. How the Family deals with these contradictions provides insight into the difficulties of maintaining a nonhierarchical, nonviolent, nonsectarian spiritual and political community.

Keeping the Peace

Political organizing has always played a role at Rainbow Gatherings. The Family's rhetorical commitment to nonviolence, for instance, is inherently political and central to the Family's doctrine. As early as 1972, the year of the first Gathering, the Rainbow Family took a public stand against government violence, drawing up a fourteen-point list of demands calling on the U.S. government to release political prisoners, respect nature, and withdraw troops from Southeast Asia, among other things (see Appendix).

Rainbows profess that the best place to start building global peace is locally, by

making Gatherings into models of peaceful coexistence and nonviolent conflict resolution. The Rainbow Family has its share, however, of child predators, rapists, mug-
gers, and thieves. Members acknowledge that whatever's "out there" in Babylon is
also "in here" at Gatherings. The Family is, after all, a microcosm of the greater society. What sets the Family apart from American municipal authorities is that while
both face violent and disruptive individuals, they respond differently. Rainbows confront violence and hate with peace and love. For many, this peace comes from within.
Rainbow Joseph Schwartzbaum explains: "If you fight evil with evil you are acting evil.
If you fight, kill the killer, kill, kill, it's a constant killing so we are caught in a process
of killing. So violence can never bring peace, war can never bring peace, hatred can
never bring love, only love can bring love, peace can bring peace" (interview 1990).

The Rainbow Family prides itself not only on its creative approaches to dealing with violence, but on providing a model for peaceful coexistence among different peoples.

> There're camps in each Gathering of born-again Christians and
> there you can come by the camp at nine A.M. and they're all sitting
> there reading their Bibles. And you know, three trees down there
> are folks sitting around at the same 9 A.M. in the morning and they're
> brewing the mushroom tea. And both of these [groups] are en-
> gaged in what to them is a religious act. . . . these groups can not
> only co-exist, but come four o'clock in the afternoon, members
> of both of these little clans can walk together into the woods and
> gather firewood together with their axes and their saws and their
> ropes for tying the sticks together and dragging them home. (Beck
> interview 1990)

The Rainbow Family is an "intentional group," that is, it has an explicit program
that rationalizes and justifies perpetuating itself (Chang 1981). Its program is inherently pacifist. Different Family members, depending on their personal disposi-
tions, pray for peace, protest and lobby for peace, or both. The Family is committed to maintaining peaceful Gatherings, even in the face of violent provocations.
An article in *All Most Broke*, a one-time Rainbow Family publication, recalls how
Family members resisted violence during a particularly difficult North American
Gathering in North Carolina:

> Of all the lessons of the 1987 Gathering, the one that tells me
> the most is that despite all the harassment and provocation on the
> part of the agents of government, 16,000 Rainbows kept the peace.
> When they (U.S. Forest Service) ticketed without notice or
> warning our early on-site vehicles—and demanded immediate
> payment of fines—no one lost their cool heads.

When they (N.C. state troopers) prevented a disabled live-in vehicle from being towed up the hill to where we could fix it, no one boiled over.

When they shut our main gate and forced everyone into a hi-pressured and foolish walk across the bridge, no one cursed them out.

When live-in vehicles were arbitrarily detained and forced to encamp on the U.S. highway, no one went home anyway.

When they (state of N.C.) reached an agreement with us, and began a "pass" system for our service vehicles, and when the very next morning they (U.S.F.S.) refused access to vehicles bearing "passes," no one blew up.

When a trailer load of watermelons had to be unloaded, carried across the bridge and reloaded, no one threw a melon thru a government windshield.

When a 9-car brigade of officers (U.S.F.S., state troopers, S.B.I., etc.) rode up the hill military-style, stopping to load shotguns in full daylight in front of children, no one reacted violently.

When our medical vehicles (with so called passes) were detained at the bridge, no one called for armed revolution.

When a vehicle with 200 gallons of distilled water for Kid Village was denied access, not one of us overreacted.

When people were indiscriminately I.D. checked on the highway in a threatening and abrasive manner, no one panicked.

When people and vehicles were searched without cause or warrant, no one slugged the illegal searchers.

When people were photoed and videoed [by the police] after requesting not to be, no one busted their camera.

When people's license plate #s were recorded by government surveillance agents, no one attacked them.

When a brother who requested the license #s not be recorded was brutally seized on-site, without warrant, and driven out, no one blockaded or stormed the arresting officers or vehicles.

When flashlights were shone repeatedly in people's eyes while loading and unloading at the bridge, no one grabbed & smashed the flashlights.

When officers made obnoxious comments about women's bodies and our children, no one fired a shot.

When our cleanup crew was likewise harassed no one ignited the ranger station.

The truth is we were provoked, goaded, button-pushed, aggravated purposely. They were waiting for us—any one of us—to take a swing—then let the violence really begin. But we didn't give it to them. 16,000 Rainbows, all 16,000 Rainbows, kept the peace. After all, that's what we're supposed to do, that's what—really—we possess, that's what we can share, and that's what, of course, those who are ruled by violence are so very afraid of. (Beck 1987)

Pentagon officials are among those who found Rainbow passivity confusing. Following the 1980 North American Gathering in West Virginia, four hundred Rainbows caravaned to Washington, D.C., where they held a demonstration for world peace at the Pentagon. The *Washington Post* reported: "Their style puzzled many Pentagon employees. 'They told us to come to work a little early in case the hippies tried to stop us from getting inside like last time,' said army sergeant Jonathan Joven. 'I don't understand these people. All they're doing is holding hands and singing. Some protest. It doesn't look like they know what they're doing'" (Sager 1980).

Om for Peace

The most common Rainbow tactic for "nonviolently" defusing crises is the formation of an "Om circle,"[1] a circle of people holding hands and chorusing "Ommmmm." Rainbows refer to this as "Omming." They form Om circles around agitated or threatening people. An Om circle, however, can be coercive in and of itself and is sometimes perceived as threatening by those not familiar with the tactic. For example, a U.S. National Park Service "Intelligence" report states, "Officers conducting foot patrols have been circled by members who hummed or chanted" (Malanka 1990a). Rainbows encircle anyone, uniformed or not, who tries to bring a weapon or alcohol into a Gathering. The Park Service report notes, however: "They will allow officer(s) to walk through without force" (Malanka 1990a). No one is above being Ommed if enough people see that person as a threat. This does not necessarily mean that the person *is* a threat.

Ed, a Rainbow from New Paltz, New York, for instance, was Ommed because he was accused by members of the "spiritual" wing of the Family of bringing "bad energy" to the Gathering by conducting political organizing on environmental issues. Ed describes the tactic as "a favorite method of the Heil Holys. If you're saying something they don't want to hear or something that requires any sort of organized actions to deal with, then suddenly the sacred Om chant will go up" (interview 1990). In cases like Ed's, the Om circle is coercive, aimed at silencing dissent. It is like being lynched by pacifists. Such abuses, however, are limited. Rainbows usually demand a good reason before Omming somebody, and suppressing dissent is unpopular and unjustifiable.

Although they are coercive, Rainbows consider Om circles "nonviolent." They point out that the key to an effective Om circle is love. Rainbows find that potentially violent confrontations are best defused by showing love. The circle, therefore, has to be loving. The idea is to nurture upset people until they see the futility of their anger, not to set up an antagonistic circle from which they feel they must escape.

Shortly after the 1984 North American Gathering, events at the Democratic National Convention in San Francisco tested Rainbow peacekeeping techniques. During a generic protest rally for "peace, justice and all things good," a group of Yippies[2] set up a table to sell newspapers and buttons. Rally organizers, who did not receive a fee or contribution from the Yippies, viewed the table as "illegal." The "official" rally "peacekeepers" therefore joined hands in a circle around the Yippie table, blocking access to it by potential customers. The Yippies, seasoned by years of confrontations with the police, were not intimidated by what they saw as "a circle of yuppies." The two groups, gathered together to call for world peace, squared off to fight until a group of Rainbows encircled the circle of "peacekeepers" who had encircled the Yippies. Smiling and looking into the eyes of the "peacekeepers," the Rainbows chanted "Om" while another group of Yippies formed a fourth circle, selling trinkets to a growing crowd of onlookers. The "peacekeepers," sensing the Rainbows meant no harm, saw the ridiculousness of the situation and dispersed, leaving the Yippies to peaceably peddle their wares.

Official "peacekeepers" at other peace rallies have requested police assistance to deal with "nonofficial" vendors selling peace-oriented T-shirts in competition with "official rally T-shirts." The scene is quite ironic, with peace activists calling in armed police to arrest other peace activists for selling peace paraphernalia at a peace demonstration. The Yippies called such peacekeepers "Peace-pigs."

The Not Really Cops Rainbow Cop Trip

The Rainbow family professes to take a fundamentally different approach to peacekeeping. Rainbow peacekeepers are "Shanti Sena." The Sanskrit phrase glosses as "peace center." In the Rainbow Family *everyone* is supposedly Shanti Sena. A person who sees a problem does not call the Shanti Sena but *becomes* the Shanti Sena. In theory, *all* Rainbows should intercede as needed, thus eliminating the need for a security force. Rainbow Family publications frequently stress the precept "WE ARE ALL PEACEMAKERS who share the responsibility of keeping this gathering safe and harmonious" (NERF 1991). The *Mini Manual for New Gatherers,* a collectively authored Rainbow Family publication, explains "Shanti-Sena means 'Peace Center.' There are no 'Rainbow Police.' We are secure because we watch out for each other. We are *all* Shanti-Sena" (Rainbow Family Tribal Council, n.d., 6).

The ideal, however, is not always the reality. Like George Orwell's fictitious pigs who proclaimed after their counterrevolution: "All animals are equal but some are more equal than others" (1964, 123), all Rainbows are Shanti Sena, but some are more Shanti Sena than others. A loosely organized Shanti Sena organization, not sanctioned by the Rainbow Family Council, does exist at North American Gatherings. They make decisions in their own covert councils. While any Rainbow can proclaim themselves Shanti Sena, only a select few may attend these councils. As a result, Rainbows currently carry two definitions of Shanti Sena: there is, first, the Shanti Sena that is within everybody, and, second, the elite Shanti Sena, who, for the sake of clarity, I will refer to as the Shanti Sena "organization."

The Shanti Sena organization is legitimized by the majority of Rainbows, who willingly take orders from them.[3] To outsiders unfamiliar with Rainbow sensitivities, the Shanti Sena organization looks like a police force, albeit a relatively genial one. A journalist in Pennsylvania, for instance, observed: "Even the most serious side of the Rainbow face had smiles. They are the members of the Shanti Sena— the police force of the Rainbows. Its members are on duty 24 hours a day to keep order within the gathering and deal with whatever problems Rainbow Family members might have in their contacts with local residents" (Clever 1986a).

Like any other "police force," the Shanti Sena organization seems preoccupied with "keeping order" and weeding out "infiltrators" and other strange agents. The same journalist adds, "Caliph [of the Shanti Sena] said the Shanti Sena has for fifteen years proven its ability to keep order among its own. There are problems, he admitted, when curious outsiders 'infiltrate[,]' but who, when unmasked, are turned over to authorities, for whatever their misdeeds might be" (Clever 1986b). Of course, according to Rainbow philosophy, there are no "outsiders." Curious neighbors are viewed as Rainbows or potential Rainbows, thus the concept of "infiltrators" goes against Rainbow beliefs.

There is a distinctly nasty side to the Shanti Sena organization. One Family member from Washington State, looking back at the 1994 Gathering, writes: "Last year's [G]athering gave me the impression that the [G]atherings are controlled by big rough men . . . who make the decisions for everyone else, and get the rubber stamp of consensus by orchestrating the councils. . . . Many people do seem to be on a power trip which is patriarchal and even violent in nature" (Anon 1995(a)). Theoretically the author could have blocked any consensus "orchestrated" by the "rough" clique. Such a block, however, would require familiarity with the Council process and a healthy dose of chutzpah. Observations such as the one above, which are common, indicate tendencies among Family members that are both antidemocratic and subversive to a nonviolent society.

The U.S. Forest Service correctly identified the Shanti Sena organization as a "power group" (Burton 1990). They have also referred to them as "an internal security force" (Superior N.F. May 30, 1990: 3). The U.S. National Park Service reports Rainbows "have their own police force" (Malanka Mar. 15, 1990). The Forest Service does, however, note that this "police force" is not quite like traditional police forces. "Rainbow police were effective in non-violent instances. Their method was to reason with people and show them love" (Lee 1984).

Not all descriptions of the Shanti Sena organization involve "love." A U.S. National Park Service "Intelligence Update" quotes their source, a self-proclaimed "Shanta Sena [sic]" member, who, sounding like a mercenary, describes his work with the "Shanta Sena" in terms Rainbows usually shun:

> According to Mr. [John] McGee, he was solicited to travel from California to assist in coordinating of the camp and participate as a member of the "Shanta Sena"[sic] or "peace warriors." Mr. McGee indicated that the Rainbow Gatherings were under tight internal controls regarding conduct, weapons, alcohol, and certain narcotics. Mr. McGee also made numerous references to his use of violence to gain compliance by Rainbow [G]athering participants. He also stated, "Things will get out of control if folks were not watched." McGee reassured us several times that he understood what our responsibilities were as they pertained to law enforcement and the possibility that arrests might be necessary. He stated that there was generally little interference. (Malanka Mar. 23, 1990)

Another self-proclaimed "member" of the Shanti Sena described to me how Shanti Sena would roll troublesome people up in their tents and drop them off deep in the woods. The use of threatened and actual violence by members of the Shanti Sena organization and individuals performing Shanti Sena duties demonstrates the pervasiveness of outside models within the Family.

Rainbow Councils regularly warn Rainbows to beware of those who identify themselves as *the* Shanti Sena. Greg Sherrill, a California Rainbow quoted in the *Bay Area Rainbow News,* cautioned people "to be forewarned of . . . the strong-arming group . . . who under the guise of "Shata-scena"[sic] physically and psychologically bum out Welcome Home" (Bushwah 1991).

The U.S. government, on the other hand, welcomes and even promotes an elite Quisling Rainbow Shanti Sena organization. The U.S. Forest Service, early in its relationship with the Family, laid down "Law Enforcement Ground Rules" for Rainbow Gatherings. At that time, they ordered local forests to "form Family Security Group to provide liaison with with [sic] Law Enforcement Teams, these individuals should be formally identified" (U.S.F.S.D.C. 1978).

Superior National Forest officials in Minnesota, who were generally cooperative during the 1990 North American Gathering, ignored Council wishes and recognized a self-proclaimed Shanti Sena organization as Rainbow Family representatives even when they were clearly acting in contempt of Council. Officials chose to negotiate and interact, not with Grey Bear, the liaison appointed by Council consensus (Grey Bear interview 1990), but with John Buffalo (Superior N.F. 1990(b); Superior N.F. 1990(c)), whom they identified in their reports as "Shanta Seena" (Superior N.F. 1990(a)). Grey Bear, a Minnesota native and first-time Gatherer, was simply described, according to Forest Service records, as "not well thought of by John Buffalo" (Superior N.F. 1990(a)).

Police officers assigned to the Gatherings, to maintain their peace of mind, often *need* to see a Shanti Sena police organization. Joseph Wetmore, a Rainbow living in Ithaca, observed, "For the police, the concept of their own obsolescence is more frightening than Rainbow's usurpation of their power. It's not Rainbow policing themselves that's scary; it's Rainbow saying we don't need police" (Wetmore interview 1991). Such an example could prove threatening to a healthy growing prison-industrial complex. Peaceability is permissible only so long as it is not infectious (Dentan 1994, 93).

Other utopian groups who nonviolently maintained peace without organized enforcers have both baffled and threatened bureaucrats in the discipline industries. One such group, the anarchist Modern Times community (Long Island, New York, 1851–1863), like the Rainbow Family, did not believe in hierarchy or government. "Crime," however, one historian noted, "was never a problem in Modern Times," it was the lack of crime that was threatening. "Lack of disorder and violence in the absence of constituted authority for such a long period is a challenge to those who believe that organized society without a 'ruler' is doomed to chaos" (Loomis 1982, 38).

Rainbows often represent Shanti Sena as a "security force" to appease law enforcement officials who are uneasy with the precepts of anarchy and unwilling to believe that people can live in peace without armed enforcers. Just as CALM will "manifest a wizard" when necessary, the Rainbow Family can produce "police" if need be to keep armed police away.[4] The U.S. Forest Service reports: "The Rainbow Family professes to have a peacekeeping group or security team called Shantisena [sic]. The Rainbow Family prefer to have this team do the internal peacekeeping at the Gathering site and to serve as parking attendants at the parking lot and will also provide some walking patrols in nearby communities to assist local law enforcement and local merchants in any problems that might arise regarding people coming to the Gathering" (Colville N.F. 1981). Bob Burton of the Forest Service, quoted in a front-page article in the *Cook County News Herald*, explained to concerned local residents how, "Traditionally they [the Rainbow Family] take care of their own problems. Their peacekeeping group, the Shanta Seena [sic], does a good job" (*Cook County News Herald* 1990a).

It is to the Rainbow Family's advantage when locals refer their Rainbow-related problems to the Rainbow Family to rectify in its own way, instead of asking the local police to handle such situations. Ron Weed, a local shopkeeper in Likely, California, for instance, told how he called the "Shanti Seena" when he found Rainbows shoplifting during the 1984 North American Gathering: "We told the Rainbow's law enforcement organization, the Shanti-seena [sic], to either control the shoplifters or the store would prosecute. The Shanti-seena posted one person outside the store and monitored the numbers" (Lee 1984). Another local businessperson recommended that colleagues "utilize the Rainbow security force, the Shanti-seena [sic]. They're very helpful" (Lee 1984).

In reality, any Rainbow helping out at a local business is Shanti Sena. Grey Bear, for instance, spent two days performing Shanti Sena duties directing parking and traffic at the Clearview General Store during the 1990 North American Gathering. He never referred to himself as a member of "the Shanti Sena," but as "a friend of Jeff," the store's owner (Grey Bear interview 1990).

Representatives from the Shanti Sena organization greet law enforcement officers at the front gate, engage them in cop talk, entertain them, and keep them from getting bored. "Bored officers," the Forest Service admits, "will initiate unnecessary problems" (Modoc N.F. 1984[a]). But some members of the Shanti Sena organization, after hours of "chillin'" with their uniformed counterparts, return to the Gathering acting much like police themselves. Since there are seldom any peacekeeping workshops for Shanti Sena volunteers, they often do not have the opportunity to learn creative methods for changing other people's behavior. Coercion with the threat of violence is still the norm in Babylon, where most Rainbows live.

At the 1990 North American Gathering, so-called Shanti Sena blocked deliveries of water[5] and demanded a bribe of fresh food before letting a food delivery pass. Snake Mountain Bear keeps a watchful eye on the "Shanti Sena": "I think that most of them are good folks. None of them are malicious. A lot of them are either Viet Nam vets or, you know, from the streets for years; and they're tough, a lot of them. And usually when they keep their cool they do a good job—but every once in a while somebody approaches them in such a manner as to trigger some negativity in them and then some of them—that's certainly not representing all of them—but some of them, will mismanage their job description to act more like a city cop than a Rainbow peacekeeper" (Bear interview 1990). Bear felt that an excess of "male energy" and a lack of communication cause many Shanti Sena shortcomings. Many Rainbows agree that women should be more active in peacekeeping at Gatherings, replacing male Shanti Sena[6] who often practice confrontation instead of understanding. Men, however, still continue to dominate the Shanti Sena organization, with members often claiming they are "in charge" of the Gatherings.

Regional Rainbow movements seek to eliminate such unofficial authority as "neohierarchical baggage" inconsistent with egalitarian anarchy. NERF, for instance, does not have a Shanti Sena "organization" and has so far effectively prevented one from coalescing. When drunks caused a problem at the front gate during a regional Gathering, a runner went to the Council Meadow to spread word of the problem. A large group of men and women, young and old, responded, going to the front gate bringing music and love rather than a spirit of conflict. Their large tranquil presence brought a feeling of harmony to the gate area, making the irate drunks feel out of place. The drunks calmed down and got bored. Some wandered into the Gathering to eat and get sober, while others went elsewhere to continue drinking.

Bear has taken measures to limit the police power of the Shanti Sena organization. At Bear's urging, the 1990 North American Gathering Council, with about two hundred people present, consensed to a policy stating that nobody could be turned over to law enforcement or mental hygiene officials without Council approval. Bear argued that as a "healing" Gathering, Rainbow should offer a creative and effective alternative to state bureaucracies. Many Rainbows feel that people who bring violence to a loving Gathering need help. Turning them over to the police would be abdicating the responsibility to provide that help. It would also be meeting violence with violence, not the Rainbow way. The policy states:

> We the Tribal Council of the Rainbow Family do declare that
> as a sanctuary, we will not turn people over to the authorities,
> police, or mental health system regardless of how abstract [sic] their
> behavior may be.
> We hereby establish a "well being center" to deal with crisis
> situations beyond CALM and Shanti Sena capabilities. No one will
> be escorted or constrained around the Gathering without appear-
> ing before the Council except for time allowed for Council to
> reconvene. (Wetmore 1990)

Bear's interest in the well-being of "mental patients" stemmed from his own experience with the mental health system:

> Back in the old days when I was mid-wifing I got locked up in the
> Vermont State Hospital. They snared me and took a couple of
> weeks out of my life basically under pretentious conditions. Be-
> cause they were saying I was practicing medicine without a license;
> and when they couldn't really find a substantial basis for a charge
> there, they began saying I was delusional and thought I was a doc-
> tor. I spent a couple of weeks there and while I was there, I no-
> ticed really horrendous treatment of the mental patients; how they
> were becoming progressively worse after they got electro-shock.
> I noticed they were deteriorating from psychotropic drugs. When
> I got out in two weeks, I vowed that I would spend the rest of my
> life confronting those kind of conditions. (Interview 1990)

He suggested referring disturbed people to a Rainbow "Well Being Center."

> Essentially the Well Being Center has got a lot of its thinking from
> the mental patients' liberation movement [which] has developed
> thousands of alternatives to psychiatry, including drop-in centers
> and housing projects operated by psychiatric inmates and past

inmates. Basically we have to accommodate their anger and their pain, to recognize their personality and honor their character. It's essentially, you know, the reason people go crazy is, for several different possibilities that I'm aware of. One of them is, *occasionally* there's chemical imbalances. . . . More often than that it's being reared by broken families, hostile environment and things of that sort. And so what we do is we try to fill in the gaps in their life which if they didn't get a lot of love in their life we give em a lot of love. Give 'em hugs. . . . We find out what they're interested in, what they're capable of doing, or want to do and what propensities they have and help them grow in those areas; and as these people start finding out what they are good for and doing it, they find out that they are good at it and then they begin to have a greater self esteem. . . . The job is to find out what's the root cause of the problem and then address that rather than control symptoms with drugs or constraint. We help people that come to the Gathering and flip out because they were drowning from alcohol or psychiatric drugs or whatever else, and so we need to determine why they're flipping out, and if it turns out that they've been taking Thorazine for ten years we might suggest that they take Thorazine a while longer and find out a better way of getting [them] off the drugs rather than going cold turkey. We might suggest that they develop a better diet, take herbs, get medical support and withdraw. You know, gradually tapering off the drugs, say 10 percent every few months. (Bear interview 1990)

Mother Nature concurred with Bear's approach. Confronted with a "child predator"[7] at the 1983 North American Gathering, she felt that putting him "back on the street" would solve nothing. She took the man, accused of masturbating in front of a child, and kept him voluntarily confined to the J.E.S.U.S. camp for the remainder of the Gathering: "I took him to [my] farm afterwards and he stayed four months with me and he told me he had been arrested twenty-one times for that. I came to find out that, when he was a little child—when he was about nine or ten years old—he and a little girl had been caught, you know, doing the things that little kids do when they're trying to understand sex. His mother had beat him, beaten him so severely that it was like, it was almost like every time he got away with it he got back at mama" (Mother Nature interview 1990). To her knowledge, the man has not been involved in a similar incident since (Mother Nature interview 1990).

Despite Bear's plans and a Council consensus declaring Gatherings as sanctuary, Shanti Sena continued, in contempt of Council, to turn people over to the authorities without Council permission during the next year's North American Gathering. The Family showed hints of hierarchy with *All Ways Free* (summer 1991) publishing a four-page diatribe by Rainbow cofounder Barry (Plunker) Adams which dismissed the aforementioned Council consensus. Adams claimed it was a "Spontaneous Consensus," which "is in variation with Long-Term Consensus." He therefore refused to adhere to the Council edict (Adams 1991). For Adams and the Shanti Sena, however, the alternatives were limited as the Family failed to establish a wellness center capable of securely handling violent individuals.

By 1995, the 1990 consensus was all but forgotten. Even without the presence of a hierarchical Shanti Sena organization at the 1995 NERF Gathering, participants debated turning over an allegedly deranged thief to local authorities. The man, accused of stealing a smoking pipe he claimed he found on the ground, soon found himself surrounded by an angry mob. A sister who was working at the information booth produced a list of items, including a 1972 Volvo, that were lost or possibly stolen at the Gathering. People demanded to search "the thieving brother's" tent, but as it turned out, he didn't have one.

In time, the mob could see only three options for dealing with the man: duct-taping him to a tree; turning him over to mental health authorities; or turning him over to the police. Two people, one a man wearing a purple toga and carrying a walking staff, and the other a barefoot woman in a quandary as to whether or not she'd need shoes in Babylon, volunteered to take the brother to a mental health facility. Some people expressed a fear that maybe the Babylonians would lock up the wrong Rainbows. A discussion ensued over who would lend a car, what state the license plates should be from, and so on. During the confusion, the thieving brother wandered off. In his absence a more Rainbowlike option emerged; someone took him home to their land to relax near their pond for a week. The alleged thief, traumatized by the ordeal, sorted his life out in peace before moving on.

"A" Camp for Alcohol Abusers

Rhetoric aside, Rainbow Gatherings are not always peaceful. North American Gatherings during the 1990s are marred by almost daily violence at the "A" Camp, or "Alcohol Camp," a North American Rainbow Gathering fixture. Alcohol is generally taboo inside Gatherings. The U.S. Forest Service dutifully notes the absence of alcohol, though they think it odd (Burton 1990). But at "A" Camp, usually located on the outer perimeter of the Gathering site, people drink alcohol freely and usually to excess.

"A" Camp is different enough from the rest of the Gathering such that both the Forest Service and the surrounding community often view Gatherings as split into the Gathering proper and "A" Camp (Wetmore 1990b). The result of non-restrictive recruiting and a respect for individual freedom, "A" Camp is a persistent problem for the Family, year after year, draining resources and disrupting Gatherings.

In Minnesota for instance, "A" Campers were among the first Rainbows to arrive, showing up in the region before a site was selected. By the time scouts consensed on a site, "A" Camp was already notorious in northeastern Minnesota, since one "A" Camper, lost on a beer run, crashed his van into an airplane (Learner interview 1990).

Violence was a regular occurrence at "A" Camp during the ensuing Gathering, occasionally spilling over into nearby Bus Village. On one occasion, local police arrested a Shanti Sena brother after he clubbed another man during a supposed Shanti Sena action at "A" Camp.[8] At the 1991 Gathering in Vermont, two women were beaten and a number of people were robbed at "A" Camp. By 1995 "A" Camp violence in New Mexico developed to involve guns and machetes, with a gunfire and a chopping at "A" Camp three weeks before the National Gathering was to officially begin. In 1996, an "A" Camper, staying in an Arkansas National Forest six weeks before the start of the National Gathering in the Ozarks, was involved in a shootout with local drunks. After his bus had allegedly been fired upon, the "A" Camper returned fire, killing one of the locals.

"A" Camp typically sets up near the front entrance to the Gathering, panhandling Rainbows as they arrive. "A" Campers often misrepresent their own money collection, which Rainbows dub the "Alcohol Hat," as the Magic Hat, thus drawing funds from the Gathering's collective coffers. During the 1990 North American Gathering, one "A" Camper referred to this collection as a "milk for the children fund." Rainbows, tired after their travels and not expecting a rip-off upon arriving "Home," often put Magic Hat money into the Alcohol Hat without question. Early in the 1990 North American Gathering, while CALM was unable to raise sufficient funds to rent a water purification system, "A" Camp was spending thousands of dollars in local stores on beer and liquor. By the start of the 1991 North American Gathering, witnesses estimated that the "A" Camp had already consumed 120 kegs of beer. They raised much of their money in a coercive manner, attempting to charge for parking, charge "admission," or offer to protect parked cars for a fee.

The scene at the "A" Camp is often violent and chaotic as "A" Campers battle and steal among themselves. One visitor explained, "While you have money and are buying [alcohol], they are your best friends; when the money is gone, you are their enemy because you are competition for the alcohol coming from the next sucker."

Many Rainbows, however, claim not to harbor personal animosity toward the "A" Campers. As one brother explained, "Well, they're our brothers.[9] I think the alcohol causes a lot of problems. I don't want to say, tell the alcohol folks 'No, you can't come,' but I don't want the alcohol people coming and getting drunk and causing problems either. So we [don't] know quite what to do" (Learner interview 1990). Other Rainbows often point out that many "A" Campers often work hard at Gatherings when they're not drunk and are on the front lines when abusive locals or authorities try to harass the Gathering. Hence they deserve respect and understanding.

"A" Camp's presence tests the Rainbow Family's nonviolent principles. The Shanti Sena brother with the club, for instance, failed the test, meeting violence with violence; other Rainbows have, over the years, tried to meet the "A" Camp drunks head on with love. Jimbo (from CALM) explains: "Most of the ["A" Camp] people have a pretty serious broken heart, and that's a real bad problem to deal with. It's a deep problem. . . . I think a lot of people do alcohol because they don't know about love and they haven't really found it in life and they kinda have lost faith and their whole reason for being alive in the first place. . . . I think ["A" Camp] needs to be approached as if there's no question that you're my brother, that you're my sister, and we love you. What can we do to help you?" (Jimbo interview 1990).

Rainbow Family "Rap 151," a tract often printed in *Howdy Folks!* invitations and other Family publications, addresses the alcohol issue:

> It has been a tradition in our family to discourage the use of alcohol on the Gathering site. There are many reasons behind this tradition. The most obvious one is that we get plenty high without the use of alcohol and hard drugs.
>
> There are more practical reasons, too. Our kids need a safe, sane environment in which to grow and flourish. We as individuals need an atmosphere of respect to maintain our health and happiness. We as a community need a sanctuary where we can work towards our goals of peace and healing on this planet. It is almost impossible for these things to exist side-by-side with alcohol abuse. If you want to have a drinking party, this is not the place. If you have an alcohol addiction that you are trying to overcome, our healers at C.A.L.M./M.A.S.H. can help you through it. (Bay Area Rainbow News 1991; *All Ways Free* summer 1991)

"Rap 151: The Flip Side" appeals to Rainbows to deal gently and respectfully with their "A" Camp brothers and sisters: "If you have any doubts about your ability to be effective and respectful, don't make the situation worse. . . . Most important, remember that it takes all colors of the spectrum to make a Rainbow. . . . It's the behavior, not the person, that is the issue here" (Bay Area Rainbow News 1991; *All Ways Free* 1991).

"A" Camp serves as a conduit to recruit self-destructive alcoholics into the Rainbow Family. Many of the Family's most energetic workers first joined the Family through "A" Camp. Rainbows view "A" Campers as being "almost home." They have come from around the continent to congregate on the perimeter of the Gathering. It's just a few more steps for them to become part of the Gathering.

Rainbows acknowledge that "A" Camp serves another useful function as well. Often local bikers and party seekers, not understanding Rainbow customs, come with a few cases or kegs of beer, to "party with the hippies." "A" Camp provides that party, freeing the rest of the Gathering from alcoholic energies. Some Rainbows see "A" Camp as a filter, sifting off what would be disruptive influences, while turning back nonbelievers who can't see past "A" Camp to what the Gathering is all about. "A" Camp is the border where the Rainbow meets Babylon. Unfortunately both cultures are at their worst here; The Rainbow Family with their "A" Camp and Shanti Sena power-trippers, and Babylon with its violent drunks, alcohol peddlers, and police.

"A" Camp is not a universal fixture at Rainbow Gatherings. It is currently unique to United States Gatherings. The Quebec Rainbow Family, for instance, has never had either an "A" Camp or an alcohol problem at Gatherings. European Rainbow Gatherings have had alcohol present, usually in the form of wine, but report few alcohol-related problems.

Peace through Violence—The Rainbow Ghetto

For the supposedly classless Gatherings, "A" camp provides an embarrassing anomaly—the dangerous decrepit neighborhood, where untouchables are ghettoized. Absent are the North Face tents, Sven Saws, Birkenstocks, stainless steel cooksets, and comfy hammocks. "A" camp is a hodgepodge of old tarps and rolls of plastic. No one is baking cookies or singing folk songs. Young Rainbows in Patagonias or tie-dyes steer a wide berth around the foul-breathed drunks. It's dangerous. It's nasty. It's all about enslavement to addiction. Most Rainbows describe it as an embarrassment.

More telling, however, is the absolute lack of anything like an "A" Camp in *any* other long-lasting utopia. While "A" Camp is a stain on the Rainbow banner, it is also testimony to an all-inclusive utopia dedicated to a healing mission. After a quarter of a century of Gatherings, drunken vibes have yet to gain ground within the Family. Gatherings are still overwhelmingly peaceful, and outside of the "A" Camp there is usually little or no drinking. The "A" Camp remains a small and isolated phenomenon, yet it has served as an important gateway, allowing drunks transcendence into a new life.

In an age when most Americans are surrendering to their own fears, surrendering to the chaos of a collapsing society they themselves helped destroy through greed and apathy, Rainbows are facing problems head on. Rather than sequester themselves in electronically fortified suburban fortresses masquerading as homes, vicariously experiencing life via television and the World Wide Web, and praying for the day when virtual reality will set them "free," Rainbows are challenging the problems within their own society. This is why they allow an "A" Camp and why they accept problem members.

While Rainbows accept violent people, they do not accept violence. They form a nonviolent society, but they are not free from violence. The Gatherings serve as a training ground where violence is discouraged; where a violence free society is evolving. Likewise, it is a nonhierarchical society that is constantly battling against the development of new hierarchies. To banish power-hungry and violent individuals, for the Rainbows, would be to admit that violence and hierarchical order can't be vanquished.

Traditionally, peace movements in North America have failed to effectively reach out to groups most affected by violence. "None of these peace groups has recruited successfully among the urban lower and under classes—the people whose lives are most painfully disrupted by violence. Pacifist ideals that appeal only to those already fairly safe from violence are not going to transform society" (Dentan 1994, 95). The Rainbow Family, however, *has* succeeded in recruiting across class boundaries. The "A" Camp testifies to that success. Whether the Family can succeed in bringing peaceability to the "A" Camp remains to be seen.

It should also be noted, that many alcoholics, including those *not* in recovery, come to Gatherings, but avoid "A" Camp. The real life model for the character "Dave," in chapter 1 ("Sunflower's Day"), for instance, is an alcoholic whose drinking is often out of control when he is away from Gatherings. At Gatherings, however, he remains sober. He refuses to interact with the "A" Campers on any level, stating, "I don't want to look into that mirror." Simply viewing the "A" Camp is enough to shock many drinkers into sobriety. At Gatherings, the choice is clear-cut—Dave felt he didn't belong in "A" Camp.

Currently, as this book goes to press, Rainbows are talking about creating a "loving 'A' Camp," with peaceful "vibes." This new improved "A" Camp, if it actually comes into being, could either mellow the drunks, wear out the do-gooders, or be so revoltingly blissful that the "A" Campers flee in disgust. The ideal can also be talked to death, with no one actually acting upon it, much like Rainbow plans for inner-city outreach.

For the foreseeable future, so long as there is an "A" Camp populated by problem drinkers whose addiction has gotten the better of them, there are going to be varying degrees of violence on the Gathering's perimeter. Ironically, the presence of this violence and its exploitation in local media helps keep the Gatherings peaceable. Historically, many Americans find pacifism "wimpish and bizarre," hence nonviolent groups like the Hutterites have had a history of sporadic repression. Groups committed to nonviolence run a risk of inviting attacks by people who don't share that commitment (Dentan 1994, 81, 93). Thanks to "A" Camp mayhem, the Rainbows, although they *are* nonviolent, are often seen as being violent. Hence, would-be sadistic bullies and other "patriotic" Americans shy away from Gatherings, fearful their violence might meet with resistance. Those who do plan on disrupting Gatherings, usually never get past "A" Camp. Peacability exists behind a real and imagined shroud of violence.

On rare occasions when violence threatens to spill over from "A" Camp to the larger Gathering, Rainbows are saved by the flexibility of their band organization, which allows them to scatter and regroup in a more peaceful time and place (Dentan 1992). The Family's uncanny ability to disperse and regroup is effective in evading violence and persecution, both from the outside world and from within.

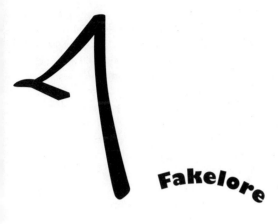

Fakelore

They want to become Indian without holding themselves accountable to Indian communities. If they did, they would have to listen to Indians telling them to stop carrying around sacred pipes, stop doing their sweat lodges, and stop appropriating our spiritual practices. Rather these New Agers see Indians as romanticized gurus who exist only to meet their consumerist needs. Consequently, they do not understand our struggles for survival and thus they can have no genuine understanding of Indian spiritual practices.

—Andrea Smith (1994, 70)

The Rainbow Family, as a spiritual manifestation, often carries neocolonial baggage. Rainbow spiritual practices frequently involve the mimicking, perverting, or outright ripping off of Native American religious rituals. As ersatz Indians, Rainbows range from silly to offensive.

Rainbow Spirituality: A Fakeloric Prophecy

Journalist Nancy Swanson, writing for a Pennsylvania newspaper, likened the lifestyle she witnessed at the 1986 North American Gathering to what she *imagined* American Indian life once was: "I have always wished that for a day I could be an invisible part of the life of an Indian tribe as they were before the settlers had introduced their diseases and bad habits. On Sunday when Pop and I visited the Rainbow Gathering along the banks of meandering Queen Run, I had the impression that my wish was being granted in some respects" (1986).

Many Rainbows would agree, seeing themselves as a contemporary incarnation of "Indians of old" (*Rainbow Oracle* 1972, 50), whom they romanticize. In various ways, Rainbow Gatherings consciously mimic imagined "Indian" ideals. Gatherings include many of the trimmings mainstream Americans expect of Indians, such as tepees, loincloths, and feathers. The Rainbow Family's Council takes a reconstructed "Indian" praxis as a model. Rainbowized "Indian" motifs pervade Rainbow iconography. *Howdy Folks!* invitations (see Appendix), for example, often conglomerate images of tepees, wigwams, feathers, and Indians in ceremonial dress. Rainbow language is full of "Indian" tropes. Many Rainbows believe their mimicry of imagined Indian ritual is the real thing, which they describe as *sacred* and *traditional*. One Rainbow explains his perception of the Family's Native American tie: "Since the Gathering[']s inception[,] traditional Native American beliefs have been among the strongest and most widely practiced[,] as can be seen in sacred sweats, pipe ceremonies, beadwork, medicine bags, and ceremony [sic] tradition lodges (tipi's [sic] etc[.]) which are the center of our sites, our counsel methods, the use of the sacred eagle feather, drums, our respect for nature and all the great spirit[']s creation, often our clothes, our trading circles, chants, stories, etc[.], etc." (Rainbow Hawk 1985).

The *Rainbow Oracle* reads: "The Family is the union of all races and all peoples; into the family is reborn the true spirit of the Indians" (*Rainbow Oracle* 1972, 52). This vision, the *Oracle* proclaims, marks "[t]he resurrection of the American Indian" (1972, 52).

Native Americans, however, are not a historic relic, but are very much a part of the here and now. The notion that the "spirit of the Indian" died and needs resurrection has long been a part of European mythology, manifested in areas of European American life as diverse as poetry, anthropology, the Cub Scouts, and the Mormons, as exemplified in the writing of Ernest and Julia Seton:

> She was introduced to us as a Mahatma from India, although born in Iowa. . . . Her eyes blazed as she said [to E. T. Seton, a white author of animal stories and one-time head of the Boy Scouts of America], in tones of authority: "Don't you know who you are?"
>
> We were all shocked into silence as she continued: "You are a Red Indian Chief, reincarnated to give the message of the Redman to the White race, so much in need of it. Why don't you get busy? Why don't you do your job? (Seton and Seton [1937] 1966, v–vi)

Despite what they view as respect for American Indian life and what they perceive as American Indian traditions, Rainbows are still in the American "mainstream" as far as how they reconstruct Native Americans. Vine Deloria, a Lakota author, writes, "The American public feels most comfortable with the mythical Indians of stereotype-land who were always THERE. These Indians are fierce, they wear feathers and grunt. . . . To be an Indian in modern American society is in a very real sense to be unreal and ahistorical" (Deloria 1970a, 10).

The *Rainbow Oracle* (1972, 50) pays homage to *Warriors of the Rainbow,* a book destined to be resurrected as a New Age classic, written by William Willoya and Vinson Brown in 1962. Willoya and Brown compare the "heros of the new age" to "the Indians of old" (1962, 77–79). Their Indians, however, are *dead,* described as "great Indians of old," "pure Indians of old," "glorious Indians of the past," "radiant Indians of old," "kind Indians of old," "joyful Indians of old," and "wise Indians of old." Contemporary Indian peoples have no role in this fable. According to Willoya and Brown, they "have been sleeping, physically conquered by the white people" (1962, 77).

For Rainbows, their supposed Native American heritage constitutes what anthropologists call a "mythic charter," which authenticates their experience. Deloria writes: "America attempted to find authenticity in American Indians, manifesting this effort in a number of diverse ways, some of which bordered on the bizarre. Many years before William Carlos Williams wrote: "The land! Don't you feel it? Doesn't it make you want to go out and lift dead Indians tenderly from their graves, to steal from them—as if it must be clinging even to their corpses—some authenticity" (Deloria 1983, 66).

Many Rainbows are not satisfied to align themselves with Native Americans, or to try to learn from them. They want to *be* Indians. A few even claim to out-Indian the Indians, claiming they are here to teach Indians how to be Indians. Rainbow Hipstory tells of a Lakota who visited the 1983 Gathering to share a prophecy from Sitting Bull. "He first came in wearing regular clothes," a hipstorian at the 1990 North American Gathering recalled, "but he was Lakota." According to Sitting Bull's alleged prophecy, "The children of the whites go back out to the mother, and bring the spirit and live in the tepee, and they bring the spirit back to the sons of the natives who are lost, and they find the spirit together and they become native." The speaker, after a pause, added, "We are native. That was, like an Indian tradition" (Hipstory July 3, 1990).

In 1992, these white "Indians," gathering in South Dakota, invited other Rainbows to come and help teach the Lakota to "grow their own vegetables." Perhaps they planned on teaching them to raise corn, potatoes, peppers, tomatoes, or a host of other Native American foods that have sustained European population growth since the American conquest (cf. Lowe 1986). The facilitators of the South Dakota Gathering, however, never got the gardening project off the ground; Lakota never got to experience the living theater comedy of a bunch of bright-eyed city white folks magically transforming their barren reservation into a fertile valley (South Dakota Rainbow 1992).

When Rainbows impersonate Indians, it causes confusion and undermines attempts by bi- and triracial isolates with Native American ancestry to affirm their Indian identities (Ryan 1993, 67–72). Similarly, Hippie-era attempts to create "tribes" and piggyback on the Native American Church's right to use peyote and other illegal sacraments in rituals undermined Native American legal battles to preserve religious freedom.

The "Hopi Prophecy"

The Native American people most salient in Rainbow myths and legends are the Hopi. Paperback versions of *Patterns of Culture* (Benedict 1934) popularized the Hopi, who were frequent subjects of anthropologists during the 1950s and 1960s, when many early Rainbows were schooled. The *Rainbow Oracle* reads: "Thus it is Foretold—The true Light Family will come, bringing the long-lost Stone Tablet— symbol of the land, and return it to the Indians" (*Rainbow Oracle* 1972, 52).

After hearing rumors of a "Hopi prophecy that the Warriors of the Rainbow are to come bearing a sacred stone tablet, a red blanket and hat," Barry Adams, a Rainbow Family founder, went to the Hopi reservation with a stone tablet, a hat, and a blanket (*Rainbow Oracle* 1972, 53). In a Rainbow Family videotape made at the 1988 North American Gathering in Texas, Adams recalls how he went in September of 1970 and met with Thomas Banyaca, telling him that "as far as I know, I'm one of those beings that you're looking for called the Rainbow." Banyaca, the sole survivor of a group of four young Hopis selected by Hopi elders in the early 1950s to interpret their message and prophecies to the outside world, didn't specifically recall Adams or his visit. He said a lot of white people "dress up in red shirts" and come knocking on his door, claiming to be the white brother of the prophecies (interview 1991). Another Rainbow would-be savior with a stone tablet arrived at the 1988 North American Gathering in Texas, driving a red car. After supposedly being shunned by the Hopis, he declared that the Rainbows were the true Hopi people (Bahana Followers interview 1990).

Rainbows have written themselves into Hopi prophecies. One supposed "Hopi prophecy" in particular seems ubiquitous on the Rainbow scene: it is posted inside Gatherings, at Gathering parking areas, and even on occasion at "A" Camp, as well as printed in each edition of the *Rainbow Peace Projects Newsletter*. The prophecy, which Rainbow Hawk, a Rainbow Peace Projects Focalizer, believes gave the Rainbow Family its name, reads: "There will come a tribe of people of all cultures, *who believe in deeds,* not words, and who will restore the earth to its former beauty. This tribe will be called Warriors of the Rainbow" (Rainbow Hawk 1990 [emphasis in original]).

The prophecy is the Rainbow Family's ultimate romantic vision. It is *not,* however, Hopi (Banyaca interview 1991). Thomas Banyaca, when interviewed for this book, was unfamiliar with the Rainbow Family and puzzled about the supposed Hopi prophecy. He speculated that it had something to do with William Willoya. "[He] came and spoke with me, then he wrote that book with [Vinson Brown]. They are the ones who put this Rainbow Warrior [concept] out and those people picked up on it." The book, *Warriors of the Rainbow,* source for the *Rainbow Oracle* (1972, 50, 69), is still often cited by Rainbows. Banyaca didn't think much of the book, though Willoya and Brown list him in their acknowledgments. As to the supposed Hopi imprimatur, Banyaca says, "It's not right. . . . We hope they will stop it."

But *All Ways Free* continues to publish a version of the prophecy, sometimes on its front page, obfuscating its attribution with the passive voice: "It is said that when the earth is weeping and the animals are dying that a tribe of people who care will come. They will be called the Warriors of the Rainbow." Robert Hunter, in writing the chronicles of the Greenpeace movement, claims Greenpeace also "attempted to fulfill an ancient North American Indian prophecy of an age when different races and nationalities would band together to defend the earth from her enemies" (1979, ix). Mexican environmental activist, New Age author, and Rainbow Alberto Ruz Buenfil quotes a variant of the same "prophecy." His version of the prophecy, also posted prominently at Gatherings, reads:

> In the moment in which the culture of the Red people would seem to be almost completely destroyed, and the rivers would be poisoned and the buffalo would be dead and the birds would start dying—in that moment there would be a spirit, an ancient spirit coming back from the Red people that would start reaching also to the White people of all different nations and religions. And this spirit would unify people around the vision of a tribe made up of members of many nations working together for the healing of the Earth. And these people would be the Rainbow Warriors. (Weinberg 1990a)

Ruz Buenfil's version also is based on *Warriors of the Rainbow.* According to Ruz Buenfil, "They [Willoya & Brown] compared prophecies from Indian nations across the continent, and *created* a scenario in which an old woman is telling her grandson [this story]" (Weinberg 1990a [emphasis mine]). Willoya and Brown write: "The story told below, we believe actually happened, though not in these exact details. We have deliberately named no tribe in this story because we want it to mean the same to all tribes, to all the Indians, for a wise old woman anywhere and a boy who had curiosity and spirit anywhere could find together this same miracle. This story makes live for us the heart of the message given us in all the great Indian prophetic visions told about in this book" (1962, 2).

Even so, the prophecy told by Ruz Buenfil isn't true to Willoya and Brown's original fabrication, nor does it appear anywhere else in *Warriors of the Rainbow*. Willoya and Brown's story ends:

> As she stopped talking, the old woman and the boy looked to the east and they saw a great rainbow flaming in the sky where a thunderstorm had passed.
>
> "The rainbow is a sign from Him who is in all things," said the old, wise one. "It is a sign of the union of all peoples like one big family. Go to the mountaintop, child of my flesh, and learn to be a Warrior of the Rainbow, for it is only by spreading love and joy to others that hate in this world can be changed to understanding and kindness, and war and destruction shall end!"
>
> And it shall come to pass afterward, that I will pour our my spirit on all flesh; your sons and your daughters shall prophecy, your old men shall dream dreams, and your young men shall see visions. Joel 2:28 (Willoya and Brown 1962, 15,16)

As the quote from "Joel" indicates, the authors are no more familiar with biblical texts than Indian ones. Their Rainbow is more likely the one in Genesis 9:12–17:

> And God said, "This is the sign of the covenant which I make between me and you, for all future generations: I set my bow in the cloud, and it shall be a sign of the covenant between me and the earth. When I bring clouds over the earth and the bow is seen in the clouds, I will remember my covenant which is between me and you and every living creature of all flesh; and the waters shall never again become a flood to destroy all flesh. When the bow is in the clouds, I will upon it and remember the everlasting covenant that is between God and every living creature of all flesh that is upon the earth." God said to Noah, "This is the sign of the covenant which I have established between me and all flesh that is upon the earth."

Far from spreading Native American spirituality, *Warriors of the Rainbow* is actually a ninety-five-page evangelical Christian tract. Crediting Christianity for creating a "great world civilization" (1962, 86), Willoya and Brown assert that all Indian prophecies actually speak of the Second Coming of Christ. Attempts to discern crypto-Christianity in "Indian" religion, like the Mormons' attempts to discover "the lost tribes of Israel" among Native Americans, are common. In 1937 Ernest and Julia Seton compiled fragments from various Native American traditions and created an Indian "Gospel" much like the Christian Gospels (1966). It is possible that this work, in which several Native Americans were involved, influenced the Rainbow Warrior myth.

Described as "Outasite" in the *Rainbow Oracle* (1972, 50), *Warriors of the Rainbow* purveys a covert anti-Semitism throughout, while evangelizing against traditional Native American spirituality. It warns Hopis not to make the same mistake as "that made by the Jews two thousand years ago when they rejected their Messiah, Jesus, because he did not bring the literal power and glory they expected," (Willoya and Brown 55) and adds: "Note that these people [the Jews] desperately needed a messiah, but that again and again they accepted the leader who brought them what they thought would be physical glory, completely neglecting and ignoring the true Messiah, Jesus, who would have brought them something much more important, spiritual glory" (87).

Still, Rainbows continue to invoke the "prophecy" from *Warriors of the Rainbow*. *All Ways Free,* as a contemporary example, quotes *Warriors of the Rainbow.* Alberto Ruz Buenfil bases his book *Rainbow Nation Without Borders* (1991) on *Warriors of the Rainbow.* He writes about the "return of a group of people called the 'Rainbow Warriors.'" Answering his own rhetorical question, Ruz Buenfil writes, "What is a Rainbow Warrior? That question was first answered for the modern world in 1962, in a book called *Warriors of the Rainbow*" (Ruz Buenfil 1991, 20). In his book, Ruz Buenfil reprints long tracts from *Warriors of the Rainbow,* including the anachronistic descriptions of "Indians of Old" and "sleeping, physically conquered" Indians (Ruz Buenfil 1991, 25). So much attention has been paid, between the Rainbow Family and the New Age movement, to Willoya and Brown's 1962 book, that it returned to print, unrevised, in 1992.

Warriors of the Rainbow has served as an archetypical inspiration for latter-day New Age spin-offs using the Rainbow symbol. The authors of two such books, Eagle Man Ed McGaa and Steven McFadden, both acknowledge Willoya and Brown—McGaa in his suggested reading list, and McFadden in his text and bibliography. In his book *Ancient Voices, Current Affairs: The Legend of the Rainbow Warriors,* McFadden alleges that "the Legend of the Rainbow Warriors" comes from Cree, Sioux (Lakota), Crow, Toltec, Aztec and Iroquois (Haudenosaunee) mythology (McFadden 1992, 9).

While Willoya and Brown's tract is surreptitiously anti-Semitic, McFadden's is decidedly racist. In McFadden's Eurocentric fantasy, "light-skinned people" have "intellect and will," while "red-skinned people" have "intuition and spiritual awareness." "Yellow and black-skinned people," having no real role in McFadden's story, are simply endowed with "gifts" (McFadden 1992, 29). The "light-skinned brothers and sisters," according to McFadden's fable, are the "reincarnated souls of the Indians who were enslaved or killed by the settlers" (McFadden 1992, 10). Ignoring for the moment that reincarnation is not a common Native American belief, McFadden's self-anointed "Indians" are practicing what many real Native Americans see as the "final phase of genocide" (Churchill 1994, 280). Following his logic, New Age whites could tell Indians, "Our forefathers didn't steal your land and resources, try to wipe out your culture and language, and practice genocide against your people. *Your* forefathers did that to *us,* because we're the *real* Indians, not you! Therefore you have no right to hoard Indian spirituality, because it is ours!" The phenomenon of white people claiming to be the true Indians is frighteningly analogous to a belief held by many Holocaust-era Nazis and contemporary neo-Nazis who, based on an obscure nineteenth-century doctrine called British Israelism, claimed that Anglo-Saxons were the true Jews spoken of in the Bible, and that modern-day Jews were the children of Satan (Reiss 1995).

New Age Indian impersonators, like Holocaust-revisionist historians, are completing the genocide by cleansing their forefathers' sins from history. They also deny the reality that they are still living privileged lives, while contemporary Indians are *still* oppressed. By becoming "Indian," by identifying with the oppressed instead of the oppressor, New Agers successfully disassociate themselves from their own cognitive dissonance. Hence there is a large market for McFadden's fabrications.

McFadden earns a living peddling his message. Rainbows, by contrast, invent "Indian teachings" but don't sell them. In keeping with the precepts of the Gathering, everything, including mythology, is freely shared. This sharing differentiates the Rainbow Family from New Agers who profit by marketing supposed "Indian teachings." One such group, which sponsors commercial "Medicine Wheel Gatherings,"[1] created the following spiritual-economic loophole for selling religion: "Under no circumstances is this sharing to be misconstrued as a "for sale" tag on Native Religion. It is intended to guide other two-leggeds in helping themselves, each other, and ultimately our Earth Mother. Monetary transaction is for lectures, workshops, entertainment, housing and meals. Ceremonies and fellowship are a private gift between all parties (elements, plants, animals, spirits and two-leggeds) involved" (Yes Educational Society 1990). The Yes Educational Society and the Bear Tribe, sponsors of the "Gathering" described above, accepted payment by check or credit card; Steven McFadden was a keynote speaker.

Author Ed McGaa, a self-proclaimed "Oglala Sioux ceremonial leader," in 1987 created a "tribe" for the New Age "Indians." In one swift but profitable move, ripping off both Native American and Rainbow Family culture, McGaa dubbed his followers the "Rainbow Tribe." His 1992 book *Rainbow Tribe: Ordinary People Journeying on the Red Road*, published by media magnate Rupert Murdoch's HarperCollins, is a how-to guide for conducting ersatz Indian rituals. In it, he instructs his followers in how to conduct "sweat lodges," "vision quests," and "spirit-calling ceremonies."

It was his friend "Joe," McGaa explains, "who came up with the name Rainbow people" (McGaa 1992, 34), an inspiration he received fifteen years after the first Rainbow Gathering. Giving Indian-wannabe Rainbows a taste of their own medicine, McGaa explains that *his* followers are the true Rainbows. In an obvious slight against the Rainbow Family, as stereotypically portrayed by the media, he identifies people who are "well meaning, are environmental [sic], are unprejudiced, and respect the ways of nature," but have "gathered together to openly use hallucinatory substances," as being banished from *his* Rainbow Tribe (McGaa 1992, 8).[2]

McGaa currently travels the New Age lecture circuit, charging members of his "tribe" from $435 to over $600 to attend five-day workshops on "Native American philosophy and spirituality" (Omega Institute 1995). Participants receive a sort of trophy for their pilgrimage; McGaa anoints them with "Lakota" names. Workshop sponsors claim that by teaching "native wisdom" to "thousands," McGaa is fulfilling Indian prophecies (Omega Institute 1995). McGaa typifies what Native American author and professor of American Indian Studies and Communication Ward Churchill calls a "plastic medicine man." Churchill writes, "Ed McGaa knows full well he is peddling a lie, that it takes a lifetime of training to become a genuine Lakota spiritual leader (which he is not), that the ceremonies he describes are at best meaningless when divorced from their proper conceptual context, and that the integrity of Lakota cultural existence is to a large extent contingent upon the people's retention of control over their spiritual knowledge." Churchill adds, "He [McGaa] has transgressed against Lakota rights and survival in every bit as serious a fashion as those hang-around-the-forts who once professed to legitimate the U.S. expropriation of the Black Hills." McGaa's only redeeming feature, according to Churchill, is that "most of the information he [McGaa] presents is too sloppy and inaccurate to be as damaging as might otherwise be the case" (Churchill 1994, 288).

Like the "hang-around-the-forts" before him, McGaa praises the early European settlers who participated in the conquest of America, writing, "I also believe there is much good in Christianity. The Christians did not wipe us out entirely. That is a fact that cannot be overlooked. Some spiritual force must have kept them from doing that" (1992, 13). Hence, in McGaa's historical interpretation, Native Americans survived extermination not because of their own strong spiritual beliefs and self-determination, but because of the benevolence of white folk.

Many New Age authors, like Rainbow Family members, have taken it upon themselves to create a version of "Native American teachings" that support their agendas. Willoya and Brown, for instance, have an evangelical agenda. Rainbows have a self-serving one, giving legitimation to their ersatz Indian spirituality. Either way, all have conveniently modified and, in some cases, outright fabricated Indian "teachings" as needed. The product is fakelore, "a synthetic product claiming to be authentic oral tradition but actually tailored for mass edification" (Dorson 1976, 5).

Rainbows, of course, haven't cornered the market on fakelore. They have merely picked up on what has developed as a literary tradition in America: "One such example of fakelore was the concept of the Noble Savage, which was used by a number of writers to score rhetorical points during their indictments of 'civilized' societies. . . . [Another] example is the celebrated address by Hiawatha [Haiyonwentha] at the formation of the Iroquois Confederacy. This 'speech' was excerpted and reworded by Longfellow, who had taken it from Schoolcraft, who had copied it from J. V. H. Clark, who had made up every word" (Robie 1986,

100). Henry Wadsworth Longfellow wrote an Americanized version of the story of Haiyonwentha, which he put to Icelandic meter as a poem. Generations of white Americans learned the poem during their schooling, believing they were gleaning something Indian. It was Longfellow's words, conjuring up the image of a long-dead [Viking] Indian, that White Raven invoked during the 1989 Rainbow Vision Council that finally led the Rainbow Gathering to Minnesota for the following year (see chapter 4).

Such synthesized Indian tales live on, even after they have been publicly exposed and discredited. So long as there is a market for fakelore, fabricated Indian tales take on a life of their own. Almost twenty years after the writings of Carlos Castaneda (Carlos César Salvadore Araña) were revealed by critics to be fictitious, and his Yaqui informant, Don Juan Matus, a hoax (de Mille 1976; 1990a; 1990b), New Agers still clamor for Castaneda.

In 1995, for instance, Bear and Company published *The Teachings of Don Carlos* by Victor Sanchez, a how-to guide for following Castaneda's "Yaqui way of knowledge." The fact that Castaneda admitted to faking the fieldwork on which his popular trilogy rests hasn't deterred his faithful following. Sanchez defends Castaneda, who, he speculates, was attacked by anthropologists jealous of his success. Confronted, however, with Castaneda's own admission of guilt, Sanchez continued to spread Castaneda's interpretation of Yaqui shamanism: "The question of whether don Juan existed or not seems to me insignificant in comparison with the ideas set forth in these books. Personally, I am not particularly interested if the ideas came from don Juan or from Castaneda" (Sanchez 1995, xiii). Hence, the dominant culture continues to embrace and spread a vision of Yaqui spirituality having little to do with Yaqui. Likewise, followers of the late New Age spiritual leader Sun Bear, excused his ersatz Indian teachings, claiming Sun Bear exercised "the shaman's ultimate gift. . . . He makes it up as he goes along" (Albanese 1990, 162).

When New Agers and Rainbows embrace a reconstructed native spirituality, even with sincere "respect," they are complicit in ethnocide. Andrea Smith, a Native American journalist, writes: "Many white New Agers continue this practice of destroying Indian spirituality. They trivialize Native American practices so that these practices lose their spiritual force, and they have the white privilege and power to make themselves heard at the expense of Native Americans. Our voices are silenced, and consequently the younger generation of Indians who are trying to find their way back to the Old Ways becomes hopelessly lost in this morass of consumerist spirituality" (1994, 70–71).

The image of Native Americans Rainbows often conjure is a Rainbow visualization of how Indians should be. Vine Deloria comments on "hippie" behavior of the late 1960s, a time when the Rainbow Family was gestating:

Hippies proudly showed us their beads and, with a knowing

smile, bid us hello in the Navajo they had learned while passing through Arizona the previous summer. We watched and wondered as they paraded by in buckskin and feathers, anxiously playing a role they could not comprehend. When the Indians of the Bay area occupied Alcatraz, the hippies descended on the island in droves, nervously scanning the horizon for a vision of man in his pristine natural state. When they found that the tribesmen had the same organizational problems as any other group might have, they left in disappointment, disillusioned with "Indianism" that had existed only in their imaginations. (1970a, 12–13)

Unfortunately, it is the Rainbow image of Indians that many people take as authentic. In creating this image, Rainbows may actually love Native American culture to death. A Montreal newspaper, for example, reported without question that Rainbow Family Gatherings represent "the fulfillment of a Hopi Indian prophecy about a 'tribe' of different peoples living in peace and harmony" (Fitterman 1994). The Indian images that Rainbows imitate are often stereotypical. The propagation of such images, according to author David Seals, is deadly: "Just about everybody would probably agree that the *image* of a culture is as important, especially in this high-tech world of instant global telecommunications, in the perception of it or of a race of people as whatever lies in the *actual* truth of that culture. Indians have often been victims of stereotyping . . . and this reduction of the image of a people kills as surely as any real-life, Wounded Knee–type massacre" (Seals 1991, 635).

Rainbows are currently exporting their vision of American Indians to Europe. Instructions on how to find the European Rainbow Gathering in Poland, for instance, admonished searchers to follow the "Hopi signs" (Forrester 1991). The same is true for French Rainbow Gatherings, where "Hopi" symbols have replaced rainbows as trail markers (*All Ways Free* summer 1990). By themselves defining and representing Indian culture, Rainbows deny Indians that right. "It is important, for reasons of ethnographic accuracy and proper respect, not to transform the lives of real peoples into utopias for the use of others. When members of powerful society use a self-serving fakeloric version of another people's history or life as a myth for their own, they may deprive that people of the chance to assert their own, differing version" (Dentan 1994, 95). The effect on Indian cultures, in the end, depends on who is listening.

While the media often report the Family's fictitious Native American mythology as authentic, the Ben Ishmael Tribe, a nineteenth-century triracial isolate, suffered the opposite fate, having their existence recorded primarily through works of "fiction" (Leaming 1993, 32–37). Hence, while an ersatz Native American culture is proclaimed real, real Ben Ishmael culture has been dismissed as fable. The result is the same—misrepresentation and confusion clouding both historical and contemporary cultural identities.

Honor the Land

It is Rainbow Family policy to honor Native American land claims and territorial sovereignty. Thus the 1991 *Howdy Folks!* reports that "Chief Homer St. Francis has invited the Rainbow Tribes to gather with the Abenaki Tribe on the Statehouse steps in Montpelier, VT on the 6th of July in a peaceful demonstration for self determination for all people" (NERF 1991). Family members often send a delegation to meet with local Indians and seek their approval before holding a Gathering, recognizing the Indians, and not the Forest Service, as having a legitimate claim on the land.

Like other white people before them, however, the Rainbows prefer to deal with Indians who will easily grant their wishes. For example, the Pitt River Tribal Council claimed the site of the 1984 North American Gathering in California's Modoc National Forest as their sovereign ancestral land, and clearly stated their objection to the Rainbows using the site. In a prepared statement, the Pitt River Tribal Council explained:

> The Rainbow Family Tribal Council are by their presence in the Mill Creek, Camp One, and Eagle Peak areas, desecrating culturally significant religious sacred grounds. . . . The Rainbow Family Tribal Council is demonstrating blatant disrespect for the Pitt River Tribe, and Tribal elders, and our religious ways and sacred lands. . . . The Pitt River Tribe, Pitt River Tribal Council declares their opposition to the uses and presence of the Rainbow Family Tribal Council and their followers, in the cultural[ly] significant religious areas, and sacred land in Hammawi territory. (Pitt River Tribal Council 1984)

The Rainbow response manifested the arrogance by which European invaders have been treating Indian peoples for five hundred years: "Yeah, these *are* sacred mountains, that's why we're going there," replied Rainbow Family cofounder Garrick Beck (Weinberg 1989b). The Rainbows decided, like White treaty writers before them, that they were dealing with the wrong Indians. Beck explained:

> We found that the Indian group was divided into different camps. You got Indian groups there that are getting a lot of government money, that elect Bureau of Indian Affairs-sponsored leaders to negotiate the tribe's resources—mining, cattle grazing, timber—and allow corporate giants to make a lot of money by

exploiting Indian lands while the Indians get a little bit of divvy-up, enough to get a pick-up truck. And it was these kinds of people who ruled in their meetings against us and told us they didn't want us there. (Weinberg 1989b)

According to Beck, the "spirituality-based Modoc Council of elders," on the other hand, was friendlier. "Of course," he noted, "there were some Indians who objected from their hearts to a bunch of white city kids camping out on their sacred mountain, as they saw it" (Weinberg 1989b). Either way, it was clear that there was no consensus to allow the Rainbow family on their land; on the contrary, there was clear opposition. The Rainbows, however, stayed. A convenient bit of fakelore was born at the 1984 Gathering, this time explaining how Pitt River "prophecies" foretold a time when "the land would be dying, and there would be a Gathering of people from around the world."

Historically, utopias, while proclaiming a more fair and just society for their followers, have been at the forefront of U.S. expansion onto contested Indian lands. One of America's first utopian visionaries, Peter Cornelius Plockhoy, who in the 1660s was centuries ahead of other reformers in preaching "compassion for the poor, uplifting education for all children, freedom of conscience, separation of church and state, and the abolition of slavery" (Miller 1993, 123), planned a community on Indian land (Miller 1993, 120).[3] Even the first Amana settlement in Ebenezer (1843), a mere six miles from the bustling terminus of the new Erie Canal system in Buffalo, New York, was located on contested Seneca land (Perkins and Wick [1891] 1975, 49). The Mormons, despite the salience of Native Americans in their mythic charter, were as brutal as any other invaders of Indian territory.

Given this history, it is not surprising that a group of Rainbows are presently attempting to organize a permanent settlement of one hundred, forty-nine-acre private farms on Maya Indian land in the Central American nation of Belize. "The Belize Project," as Timothy McClure, its organizer, calls it, would be situated on government-recognized Maya reservation land. The proposed Rainbow site falls within the confines of an area that the local (Belize) Toledo Maya Cultural Council is fighting to have set aside as a Maya homeland. McClure, however, makes no mention of this claim. Instead, he alludes to the land's being abandoned, writing: "Though the land may have been abandoned by the people who must have once lived there." McClure does make reference to the fact that this "abandoned land" might not be quite so abandoned. Like colonial missionaries before him, he promises that settlers will "go out of our way to help the indigenous people in every way we can, *especially those who want to become a part of our way of life*" (McClure 1994, 16 [emphasis mine]).

McClure's Belize project is divinely inspired by the standby Rainbow Family prophecy, this time attributed to the Haudenosaunee and Abenaki as well as the Hopi nations. McClure boldly writes, "I am one of the Warriors of the Rainbow who, as prophecied [*sic*] by the Abenaki, the Iroquois and the Hopi, have returned to Earth as ordinary people of all colors who are to find each other and become One People again who will live together on The Land, and create a spiritual community that will foster a new culture in alignment with spirit, and in harmony with The Earth" (McClure 1994, 11).

For their 1990 Gathering in New York State, the North East Rainbow Family (NERF) sent a delegation to the Onondaga Nation near Syracuse, to seek permission to Gather in the Finger Lakes National Forest. The delegates returned, claiming to have received the approval of the "elders." Oren Lyons, an Onondaga chief who serves as Faithkeeper of the Grand Council of Chiefs of the Haudenosaunee ("Iroquois"), was unfamiliar with the Rainbow visit and had no idea who they spoke with. Had they spoken with him, he said, he would have told them to "go see the Cayugas" (Lyons interview 1991). The Finger Lakes National Forest, is, after all, on Cayuga, not Onondaga, land.

The Quebec Rainbow Family extended themselves an invitation to gather, not on public land, but on Montagnais Indian reservation land. Only after doing so did they tell the Montagnais they were coming. The Rainbows then asked Indian leaders where on the reservation they should set up the Gathering. The Montagnais sent them to a contested area that a local construction company was using as a gravel mine and dump for construction debris. The Indians used an adjacent area for fishing and drinking beer, while doing a bit of dumping themselves on the Rainbow site. The Rainbows believed the area was "sacred" Indian land (Louie interview 1990). A Montagnais visitor told me, however, "No, it is, how you say, a dump." Despite being surrounded by tons of trash and debris, few Rainbows accepted the fact that they camped on a dump.

Rainbow culture, when not attempting to pass itself off as the spiritual heir apparent of imagined Indian culture, is in fact compatible with many Native American traditions. For this reason, a significant number of Native Americans frequent the Gatherings, which are somewhat akin to powwows. The Family's struggle to balance politics and spirituality is crucial in Rainbow relations with Native Americans. Problems arise when Rainbows try to seize what they perceive as Indian spirituality. When Rainbows respectfully align themselves with American Indian *political* struggles, however, relations become amicable.

In 1984, for instance, a delegation of Rainbows stayed in the area after the Gathering to attend an Indian-sponsored conference on the Pitt River. In 1985, at the invitation of local Indian activists, Rainbows went to St. Louis after the Gathering to help establish a support encampment during Leonard Peltier's appeal trial. The 1990 Rainbow Thanksgiving Council "consensed" that publicizing and organizing resistance to the James Bay II hydro project, which would flood thousands of miles of Cree land, would be a focal theme for the 1991 Gathering. Rainbows have also been very active in the Big Mountain support movement, helping to organize resistance to the forced relocation of the Dineh ("Navajo").

Fakeloric or not, many Native Americans recognize that Rainbows, with their deep respect for "mother earth," have their hearts in the right place. Heart Warrior Chosa, an Ojibwa woman who ran for governor of Minnesota in 1990 as a fringe candidate, participated in the same year's North American Gathering. She described the Rainbow Family as "people that have stepped back and seen what's happening in the culture and are searching for something better. They have a vision. Something for all people" (Chosa interview 1990).

Similarly, Gillette Wingel, an Ojibwa, paid an unplanned visit to the 1990 North American Gathering after the police mistook him for a Rainbow and stopped to question him as he hitchhiked toward Isle Royale National Park, north of the Gathering site.[4] After ascertaining that he was not a Rainbow, police officers continued to question him. Wingel recalls:

> So then they asked me why I was going to Isle Royale. I said I was going there to do my vision quest. So [they] asked me how the vision quest was done, I told [them] it would take at least four days, and gave [them] a general idea what was involved, the procedures of the vision quest in terms of setting up the lodge. I didn't tell them what I expected to see, or things like that. . . . I told them it was part of my ritual and they really didn't have the right to know. And as long as I wasn't going to the Rainbow Gathering they felt, you know, I wasn't part of their mission or their purpose. (Wingel interview 1990)

The officers gave Wingel a cup of coffee. They told him his vision quest sounded dangerous and suggested he'd be better off going to the Rainbow Gathering. They then offered him a ride as far as the trailhead to the Gathering. Since the Gathering was basically on his way, and with his curiosity now piqued, Wingel decided "to check it out." He only planned to stay for "an hour or so" before continuing north. When he arrived at the Gathering, however, he noticed that it bore a resemblance to a "recurring dream" he had been having and had recently written down, so he decided to stay. After four days, he felt that the Rainbow Family had a mission: "I think the mission [of the Rainbow Family] is to set an example on the philosophy of life that the Indian people had at one time. Creed, code, moral code that governed their lives . . . which they themselves developed by listening and watching the animals, watching nature in general. . . . The Rainbow Family [will] gradually be a vanguard to reach out to others . . . with some spiritual consciousness and eventually grow to the homes of the rich people" (Wingel interview 1990).

Wingel was popular at the Gathering, bringing a message many Rainbows wanted to hear. He was hopeful that Rainbows could respectfully learn more about various Indian ways: "I certainly don't see too much of the Indian ways incorporated [in Rainbow] cause I believe, a great part of it may not apply to non-Indians. They can't ingest it all at once, they have to be given this piecemeal, piece by piece. It shouldn't be forced down on them like the non-Indians forced their religions and values upon the Indian peoples. We've learned that. Tell them they have to take it piece by piece, ingest it, understand it, be conscious of it, it's growth" (interview 1990).

Wingel and Chosa are just two of many Indians who have encountered the Rainbow Family. While they are sympathetic, others are disgusted. Many Native Americans just don't want to be bothered with it. Without fakelore, however, the Rainbow Family would probably draw more sympathetic Native Americans.

From Ethnocide to a Multispiritual Utopia

Ethnocide, even with the best of intentions, is still ethnocide. Native Americans are adamant that the theft and desecration of their culture and sacred spiritual beliefs is nothing short of genocide. No matter what the intention, it represents the eradication of their identities as indigenous peoples. The Dakota, Lakota, and Nakota Nations addressed the point in June of 1993, when they ratified a "Declaration of War Against Exploiters of Lakota Spirituality." In it they decry having their "most precious Lakota ceremonies and spiritual practices desecrated, mocked, and abused by non-Indian "wannabes," hucksters, cultists, commercial profiteers, and self-styled "New Age Shamans." Such "pseudo-religious hodge-podge," they assert, "compromises a momentous obstacle in the struggle of traditional Lakota people for an adequate public appraisal of the legitimate political, legal, and spiritual needs of real Lakota people" (Churchill 1994, 274–75).[5]

The Rainbows, with their invented "Indian" myths, are clearly part of the problem facing Native North America. The appropriation of Native American culture, however, predates both the Rainbow Family and the New Age movement, going back to the first European settlements in the Americas. Many historians believe, for instance, that the early American colonists at Roanoke, who subsequently disappeared leaving only a cryptic message, "Gone to Croatan," actually abandoned their settlement to join up with the Croatan Indians. American history and folklore is rife with stories of mountain men and other assorted dropouts who have run off to the wilds, to live either with, or like, supposed Indians. "Cultural Primitivism," the disenchantment of the "civilized" with "civilization," predates the American conquest, having roots extending back to the beginnings of European "civilization" (Lovejoy and Boas [1935] 1965, 288). When it comes to playing Indian, the Rainbows are not that far from mainstream America.

Rainbows are now faced with the opportunity to stop the game; to take a *political* stance against the destruction of native cultures. The Center for the Spirit,[6] a nonprofit organization of Native Americans united to preserve Indian religious traditions, asks "all those who care about Indian people in our struggle for justice and peace to help us put an end to spiritual genocide. We urge you to protest against 'plastic medicine men' and hucksters wherever they appear in public; to lend them no degree of credibility; and to warn your friends who, through ignorance or naïveté, are in danger of being swindled by these con artists" (Churchill 1994, 281). Rainbows are at a threshold. Whether they will take action against fakeloric cultural appropriation, or continue to bask in the fantasy of being Indian, remains to be seen.

"Indianism," while the most obvious and prevalent manifestation of Rainbow spirituality, is certainly not the *only* religious belief in the Family. Family members represent most of the world's major religions, and diverse religious ceremonies and practices are common at Gatherings. It is not uncommon at a North American Gathering, for instance, to stumble upon various Christian denominations, Muslims, Jews, Hindus, Buddhists, Bahá'ís, Krishnas and assorted Pagans. Many, however, relate their practices in one fashion or another to supposed Indian practices. A rabbi at a Rainbow Gathering, for example, explained how Jewish Sabbath candles represent a nomadic people's version of a "tribal fire." He hadn't, however, conjured up any drums.

Fakeloric and sometimes arrogant, the Rainbow Family's relations with Native Americans are far from ideal. The Rainbow Family's Indian roots are weak, at best. Yet it is important to look past the fakelore, to see Rainbow culture as Rainbow culture, not as ersatz Indian culture. When not pretending to be Indian, it is strong, multicultural, and multispiritual. Likewise, the Rainbow message of peaceful coexistence with one another, other peoples, other species, and the environment merits respect.

The Mediated Rainbow:
The American Media Look at the Rainbow Family

All of us at one time or another have read a newspaper story or seen a news broadcast that we know misses the real story. Perhaps we have been present at an event, only to find the next day's news account far removed from our firsthand experience. The more one understands about the world, the more one sees how our news media deliberately or inadvertently fudge the facts and distort key issues.

—Martin A. Lee and Norman Solomon, *Unreliable Sources: A Guide to Detecting Bias in News Media*

People learn about the Rainbow Family and vicariously experience the Gatherings through the media. Since most people who read articles, watch television, or listen to radio news reports about the Family never attend a Rainbow Family event or even talk with a Rainbow Family member, their perception of the Family rests on these reports. Likewise, their impressions of the Gatherings stem entirely from media reports.

Creating Opinion

Since most Americans are unfamiliar with the existence of the Rainbow Family, it constitutes what the former director of social research for the CBS television network calls a "new issue":

Mass communication is extremely effective . . . in the creation of opinion on new issues. By "new issues" I mean issues on which the individual has no opinion and on which his friends and fellow group members have no opinion. The reason for the effectiveness of mass communications in creating opinions on new issues is pretty obvious: The individual has no predisposition to defend, and so the communication falls, as it were, on defenseless soil. And once the opinion is created, then it is this new opinion which becomes easy to reinforce and hard to change. This process of opinion creation is strongest, by the way, when the person has no other source of information on the topic to use as a touchstone. (Schiller 1973, 166–67)

Media descriptions of the Rainbow Family are therefore potent. They take root as uncontested fact in the minds of media consumers unfamiliar with the Family. Since negative press reports fall on such "defenseless soil," the way local media present the Family before a Gathering is crucial for community relations. When Rainbow Family members appear in a community where the press has portrayed them negatively, they face the difficult task of trying to change public opinion. Positive press reports in local papers, on the other hand, pave the way for a smooth reception.

The most common device used for creating a negative press portrayal of the Rainbow Family is biased language. A media critic points out: "It is the choice of just the right adjective or verb to sum up a situation that evokes from the receiver the response the communicator feels should be adopted toward a story. . . . The word and the situation it describes become almost inseparable, so that the use of the word triggers a standardized response in the receiver. . . . Language patterns stereotype both the situation and the person they are applied to" (O'Hara 1961, 229–40). It is easy to see how the language journalists choose to describe the Family may emit subtle negative signals. The media tend to anachronize the Rainbow Family (and the environmental and antimilitarist movements of the 1990s) as remnants of the 1960s (Aslam 1990, 24; Hagar 1990, 34).

Stuck in the 1960s

The twenty-four stories (twenty-two about Rainbow Gatherings, and two about a mother who killed her teenage son to keep him from associating with the Rainbow Family)[1] sent out over the United Press International (UPI) wires in the mid- to late 1980s, without exception, are full of 1960s references. In the lead sentences of all the stories, the most common descriptives of Rainbow Family members were "aging hippies" (four articles) or "middle-aged hippies" (four articles). The next-most-popular descriptive (three articles) was "1960s style hippies." This bloated descriptive serves to remind readers that "hippies" and thus, Rainbows, are anachronisms. The descriptive term "hippies" stood alone in two lead sentences, making it the fourth-most-popular descriptive. "Erstwhile hippies," "neo-hippies," and "hippie like folk" each appeared once, characterizing the diverse Rainbow Family as well as the phrase "middle-aged white folks" describes the population of the United States.

These descriptives link the Rainbow Family to a bygone era, signaling to the reader that Rainbows are not to be taken seriously in the contemporary world. Likewise, readers need not take any Rainbow Family philosophies or beliefs seriously. The media can thereby ignore, for instance, the Family's successes with nonviolent conflict resolution, which, if taken seriously, might provide both an inspiration and an example for a violence-ridden society. The media also ignore the legal challenges and threats that government agencies pose to the Family's right to gather (see chapter 10). Relegating the Gatherings to the past obscures the implications these challenges have for the rights of other Americans.

Besides the "hippie" theme, the "flower child" motif was also popular in UPI's lead sentences. While one article described the Rainbows as "flower children," another described them oxymoronically as "grown up flower children" and yet another as "grown up flower children of the 1960s." UPI also refers to Rainbows as "yesteryear's flower children" or "latter day flower children." In another article, the author simply calls them "flower children of the 1960's," as if they were miraculously preserved specimens, still children after all these years.

Key to the phrase "flower child" is the word "child."[2] The message, that these people have not grown up or matured, supports paternalistic government attitudes about having to *manage* and *regulate* Rainbow Gatherings. It also suggests that their concerns, and the solutions they have found to human problems, are beneath the attention of serious people, the same way adults dismiss or trivialize children's concerns and plans. The Rainbow aversion to hierarchy (see chapter 3) becomes a manifestation of childish immaturity, as in UPI's phrase "leaderless flower children."

The idea is that, while Rainbows age, they never mature into responsible adults. They become, in the lead sentences of two articles, "aging flower children." One article describes the Rainbows as "flower children, many now in their 40s and 50s" (UPI July 1, 1987). When these flower children procreate, they don't give birth to "babies" but to "new flower children" (UPI July 4, 1984).

The "aging" in the UPI articles is not a mellowing, comparable to fine wine, but more of a withering. Ugliness lies just below the surface in two lead sentences about official orders for Rainbows to *hide* their *aging* bodies. One reads: "Authorities ordered more than 5,000 aging flower children gathered in a national forest Wednesday to stay in the woods away from public view if they must go nude" (UPI July 1, 1987). The other: "More than 5,000 aging flower children were told to hide their nudity by the U.S. forest service" (UPI July 2, 1987).

The verbs to describe Rainbow activity support a picture of childish feckless-ness. Rainbows in UPI articles "romped," "frolicked," "milled about," and "lazed." While "lazed" was the most popular verb, "ragtag" was the most popular adjec-tive to describe Rainbow people. The following UPI story lead demonstrates many of these word usages:

> Thousands of leaderless "flower children" have obtained a court judgment that allows them to romp at will in the Great Smoky Mountains by promising a federal judge they will clean up behind themselves.
>
> Representatives of the Rainbow Family[,] a ragtag collection of aging hippies, Hare Krishnas and assorted flower children signed a 23–item agreement Thursday with the state of North Carolina to abide by court-approved sanitation requirements during their week-long frolic in the mountains. (Perkinson 1987d)

One UPI article covers both "swarming mosquitos," and "swarms of Rainbows" descending upon Zavala, Texas (UPI July 3, 1988). The analogy is obvious: the "odd human scenery" (UPI July 3, 1987) that mysteriously "had collected" (UPI July 03, 1987) in Texas were pests. UPI's anachronizing coverage of the Rainbow Family is the norm among the mass media. All four *New York Times* pieces about the Rainbow Family published during the same period, used the term "hippie" in a headline, as does the only *London Times* piece (Morgan 1987). These "hippie-style" descriptives trivialize Gatherings, stressing dress, language, age, and style over politics and ideals (Gitlin 1980, 23).

Some Rainbows, however, use the word "hippie" affectionately in familiar con-versation, much as some African Americans use the word "nigga" or Polish-Ameri-cans use the word "Polack." This usage has led publications such as the *New York Times* to refer to Rainbows as "self-described hippies" (Belkin 1988a). Although an article like this, titled "Hippies Find a Way in a Texas Court," is acceptable for Rainbows, it would be unthinkable for the *Times* to treat Polish Americans or African Americans, for instance, the same way. An article titled, for example, "Polacks Find a Way in a Texas Court," which begins with a reference to "self-described Polacks" would be clearly unacceptable. Equally unthinkable would be phrases like "aging Polacks," "neo Polacks," "1960s-style Polacks," and "Polack-like folks."

On July 5, 1988, the *New York Times* published another piece about "self-de-scribed hippies," this time stereotyping Texans as well as Rainbows (Belkin 1988b). Writing that "Texas made it clear that they did not want the Rainbow Family here," the reporter backed up her point by quoting a local resident who, she says, "had arrived by pleasure boat to stare at the Rainbows." According to her source,

"These people [the Rainbows] are no-good hippies and we should run them out of town." She made no mention, however, of the many locals who were using their boats to ferry Rainbows and their supplies around a Forest Service roadblock (1990 Hipstory), nor does she quote any Texans who had positive words for the Rainbows (Nather 1988). She does add a bit of condescending humor about Texans who came to "stare" at the Rainbows, attributing the quote "We are not animals in the zoo" to a Rainbow named Running Goose.

A July 9, 1982, *New York Times* article, "Holdover hippies meet for their annual fling," kept returning to the theme that the Rainbow Family was the last gasp of a dead subculture. The lead describes the Gathering as "a scene from the past." The fact that Rainbow Gatherings continued to grow in number and size around the world in the years since the article was published would suggest that "a scene from the future" might have been an equally appropriate description.[3]

Rainbow Family members, according to this reporter, were a "group of counter-culture advocates, religious cultists and shaggy, barefoot folks who used to be called hippies." The supposed Rainbow Family comprised both "aging remnants of the flower generation" and "teenagers too young to remember Woodstock." The teenagers, whose presence suggests that the Rainbow Family is an ongoing group, were referred to as "young recruits of a subculture most now regard as a relic." Without any attribution, it is impossible to tell if this "most" refers to the author's colleagues at the *Times,* his friends, people of his social background, or the readers who relied on him for their information about the Rainbow Family. These Rainbow teens are contrasted with "*American* young people," who, the article points out, "have shifted to a decidedly more conservative track" (emphasis mine).

All of the above quotes appeared in the first four paragraphs of the *Times* article. Most readers who skim the paper will read only the headline and these first few paragraphs, then move on to the next story. Editors normally "cut" an article from the bottom up, often without reading the cut paragraphs. Experienced reporters write with this practice in mind, placing their most important facts early on in their articles. Most readers have learned to read the same way, scanning the lead sentences and cutting out the rest. In the case of this *Times* article, had they read on, they would have seen a different picture. After four paragraphs of clichés, the author proceeded to draw a somewhat more accurate description of the Rainbow Gathering.

By the seventh paragraph, the "shaggy," "barefoot," "counter-cultural" "religious cultists" of the second paragraph, miraculously became people who had chosen "what could broadly be described as an alternative way of life," as well as "students" and professionals, albeit "self described" professionals. Despite his conventional biases, the reporter made an attempt to show the Gathering in a somewhat positive light, quoting local residents who said the Rainbows "behaved real respectable" and told how "the situation could be a lot worse." He even contradicted his initial descriptions by quoting a state trooper about how "these people here" differ from folks "back in the 60s."

Similarly, after the usual "hippie" and "flower power" rhetoric of the headline and lead paragraph in a July 7, 1980, New York Times article, readers encountered an honest attempt at describing the imagery of a Rainbow Gathering. The unnamed author wrote, "Tepees appeared, dulcimer and fiddle music wafted through the trees, and blissful talk of world harmony and a new American tribe could be heard throughout the sprawling camp."

A major problem plaguing national media coverage of the Rainbow Family (and other complex stories as well) is the lack of time and resources editors allow journalists for research. Reporters with little or no time to spend at the Gatherings often revert to stereotyping, instead of actually understanding, the Rainbow Family. Since they know little about the Family, and have no time to learn about them, they lump them into what they see as the closest familiar category: the defunct hippie movement.

One of the most widely read pieces about the Rainbow Family was a 1988 Newsweek article, "A Fracas over the Rainbows: Hippies in East Texas" (Baker and Drew 1988, 31). It began with the standard canned fare: "Aging hippies from the 1960's plan to invade national forestland. . . ." The article continued on to warn that Rainbows constituted "a hazard to the forest," and quoted a Forest Service agent who explained how "their [Rainbows'] brains are baked." Above the article was a picture, not of a Rainbow, but of a local Texas biker with a can of beer prominently displayed in the foreground; so prominently displayed, in fact, that the can was larger than the biker's head.

Forest Service records show that Lisa Drew, the local Newsweek researcher for the story, spent less than four hours at the site of the early Rainbow Seed Camp, checking in and out at a Forest Service "command post" (US NFS Texas Telecopy Message June 17 and 13, 1988). The story, which ended with an ominous warning about how the Rainbows would be "fresh meat" for chiggers, ticks, mosquitoes, snakes, rabid raccoons, skunks, and foxes, never quoted any Rainbow members or made any effort to describe the Rainbow Gathering or its purposes.

Media for the 1990s

As the 1980s gave way to the '90s, the Family continued to evolve. North America's first Zippie Raves, for instance, were held at Rainbow Gatherings (cf. Ferguson 1995). Rainbow children brought up within the Family became adults, active both in Rainbow Councils and in communities away from the Gatherings. The Family had hit the twenty-five-year mark, still very much alive and growing. What didn't evolve or mature, however, was press coverage of the Family. Ironically it is *not* the Rainbow Family, but the American press that is stuck in the hippie era.

The *real* throwbacks, having given up typewriters for word processors years earlier, were still pounding out the same tired old anachronisms on their spiffy new keyboards. To the *Boston Globe* the Rainbows are "never-say-die hippies" (Saunders 1994b) and "a loosely organized group of '60s hippie holdouts" (Saunders 1994a). The *San Diego Union-Tribune* calls them "graying hippies" (Berliner 1994). The *Denver Post* calls Rainbows "modern hippies" (Seipel 1994) while the *Rocky Mountain News* refers to them as "latter-day hippies" (Frazier 1994), "1960s-styled counterculture freaks," and "that offbeat band of hippies" (Foster 1994). According to the Gannett News Service, the Family is more than "offbeat," it's "part of the nation's largest band of hippies" (Wagster 1993). The Unification Church's *Washington Times* calls them "a ragtag band of neo-hippies" (Richardson 1994).

In Florida the *Orlando Sentinel Tribune* says, "It's a scene straight out of the 1960s," with "fortysomething flower children" (Campbell 1992). The *Tampa Tribune* describes the Family as "Fading freaks" and "leftover hippies from the 1960's" (Campbell and Murphy 1995). Ironically, in the same article, the authors complain that "there seem to be fewer legitimate hippies" since "the bulk of this year's crew at the Rainbow gathering is between 17 and 25 years old—some second—and third-generation followers" (Campbell and Murphy 1995). Though left over from the 1960s, most are only seventeen to twenty-five years old; indeed an impressive piece of Rainbow magic.

The *Bergen* (New Jersey) *Record* defines Rainbow Family members as "a Woodstock-style grouping of aging Flower Children, Aquarians, New Age hippies, Dead Head retreads, and," interestingly enough, "just about anyone else into sharing, caring, and nurturing" (Gibson 1994). The *Washington Post,* striving to invent new clichés for the 1990s, calls the Gathering "an annual celebration of woolly-headed idealism and primitive collectivism" (Leiby 1994).

Small Towns—Big Stories

Working with scattered and often erroneous bits of information, many news articles failed to provide readers accurate information about the Rainbow Family. On a local level, the lack of reliable information and the proliferation of misinformation can lead to misconceptions and fear in small communities where Rainbow Gatherings are planned.

While categorically trivialized as *fluff* in the national media, Rainbow stories are *hard news* in the local press near Gathering sites. Jack Becklund, a columnist for the Grand Marais (pop. 1,200), Minnesota, weekly *Cook County News-Herald* illustrated this point in his July 2, 1990, "Uffda!" column. Becklund explained why it was important to give thorough coverage to the 1990 North American Gathering held in Cook County:

> The simple answer is that the Rainbow Gathering is news. It's the number one topic in restaurants, service stations, and homes around the county. There are stories and jokes being told from Schroeder to Grand Marais and beyond. . . .
>
> In a couple of weeks, when this entire event starts to wind down, we'll begin to realize that the Gathering was a major historic event. As the years go by, it will pass into that fabric of folklore that makes our county so colorful.

For small quiet remote rural communities, Gatherings are monumental events, searing their way into local history. A 1994 article in the *Charleston Gazette* about life in the small West Virginia town of Dyer, for instance, begins with "You won't find it on most maps, and there aren't any signs when you get there." The article goes on to observe, "Folks still marvel at the Rainbow Family, who held their annual counterculture gathering a few miles down the road in 1980" (Byers Aug. 29, 1994).

Local media, with a stake in unearthing the details of the Rainbow Gatherings, have produced in-depth reports about the Family. On January 8, 1990, the *Cook County News-Herald* published a front-page story headlined "Hippie Happening May Happen Here." The story, which "warns" of a possible Rainbow Gathering in Cook County, the eventual site for the 1990 Gathering, grew entirely out of a January 2, 1990, informational meeting orchestrated by Cook County sheriff John Lyght. At that meeting, Sheriff Lyght presented a hostile Forest Service video documentary of the 1987 Rainbow Gathering in North Carolina. The *News-Herald* cites the video and warns readers that "the Rainbow Family believes that the only rule is that there are no rules." This line, which has appeared verbatim in news accounts of the Rainbow Family across the country, comes directly from the narration of the Forest Service video and *not* from any Rainbow Family member.

According to Forest Service narration, "Law enforcement personnel were advised that the group believes in the power of intimidation . . . , [that] some group members also have confrontational attitudes, and that incidents involving locals and Family members occur." Based on the Forest Service misinformation, the *News-Herald* advised frightened readers that "some [Rainbow Family] members also have extensive criminal records" and could be expected to leave garbage and environmental damage in their wake.

The *News-Herald* report could have been far more hostile had the paper chosen also to quote Sheriff Lyght. Lyght presented a truly bizarre description of the Rainbow Family to local politicians and the press, explaining: "40% of them are real up-to-date people, and this family consists of mostly doctors, lawyers, judges, law enforcement people." The other 60 percent, he added, "are the cruddy ruddy type that we have to deal with. And they're noted for bringing in drugs, er, child molesting, and anything that's not legal" (Nelson, PAC-13 video 1990).

This horrific mélange of lawyers and child molesters could run wild, according to Lyght, because "the Forest Service is kind of reluctant to enforce too much of the laws because word is they've lost in courts, back in Washington. They've lost cases on it." Lyght speculated that, since the Rainbow Family included "judges, lawyers, and chief law enforcement people," a fifth column of sitting judges was on their side. Lyght said the Rainbow Family was "quite an organization" and promised to keep folks "well abreasted" [sic] of the situation.

The *Cook County News-Herald* was edited at that time by Shawn Perich, a freelance "outdoors" writer and editor for a "sportsman's" publication. Perich, an experienced magazine journalist, formerly based in Atlanta and Minneapolis, did not leave his wits behind when he moved up to what the *News-Herald* refers to as "Minnesota's most beautiful county."

Shortly after the inflammatory meeting with Lyght, Perich was sitting at his desk at the *News-Herald* when a couple of local dog mushers[4] spotted his notes from the meeting. One musher, seeing that Perich was writing about the Rainbow Family, produced a copy of *All Ways Free,* a Rainbow publication. Perich now had two contradicting stories. Perich decided to put together two articles, "one from the official point of view, and one from spending an hour or two gazing through *All Ways Free* and some of the press clips from Texas" (Perich interview 1990). He ran the two contradictory pieces side by side on the front page on January 8, 1990. The piece based on *All Ways Free,* entitled "Publication Depicts Rainbows in Different Light," states: "Negative impacts of Rainbow Family gatherings may be overstated by the Forest Service and law enforcement agencies, according to legitimate news accounts that were reproduced in the winter 1989 issue of All Ways Free." Perich went on to add:

> Intensive drug enforcement efforts [at the 1988 Gathering in Texas], including dope sniffing canines, turned up only small amounts of marijuana. Law enforcement personnel at the gathering included the U.S. Forest Service, U.S. marshals, the U.S. Customs Service, state troopers, sheriff's deputies, district attorney's office officials and local constables. Apparently, the Rainbows caused no trouble. Several Texas editorials, including ones from the newspaper where the Gathering occurred, were favorable toward the Family and sarcastic about the excessive law enforcement coverage.
>
> Cleanup after the event apparently wasn't a problem either. One account quoted the local district ranger as saying, "In all honesty, they left the place cleaner than they found it."

All told, in 1990 the *Cook County News-Herald* published twenty-eight articles and columns wholly or partly about the Rainbow Gathering. Perich said, "The only thing we decided to do as a paper was not to editorialize one way or the other until after it was over, because it was new for us, it was new for everybody, we had to see how it would go" (interview 1990). True to his word, Perich refrained from writing any editorials either supporting or condemning a people and an event he was learning about for the first time.

Jack Becklund, a *News-Herald* columnist, looked forward to the Gathering:

> A lot of media attention will be focused on Cook County and Grand Marais. How we as hosts behave under the glare will determine in large part whether we gain a long range benefit in tourism. It doesn't pay to go around telling visiting reporters that you hope the mosquitos and flies will carry off the entire encampment.
>
> Call me naive, call me an optimist, but I for one am kind of excited that the Rainbows are probably coming to Cook County. I say probably, because nothing is etched in stone. Their impact on our usual tourist business will probably be minimal because they select isolated campsites.
>
> Call 'em neo-hippies or counter-culturalists, they have at least one thing in common with most of us who live in Cook County. They enjoy the woods and have determined, after considerable study, that Cook County's the best place to go camping and spend a summer vacation in all of Minnesota. (1990a, 4)

The *Times-Herald's* reporting was a respectable attempt at objectivity mixed with an old-fashioned bias for hometown values. The July 9, 1990, edition, for example, sported two cover stories about Fourth of July celebrations. One described the annual Cannon Shoot in the town of Tofte as entailing a "sizable crowd," gathered to watch four cannons blast concrete-filled beer cans and red, white, and blue steel pegs at a "pirate ship sailing a couple of hundred yards off-shore." When the "ship," or more accurately, the raft, finally sank, the crowd moved over to the highway to watch a parade of fire trucks, "hot rods," and a "kids battalion." The headline described this ritual as "An all-day Festival."

Another headline described the Rainbow Gathering taking place a few miles away as "A Weird Fourth." The article began, "The last place you'd ever expect to meet anyone you know is at the Hare Krishna kitchen at the Rainbow gathering." This style established Perich, like other people from his community, as an outsider at the Gathering. As such, he was not alienated from his readership. He reported the Gathering as accurately as he could but was still clearly taking precautions not to go native.

Working closely with Perich was Holly Nelson, who, with his wife Janet, operates Grand Marais's public access cable television station, PAC-13, from the rear room of their Radio Shack store. Holly Nelson and his video camera became regular fixtures at the 1990 Gathering as he wandered from camp to camp conducting interviews. He aimed to document, for posterity, one of the most colorful events in Cook County's history. The Nelsons' motives, though, went beyond aesthetics. Janet Nelson writes: "We felt our purpose was to calm our area down, we are a small Scandinavian [community], far from everyday fears of cities, protected from the big world and guess we want our little world to stay little and calm. The thought of 10,000 to 20,000 people moving in was really mind-boggling. The people were scared and could not believe it was possible. This is three times more than we have in our whole county" (1990). With their straightforward reporting, PAC-13 and the *Cook County News-Herald* derailed Lyght's misinformation campaign and laid the groundwork for a tranquil summer of cooperation between the Rainbow Family and the people of Cook County.

The daily *Duluth News-Tribune,* whose service area includes Cook County, published forty-two articles and one editorial about the 1990 Rainbow Gathering. *News-Tribune* editors never used any derogatory terms like "hippie" or "flower child" in their headlines. Instead they used the term "Rainbow" in thirty-three headlines—a descriptive never used at the time in a *New York Times* headlines to describe the Rainbow Family.[5] Not content with the national media practice of hiking in for a few photo opportunities and a random interview and then returning before dark to the world of restaurants and expense accounts, *News-Tribune* reporters Julie Gravelle, Susan Stanich, and photographer Clara Wu decided to join the Gathering and camp at a Rainbow encampment. The trio arrived at the Gathering site at about 11 P.M. on Wednesday, June 20, after covering a public informational meeting about the Rainbow Gathering in Grand Marais, the county seat. After waiting for some time in the mud, they unceremoniously rode with their canoe and gear from the parking area through the pouring rain in the back of an open pickup truck, to be deposited at the info center, where the road ended and the trail system began. They eventually made their way to Buffalo Camp (described in chapter 1, "Sunflower's Day"), where they made camp.

Although they only stayed one day (during the setup stage of the Gathering), they experienced the Gathering as participants and witnessed it as a twenty-four-hour system. They pitched a tent in the pouring rain, ate Rainbow food, and presumably used Rainbow latrines. They listened to music huddled under tarps with Rainbow Family members. They spent their day exploring the various camps. They made friends, interviewed people, and jotted down observations. Four days later, on June 24, 1990, the *News-Tribune* published a collection of five articles by Gravelle and Stanich. They quoted Forest Service spokesperson Bob Burton three times about how the Rainbow Family cleaned up sites in the past and how he expected the Gathering to be a good experience for both the Rainbow Family and the Forest Service. Except for Burton and one friendly minister, all of the quotes in the articles were from Rainbow Family members. Gravelle and Stanich verified Family members' descriptions of the Gathering with their own firsthand observations.

While the *New York Times* published official accounts of overflowing latrines and cliché descriptions of people's clothes, Gravelle and Stanich write: "Water drips from the motionless maples, cedars and birches, hitting the thick undergrowth and fallen, mossy logs with a spatting that echoes loudly in the deep silence. Ahead, beyond where the path cuts into the thick woods, you might hear a voice from a campsite too far off to see. Eventually, you glimpse the smoke or sniff the potatoes baking in a kitchen ahead."

Part of the success they had in conveying the feelings of the Gathering to readers throughout northern Minnesota lay in their willingness to try to glean individual moments from the Gathering, recreating them in print.

> True Story stands in a shaft of morning sunlight, singing his heart out to the sky, accompanying himself capably on a guitar. He's in tune musically, and he's also moving harmoniously in other ways, says his wife of three weeks, Colleen.
>
> Watching him affectionately, Colleen explains: True Story was a prisoner of war in Vietnam.

Another paragraph describes their ride in: "The pickup is packed with rain-soaked travelers and as it passes a bicyclist on the road, everyone yells: 'Weeeee loooooove yooooou.' The man returns the greeting before disappearing over the hill."

Seemingly, their most difficult task was defining the Rainbow Family. This was the only instance in the five articles of their using the word "hippie" outside of a quote: "The Rainbow Family is an unorganized group of individuals and movements linked in what its members call a tribal community. This mix of middle-aged hippies, people successful in the mainstream world, young New Agers, drop-outs, off-beat religious types, Deadheads—fans of the Grateful Dead rock band—and homeless people share material goods and a philosophy of tolerance, respect and the need for balance in the natural and spiritual worlds." Overall, the *News-Tribune's* reporting stood in sharp contrast to the national media's. Reporters used "hippie" in only a handful of instances in the forty-two pieces printed. These uses were primarily early on in the reporting, before many Rainbow Family members had arrived in the area.

This difference in reporting reflects the fact that, in general, the tenor of the press coverage is directly related to the amount of contact reporters and editors have with Rainbow Family members. Those with little contact are more likely to be condescending. The national press usually expends little effort on what it regards as fluff pieces and therefore leaves negative stereotypes unchallenged. On the local level, where the Rainbow Gathering is a major story, additional coverage often exonerates the Family from the negative preconceptions held by many outsiders.

The Minnesota papers did not have a monopoly on fair and open reporting of Rainbow events. Many small community newspapers transcended their fears about the Family as reporters gained familiarity with Rainbows. The newspapers in the area surrounding the Allegheny National Forest in conservative northeastern Pennsylvania and the "Southern" Tier of Western New York exemplify such coverage.

Forest Service officials from the Allegheny National Forest took a decidedly hands-off approach to the media. While available for comment when journalists sought them out,[6] Allegheny officials did not try to shape media coverage. The Allegheny National Forest's "Operating Procedures" for the 1986 Gathering stated that the "F.S. will not make arrangements for, or accompany news media." As a result, local coverage of the 1986 Gathering was mostly fair and accurate. The *Ridgeway Record* put the Gathering into terms familiar to local readers: "That spirit of volunteerism appears to be how the entire affair is carried off, with a central core of individuals—again volunteers—acting as 'council' to make a site decision and then again to run the day-to-day affairs of the Gathering" (Bishop 1986).

The *Forest Press,* of Tionesta, Pennsylvania, headlined an article about the upcoming Gathering, "Peace, Healing Rainbow Theme" (1986). The *Warren Times Observer* used the friendly headline "Everyone Belongs" (Morrison 1986). Headlines in the *Valley Voice,* of Sheffield, Pennsylvania, included "A Place For All Who Come: A Concern For The Earth; A Job For All Who Will Work; A Home In The Wilderness," and "Peace, Justice and Love" for a photo series they presented (July 4, 1986). Even the *Philadelphia Inquirer* used sympathetic headlines: "A Communal Gathering; Over the 4th, Harmony in a Pa. Forest" (Naedele 1986).

Having experienced a North American Gathering on their turf in 1986, the local press was familiar with the Rainbow Family when in 1988 they learned that a regional Gathering would be held on the site of the 1986 Gathering. Tom Curtin, a writer for the *Valley Voice* of Sheffield, started his article by writing, "They're back! The Rainbow People have returned to the scene of a former encampment, something they rarely ever do" (1988). This was not a cause for alarm, however, but a source of pride. He continued: "Many members of this loosely defined group traveled great distances from other regions to return to the lovely wooded campsite they remembered along gently shimmering Queen Creek." Contrasting the poor treatment the Rainbows received during the previous month in Texas, Curtin wrote proudly, "[Rainbows] had nothing but praise for U.S. Forest officials at the Allegheny National Forest with whom they feel they have excellent relations. This combined with the desirability of the campsite as well as the friendliness of the local people allegedly brought them back to this area" (1988).

Telling his readers about the upcoming Gathering, the managing editor of the *Olean Times Herald* reminisced about the 1986 Gathering when Rainbows passing through Olean, New York, were the butts of "uncomplimentary comments from people who should have known better" (Heimel 1988). He added: "These 'Rainbow People' seem pretty harmless to me. I have a lot more respect for a person who can draw his fulfillment from Mother Nature and communion with other human beings than I do for somebody who parks his carcass in an easy chair every night, absorbing video rays designed to control how he thinks and what he buys." These excerpts from the Pennsylvania and Minnesota press mirror a historical trend where small local independent media organs have traditionally been more open and accepting of utopian communities than their big city counterparts.

Over the years, however, even a few major market papers on occasion produced accurate well-researched reports on the Rainbow Family. In 1992, for instance, Matthew Gilbert, a reporter with the *Boston Globe* broke from tradition and camped with the Rainbows in Colorado. Like his Minnesota colleagues, Gilbert's descriptions were vivid, conveying the essence of the Gathering: "Late into the night, and through to morning, I could hear drumming in my tent, literally blowing to me on the wind, coming and going like waves. Sometimes laughter would blow in on top of the drumming, crazy laughs and hoots that were frightening and ecstatic. Early on, my fears of sleeplessness vanished, as the drumming and laughing seeped into my dreams, and my sleep washed back and forth with the waves of sound" (Gilbert 1992). Gilbert's writing, however, did not exemplify the type of reporting elements within the Forest Service wanted to see.

Official Sources

Media distortion of the Rainbow Family stems in part from overreliance on government spokespersons. This problem plagues not only coverage of Rainbow Gatherings but mass media coverage in general. A study of 2,850 articles printed in the United States' two newspapers of record, the *New York Times* and the *Washington Post*, for example, found that 78 percent of those articles relied primarily on official utterings (Parenti 1986, 51). The "objectivity" most mainstream American journalists adhere to involves an acceptance of "neutral" official voices (Bagdikian 1983, 182). Much of UPI's reporting of Rainbow activities, for example, relies on information not from Gathering participants but from law enforcement officials unfamiliar with the Family.

Time constraints make reporters inclined to use familiar accessible sources; this usually means a call to the local police or government agency with jurisdiction over the geographic area of the Gathering. Often the main sources cited for quick one-line summations of Rainbow culture are rural law enforcement officials who have only recently heard of Rainbow Gatherings, and whose sole contact with the Family is through law enforcement details assigned to the perimeter of the Gathering. Documents released by the United States National Forest Service in accordance with the Freedom of Information Act (F.O.I.A.) document the multitude of press contacts over the years with the Forest Service to obtain information about the Rainbow Family. This type of reporting circumvents the only people who can provide a firsthand understanding of the subject.

The most comprehensive UPI article of the twenty-four I analyzed for this chapter relied on Forest Service and police spokespeople for about 80 percent of its material. Twelve of the quotes in this June 30, 1987, piece were from officials; three were from Rainbows. A July 4, 1984, UPI article stated: "While there have been a few minor arrests and a few complaints of police harassment in the parking lot, both sides have agreed that the Gathering has been a peaceful one." The phrase "both sides" fosters the impression that the Rainbow Family is in conflict with the authorities. Ironically, after introducing this phrase, the reporters proceeded to quote official sources six times, never referring to any Rainbow sources. Another UPI article, dated July 6, 1985, which quoted only an official source, provided one of the more comical media descriptions of the Rainbow Family to date: "The Rainbows are a loose-knit group of latter day flower children, who believe in communing with nature either naked or with the use of marijuana."

Many officials focus primarily on "problems." The "Incident Command" model used to "manage" Rainbow Gatherings in National Forests, for example, follows the model used to coordinate fire fighting. Some officials view Rainbows, like wildfires, as problems that they hope will die down without a major impact. This view rates Gatherings not for their positive value, but simply on how problematic they are. If an event is free of mishaps, as was the 1988 Regional Gathering in Pennsylvania, then it is, in the words of the official source for the *Buffalo News,* a forest ranger, "uneventful" (Madore, 1988a). Within a week, the *Buffalo News* fully absorbed the official version of what constituted eventfulness, reporting, "A week long Gathering of about 700 hippies in the Allegheny National Forest has been relatively uneventful, with only a couple of arrests for possession of drugs and none for public nudity" (Madore 1988b). They contrasted the Allegheny Gathering with a more "eventful" one in 1980, when "two Rainbow women were murdered during a West Virginia encampment" (Madore 1988a).

The meaning and events of the Gatherings become obscure, as journalists conform them to the crime/mayhem model of reporting. The women, incidentally, were not murdered *at* the West Virginia Gathering, but while hitchhiking en route (Mullins 1980; Monongahela National Forest 1980). Had the *Buffalo News* reporters been able to escape their reliance on official sources and their fixation with dividing the world into criminals and victims, they might have recalled the West Virginia Rainbow Gathering, not for the murders that *didn't* happen there, but perhaps for the day the Rainbows danced and played fiddle with the good folks of Richwood, West Virginia.

Relying on official sources, news media publish such nondescriptive descriptions of the Rainbow Family as that of Modoc County (California) sheriff Ray Sweet, whom UPI quoted as saying, "They're of all ages, sizes and shapes and a lot of them have children with them" (UPI July 2, 1984). As useless as this description seems, it is the only accurate description of Rainbow people in the UPI article. According to the article, "The ages of the hippies range from the late 30's to the early 40's," quite a narrow range for a group of 25,000. The reporters did, however, note an exception: "But one, who calls himself Hairy Man, claims to be 60" (UPI July 2, 1984). The *Los Angeles Times* offered a more accurate description of the previous year's North American Gathering, when on July 10, 1983, they described participants as ranging in age from "infancy to elderly."

Government Media Management

The following words are from the Forest Service's 1990 Chief Incident Information Officer's description of the Rainbow Family.

> Although they do nothing substantive other than gather, Rainbow family Gatherings are media events that are covered by newspapers with the stature of the Los Angeles Times and the Philadelphia Inquirer. They will also receive significant local newspaper and television coverage and perhaps even warrant a T.V. network spot. Some feel that a concerted effort should be made to have a Gathering reported from the viewpoint of the Forest Service. The Rainbows, in contrast, would like to have events reported so that they are shown in a positive light. In either case efforts are probably viewed by the media as attempts to manage the news, something that is not well received. A better approach would be to set up a media information center, provide assistance when requested and offer to accompany reporters on their visits to the site. This approach would, in all probability, yield well balanced coverage. (Burton, United States Forest Service 1990)

This report serves as a reference for the Forest Service in general. Its views, while progressive by Forest Service standards, assume that showing the Family in a positive light would somehow undercut the Forest Service. The official goal remains for the media to denigrate the Rainbow Family.

The narrator of the Forest Service video presentation of the 1987 North Carolina Gathering, supposedly a training film, alludes to attempts to manage and manipulate information, stating, "We brought the media in very quickly for the event. That is, we made several contacts initially, took the media folks on the ground to explain to them what was going on and give them details. We thought we were very successful in working with the media for this event."

To illustrate this "success," the video shows a number of newspaper headlines:

"Ousted Rainbow Family Member says Gatherings No Longer Peaceful," "Nude Woman Runs Amok," "Forest Service Ranger Hurt," "Officials Try to Stop Forest Gathering as Counterculture Group Blocks Road," "Two Rainbow Members Arrested," "Rainbows Say They Blocked Forest Road to Halt 'Armed Posse,'" "Rainbows File Complaint Against Police State," and "Rainbow Tribe Sent Packing." While the Forest Service has no overt national media policy regarding the Rainbow Family, local districts supervising the individual forests that host the Gatherings do. These policies vary greatly from forest to forest, as do the overall "management" plans the forest managers devise for the Gatherings.

Forest Service officials in California, for example, took steps to block publication of a news article (Modoc N.F. 1984). The forest supervisor also issued a "media direction" [sic] which suggested to reporters that they not report about certain aspects of the Gathering, such as "Gathering activities" or the use of "Forest Service agents" (Modoc N.F., 1984). Minnesota rangers opened a media center as a part of their Incident Command Center, to meet the media's preference for readily accessible official accounts. In contrast to his California counterpart, the Information Officer informed reporters, however, that the local Forest Service had decided to cooperate with the Rainbow Family. While providing the schedule and phone number for the Forest Service's media center, he wrote, "The Rainbow Family also has an information tent, which is located in the main Gathering area. Media personnel are encouraged to stop there. The Rainbows will be happy to provide you with a personal tour and general information" (Superior N.F. June 22, 1990). The resulting coverage, according to the Forest Service "situation report," was "factual and accurate" (Superior N.F. June 28, 1990).

Not everybody at the Forest Service, however, was happy with "factual and accurate" coverage. On June 30, 1990, in a "coordinating meeting," local Forest Service personnel voiced concerns that "info. for reporters coming from Rainbows" led to "sensationalistic reports." They suggested that the media work instead with local resort owners to get the "true story" (Superior N.F. June 30, 1990). One ranger, in her critique of the Gathering, appeared to feel slighted by the media, complaining, "I would take a more pro-active approach with the media. They only got the Rainbow story. It seemed like a good time to plug ICS (Incident Command System) operations and the teamwork involved. Our side of the story didn't get told" (Bergerson 1990). Apparently reporters preferred the colorful hoopla of the Gathering to Forest Service bureaucrats sitting in a motel.[7]

Some Forest Service officials want the media to ignore the Rainbows all together. A Nevada Forest Service report on the 1989 Gathering in the Humboldt National Forest suggested: "In some cases the lack of media coverage can be a benefit to the management of the Gathering" (Humboldt N.F. 1989). Still one official disagreed: "How can we keep it from the press? And is it potentially more damaging not to give them the facts from the F.S. point of view before the issues are clouded by the lies of the Rainbows? Also, we must remember that the media will sensationalize when they don't have access to the Official spokes person or persons at an incident" (Humboldt N.F. 1989). The preemptive information strike suggested by this official would be much like Sheriff Lyght's campaign the following year. In fact, the most sensationalistic reporting usually appears early on in the cycle of a Gathering, when the press has access *only* to "official" sources.

During the 1988 Rainbow Gathering in Texas, the Forest Service, in cooperation with U.S. Customs, the U.S. Marshall's Office and the local sheriff's office, staged what they referred to as a "media event" for the press (US NFS Texas June 21, 1988). To highlight a supposed Rainbow "drug" threat, officials treated the assembled press corps to a display of trained drug interdiction dogs sniffing Rainbow vehicles, whose annoyed owners were forced to stop for the show. So orchestrated was the media coordination at the Texas Gathering that Forest Service policy makers forbade ordinary Rangers to talk with reporters (US NFS Texas July 4, 1988). Rangers were ordered to refer media representatives to a Public Affairs Officer (PAO).

The use of PAOs to "coordinate" media is not limited to the National Forest Service. The National Park Service, planning for a 1990 regional Gathering at the Big South Fork National River and Recreation Area (NRRA), decided to assign a PAO to the "incident" when the Rainbow population reached two hundred people (Big South Fork NRRA 1990). The PAO would, incidentally, be accompanied by twenty-four Rangers, three narcotics agents, and nineteen other officials.

This highly structured organization proved self-defeating at the 1988 Gathering. When PAOs were not present, obediently gagged rangers stood helplessly by as talkative Rainbows chatted with reporters. In one instance forest rangers explained to a television news crew that to talk to somebody from the Forest Service they would have to do it by telephone. The reporters then turned to an available Rainbow for comment (US NFS Texas June 21, 1988).

In time, the Rainbows broke through governmental news management and reached the people of East Texas. David Nather, a *Dallas Morning News* reporter, sampled local thoughts:

> "You know all the bad publicity that preceded it, and it was nothing like that at all," said Rachel Creamer, owner of the R&R Quick Stop convenience store on highway 69 in Zavalla, where Rainbow Family members came throughout the weekend to buy groceries and use the pay telephone.
>
> "They were real nice. They were from all different places. Some of them were a blast to talk to."
>
> "They were just a bunch of people camping out and all," added Jack Bates, who lives in a retirement community at nearby Caney Creek. "They never did give anyone no problem out there."
>
> Law enforcement officials said the Gathering wasn't the drug-crazed, destructive orgy they had expected, but added that it wasn't something they would have attended on their own. (Nather 1988)

Drug-Crazed Media

Fanned by official propaganda, people expect Rainbow Gatherings to be "drug-crazed." *Newsweek,* for example, alleges "every drug but heroin has *reportedly* been used at Gatherings" (Baker and Drew, 1988 [emphasis mine]). *Newsweek* does not mention, however, who was doing the "reporting."

A week before the 1987 Gathering, the Associated Press touted a story that appeared in the *Hendersonville Times-News* and other newspapers (Associated Press, 1987b) based on an article in the *Asheville Citizen* (Davis 1987), which in turn rested entirely on the testimony of an angry transient expelled from the Rainbow Seed Camp for allegedly assaulting a child. The AP piece identified the man as a "former leader of the Rainbow Family" and "the unofficial spokesman of the Rainbow Family Gathering." Their source told how the Gatherings were co-opted thirteen years earlier and were now inundated with "bad drugs, bad people" and "bad feelings":

> "The people here this week are here for the sex; they're here for the rock and roll," he said.
> Thai suspects more problems as others arrive, trade needles and engage in casual sex with people they don't know in the "boogie meadow." A field where members exchange drugs and bodies, the meadow could be a breeding ground for incurable diseases, he said.
> "It's going to be dangerous, horrible," he said.

Despite his promotion by the Associated Press, "Thai" was clearly neither a "leader" nor a spokesperson for the Rainbow Family. The AP's own article earlier in the month, appearing in the *Hendersonville Times-News* on June 3, 1987, reported that to identify the Rainbow Family's leader, a Rainbow pointed to the sun. Had "Thai" denounced the Forest Service or the State Police for their mistreatment of the Rainbow Family, the AP[8] might not have devoted an entire article to him. Touting a line editors wanted to hear, however, made him a "leader."[9]

The characters in news stories about the Rainbow Family oftentimes don't even have to be definitively associated with the Family. For the *Rocky Mountain News* and the *Denver Post,* Rainbow-literate since the nearby 1992 North American Gathering, anyone deviating from the mall-to-car path may be labeled a Rainbow, whether their actions are constructive or disruptive. The *Rocky Mountain News* referred to anti-KKK protesters as "Rainbow Family-type people" (McCullen 1995). When retail business died down in Boulder's shopping district, the *Denver Post* blamed "local punkers and visiting Rainbow Family hippies" for driving away customers by "ranting about peace and rights" (George 1994). Such free use of the Rainbow Family title further confuses already distorted press reports.

Like the AP, the Forest Service also promotes a supposed Rainbow Family connection with illegal drugs. The Forest Service video presentation of the 1987

Gathering, widely disseminated to the media, showed the Gathering's main meadow on July 4, filled with people. Smoke from campfires mixed with mist hung low over the crowd in the humid air. The voice-over commented that the low cloud is "certainly not from wood smoke but is marijuana usage there on the site." Similarly, Sheriff Lyght in Minnesota showed local politicians and press a picture of a small Rainbow encampment with a plume of smoke rising from the campfire, saying, "Notice that the smoke in the background isn't just smoke from campfires" (Nelson PAC-13 Video 1990). Lyght warned that the Rainbows would be bringing "bales" of marijuana, as well as cocaine (Nelson PAC-13 Video 1990). Of course it is understandable, after viewing the video, where Lyght's theory about "bales" of marijuana originated, since it would certainly take many bales of the weed to create the supposed marijuana smog alleged by the Forest Service video.

While some Rainbows do use illegal substances at the Gatherings, the drug-crazed phantasmagoria of the national media and some Forest Service sources is chimerical. Hard drugs, the white-powder variety usually associated with the violent drug trade, are virtually absent. Marijuana, fungi, and LSD are the drugs of choice for those seeking an artificial high. While these substances are used and shared by some Rainbows, selling them is taboo. Neither government nor media has demonstrated any more substance abuse at Rainbow Gatherings than in mainstream communities of similar size.

The greatest danger of government/media propaganda linking Rainbows with hard drugs is that it may become self-fulfilling. News stories promising a "drug party" lure people looking for one. Likewise, stories that promise an open market for buying and selling illegal drugs attract drug buyers and sellers. Thus local teenagers, expecting drugs at the Minnesota Gathering, came wearing signs reading "dose me." Such clowning disrupts an ostensibly spiritual event and gives the media and government the opportunity to link Gatherings with drug abuse.

National reporting of Rainbow Gatherings ignores their successful detoxification and drug/alcohol rehabilitation programs. In a media environment habitually producing stories of innocents going to Rainbow Gatherings and getting turned on to dangerous drugs, stories of addicted persons going to Rainbow Gatherings to get off drugs just don't fit. The "alternative media," on the other hand, does report this facet of the Gatherings.

High Times, a magazine critics often associate with illegal drug use, devoted its sixteenth-anniversary issue to articles about the Rainbow Family. Although "*High Times*" supposedly "was to drugs what *Playboy* was to sex" (Anderson 1981, 13), editor Steven Hager writes:

> After five days in paradise, I'm reluctant to leave. . . .
> There are many aspects of Rainbow that continue to impress me after I leave. I realize I went the entire time without a beer or any other drug, and didn't miss them at all. Because I was constantly being bombarded with love vibes, my consciousness was already

> altered. I was on a natural ecstasy and didn't have the urge to do
> drugs, even though they were offered free on several occasions.
> (Hager 1990, 69)

For their centerfold spread, often devoted to the "bud of the month," *High Times* used a photo of the July 4 noon circle at the North Carolina Gathering, upon which they superimposed the phrase "Natural High." Ironically, it was the same July 4, 1987, noon circle that the 1987 Forest Service video described as fogged in under a cloud of "marijuana smoke."

Hager asked a question national media overlooked: "The Rainbow Family teaches respect for Mother Earth, respect for elders, and, most important, respect for peaceful co-existence. So why is the government spending millions of dollars harassing them?" (Oct. 1990, 34). The Rainbow Family has endured, according to Hager, "18 years of media misrepresentation and government oppression," with the Family dismissed as "an embarrassing anachronism—the last of the hippies."

Journalists affiliated with the alternative press are comfortable enough as fellow travelers in the counterculture to see past clichés. Presumably most *High Times* correspondents are familiar enough with the drug culture to recognize that Rainbow Gatherings do not center on drugs (see, e.g., Anderson 1981, 174–79). Likewise, alternative press reporters such as Bill Weinberg, who as a political columnist for the New York weekly *Downtown* reported extensively on the Family, recognize the uniqueness and complexity of Rainbow politics. Unlike his mystified counterparts in the mainstream press, Weinberg had no difficulty understanding the Family. All he had to do was *listen* when they spoke.

While it is the alternative press and small local newspapers, and not the mainstream press, that provide the most accurate coverage of the Family, it is the mainstream press that the Family must cultivate to bring its message to the general population. This will be difficult, since the mainstream press, acting as a cheering squad for the status quo, has traditionally lambasted fringe social groups. "If it bleeds it leads" journalism places little value on a group of people whose main purpose is to assemble *peaceably*. In the words of the *Buffalo News* (Madore 1988b), it is an "uneventful" event. Peaceability makes for poor copy.

What makes the Gatherings "newsworthy" are the aberrations: the drunk who was arrested, the traveler who was busted, or the person who was injured. Matthew Gilbert of the *Boston Globe,* writing a rare comprehensive piece about the Family, warned how "the event [Gathering] is vulnerable to ridicule and bad press" (Gilbert 1992). He tells how "journalists have generally fashioned Rainbow stories around the accidental deaths, or the drug busts, or the muddy nudity of the flailing, dancing fanatics" (Gilbert 1992).

Such inaccurate press coverage has always dogged nonexclusive utopian communities. The Modern Times anarchist community (1851–1863), which included a few "harmless eccentrics" among its members, exemplifies such press ridicule in the nineteenth century. One historical account recalls, "These eccentrics were harmless enough in themselves—there were, for instance, a polygamist and a nudist—but journalists in search of sensational news focused their attention upon them until it seemed to the public that there could not be a normal human being in the village. . . . Such publicity brought nothing but a troublesome notoriety to the colony, which eventually sought to avoid further experiences of the same kind by changing its name" (Holloway 1951, 157).

Negative coverage transcends not only time, but geography as well. Today European Rainbow Family members are having many of the same difficulties with the media as their American counterparts. One Rainbow at the 1992 European Gathering in Poland told the press, "We don't want the television here. . . . everything I've ever read or seen about the Rainbow [Family] in the media has been lies" (Mrozowski 1992).

All groups are composed of more articulate and less articulate members. Journalists decide how they want to portray the group, then select spokespersons from the group whose mediated images will best support that predetermined portrayal. Hence, media bias is easy to detect by observing who journalists choose to anoint as "spokespersons." The Rainbow Family Council has a media policy, often mentioned but seldom followed, that evolved to combat such media manipulations. The policy suggests the use of a Media Council to provide "representative" groups of three or four spokespeople who will be interviewed together. These people, however, cannot speak for the Family. Only a Council Consensus can be attributed to the Family. Rainbows hope that using small groups for interviews will keep individual egos in check. To keep the media from creating their own Rainbow "leadership," Family members who are interviewed more than once, the policy states, should "drop back" and pass the ball to others.

This policy, however, is not adhered to. Journalists have no difficulty, given a crowd of thousands of Rainbows, in finding the caricature that best fits their story. Hence, images of local drunks sporting beer cans or Deadheads panhandling for LSD in the parking lots often wind up in the media as Rainbow Family depictions. Even hardworking Family members, enchanted by the media limelight, will drone on and on for the cameras. Without an understanding of how to speak in soundbites, however, their words are often twisted as journalists quote them out of context.

To get an accurate picture of the Rainbow Family from the mass media one would have to read, watch, and listen to many reports. It would involve a lot of reading between the lines; past the fear, confusion, hatred, or infatuation; past rhetoric, stereotypes, and propaganda. Accurate information is often available, but it is obfuscated in a sea of misinformation. The challenge for the Rainbow Family is to survive the misinformation, to demand that news reporters depict the Family accurately, and to resist becoming the Rainbow Family that the news reports attempt to create. So far they have been successful.

CLEANUP STARTS WHEN YOU ARRIVE AT THE GATHERING. Remember: if you pack it in, you're going to have to pack it out, so travel as lightly as you can. Always pick up any litter or cigarette butts you find on the trail. Separate all trash for recycling at your neighborhood Garbage Yoga Station. Tote a bag or two of garbage anytime you leave the site. At the end of ou[r] stay, please help clean up by carrying out more than you carried in. Work crews are needed to stay on the site for cleanup, to reseed the meadows, and return the land to its natural state. It is our tradition to leave the gathering site cleaner and even more beautiful than we found it.

—*Howdy Folks!* (NERF 1991)

Rural communities faced with the prospect of a Rainbow Gathering or, as the first media reports usually portray it, an "onslaught" of "hippies" "invading" their area, are understandably apprehensive. They fear bad physical, social, and economic impacts, ranging from the destruction of the forest to the possible loss of tourism revenue and the corruption of local youths. Rainbows are generally sensitive to these concerns. Since they view the Gatherings as a model for a new society, they want them to be well received by all who come in contact with them. Hence, restoring the environment, removing trash from the site, and creating and maintaining good relations with their neighbors are Rainbow priorities.

Cleanup

One reason the U.S. Forest Service has failed to legally bar Rainbow Gatherings is the Family's quarter-century-long track record for respecting the land on which they hold Gatherings.

Some Rainbows work cleanup year after year—a difficult and often thankless task. The Seed Camp (setup) crew finds rewards in watching the Gathering grow, with new faces arriving every day to appreciate their work. The cleanup crew, by contrast, is left working in a postapocalyptic environment. The Gathering site, two weeks after the official end of the Gathering, resembles my neighborhood on the East Side of Buffalo, New York, where old-timers sometimes think they still hear music and conversation from boarded-up taverns and vacant lots. Both are ghost towns, haunted by memories of better times. A key difference, however, is that while in the city buildings decay and eventually collapse, at former Rainbow encampments, animals return and flowers grow. Nature replaces the colorful celebratory decor of the Rainbow camps with a Rainbow of wildflowers, growing in to erase trails and camps as the natural environment reclaims the Gathering site.

Despite stated egalitarianism and environmentalism, the Family, like their counterparts in Babylon, leave the dirty work of cleaning up after the multitudes in the hands of a small group. A member of the Minnesota cleanup crew, while hauling trash from the site, explained how he hoped the Family will one day "evolve" and realize its ideals: "Here we are living in industrial America. We do produce this garbage, and here we are trying to figure out what to do with it. One of these years we are going to have a Gathering and everyone's going to take home what they brought, but the Gathering hasn't evolved that far yet" (Nelson 1990 Video).

The Family disseminates Rap 701 (see Appendix), the reciprocal of Rap 107 (see chapter 4). Where Rap 107 welcomes people to the Gathering and gives a crash course on Gathering etiquette, Rap 701 wishes folks "Happy Trails" and provides instructions for breaking camp.

In 1990 the Forest Service created its own "Rehabilitation Plan" for Rainbow Gatherings. The plan, which they devised to give "general guidance" to the Rainbows, is essentially the same as Rap 701 and other Rainbow Family cleanup plans dating back to the 1970s (Superior National Forest 1990).

At the 1990 Gathering, for example, Rainbows who remained on-site after July 8 automatically became part of the cleanup crew, as in other years. The July 9 Council named a tool-keeper to facilitate efficient use of tools, and a massage therapist to restore workers' energy. The Cleanup Council felt that no one should go home drained. Volunteers also formed an automobile mechanics' crew to tackle the problem of dead vehicles in the parking areas. CALM and Banking Council continued to function, as their services were needed until the last of the cleanup crew left. The Minnesota cleanup impressed Paul Flood, the Forest Service liaison to the cleanup crew, who in mid-July reported: "All the garbage is really out of the woods. . . . We're down to one kitchen. All the other kitchens have been torn down, the rock rings dispersed, the compost pits and latrines have all been filled up. So the facilities that have been set up here are looking great, quite good, returning the land back to normal. . . . It looks pretty clean for all intents and purposes" (Nelson 1990 Video).

Although the Minnesota cleanup crew followed both Forest Service and Rap 701 guidelines, bears returned to the site in force and dug up compost from many major kitchens. According to Tofte District Ranger Larry Dawson, they spread food, cans, and broken glass, a mess that included items that were not supposed to be buried in the first place (Perich 1990d). By November, trash was beginning to cover the site of the June-July Gathering, heavily visited by hunters and local post-Rainbow curiosity seekers. Rangers also found a Rainbow latrine cover near the former "A-Camp" and an uncovered latrine at the former campsite of the "Gate Crew."

The focalizers' network reproduced and distributed a story about the trash, written in the local Grand Marais, Minnesota newspaper (Perich 1990d). Regional Councils around the United States decided not to contest responsibility for the garbage but instead to publicize the situation in Rainbow circles and organize a final cleanup: "I can't tell how true this article is, but whatever the problem is, the solution is to get together and work it out as a Family. Please Council about it and Take action. I am doing the same. Hopefully, we have not disrespected the Earth, or the People of the area, or the Spirit of Our Gathering. If we have, we must set it right" (Thumper Dec. 5., 90). Minnesota Rainbows called an on-site Council for May of 1991 to facilitate the completion of cleanup after the spring thaw. Family members said they would continue to clean up the site, embarrassed that the folks in Minnesota weren't as pleased as Lloyd Swager, for example, a Forest Service district ranger, who, describing the cleanup after the 1976 North American Gathering in Montana, said: "It's still amazing to me. We searched that area with a fine tooth comb, including the parking lot and we couldn't come up with anything. Not even a scrap of paper" (*Great Falls Tribune* 1976).

The Forest Service and local reporters recognize that the Rainbow Family often leaves the sites of the massive Gatherings in better shape than they found them. The *Tygart Valley Press* of Elkins, West Virginia, described cleanup after the 1980 North American Gathering: "Refuse from the Gathering was carefully collected at several stations, separate containers being used for compostable garbage (which was later buried), recyclable metal, glass, and burnables. The metal and glass were carried out to be recycled, although much of it did not come from the Rainbow Gathering, but had been left by previous campers. The Rainbow Family will leave the campsite much cleaner than they found it" (Teter 1980). Similarly, the Environmental Analysis Report for the 1978 North American Rainbow Gathering in Oregon noted: "It is likely that some of the rehabilitation work planned in terms of grass seeding and de-compaction will improve portions of the area within the Big Camas parking area that have been previously overused" (Umpqua National Forest 1978, 7).

Bruce Platt of the Mark Twain National Forest in Missouri, host of the 1985 North American Gathering, said, "It looks better, quite frankly, than it did when they arrived"[1] (Bishop 1985). Lake County (Minnesota) undersheriff Harold Paulseth admitted to a local community meeting that Rainbows leave the forest in better shape than the Boy Scouts (*Duluth News Tribune* 1990c). After the 1984 North American Gathering in California, the local press reported Rainbows were removing trash dating back to the 1950s (Holloway 1984; Toussaint 1984). At times Forest Service officials learned new techniques by observing Rainbow Family cleanup. Forest Service wildlife biologist Gertsch said, "Family members taught the Forest Service a new trick, burying 'willow waddles' [wattles] in wet areas of the meadow." Gertsch explained, "The bundles of willow branches soaked in water would sprout, providing vegetation to stabilize the soil" (Hallinan 1978).

Writing about the 1986 Gathering, a local journalist stressed the positive impact of the Gathering, claiming Rainbows left "only footsteps & money." The article quoted forest ranger James Schuler as stating that the Rainbow Family members "are the most environmental[ly] conscious people I have ever dealt with" (Clever 1986b). The same article cited a local game officer and a deputy sheriff as "very much impressed by the neatness of the entire area," noting "that cigarette smokers stripped their butts of paper and filter for proper disposal before recycling the remaining tobacco to the ground."

Their experiences in 1986 made Allegheny rangers confident about the Rainbow Family's ability to care for the land. When a regional Gathering was held on the same tract of land in 1988, the Supervisor of the Allegheny National Forest wrote:

> Our experience with the Rainbow people during their Gathering on the Allegheny National Forest in 1986 demonstrated to us that they do care for the land. In 1986 they faithfully carried out all stipulations to protect the environment as listed in the operating plan that had been agreed to by both parties. No significant or adverse environmental damage occurred to the Gathering site.
>
> I personally visited the site two weeks ago and found it to be in very good condition. Based upon my discussions with the Rainbow leadership, I anticipate the same level of cooperation at this year's Gathering. (Wright 1988a)

Capitalizing on the Rainbow Family's love for the land, budget-conscious Allegheny rangers engaged Family members as volunteers in a tree-planting program on the Gathering site. The Allegheny National Forest's report on the 1988 Regional Gathering noted:

> During the middle of the week, the tree planting project was begun with Family members. The District had obtained 300 Chi-

nese Chestnut seedlings and fence material. The trees and fence were delivered to the trailhead where they were brought down to the site by Family members. Over the next few days, all 300 seedlings were planted and fenced throughout the Gathering area, along the Queen Creek valley, and along the FR 552 parking area. . . .

For many Family members, this was their first opportunity to perform work on a National Forest. These people were assisted by several Family members who had planted trees professionally on F.S. contracts. The quality of the work was very high and the care taken with the trees was exceptional. In general, this proved to be a very enjoyable experience for the Family members who participated and a unique way of accomplishing beneficial wildlife habitat work for the District. (Colaninno and Dunshie Sept. 1988)

Such projects give Rainbows a way to return a gift to the local areas hosting the Gatherings. Similar cooperative projects have taken place at NERF Gatherings in Vermont and New York in 1988, 1989, 1990, and 1995, where local forest officials have approached the Rainbow Family in an atmosphere of respect and cooperation.

The situation in North Carolina at the 1987 North American Gathering, by contrast, was anything but cooperative. Since this was the only Rainbow Gathering where cleanup and rehabilitation were never completed, it deserves mention. The failure to fully restore the site resulted from state and federal government harassment of the cleanup crew. This puzzling behavior, it turned out, was part of an attempt to prevent the Texas Gathering in 1988, by provoking a poor cleanup in 1987 (see chapter 10).

In 1990 Cook County (Minnesota) sheriff John Lyght showed the Forest Service video of the refuse left in North Carolina as part of a Rainbow background briefing he presented to local elected officials (Nelson 1990 video). Lyght was so upset by what he saw in the video that, in a letter to U.S. Representative James Oberstar, he suggested calling in "the Marines" to help his department during the Gathering. The letter also accused the Rainbow Family of leaving open latrines and hundreds of pounds of garbage at the previous year's Nevada Gathering site (Lyght 1990). Roderick Howard, the district ranger in Nevada, however, contradicted Lyght, reporting in a memo that the cleanup of the area was "excellent" (July 27, 1989).

Lyght's letter and the Forest Service's legal efforts to thwart the 1988 Gathering emphasize to Rainbows the tactical importance of their long-standing tradition of leaving the land better than they found it. Rainbows, however, clean up and rehabilitate the land out of respect for the earth, which for them, is stronger than their respect for the laws of governments.

Even the dilemma of holding a Gathering in a dump did not deter Rainbow Family cleanup efforts. Rainbows at the 1990 Quebec Gathering consensed to use scarce

Magic Hat funds to contract with a local construction company to haul a massive dumpster to the site. The prospect that the wastes, some of which were hazardous,[2] would only be hauled off to a similar site to be dumped once again, didn't deter Quebecois Rainbows from their project.

During Gatherings, Rainbows usually bring their garbage to recycling centers known as "neighborhood garbage Yoga stations" set up at major kitchens and camps. The stations, originally established in the 1970s by Swami Mommy, the Rainbow garbage guru, divide garbage into seven "Chakras": Free; Lost 'n' Found; Plastic; Compost; Paper; Paper; Glass; and Metal (Swami Mommy n.d.). Rainbows not only bring their garbage to these centers, but mine them for resources as needed during the Gathering. An old soup can, for instance, can become a cup. With a hole poked near the top, it can be conveniently tied to a belt loop. An old coffee can with a plastic lid is ideal for keeping toilet paper dry.

Rainbows burn all paper that is not reused or conveniently recycled. They bury the compost. Swami Mommy suggests urinating on compost pits as the nitrogen helps break the compost down to rich soil. People remove other materials from the site as they leave, with the remainder being removed at the end of the Gathering by the Cleanup Crew. The Cleanup Crew brings nonrecyclable trash to local dumps, where the Magic Hat pays dump fees. They bring recyclables to recycling centers when such facilities exist within a reasonable distance; otherwise recyclables are also taken to dumps. There have been some instances, however, when the cleanup crew incinerated all garbage on-site, sending up plumes of black smoke, when the Magic Hat lacked funds for trash removal.

Community Relations

Many people who pitch in and participate at Gatherings are from the local rural communities near where Gatherings occur. Rainbow Family relations with these communities often start out shaky but end well. The 1984 North American Gathering, held in Modoc County, California, exemplifies a large Gathering's impact on a small rural community. The Forest Service estimated peak attendance at twenty-three thousand people (Lee 1984); Family members thought that, all told, from twenty-five to thirty thousand people attended. The closest town, Likely, by contrast, comprised only a handful of buildings. The total population of Modoc County was only about nine thousand.

Modoc County locals feared the worst, expecting "hippies" to overrun the local social services office and bankrupt the county with requests for public assistance. The Rainbow Family is sensitive to the concern that the influx of a large service population can severely strain the resources of a small community. Its policy has always been to spread the word among Family members not to apply for assistance of any sort in the area of the Gathering. At the 1984 Gathering, Rainbows gave form letters to the department of social services, directing any Family members who might wander that way over to the Gathering, where they would receive food and shelter (*Modoc County Record* 1984). Magic Hat money, typically five dollars per hitchhiker and twenty dollars per car, often finances the departure of destitute stragglers at the end of cleanup, assuring that they can leave the community and not stay as a burden.

Local business people in Modoc County, surveyed by the Forest Service after the Gathering, were generally pleased with the Rainbows (Lee 1984):

> Jerry's Restaurant—Volume of business definitely increased. According to Johnson [manager], "Our restaurant made good money while the Rainbows were here. . . . All three shifts were up." Johnson said the Rainbows were well mannered, well educated, very patient, and good tippers. . . . Johnson felt it was a unique experience for community through exposure to a different culture.
>
> Beacon Coffee Shop— . . . "They were nice, well-behaved and good tippers[.]" The restaurant had no regular customer complaint about their presence.
>
> Texaco [station]—Hunter [attendant] felt the station had little problem with the Rainbows, they were generally nice people. Early-on they used the restrooms to bathe, and the station was "constantly cleaning" them. The Rainbows, commonly dubbed the "Dumpster Divers," raided the garbage bins located on the premises which was objectionable to his patrons and the local community. The station chose to lock the garbage bins, and post "Customer Use Only" signs on the restroom doors. Rainbows honored the signs.
>
> Presty's Market—Presty said, "If I knew for sure where the Rainbows were meeting next year, I'd buy a store there." Sales were up. Presty did catch a couple of people shoplifting but he felt that should be expected considering the increased number of people in the community. Rainbows didn't buy foods in bulk but purchased lots of fruits, vegetables, canned rolling tobacco, and Snickers. (Lee 1984)

Rainbows volunteered to wait tables at the Most Likely Cafe in Likely, easing the workload on overburdened waitresses. One Rainbow sister stayed after the Gathering, having landed a job as waitress there (Modoc National Forest 1984).

The aftermath of the next year's North American Gathering in Missouri was similar.

> Some businessmen in Viburnum, the nearest town to the [Rainbow] encampment, reported the Rainbow People provided a

needed "shot in the arm" for the local economy at a time when lay-offs were taking place in the local mining industry.

One store owner told the newspaper that he logged $35,000 to $40,000 in additional sales during the one month the Rainbow People were in camp. A grocery store owner said there had been some shoplifting in his store, but a representative of the Rainbow People gave him a check to cover most of his losses. (Hayes 1986)

The 1990 Gathering again gave local businesses an economic boost. Businesspeople initially feared that the bad press the Gathering was receiving would frighten away tourists and cut into the hotel business (Latz interview 1990). However, both Rainbows and Forest Service officials assigned to the Gathering rented hotel rooms, thus compensating for any lost business. Retailers praised the Rainbows:

"I hate to sound like the Rainbow Chamber of Commerce, but they really have been great," [store owner] Barb Puch said. "We haven't had any problems." . . .

Many tourists stop and pick lilacs at a large bush outside the store's window, almost never asking for permission, the Puchs said. Dozens of Rainbows have stopped for a flower, and all have asked permission. One Rainbow who bought gas [even] asked permission to empty the water from his cooler onto the store's front lawn. (Myers 1990e)

Across the Road at the Clearview General Store, owner Jeff Latz shut off his spigot, fearing Rainbows would run his well dry. Things got hectic around his store, as Rainbow traffic doubled his business. Jeff felt it was a good experience, but not one he'd like to repeat again soon. He did say he'd like to attend a Gathering, however, if one was held in the area, this time as a participant, not a merchant (Latz interview 1990).

Communities not only in the United States but also in Europe have discovered the economic benefits of hosting a Rainbow Gathering. According to the *Irish Times,* the 1993 European Gathering in Ireland "has amazed and intrigued the local community, who have heaped praise on the [G]athering which has brought much needed business to the area." In Ireland, local officials hoped to use the Gathering as a magnet for developing tourism (O'Halloran 1993).

Gatherings expose otherwise isolated populations to diverse lifestyles, offering a crash course in cultural pluralism, anarchy, and a congeries of alternative lifestyles and spiritual beliefs. Terms like "Dumpster Diving," "Faerie Camp," and "Shanti Sena" become household words. Even so, the media and the talk in the local diners and convenience stores always seem to focus on nudity.

New Cultures—Naked People

Sheriff John Lyght was particularly disturbed by the nudity at the 1990 North American Gathering, complaining: "We all got bodies. We all got certain parts of our bodies. *Keep 'em covered!* I got into a discussion with a lady down there [at the Gathering] the other day. She said it's normal for women to walk around topless and for men to walk around with nothing. It's not normal. I'm sixty-two years old and I wasn't brought up that way" (Lyght interview July 11, 1990).

Rainbow Family members, however, don't find nudity offensive. One Rainbow explained to a reporter:

> The nakedness that's going on up there [at the Gathering site] is very, innocent. People are holding hands and walking through pastures and putting their feet in the water and laughing and playing zithers! It looks more like Heaven! You want to see some nasty nakedness, you go to your local super-market and you pick up one of those magazines. . . . What's going on up on the mountain is a very different kind of nakedness—it's an appreciation for the feel of sunlight, or being able to skinny-dip! And I'll tell you, I don't think there's a single cop or judge or housewife in rural America that hasn't gone skinny-dipping at one time or another! (Weinberg 1989b)

Doug Irwin, the supervisor of Limestone Township (Tidioute, Pennsylvania), visited the 1986 North American Gathering in Pennsylvania with his son. Irwin quickly felt at home among the naked Rainbows: Irwin "commented that it would have taken very little to 'be one of them' as far as nudity was concerned, and he said he doubted that he would have been embarrassed had he gone nude. He indicated he would be very much interested in learning where the 1987 gathering will be, so he can plan to spend his vacation there with his family" (Clever 1986b).

Locals, regardless of their stance on nudity, study the situation keenly. They often ring swimming holes at Gatherings in various states of dress or undress, with an occasional beer, cans of soda pop, or cameras in hand. Eventually, many relax. Don Teter, a reporter for the *Tygart Valley Press* in West Virginia, writes:

> And what did your intrepid reporter do when faced with the spectacle of several hundred skinny-dippers? Why, the only sensible thing. I stripped down and joined them, and I still have the sun burned rear to prove it. The swimming hole was also one of the most popular spots for visits by curious locals, who stood around on the shores in small groups, giggling and making little jokes among themselves, or taking pictures for posterity. The Rainbow people

generally went about their business as if they weren't being watched by a captive audience, which only non-pluses the spectators more. The fact that was obvious to all of us naked people was that the only ones who looked silly were those standing around with their clothes on. (1980)

Like many Gatherings over the years, the 1980 North American Gathering in West Virginia began as a tense and hostile situation. The local community expressed strong anti-Rainbow sentiments. Those views changed, however, once the local folks actually met the Rainbows. Water Singing on the Rocks, a CALM. volunteer, recalled a town meeting that began in hostility, but ended with Rainbows and locals joining hands in a large circle (Water interview 1990). The *New York Times* reported: "More than 100 local residents turned out . . . in Richwood, to see a Rainbow Family slide show, which was followed by questions and answers. While some were a little stunned by such Rainbow exotica as a young man who introduced himself as 'Water Singing on the Rocks,' the meeting ended with Rainbows and Richwood residents alike joining hands and singing the old hymn "Will the Circle Be Unbroken?" (July 7, 1980).

The year 1980 also saw a tragic event in Rainbow history. Two Rainbow sisters hitchhiking to the Gathering were murdered. Their bodies, which had been neither robbed nor sexually molested, were dumped near the Seed Camp site. It was an execution: "When this horrible act against us occurred, the local people came out. They said, 'We love you, we are not those people.' On the 4th [of July], 8,000 Rainbows, and about an equal number of local citizen Rainbows came together. . . . Generations meeting generations. Interface. It's one of the truths of this Gathering; that we interface with local citizens here, in a way that the people in Washington, D.C., the people who are glued to their T.V. sets in suburban America, have no idea" (Hipstory July 3, 1990).

In 1988, East Texas locals showed the Rainbows some Texas hospitality, sympathizing with them after seeing how the Rainbows were being systematically harassed by the federal government. Dozens of Texans risked having their boats confiscated in order to ferry supplies and people around a Forest Service roadblock. Many of those locals eventually became Rainbows: "They come back again and again and they gather with us. . . . You can tell that they're different because they're here with their short hair and their, you know their, their Texas style of dress, and their accent. They're now with us. Different color of the Rainbow, distinctly different color, but they're here. And they love us" (Harmony interview 1990).

Like the Texans who comprised the "Rainbow Navy," rural neighbors have, at different junctures in history, come out in support of their utopian neighbors. In 1850, for instance, Illinois's Bishop Hill community was protected from an angry mob from Chicago by neighbors who respected them for their industrious work ethic (Holloway 1951, 166). In another example, central New York's Oneida community was defended by neighbors who signed testimonies as character witnesses for the Oneidans when the community was assailed in court for its practice of group marriage.

What makes the Rainbow case unique is the short time the nomadic Family has to get acquainted with its neighbors. While Bishop Hill and Oneida cultivated a relationship with their defenders over years, the Rainbow Family shared only three weeks of history with their Texan supporters. Likewise, within weeks, Minnesotans considered their bizarre guests as kin. A Grand Marais, Minnesota, gas station attendant, for example, gave local residents a four-cent-per-gallon discount on gas prices seasonally inflated for tourists. Rainbows, without asking, automatically got the local price. The attendant explained that since Rainbows weren't "tourists," she viewed them, at least at her gas station, as locals. Many Rainbows spend over a month at the Gathering, setting it up and then cleaning up afterwards. During that period they make regular trips into nearby towns, buying supplies, visiting restaurants, and so on. These Rainbows, who become regular fixtures in town, see a side of the community and meet a cross-section of residents that casual travelers seldom do. Rainbows participate in town meetings, negotiate with local government agencies, and make wholesale purchases from local businesses. It is hard to learn more about a community without actually living in it. The education goes both ways: Rainbows bring alien culture to the American heartland, but they learn something from each area they visit.

Conservative Values

The strong support the Rainbow Family has found in traditionally conservative enclaves of rural America reflects a shared set of values about hard work, independence, self-sufficiency, and elemental freedom. These values transcend glaring surface differences. Many rural Americans, already alienated from the consumerist commuter lifestyle of the suburbs, appreciate the personal freedom Rainbows foster. Bob Scott, a North Carolina journalist, explains: "I was impressed by the Family members because I believe they are doing something that all of us, even conservatives like myself, have dreamed of doing sometime—saying the heck with material things and the mortgage, and running off to live wherever the spirit and the winds and an old Volkswagen bus will take us" (Scott 1987). Many social aspects of the Gatherings also appeal to conservative middle America. Scott noted, "Their friendliness and the politeness of their children make a good impression. I didn't hear a radio or television, but I did see some books—something not often found in today's campgrounds" (1987). It is this common ground that has traditionally bound utopians to their country neighbors.

The Farm, a countercultural community in rural Summertown, Tennessee, traces its origins to many of the same social movements as the Rainbow Family.

Like their Rainbow cousins, their community relations have been exemplary since their inception in the early 1970s.[3] Neighbors came to know the Farm folks as being, "in their own fashion—pious, moralistic, and orthodox" (Egerton 1977, 11). Homer Sanders, one of the first neighbors to meet Farm founder Stephen Gaskin and company, came with his shotgun in hand, intent on driving the invading "hippies" away. After speaking with Gaskin, however, he changed his mind and turned his shotgun on another neighbor who was giving Farm folks a hard time, only to be dissuaded by Gaskin from using violence. In time, Sanders went on to teach the "hippies" how to make cane molasses and mill lumber (Gaskin interview 1994a).

This Tennessee scene was not unlike that of a century earlier, when rural Tennessee neighbors embraced the Ruskin Cooperative Community. Like the folks in Summertown a century later, "[o]nce-hostile neighbors had begun to admire the industriousness of the Ruskinites, to trade with them, and even on occasion to socialize with them" (Egerton 1977, 75). In the end, when the colony broke up, fifteen hundred local residents showed up to see them off at their final July Fourth celebration (Fogarty 1990, 160).

Rainbows, like the Farm and the Ruskinites, make friends in the oddest places. In 1994, Rainbows and Wyoming cattle ranchers found common ground in their mutual mistrust of the federal government. Both the cattle ranchers and the Rainbows were united in opposing proposed federal regulations that would have restricted their use of forest lands. What resulted was a bizarre orgy of mutual admiration among an odd array of bedfellows. Pacifist vegetarian Rainbows, for instance, praised the National Rifle Association for its hand in fighting the proposed regulations, while cattle-grazing Wyoming ranchers admonished "mankind" to "take a lesson from the Rainbows" about "love and respect for the land" (Associated Press 1994).

Sociologist Rosabeth Moss Kanter observes that "the commune operates to serve first and foremost its own members; any benefits it provides to the outside are generally secondary. . . . Relations among members of the community are more important than relations of members or the community to the outside world" (Kanter 1972, 3). Both the Farm and the Rainbow Family, however, stress good relations with the outside world. Because both communities, like utopians before them, see themselves as a model for reforming Babylon, they feel their behavior must be exemplary. The Farm, over the years, has provided technical assistance, an ambulance service, and health care to their rural neighbors, as well as organizing an international relief program active around the world. Rainbows have always opened their healing Gatherings to all who wanted to come, providing food, shelter, and medical care for anybody who arrives.

Living near a community such as the Farm or a Rainbow Gathering provides advantages. Neighbors benefit both from services the communities render and from the cultural benefits and entertainment they provide. While such benefits have been enjoyed throughout utopian history (Holloway 1951, 223–24), the

Rainbow Family, as a nomadic group, adds a twist. They bring the mountain to the people. The odd array of spiritual beliefs, cuisines, music, and dance that the Family encompasses exposes small rural communities to a side of the world that otherwise would go unseen.

Fight, Flight, or Accommodate

Historically, relationships between utopian communities and their neighbors have been both sweet and sour. Bad relations can result from a reactionary close-minded community of neighbors, an insensitive utopia, or a combination of the two. When relations turn sour, the utopians have traditionally chosen among three possible responses; fight, flight, or accommodation. When push came to shove, the Oneidans, for example, gave up their controversial practice of group marriage, rather than continue to defend the custom before hostile detractors. Hence, though they opted for a peaceful solution, it came at the expense of sacrificing a central tenet in their ideology.

Other groups have chosen to flee when faced with hostile neighbors. The Hutterites, for instance, suffered greatly when, due to their pacifist conscientious objections to fighting in World War I, they fell victim to violent attacks and looting. In response, they fled to Canada, where they resettled in Manitoba. Likewise, over five thousand Mormons fled Missouri in 1838, after non-Mormons, annoyed at Mormon predictions of Missouri's becoming a Mormon state, began to persecute them (Hayden 1976, 113).

Rainbows practice varying degrees of fight, flight, and accommodation when faced with hostile adversaries. Rainbows will try to accommodate neighbors so long as the accommodation doesn't violate Family principles. Hence, in 1990, Quebec Rainbows discouraged nudity at their regional Gathering in the belief that such nudity offended area Indians.[4] On other occasions Rainbows avoided Gathering in areas that were cherished by locals, detoured traffic away from residential roads, and so on. Such accommodations were possible, since no Rainbow tenets were violated.

Rainbows will also fight, mostly in the form of nonviolent civil disobedience, when their right to Gather is challenged. Such battles usually place the Rainbows at odds with government agencies, and not local people. Rainbows will also fight rhetorically, when they feel they have been wronged or slandered. Hence, Rainbows will show up at local town meetings to defend themselves against what they see as false accusations. Again, these accusations usually originate in the press or with government officials, and not with local people. Often it has been through the help and support of local people that the Family has been able to triumph peaceably in the face of government efforts to thwart the Gatherings.

The emergence of private right-wing armies, or "militias," in the United States threatens to complicate Rainbow-community relations. Rural militias often claim proprietary rights over public lands and, like the Rainbows, challenge Forest Service stewardship over those lands. How they will react to the Family gathering on "their" land remains to be seen. If militias view the Rainbows as "invading" *their* turf with the blessing and protection of the federal government they might intercede to "stop" the Rainbows. On the other hand, if the government moves against the Rainbows first, the militias could just as easily move to support the Rainbow Family's right to gather on public lands without government harassment, as locals did in Texas in 1988. The continued growth of the militia movement makes either scenario increasingly likely. Since the Rainbow Family is nomadic, however, there is little chance of a long-term standoff either with the government or the militias.

Rainbow relationships with their neighbors are temporary. Being aware of this transience allows both Rainbows and locals to be more tolerant. The fact that the Rainbows will soon be leaving often prompts local curiosity seekers to venture forth to meet the Family and experience the Gathering, lest they miss local history in the making. Some neighbors, however, once introduced to the Rainbows, establish a long-term relationship with the Family, traveling to Gatherings themselves. Hence, through positive community relations, Rainbows recruit members from the regions where they have Gathered. At the 1993 Gathering in Alabama, for example, local teenagers started frequenting the Gathering. Within a week they were helping cook in kitchens, haul water, and work with CALM. At least one returned to the Family at the next year's Gathering in Wyoming, claiming Rainbow had "changed his life." If nothing else, it broadened his horizons, as it does for many other visitors.

Each new Gathering, taking place in a different geographic region, brings the Rainbow message of peaceful coexistence to a new audience. More common ground is discovered as locals and Rainbows both learn a little about each other and themselves. Unlike the 1960s hippie movement, the Rainbow Family has been successful in creating and maintaining good relationships with the mainstream world. The 1960s-era "fuck the pigs" images, like the sixties images of construction workers beating hippies, have fallen by the wayside, replaced by images of middle Americans and Rainbows holding hands and singing. This is the Rainbow revolution that the Family hopes to carry forth into the twenty-first century.

10

The Rainbow and the U.S. Government

Congress shall make no law respecting an establishment of
religion, or prohibiting the free exercise thereof; or abridging
the freedom of speech, or of the press, or the right of the
people peaceably to assemble, and to petition the Government
for a redress of grievances

—U.S. Constitution, First Amendment, 1791

It is essential that the Gathering be viewed as a group of
persons exercising their legitimate right to use the National
Forest and that it be treated in this way. Law enforcement and
other functions must be viewed from that perspective

—James Schuler, Sheffield district ranger, Allegheny National
Forest (Feb. 27, 1987)

In the United States, almost all Rainbow Gatherings are on public land,
usually U.S. National Forest Service land. While Forest Service land is relatively
abundant and often beautiful, Rainbows gather on public land as a statement, sus-
taining a bond to the land and exercising their inalienable right to peaceably assemble. They avoid gathering on private land to escape the class distinction between landowners and tenants. Since public lands are ostensibly held in trust,
everyone shares equally in their ownership. Gathering on public lands, however,
requires the Rainbow Family to interface with government bureaucracies.

The relationship between the Rainbow Family and the U.S. government is often trying for all parties involved. Rainbow egalitarianism frustrates bureaucrats to whom, apparently, no one is in charge. From their first encounters with the Family in 1972, United States government agencies have insisted that the Rainbow Family produce leaders with whom they can negotiate. The Rainbow Family Council, ideologically opposed to hierarchy, steadfastly refuses to provide any. Rainbows point out that there are no leaders to "sell out" their interests. The Council does appoint "liaisons" to facilitate communications with government officials. Liaisons, however, have no authority to speak for the Family. The full Council must approve all decisions, including those involving government agencies.

The bureaucrats who run the Forest Service, the governmental agency that has the most dealings with the Rainbow Family, understand bureaucracies, not participatory democracies like the Rainbow Family, where members do *not* yield their voices to representatives. The Family's refusal to appoint leaders seems to Forest Service officials like a ploy to thwart prosecution and intimidation. Forest Service officials sometimes try to identify people, usually men, as "leaders" or "organizers," and then proceed to work with them as if they actually were leaders. At the 1989 Gathering in Nevada, law enforcement officers filed an intelligence report with the Forest Service identifying people[1] in the early Seed Camp by name, categorizing each person as an "organizer," a "laborer," or "security" (Lotspeich 1989), much as a child would try to sort out who's who in an ant farm. On other occasions, the Forest Service has simply been hostile and abusive, attempting to stop Gatherings from occurring altogether.

Harassles and Justice

How the Forest Service will react to Gatherings from year to year is unpredictable. The Forest Service is decentralized. Authority is vested in a hierarchy of regions, forests, and finally, districts. Regions operate somewhat autonomously from the national organization, each developing its own plan for working with or combating the Family. In 1983, for instance, the Forest Service took a "hands-off" approach to the North American Gathering. They spent eight thousand dollars (Lee 1984) monitoring the event, which ran smoothly; a high point in Forest Service/Rainbow relations. In 1987, however, the Forest Service spent $270,156 (Rickerson et al. 1987, G-1) to harass and disrupt the Gathering, ticketing or arresting people for 311 predominantly vehicle related violations (Rickerson et al. 1987, E-3), as well as nudity.

The year 1987 was a benchmark for the Rainbow Family. Diarrhea reportedly affected "61.7%" of Gathering participants.[2] The causes of the epidemic are unknown. A number of Rainbows reported seeing an airplane spraying the area early in the Gathering (Adams 1988), a report that the Centers For Disease Control duly noted (Wharton and Spiegel 1987). Exceptionally unsanitary conditions and contaminated water sources at the Krishna Kitchen[3] could have introduced the infection. Uncovered latrines throughout the Gathering and a general lack of potable water also may have contributed to it.

The 1987 diarrhea outbreak and failure to clean up the Gathering site provided a plausible pretext for the Forest Service to try to get a court order prohibiting the following year's North American Gathering in Texas (Greenfeather and Water 1988). Appearing before Chief Federal Judge William Wayne Justice, U.S. Justice Department attorneys argued for a restraining order on number of grounds, calling the Gathering a health threat, an environmental threat, and a nuisance.

A lawyer representing the Rainbow Family as a defendant class argued that Forest Service interference caused most of the health and cleanup problems at the North Carolina Gathering. The Forest Service, for instance, stopped vehicles carrying fresh water and supply trucks carrying plywood for latrine covers, refusing to let them pass a roadblock and bring their supplies to the Gathering site. Likewise, the Forest Service barred trucks carrying piping and barrels for gravity-fed shower systems (*U.S.A. v. Rainbow Family* L-88-68-CA: 589, 591). The Forest Service also discouraged doctors from helping at the Gathering. Water, a Rainbow CALM volunteer, explained to Judge Justice:

> We had a doctor from North Carolina, a lady doctor, who came to take part in the [G]athering who brought a whole lot of supplies. They intimidated her. They threatened her. They told her she was crazy to involve herself with the Rainbow Family. She still said she wanted to come in. They told her fine, but they were going to search through all her things and they started very carelessly searching through her things. They got her so upset that she did, indeed, leave and did not come into the gathering or bring her supplies. (*U.S.A. v. Rainbow Family* L-88-68-CA: 589–91)

The Forest Service also refused entry to an ambulance responding to an emergency call as well as garbage trucks hauling trash from the site (*U.S.A. v. Rainbow Family* L-88-68-CA: 589–91). The cleanup ended prematurely when the Forest Service arrested the cleanup crew, who were still working at the end of July, collecting the trash bottlenecked on the site. The Forest Service, adding an Orwellian twist to the story, referred to their 1987 stance as "The Good Host approach" (Rickerson et al. 1987, 5). Judge Justice concluded:

> Indeed, the evidence record developed at the three sets of hearings lends substantial credence to one of the arguments advanced by the defendants, that the health and other problems seen at the 1987 Summer Gathering in North Carolina were exceptional and

> traceable—at least in part—to a hostile and adversarial relation-
> ship between the government and the Rainbow Family. . . . Indeed,
> the government did not offer any evidence of major health, safety,
> or environmental problems from other past Rainbow Family gath-
> erings, except for the 1987 gathering in North Carolina. (Justice
> 1989, 26, 27)

Justice also dismissed the Forest Service's contention that halting the Gathering
would protect the environment, pointing out that even the 1987 Gathering in
North Carolina, had "not resulted in serious or irreparable harm or damage to
the environment or to public property, as the government contends" (Justice
1988b, 29). When the Forest Service attempted to invoke the National Environmental Protection Act (NEPA) in asking for a federal injunction against the Gathering, Justice responded:

> While it is commendable that the F.S. is concerned about possible
> adverse environmental effects, there is reason to question the
> government's good faith in raising this argument at this time. . . .
> Although NEPA is unquestionably constitutional, even an oth-
> erwise valid statute cannot be applied in a manner designed to
> suppress First Amendment activity, or out of hostility to a particular
> group. (Justice 1988b, 21)

Sign No Permits

A major source of contention between the Rainbow Family and the Forest Service is the Family's refusal to apply for or accept a permit to use the National Forests. Rainbows contend that "we do not need anyone's permission to
gather," explaining, "we sign away our right to peaceably assemble when we sign
permits" (Legaliaison 1990).

Rainbows, however, first tried working within the permit system. From 1976
through 1981, Rainbows tried signing permits, but found that arbitrary permit
stipulations made getting a permit so "difficult and complex" as to impede their
right to gather (Hipstory July 3, 1990): "We were faced with impossible permit
demands covering lighted parking lots, flush toilets, gigantic insurance premiums,
performance bonds, hired policepeople, outsize [sic] (immense) water storage,
enclosed kitchens, state-certified parking attendants, and so on. Each of those
five years we ceaselessly negotiated, compromised, worked out arrangements
and agreements" (Legaliaison 1991). Eventually the Family gave up on the permit
system: "We just quit getting permits, saying, "It's permitted under the natural
laws of the universe and the constitution. . . . [The] Constitution doesn't give us

the right to assemble. It guarantees our right to assemble will be protected by law" (Hipstory July 3, 1990).

The Forest Service continually amends permit regulations specifically to hinder Rainbow Gatherings. A federal court in Arizona, for instance, found such an amended regulation unconstitutional in 1986 (*United States of America v. Gideon Israel*) after the Forest Service attempted to enforce it at a regional Rainbow Gathering. That regulation required groups of ten or more people who gather on Forest Service land "for the purpose of expression or exchange of views or judgments" to apply for a special use permit (*United States of America v. Gideon Israel*).

The Forest Service redrafted these regulations, changing the maximum number of persons gathering from ten to twenty-five. They introduced the new regulation, without the usual thirty-day notice and comment period required by federal law, on May 10, 1988, about the time Rainbows started to arrive in Texas. Within hours of publication, the Forest Service initiated proceedings against the Family, based on the new regulations. They argued that the "emergency" the Gathering threatened justified waiving due process (Justice 1988a, 19).

The new regulations closely resembled the unconstitutional 1986 ones. Attempting to enforce the new rules in federal court in Texas, government lawyers neglected to mention that another federal court had voided the earlier ones (Justice 1989, 15). An angry Judge Justice ruled:

> The amendments to the special use permit regulations did little to correct the constitutional deficiencies of the earlier regulations. . . .
>
> Indeed, there is substantial support for the defendant's argument that the government has acted with hostility to the Rainbow Family, in seeking to enforce the special use permit regulations before the 1988 gatherings. (Justice 1989, 16–17, 27)

He also condemned the Forest Service for singling out the Family for special treatment.

> Forest Service officials could not identify other groups that were similarly required to submit the type of detailed application. . . .
>
> The manner in which the amended permit regulations were adopted, as "emergency" regulations on the eve of the Rainbow Family gathering, without prior public notice or comment . . . bespeaks of agency action directed specifically at the Rainbow Family gathering. The fact that the amended regulations add an additional requirement for a permit which does not appear in the earlier regulations, and which seems to be uniquely applicable to the Rainbow Family,[4] while retaining a *constitutionally repugnant* per-

mit scheme that singles out expressive activity for special treatment, further support this impression that the F.S. has not been motivated in this litigation solely out of concern for the public health and safety; but rather has been motivated, at least to some degree, by hostility to the Rainbow Family. (Justice 1989, 28–29 [emphasis mine])

The judge awarded the Rainbow Family $13,669.09, to be paid by the plaintiff, the U.S. Attorney's Office, for costs and attorneys' fees incurred during the ordeal.

Despite Justice's rulings, the Forest Service continued to harass the Texas Gathering, much as they did during the previous year's Gathering in North Carolina. Forest Service Special Agent Billy Ball,[5] a former Dallas narcotics agent who served with the Armed Forces Police during the Watts riots, was present at both Gatherings. Water Singing-on-the-Rocks testified before Judge Justice that Ball, in 1987, threatened the Rainbow Family, promising that the Forest Service would make sure that the Rainbow Family wouldn't have a successful Gathering in 1988 (U.S.A. v. Rainbow L-88-68-CA: 591–92). Indeed, the Forest Service appointed the pugnacious Ball to the post of incident commander in charge of the 1988 Rainbow Gathering.

At the behest of the U.S. Attorney's office (Wortham 1988), Forest Service agents videotaped people and proceedings at the 1988 Gathering, as they did the previous year in North Carolina, in violation of Forest Service regulation 0.735-11(b)(7),[6] which prohibits covert videotaping. They also insisted on controlling access to the Gathering, allowing a drunken local to drive his Jeep in, run over, and nearly kill Noguns, a Rainbow sister. Noguns, who chose to forgive the driver instead of pressing charges, was incapacitated for nearly a year afterwards.

The site itself was not the Rainbow's first choice. They were considering another site when, allegedly at Ball's behest, a Forest Service crew began an odd destruction/construction project. According to witnesses, shortly after Rainbows selected a site, a Forest Service work crew came and started knocking down trees, bringing in electric lines, and building a concrete structure. They also bulldozed two roads right into the central Gathering meadow. Garrick Beck recalls: "Forest Service enforcement agent Billy Ball did more damage to the National Forest in that afternoon with that bulldozer than the Gatherings could do between 1972 and 2072! So the whole camp up and moved. Who knows what this guy's planning? He's building a cement compound! He's putting up barbed wire! We felt like he was dangerous to us" (Weinberg 1989c).

The Drug Factor

In the 1988 court case, the Forest Service repeated a familiar charge: Rainbow Gatherings are a haven for illicit drug use. Such charges, as James Ridgeway notes in the *Village Voice,* were common: "Dope is replacing communism as both the rationale for American hegemony abroad and for a crackdown against minorities and dissidents here at home. Where 'national security' and 'terrorism' once were enough to get an FBI investigation going against U.S. citizens, now it's all in the name of epidemiology" (Ridgeway 1989).

Despite a quarter century of dismal results, the Forest Service, year after year, encourages local police agencies to conduct "probable cause" vehicle inspections for illegal drugs at Rainbow Gatherings (e.g., Wright 1988b, 4). The Forest Service has even *paid* local police agencies to engage in such harassment. In 1986, for example, the Forest Service contracted with the Pennsylvania State Police, paying them about thirteen thousand dollars for services rendered at the Rainbow Gathering (Carpenter 1986). After years of searching thousands of vehicles, a constitutionally shaky act, cooperating police agencies failed to turn up any significant quantity of illicit hard drugs. The amount of marijuana and soft drugs confiscated, Rainbows point out, is statistically normal for the number of vehicles searched. Even the Forest Service admits that the incidence of crime at Gatherings is "*remarkably low considering the size of these gatherings*" (Okanogan National Forest 1981, 5 [emphasis in original]).

The "Good Host" approach to the 1989 North American Gathering in Nevada involved equipping police with drug-sniffing dogs, although the Forest Service conceded that "the Family does not advocate the use of hard drugs or alcohol and supports the rehabilitation of anyone addicted" (Jarbidge 1989, 1). Nonetheless, Forest Service records remark:

> The Sheriff's Office was able to borrow two "drug dogs" and these became very valuable tools during the [G]athering. Many vehicles were checked by the drug dogs, some after being stopped for traffic infractions and some that stopped to ask for directions or for other information from patrol units along the road. (Hawkins 1989)

> Local law enforcement provided intermittent informational check points, at which time general information was provided to those individuals interested in the Gathering. Also at this time, if probably [sic] cause developed, individuals were arrested. (Watson 1989, 26)

Despite the vigilance of the "good hosts," relatively few Rainbows were found to be carrying drugs. Officials dismissed their low arrest tally as evidence, not that the Rainbows weren't the drug fiends officials portrayed them as, but that they must instead be cagey drug traffickers. Agents theorized that Rainbows must have somehow set up "information stations" on the road to warn people about the dogs. Hence, the dogs, in this scenario, "did deter some that might have brought drugs into the area," thus justifying Forest Service expenditures (Hawkins 1989). Police, however, never found these "information stations" that supposedly dotted America's highways.

Agents from the Nevada Division of Forestry, the U.S. Border Patrol, the U.S. Fish and Wildlife Service, the U.S. Bureau of Land Management, the Department of Defense, the Nevada Brand Inspector, the office of the Governor of Nevada, the Department of Human Resources Health Division, the Nevada Department of Emergency Services, the Nevada Highway Patrol, the Idaho Highway Patrol, the Nevada Department of Wildlife, and a number of sheriffs' agencies and police departments from Nevada and Idaho were involved in "administering" the 1989 Gathering in Nevada (Jarbidge Ranger District Reports 1989). A Nevada Department of Wildlife official cautioned his agents on patrol at the Gathering site to "Take extra ammunition, handcuffs and film," adding, "Keep your head down" and "telephone a report to me as soon as you get back to the World."[7]

In 1990, the government spent about $310,000 on the North American Rainbow Gathering in Minnesota (Joens 1990b; Tofte 1990). Almost $180,000 of this money went to agencies other than the Forest Service (*Cook County News-Herald* 1990e; Joens 1990b; Tofte 1990). The state police, using a drug-sniffing dog borrowed from U.S. Customs, inspected 1,113 vehicles on Highway 61 approaching the Gathering. They made sixteen drug-related arrests and issued a host of vehicle-related citations. Rainbows, however, accounted for only 19 percent of these citations and arrests (Joens 1990b; Tofte 1990; *Cook County News-Herald* 1990e; Superior National Forest reports 1990). The rest were presumably tourists and locals. One local resident wrote: "Now that such a fuss has been made on the 'bust' of about ten 'Rainbows' for minor drug charges, let's stop and think. If the 'Patrol' set up their 'roadblock' in the same area on any given holiday the outcome would be the same, Rainbows or no" (Osgood 1990). Another area resident questioned the expense of the police action: "I think one has to seriously consider the reaction [or] perhaps more accurately the overreaction of the law enforcement community to what was essentially a legal gathering of non-typical people. . . . Regarding drug possession, that is a crime and scourge on our society. People who peddle or use should be put away, period. However, one had to ponder if the extra law enforcement funds could have been more wisely used in sweeping parts of the Twin Cities for crack houses rather than busting a few hippies for pot" (Wasik 1990).

A local columnist with the *Cook County News-Herald* observed that one of the most noticeable aspects of the Rainbow Gathering was the proliferation of law enforcement people. As she drove home one day she passed sixteen patrol cars driving on the desolate stretch of road; another nine were parked. A friend of hers counted thirty-two on a similar outing (Blank 1990). The density of state police cruisers became so high on July 1 that a solitary moose crossing Highway 61 managed to destroy one and heavily damage a second (*Cook County News-Herald* 1990c).

Such scenes, however, are commonplace near Gatherings. While Rainbows have grown accustomed to such harassment, many locals are outraged. At a 1993

Gathering in Kentucky, local papers reported that police had issued 382 citations and arrested 69 people by July 6, mostly for minor traffic violations. A Somerset, Kentucky, attorney writes: "I thought it was a terrible waste of taxpayers' money on the Fourth of July weekend to harass a group of people who appear to be engaging in conduct no more seditious than to offer prayers for world peace" (Haukebo 1993). The mayor and assorted residents of Big Piney, Wyoming, the site of the 1994 North American Gathering, complained that police were being "overzealous" in issuing citations during the Gathering while menacing local motorists (*Casper* [Wyo.] *Star-Trib* 1994). Similarly, Vermont residents complained that their community was turned into a "police state" during the 1991 North American Rainbow Gathering.

Government attempts to connect the Family to drug trafficking are relentless. A "peculiar van" traveling at 9 P.M. one evening near the 1984 North American Gathering, for example, put the Forest Service on alert: "Administrative Officer says it could be the route for drug traffic, will send up information to Incident Command" (Modoc National Forest 1984). The lack of any evidence linking the Family with drug trafficking does not exonerate them. The Forest Service seemingly concludes that Rainbows are just too sly to be caught. Police units in cooperation with the Forest Service have planted undercover officers in the Gatherings, ostensibly looking for drug dealing, although the limits of their surveillance and record keeping is uncertain (e.g., Wright 1988, 4,5). Despite Forest Service allegations linking the Family to illicit drugs, the U.S. Drug Enforcement Administration (DEA) seems to see no threat in the Rainbow Family, claiming not even to maintain records on the Rainbow Family (Langer 1990; Huff 1991).

The Federal Bureau of Investigation (FBI), in an internal memo, went as far as to add charges of child prostitution to allegations of drug trafficking: "The Rainbow Family is reported to be a group involved in the interstate transportation of white minor males for the purposes of prostitution and also transporting drugs interstate. . . . Runaways that are recruited by the Rainbow Family must help with the living expenses, therefore they must sell drugs and/or hustle as prostitutes" (FBI 1983). The memo, while utilizing the passive voice to obfuscate its source, offers no evidence to support these charges.

Bureaucrats find political justification for general surveillance of the Rainbow Family. The Forest Service not only allows but encourages other government agencies to spy on Rainbows. For example, after learning that some Family members were planning a peace demonstration at the Pentagon, the Forest Service extended an invitation to Detective K. R. Green of the National Park Service, suggesting: "You might want to consider planting an agent amongst the Rainbow Family at the Gathering to gather intelligence on their Pentagon demonstration proposal. We will cooperate every way possible and would welcome any additional intelligence your agent would come up with" (Ziegler 1980).

The Forest Service encouraged the California Bureau of Organized Crime and

Criminal Intelligence to spy on the 1984 Gathering, collecting data on Rainbow participation in demonstrations slated for the 1984 Democratic Convention in San Francisco as well as the Olympics in Los Angeles. The Forest Service promised "full cooperation and assistance in the intelligence phase and thereafter" (Smith 1984). Rainbows, like other targets of government surveillance, have developed an acute sense of paranoia.[8]

Despite fruitless surveillance, Forest Service officials suspect Rainbows are getting away with criminal activity, claiming that a double standard lets Rainbows openly commit crimes the local citizenry cannot. This, they say, enrages local citizens who supposedly either cry out for either tougher enforcement against the Rainbows or relaxed enforcement directed against locals (e.g., Rickerson et al. 1987, 15). A California Forest Service official wrote: "It is easy to see why the general public cannot understand how we could let an anarchist group of people use the Forests for dubious purposes" (Lee 1984). Government attorneys raised this issue of a "double standard" in the 1988 suit against the Rainbow Family. Judge Justice ruled:

> The government has also alleged that, as a result of its purported inability to enforce F.S. regulations at the Rainbow Family gathering in North Carolina, citizens in the surrounding area felt that a "double standard" existed, in which regulations were enforced against themselves, but not against the Rainbow Family. Other than hearsay, however, no competent evidence was presented in this regard; and, particularly, there was no showing that some lasting or irreparable impact resulted. The apparently uncompromising attitude of the government toward the defendants in this litigation would, it seems, eliminate any possible suspicion that the government is treating the Rainbow Family more favorably than local residents of East Texas. (Justice 1988b, 32)

An Expensive Game

The government's campaign against the Rainbow Family is expensive. At the 1989 North American Gathering, for example, various agencies (excluding the Forest Service) clocked 38,940 miles, driving government vehicles around the perimeter of the Gathering (Jarbidge Ranger District reports 1989; Watson 1989, 27). The Forest Service reimbursed the Elko County, Nevada, Sheriff's Department, for example, fifty cents per mile for vehicle usage, nearly double the regular federal rate (Inman 1989). They budgeted for an additional thirty thousand miles of driving by Forest Service employees (Jarbidge Ranger District reports 1989).

Not wanting their employees to be mistaken for Rainbows, the government spent

$1,821 on new uniforms (Jarbidge Ranger District reports 1989). Catering for the government team cost $21,000 (Jarbidge Ranger District reports 1989). They spent $603.25 and $2,000 to rent planes and helicopters respectively (Jarbidge Ranger District reports 1989), presumably to fly over the Gathering, despite Rainbow complaints about the flights and government denials about flying over the sites.[9]

The Forest Service budgeted $15,000 to feed and lodge employees working at the 1990 North American Gathering in Minnesota, putting some agents up in condos. Federal bureaucrats were on hand to handle any problems the team might face, such as when a resort didn't accept Diner's Club cards. Although the restaurant did take the card, it dropped "the special meal" from the menu, creating more problems. An alert government planner saved the day, however, suggesting "everyone will/can order off the menu" (Christiansen 1990). Marty, a Forest Service employee, had laundry duty for the detail. Forest Officials even designated a special trash can for "official trash" (Superior National Forest reports and meeting notes 1990).

Forest Service administrators, worried that the assignment might still prove too stressful for rangers, suggested "rest and hippy-less [sic] days." Meeting notes of the Superior National Forest show that a rest and relaxation (R&R) program was established by the Forest Service to help the rangers through their "hippy-less" days, offering gondola rides, bike and "unmarked" van rentals, canoe tripping into the Boundary Waters Canoe Area, horseback riding, and "Beaver Flights" (1990).

Rainbow phobia is a windfall for law enforcement agents whose salaries are often paid by the Forest Service (e.g., Inman 1989). Despite ample Forest Service documentation demonstrating the tranquillity of the Gatherings, Mike Presti, an Elko County Sheriff's "Special Reserves" officer, earned $1,286.48 as a "bodyguard" for state of Nevada health specialist Scott Marteney as he collected water samples and examined latrines at the 1989 North American Gathering (Jarbidge Ranger District reports 1989; Marteney 1989). Detective Curtis Watson, who earned $2,162.30 policing the 1989 Gathering, recommended that law enforcement officials must be "involved in every contact" when "one of these groups that has in the past shown a propensity to radical behavior" like "stated anarchy" gathers in a National Forest (Jarbidge Ranger District reports 1989; Watson 1989, 29). Forest Service Special Agent Charles E. Hawkins, who earned $2,800 for his work at the same Gathering alleged in a letter that officers were "constantly harassed, baited and taunted by the people attending the Rainbow Family Gathering," who he claimed abused their children (July 12, 1989).

Special Agent Tommy C. LaNier, who earned $4,700 for policing the 1989 Gathering argued for an even more visible law enforcement presence at future Gatherings (Jarbidge Ranger District reports 1989; LaNier 1989). Cook County, Minnesota, sheriff John Lyght, who warned U.S. Representative James Oberstar that Rainbows would walk around town nude, destroy the land, drive tourists away, and import "bales" of marijuana, considered calling in "the National Guard or

Marines" to deal with the Gathering (Lyght 1990). During the Gathering, Lyght, who actively spread fear of the Rainbows around his community, earned $3,120 in overtime; three of his deputies earned a total of about $10,000 in overtime pay[10] (*Cook County News-Herald* 1991).

Paternalism

It is almost impossible to institutionalize structural links between societies organized into relatively permanent hierarchies like the United States government, and those in which egalitarian social relations prevail, like the Rainbow Family. The inevitable mutual misunderstandings generate mutual suspicion. This suspicion leads to evasiveness and strategic obfuscation. These tactics eventually lead to frustration, which both sides express in irritation and mockery, at least when the other party is absent. Parallels to government/Rainbow relations exist, for example, between Malays and Orang Asli in West Malaysia and between Bantu and BaMbuti in Zaire (Dentan and Endicott 1997; Turnbull 1962). A common result, already described here, is that the hierarchical people recognize (i.e., create) "leaders" with whom they can deal comfortably, although those leaders have no authority from "their" people to represent them (cf. Benjamin 1968; Dentan 1979). Other tactics include treating the egalitarian people as a chronic problem, a sort of social itch.

Egalitarian peoples, despite their relative powerlessness, are difficult to manipulate and control. The analogy with parent-child relations is almost inescapable (cf. Douglas 1973). Manipulation and control by the dominant hierarchy often takes the form of benevolent paternalism. Thus white South Africans, for example, regard Bantu as "childlike," even though they shy away from describing their own children as "like Bantu" (Kuper 1960, 539). Similarly, Forest Service bureaucrats rationalize their actions as necessary to protect Rainbows from themselves. One Forest Service report about the Rainbow Family includes the following stanzas from a poem by a forest ranger which illustrates this attitude:

> They seem a funny people
> to me and others too.
> You'd like to help them if you could
> You don't know what to do. . . .
>
> Our job as Forest People
> Is to help them get along;
> And hope that in the process
> They'll not do things real wrong
> (Jarbidge Ranger District 1989)

Sheriff John Lyght described the Rainbow Family as "just like little kids" (Lyght interview 1990). For an April 1990 Regional Gathering at the Big South Fork NRRA, the National Park Service generated a series of "Intelligence" reports about the Rainbow Family, along with the usual pile of paperwork to justify expenditures. All the reports refer to Rainbow Family members as "The Rainbow Children," quite a different take from the media's "aging hippies." This error, reminiscent of the 1960s media-blessed "Flower Children," occurred in spite of the fact that they possessed, in their "Intelligence" file, the Rainbow Family *Howdy Folks!* flyer announcing the Gathering of the "Rainbow Family of Living Light," not the "Rainbow Children."

The Two Faces of Government

The Forest Service reacts to news of an impending Rainbow Gathering by declaring it an "Incident," and appointing an "Incident Command Team," a top-down archetypal hierarchical structure. These teams alternate between the "heavy-handed approach" at "managing" Rainbow events (Filius 1990), and a more relaxed approach that involves seemingly friendly and cooperative law enforcement. The amicability, however, is often tactical. Recommendations for dealing with the Rainbow Family, released in 1984, point out that "Rainbows are quick to disdain people who talk and act like bureaucrats" (Lee 1984). The report suggests that bureaucrats put on friendlier faces and pick wily people to work with the Rainbows: "It is important that these individuals are selected on their ability to communicate, negotiate, and *manipulate*" (Lee 1984 [emphasis mine]).

The failure of the heavy-handed approach has led the Forest Service to rely more on ostensibly amicable "manipulation" to control Rainbows. Agents should appeal to Rainbow values. A Forest Service report advises: "Base arguments from a Rainbow standpoint. They have strong ethics, though different from most. Laws, regulations, government, capitalistic interests are disdained. They respect the earth, nature, Native American[s], and opinions of individuals" (Lee 1984). This memo suggests that to deal with the Rainbow Family, Forest Service officials must forgo more traditional values, and feign respect for the earth and its inhabitants. Hence, for a short period, the Forest ceases to be a "resource" to be controlled or "impacted" and becomes a living ecosystem to be preserved.

Besides posing as friends, the Forest Service tries to recruit the Family's supposed allies. For example, in 1984, the Forest Service petitioned their longtime adversary the Sierra Club to lobby the Family to camp at "Camp One" rather than "Mill Creek" (Strickland 1984). The Sierra Club, which has since charged that the Forest Service is "managing our national forests as though they were outdoor warehouses of living trees, held in inventory until the lumber companies are ready to take delivery" (Fischer 1991), complied, asking the Rainbows to leave Mill Creek (Weidert 1984).

When the Family responds to friendly gestures with cooperation, Forest Service officials applaud their successful manipulation of the Rainbows. For example, at a regional Gathering in Pennsylvania in 1988, Rainbow volunteers helped the Forest Service plant and fence three hundred Chinese chestnut trees. Rainbows usually organize such projects to repay the Forest for its hospitality and build a friendly relationship. While the project served, according to the Forest Service, as "a very successful means of solidifying a strong working relationship with the Family," it also "greatly assisted in getting compliance in other unrelated aspects of the Operating Agreement" (Colaninno and Dunshie 1988, 6). The trees, planted too late in the season and not maintained by the Forest Service, all died.

Similarly, in 1989, Rainbows complained about the dust and dangers caused by frequent patrols of police cars through Bus Village. Enforcement officers switched to horseback, ostensibly as a conciliatory gesture. In the supposed privacy of memos, however, bureaucrats congratulated themselves: "The horses were both respected and feared," and they "placed officers at a height advantage so that they could observe any areas of potential problems" (Watson 1989).

The amicable pose stems from the Forest Service's hard-won understanding of the Rainbow Family and their Gatherings. This understanding, though not pervasive, is sometimes sophisticated, as in a 1978 report: "The first point that should be remembered is that many of the Family members have a basic distrust of "the bureaucracy" and do not expect most agency personnel to level with them. Based on some of their experiences this may very well be warranted. . . . As a consequence, one of the first obstacles to overcome is this lack of trust" (Martin 1978). The same report notes the inappropriateness of trying to find "leaders" with whom to deal:

> When working with the Family, it is important to keep in mind that their "organization" is quite democratic in nature, and no chain of command exists and no one person is going to "give the orders." Generally, decisions are group decisions and will only be implemented by those who are committed to that decision. However, there are specific individuals who accept more responsibility than others, and once permit administrators can identify them, they are generally the ones that can be counted on to get things done. The interesting thing is that during the course of the Gathering, different individuals keep appearing to fit this category, and the ones that were responding one day may move out of the picture for a time and someone else will assume their responsibilities. (Martin 1978)

This report outlines various aspects of the Gathering, potential problems, and possible peaceful solutions. It also points out how Gatherings could benefit Forest Service personnel: "In conclusion, the energy and effort expended during this period were rewarding and interesting in many ways. It is felt that this type of legitimate use provides a different perspective to those involved with its administration, and tends to broaden one's horizons, which may assist in dealing more effectively with the more traditional uses that occur within the National Forest System" (Martin 1978). The author of the 1978 report noted that "it is essential to try and understand the culture and organization of the Family and to develop a mutual trust level early in the relationship. If these two things are accomplished," he pointed out, "more than likely everyone's objectives will be met" (Martin 1978).

Some Love for the Law—and Cops Gone Native

Ideally, the Rainbow Family treats armed or intolerant law officers and Forest Service officials like anyone else who acts inappropriately at a Gathering, by just "showing them a bit more love" in order to "harmonize" them. Rainbows have repeatedly made it clear that unarmed and tolerant police and Forest Service officials *are* welcome at Gatherings. Indeed, some Rainbows argue that cops and bureaucrats need the tranquillity of the Gathering more than most other Rainbows. One officer told the *New York Times*: "Back in the 60's, people like these used to call you 'pig,' . . . But these people here come up to you and say, 'I love you, officer,' or 'Officer, have you been hugged today?'" (Schmidt 1982).

This loving approach often works. After a few days at the Gathering, Rangers and police officers often can be found sitting comfortably, sharing coffee or tea with their Rainbow brothers and sisters, calmly conversing with naked Rainbows at the swim hole or collecting berries for a kitchen. One Nevada ranger, Rod Howard, after a trip into the 1989 Gathering site, wrote, "I had not seen anything in the Hole [Robinson Hole, the site of the Gathering] that scared me. I think the tension is artificially high and could be downgraded" (Howard 1989a). On the following day, he added, "I feel no danger with these people what so ever . . . I don't think they are hippies. I think [they are] here for a Love[-]in party" (Howard 1989a). Howard explained, "These people need to be treated much like the early Indians. We can fight them, or work with them and tolerate them" (Howard 1989a). Real sympathy, as opposed to feigned friendliness, however, violated Forest Service guidelines. Ranger Howard writes: "During evening briefing I recommended that we have several people in the Hole shaking hands and building good will on the fourth. I further stated I would like to be in the circle. . . . The I.C. [Incident Commander] and ops [Operations] chief said they would rather I not go into the hole, that the time for negotiations were past and these people were not to be trusted" (Howard 1989a). Howard eventually spent the fourth on "the rim" overlooking the main circle area, wishing he could be closer (Howard 1989a).

Howard was even momentarily taken for a Rainbow, reporting; "The Forest officer stopping us was in our faces before realizing who we were" (Howard

1989a). On the following day, he observed of the police: "I think trying to restrain well trained, disciplined, and dedicated law officers is like trying to ask a bird dog not to hunt during the summer when the birds are on the nest or have chicks" (Howard 1989a). While criticizing the police, Howard seemingly became more comfortable with the Rainbows. On July sixth, he wrote, "[Another ranger] and I spent the day in Robinson Hole. We were warmly greeted. Most people were very friendly and wanted to talk. The atmosphere was one of a holy experience" (Howard 1989a).

Rainbow Gatherings have become popular with some Forest Service employees. For the NERF Gathering in Vermont in 1989, all the law enforcement slots were filled, with the local Forest Service compiling a stand-by list for law enforcement personnel volunteering for the popular assignment (Laflam 1989a). Similarly, the supervisor for the Colville National Forest in Washington, which hosted the 1981 North American Gathering, had to order that only personnel on official business could attend the Gathering on Forest Service time (Shenk 1981). At the 1990 NERF Gathering near Ithaca, New York, local off-duty law officers, many accompanied by their families, visited freely.

Many Forest Service personnel who got to know Family members and who spent time at Gatherings, look back on them fondly, as these three reports indicate:

> The 1988 New England Regional Rainbow Family Gathering is now history, and I would categorize it [as] a bright chapter in the annals of the Rochester Ranger District. . . . The event is over. New (England) ground has been broken and a seed planted. (Lundberg 1988)

> I totally enjoyed my involvement with the Gathering. It felt "good" to walk through the Gathering, making friends with the participants, learning from them as well as educating them about the F.S. and having them look at me not as a threat in a uniform with a badge but as a friend, even though I was wearing a uniform with a badge. (Laflam 1989b)

> Persons in town generally had a positive attitude toward the event and were well treated by the visitors. . . . We were able to put together a [F.S.] team that worked together very well and genuinely enjoyed the experience of the Gathering. (Schuler 1987)

Law enforcement personnel, however, who often never get past "A" Camp, have mixed reactions. While some officers are open to learning what the Rainbow Family is about, others cling to their prejudices. A former Pennsylvania police officer wrote, "I thank God that I don't have to patrol the area where these people are having their nudist occult drug party" (Swanson 1988).

Law enforcement officers, in general, tend to be less tolerant of, and more abusive to, Rainbows than are other government officials. Forest Service records often admit the "differences in approaches and attitudes between the law enforcement folks and the rest of the [Forest Service] team" (e.g., Bergerson 1990). There is also often a problem between the Forest Service and local police agencies who, once called in, cannot be controlled. One Forest Service official suggested to co-workers, "Build a relationship with law enforcement agencies early on and involve them. *Don't let them dictate how it will be run.* The Forest Service needs to maintain control. This will be a very difficult job" (Lee 1984). The same report also warned against assigning too many law enforcement officers to the Gathering: "It is costly and historically has not been needed. Bored officers will initiate unnecessary problems" (Lee 1984). This report, published in 1984, had little effect on Forest Service policies, which still encourage, and often pay for, a large police presence at the Gatherings.

Persecution and Survival

The 1978 report cited earlier demonstrates that the Forest Service *can* understand the Family well enough to work with it peaceably and *has* understood the Family for most of its existence. The subsequent failure to benefit from such reports is puzzling. The involvement of a myriad of federal agencies—ranging from the Federal Emergency Management Agency (FEMA) to the Border Patrol—may impede the transmission of understanding. A bureaucratic mind-set against apparent anarchy and untidiness may also play a part.

The Forest Service is still trying to introduce and implement new regulations aimed specifically at the Rainbow Family, despite the unconstitutionality of its previous attempts in Arizona and Texas. The need for new regulations, however, is unclear in light of the federal judicial ruling stating that "the government otherwise has available to it a panoply of statutory and regulatory grounds to prevent the alleged harms posed by a gathering" (Justice 1988a, 48).

In 1993 the Forest Service began drafting yet another version of the same regulations. The newest regulations (36 CFR Parts 251/261), introduced in 1995, pay lip service to the First Amendment of the U.S. constitution, stating, "It is well established that the government may enforce reasonable time, place, and manner restrictions on First Amendment activities." The new proposals go on to require special use permits for all noncommercial gatherings of twenty-five or more people, and, especially frightening to Rainbows, require a permit for distributing literature. The new regulations also broaden federal police powers within National Forests, making it easier for officials to close forests to the public.

In the Forest Service, the Rainbow Family has a powerful adversary. This enmity, however, has served more to strengthen the Family than to harm it. "Facing a common enemy binds people together," according to Kanter, who observed that, "a slightly higher proportion of successful than unsuccessful nineteenth-century groups suffered through these [persecution] experiences" (Kanter 1972, 102–3). Persecution against utopian groups, in Kanter's view, is a sort of "social vaccination": "Through the experience of persecution and conflict, defenses are built up and strengthened, so that the group is made immune to (prepared for) future and more extreme attacks on it. . . . If a group has experienced persecution, then it should be able to withstand other kinds of threats to existence, such as natural disasters, famines, and epidemics." Being perceived as a threat by its adversaries also increases group self-esteem, thus strengthening it in the face of disaster (Kanter 1972, 102–3).

The Rainbow Family, enjoying the flexibility of a band society, dissolving and regrouping while maintaining a cohesive identity, has withstood government harassment, both in the United States and abroad. Such attacks, rather than deterring the Rainbows, have served in the long run to unite the Family, which was born in an act of civil disobedience in 1972. The Family's persistence could be related to its oppression: "Both the source and the continued existence of a people appear to lie in an 'oppositional process,' that is, 'a continued conflict between these peoples and the controllers of the surrounding state apparatus'" (Spicer 1971). Rainbow publications and on-line computer bulletin boards celebrate the Family's triumphs over its adversaries. The absence of leaders protects the Family from co-optation. In one form or another it will win: attacks against the Family, while hurting individuals, are more of a nuisance than a fatal threat.

In a society devoted to commonly accepted conservative American ideals, it would be the Forest Service's responsibility not to harass campers, but to coordinate law enforcement activities within their jurisdictions so as to not infringe on the Rainbow Family's constitutional right to Gather. Selective enforcement of vehicle laws and the invocation of drug-related hysteria against the Rainbows flout that responsibility. In such a society, the Forest Service would respect the Rainbow Family's right to privacy by curtailing video surveillance and the use of undercover agents against the Rainbow Family.

The government war against the Rainbow Family involves more than the fear of drugs or abhorrence of supposed environmental degradation. It transcends the administrative boundaries of the Forest Service. It is a clear and consistent pattern of harassment by a government without a mandate, of a people without a land.

The issues involved here go beyond the persecution of Rainbows camping in National Forests. Recent civil rights abuses and the emergence of armed citizens' groups demonstrate a pervasive contempt for traditional American ideals on the part of government bureaucrats, and a reactive reactionary backlash on the part of the governed. If the people who rule America do not act with restraint and respect, they will lose—are losing—the reciprocal respect that legitimizes their rule.

Conclusion: Endless Summer

Utopia is the imaginary society in which humankind's deepest
yearnings, noblest dreams, and highest aspirations come to
fulfillment, where all physical, social and spiritual forces work
together, in harmony, to permit the attainment of everything
people find necessary and desirable. In the imagined utopia,
people work and live together closely and cooperatively, in a
social order that is self-created and self-chosen rather than
externally imposed, yet one that also operates according to a
higher law of natural and spiritual laws.

—Rosabeth Moss Kanter (1972)

The Rainbow Family is a growing and evolving contemporary movement,
not the anachronism that press reports imagine. It is an idealistic utopian movement with a vision of a world driven by love and cooperation, free of violence and
competition. It is an egalitarian vision of a world without leaders, without oppres-
sors, or oppressed peoples. The Family is decentralized, with Gatherings and events
throughout the world. There is no central organization to be subverted or destroyed. It is a movement, not an organization. Its strength lies with individuals
who make up the Gatherings.

The Family attracts a core of young participants who see the Rainbow "vision" as
an alternative to pessimism, apathy, the cynical promises of demagogic politicians, or
the sectarian divisiveness of revolutionary politics. Like the Rainbows who organized
the first North American Gatherings, those participating now are also spreading the

Rainbow vision, this time to the world.[1] The Family crosses cultural and geographic boundaries, with Gatherings ranging from Eastern Europe to Latin America. Regional Gatherings in North America are bringing the Rainbow vision within reach of every population center. They encourage bioregionalism, promote a sensitivity to local environmental conditions, and help foster communication between organizations and individuals involved in myriad progressive causes. The European Gatherings celebrate cultural diversity while mocking international boundaries. Against the backdrop of Eastern European ethnic strife, nationalism, and xenophobia, the Gatherings celebrate human unity and cooperation.

Seeking a Perfect Model

The Rainbow Family is a utopian experiment in the classic sense: perpetually exploring new ways to perfect an imperfect reality. True utopia, the perfect society, however, exists only as an imagined state, a romantic vision. The word *utopia* comes from Greek. The literal meaning is "no place."[2] In reality, utopia "is not a perfect place, but the aspiration to create one; it is oriented to the future rather than to the past or the present, and its virtue is not in what it has achieved but in what it is willing to attempt" (Egerton 1977, 87). True utopia, given the limited current level of human social evolution, will remain elusive. Rainbows, however, won't give up on that dream, seeing themselves as a catalyst for evolutionary change.

The Rainbow Family, like their utopian predecessors, shares a vision to create a working model for a better, more equitable society. Through such a model they hope to demonstrate the viability of cooperative principles and create an environment where people from all walks of life can "drop out" of mainstream society, if only for a day or a week, and experience a new way of living. Like their counterparts in the 1800s who, "[i]nstead of trying to change society from within, by parliamentary reform or by violent revolution, . . . tried to set up models of ideal commonwealths, thus providing examples which they hoped the world would follow" (Holloway 1951, 18), Rainbows seek to create a working model for reform. After a quarter of a century, the Rainbow Family is still working to perfect and make operational their model.

Like Robert Owen, who "was convinced that the truth of his principles and the advantages of communism would spread from Community to Community, from State to State, from Continent to Continent, finally overshadowing [sic] the whole earth" (Holloway 1951, 105), Rainbows hope that all the earth's peoples will eventually adopt their model. Utopians and communards throughout history saw themselves as "social architects," seeking to redesign society (Hayden 1976, 9). "All believed that social change could best be stimulated through the organization and construction of a single ideal community, a model which could be duplicated throughout the country" (Holloway 1951, 9).

Even skeptics admit the success of the Rainbow model. *Time* magazine, for example, writes: "For a tribe of peace-and-love anarchists with no structure and no leaders (their Council is anyone who shows up at Main Circle), the Rainbows' disorganization is surprisingly effective" (Skow, 1991). State government officials in California looked toward the Rainbow infrastructure as a model for the possible resettlement of San Francisco residents to the countryside in the event of an emergency (Lee 1984).

Rainbow child rearing lets children voice their concerns and participate in planning their own activities and menu at Kiddie Village. Since Rainbow children are encouraged to speak their minds, the Council discusses and acts upon issues like child molestation instead of sweeping them under the carpet. Rainbows teach children that they are important, and they know that adults will listen to them. There is a healthy dialogue between generations. Unlike American communities where municipal and school authorities subject children to curfews and random searches, Rainbows do not fear their children.

Gatherings demonstrate the effectiveness of nonviolent crisis intervention. Rainbow Gatherings are overwhelmingly peaceful, with remarkably few problems for such large events. Problems such as those which crop up at "A" Camp challenge nonviolence, providing an opportunity to prove its effectiveness. Many Rainbows view both the courts and the penal systems as "violent" in the sense that they depend on punishment. Rainbows are searching for alternatives to turning troubled people over to the state. Their aim is to heal them, ending their violence and helping them grow.

A Unique Utopia

The Rainbow Family is unique among utopian societies. As a band society it practices "fission-fusion" (Dentan 1992; Dentan 1994; Fix 1975; Neel et al. 1964), dissolving into the dominant society and regrouping again as a community in a different locale. The freedom that the Family experiences at Gatherings is temporary, yet comprehensive. Within their Temporary Autonomous Zone (Bey 1991) or "refuge" (Dentan 1992), Rainbows enjoy a level of freedom unobtainable in a stationary community which must interface over a long period of time with mortgage holders, neighbors and local governments. In many ways, it is more like a "twelve-step group" than a utopian movement (Dentan 1992).

The Rainbow Family shares few traits with what historians and sociologists traditionally identify as successful utopian communities. It has no permanent settlement or land base; no assets; no formal organization, charismatic prophet, hierarchy, or identifiable leadership; it is nonsectarian and maintains no selective criteria to determine membership; requires no material investment or personal sacrifice from recruits; has no work routines or requirements; does not encourage, discourage, or attempt to coordinate sexual relations; does not require any ideological conversion nor attempt to control child rearing. By all indications, looking at historical precedents, the Family should have collapsed shortly after its inception in the early 1970s.

Whereas utopians have striven for order and are characterized by "conscious planning and coordination, whereby the welfare of every member is insured" (Kanter 1972: 39, cf. Dentan 1994), Rainbows thrive in their own cohesive brand of chaos. In many utopian communities, all life functions are planned and coordinated by the leadership, including eating, sleeping, praying, loving, working, and playing (Kanter 1972, 40). "In many communes there is a decision making body that effectively coordinates members' lives, informing them when and where to eat and sleep, sometimes with whom to make love, and usually what hours and tasks at which to work" (Kanter 1972, 40). These decision makers have often been "charismatic leaders" or "prophets" with a supposed divine sanction for leadership (Wallace 1956, 273–74, 279).

Traditionally, the larger the community, the more centralized the decision making. Even the largest Rainbow Gatherings, with thirty thousand members, however, remain decentralized and nonhierarchical. Such non-organization is usually associated with failed utopian experiments. "The most enduring communes were also the most centralized and the most tightly controlled" (Kanter 1972, 129). Yet it is the Rainbow Family's lack of centralized control that has allowed it to both endure and flourish. Other communities, or even nations, become bogged down in perpetual power struggles for control of a centralized hierarchy. Such infighting often leads to fractures within groups, as those who are estranged from the power base either leave the group to start their own organizations, or try to undermine group leadership. Likewise, leaders resort to favoritism, rewarding and strengthening their followers with patronage perks, to keep their political organization thriving. Internal power struggles contributed to the demise, for example, of many well-known nineteenth-century utopian communities such as Nashoba, Bishop Hill, Skaneateles, and New Harmony (Kanter 1972, 140; Fogarty 1990, 175).[3] Even Alcoholics Anonymous, in 1995, was showing signs of internal strain. The Rainbow Family's consensus Council, by comparison, does not estrange dissenters. Since everybody is supposedly included in all decisions, revolution becomes obsolete. With no one *in* power, no one is *out* of power.

Successful utopian communities have often asked that perspective members make some sort of sacrifice in order to become a member. The sacrifice, whether represented by an economic investment in the community, a vow of sexual abstinence, or a vow of poverty, serves to strengthen the community by placing a value on membership. Hence, according to cognitive consistency theories, the more it costs to be a member, the more valuable membership becomes. Members with an investment in the community will be less likely to leave it, making for a more stable population.

The tradition of sacrifice dates back to the beginnings of the American utopian movement. The Labadist colony at Bohemia Manor (Maryland 1683–1722 or later), for example, would not let members heat their rooms, food was purposefully prepared unpalatably, meals were taken in silence, and new members had to donate all of their worldly goods to the collective. By standards of longevity, the community was a success, lasting four decades (Miller 1993, 124). Rainbows by comparison make few demands on new recruits.[4] Contributions are voluntary. Wealthy Rainbows are free to hoard their wealth.

Other successful utopian communities have required members to renounce relationships that could possibly undermine group cohesiveness by, for example, posing a conflict of loyalties. Thus Alcoholics Anonymous members shun "wet people and wet places" (Dentan 1994). Rainbows, however, decry renunciation, seeing the task of forming a cohesive bond between different peoples as a major group goal. Hence, the Family consists of vegetarians and hunters; pacifists and National Rifle Association members; anarchists, socialists, and Republicans; Christians, pagans, and atheists; cops and robbers, all celebrating life together. While they share values such as a broad commitment to nonviolence and nonhierarchical governance at Gatherings, they sometimes choose not to, or cannot, practice these values as individuals away from Gatherings.

Traditionally, successful utopian communities remained small, not being able to absorb large numbers of recruits (Barkun 1986, 63). This stemmed from their inability to culturally assimilate large groups of new recruits and to care for their physical needs. The Family, by comparison, has had many successes assimilating large groups of newcomers into their Gatherings. It is not unusual for Gatherings near large urban areas to attract a population, half or more of whom are newcomers or "tourists." Even under this stress, however, Gatherings have remained cohesive and kept their identity. This is because the Rainbow doctrine is relatively simple and easy to accept. Volunteers at the front gate, for instance, educate newcomers with a basic Rap 107 explaining the noncommercial, nonviolent alcohol-free (except "A" Camp) Gathering environment. Within a short time, newcomers become familiar enough with basic Rainbow values that they can educate later arrivals. Hence it is conceivable that someone who arrives at 10 A.M. could be a full-fledged Rainbow by noon, providing information to newcomers. In this way Rainbow ideology can spread like a virus. Misleading media reports, however, often cause newcomers to have a confused image of the Family, thus making the process of assimilating them more difficult.

During the utopian heyday of the nineteenth century, the vast majority of successful communities were sectarian, only accepting members with a common religious or ethnic heritage. "Apart from the Shakers, the most firmly established and longest-lived communities in America were all German sectarian groups" (Holloway 1951, 159). Most utopias restricted recruiting to a narrowly stratified group with common religious beliefs, ethnic identification, class status, or political outlook.

While Rainbows share a broad-based worldview of a peaceful environmentally sustainable society, they are firmly nonsectarian and pride themselves on their attempts to attract a diversified multicultural membership. Rather than hindering the Family's success, such diversity has been key both to the Family's growth and to the warm reception they have received in many parts of the country. The latter is because, wherever the Family goes, locals will share affinity with some Rainbow sub-group. Hence, Christian Texans, for instance, disturbed by rumors that the Rainbow Family members were all pagans or atheists, were relieved to find Baptists among the Family. Likewise, rural residents were relieved to find farmers among the Rainbows, and so on.

The downside of the Family's inclusiveness is the presence of a disruptive and often violent "A" Camp at American Rainbow Gatherings. Traditionally, utopian communities have excluded such people. Peter Cornelius Plockhoy, who in 1663 founded the first non-native North American utopia, for example, wrote, "We desire no wild cursers, drunkards or other strange people in our community" (Miller 1993, 121). Most Rainbows, however, while sharing a disdain for the violent drunken antics of "A" Camp, see healing "A" Campers as part of their mission. To refuse to help brothers and sisters in need goes against Rainbow doctrine, even if the people in question don't recognize the need for help, refuse help and victimize Family members. The presence of violent drunks has been associated with the downfall of utopian projects like Earth People's Park in Norton, Vermont, which died in the late 1980s. The Rainbow Family, however, has thrived despite "A" Camp, integrating some former "A" Campers into the main Gatherings, where they are now productive Family members.

Utopian communities have also collapsed because they were either too successful economically or, antithetically, because they were too poor. Economically successful communities, after becoming prosperous, historically have tended to abandon communal ideals, in favor of distributing communal assets through privatization (Hollaway 1951, 48; Oved 1988, 442; Kanter 1972, 158). Many of these colonies faced ideological conflicts between older members with a deeper commitment to communal ideals and newer members who were at least partially attracted by the wealth of the community. As communal assets grew more valuable, the arguments as to how they should be divided or invested grew more intense. Eventually, in most cases, assets were finally divided among members.

The Rainbow Family, by comparison, has no assets. The Family's lack of a centralized organization ensures that it will never have any assets. Hence, the Family is not likely to become engaged in a fight over assets. While individual Rainbows might be economically successful, and in turn be generous in donating to the Magic Hat, their assets are not communal or under Council jurisdiction. Magic Hat money, the closest thing the Family has to collective wealth, goes for consumable resources, usually food, before it ever amounts to much.

Sporadically, Family members have attempted to raise money to purchase a collective water supply system. Plans, at one time, called for constructing a massive truck-based carbon filtration system and purchasing miles of plastic piping. Had these failed plans been successful, they would have threatened Family cohesiveness as Council debated where the system should be stored, to which regional Gatherings it should go, and so on. The limited water systems the Magic Hat bought in the past disappeared after Gatherings, sometimes to reappear at future Gatherings or as donations to nonprofit groups or booty for thieves. Individual Kitchen Councils, however, have obtained resources such as water filters and cooking equipment and successfully cared for these resources between Gatherings. So far, the Family as a whole has not accumulated resources.

Utopian communities have also failed because they couldn't lift themselves from poverty, couldn't provide adequate material conditions for their members. The Rainbow Family, as a nomadic band, faces no such challenges. The Family is not responsible for providing year-round shelter and care for its members, and its inability to do so isn't construed as a failure. If food at one Gathering is in short supply, the situation is only temporary. Rainbows often trade stories of poor Seed Camps where members subsisted on one sort or another of gruel for a week or so. These conditions usually got better with the arrival of "yuppie" (employed) Rainbows who showed up later on in the Gatherings with food or money. In the rare instance where an entire Gathering went "hungry,"[5] the situation ended at the conclusion of the Gathering, with the Family regrouping elsewhere under better circumstances. Hence Rainbows have never faced prolonged hardships like those faced by frontier utopians existing as truly self-sufficient communities.[6]

Nomadic versus Permanent: A Comparison to the Farm

To understand the dynamics of the Family's nomadic existence, it seems useful to compare the Rainbows to a permanent land-based utopian community. For comparison, I have chosen to look at the Farm in Summertown, Tennessee,[7] the twentieth century's largest single cooperative utopian community.[8] They settled in Summertown in 1971, a year before the first Rainbow Gathering. Transplants from San Francisco's Haight-Ashbury "hip" scene, they arrived in a caravan of fifty or so brightly painted live-in school buses. They were a bunch of city folks planning to grow their own food, get high, groove on the land, and teach the world how to live in peace. According to their one-time spiritual mentor, Stephen Gaskin, the Farm was to be a demonstration project for a sustainable future—a nonviolent ecofriendly cooperative community of pioneers ushering in a new age.

By the early 1980s, when most other '60s-era communal experiments were fading, its population swelled to almost fifteen hundred people, who pooled their incomes and savings into a common coffer. Besides farming portions of their seventeen hundred acres in Tennessee, they had satellite farming operations in ten states, Canada, France, and Ireland. They ran relief operations in Central America, the Caribbean, Africa, Bangladesh, and the South Bronx through a worldwide operation in constant communication with Tennessee via ham television and radio. They invented Ice Bean, ran a school, pioneered vegan cookery, and started a publishing company, an electronics firm, a "soy dairy," and a construction business. Farm midwives earned worldwide recognition as leaders in the midwifery revival and the respect of the local medical establishment for their excellent birthing record.

While there is little interaction between the Farm and the Rainbow Family, Farm founder Stephen Gaskin sees the two groups as "cousins," evolving from the same general movement (Gaskin interview 1994). Hence, although very few Farm members have been to Gatherings, they feel an affinity with the Family. Likewise, Rainbows talk positively about the Farm, though few have ever visited.

Although the Farm is still prospering today, they abandoned their communal economy in 1983 after falling more than one million dollars in debt during the American farm crisis of the late 1970s, despite hard work and excellent crops (Bates 1993; Traugot 1994, 60–64; Farm Oral History 1994). Their other cash producer, a collective construction company, itself all but idle during the Reagan recession, failed to pull them from the brink of bankruptcy. The Farm was in trouble, ironically, not because their experimental collectivism failed, but because of failures within the greater capitalist economy.

To pay off their debt, the board of directors developed a plan, ratified by a vote of the membership after much debate, to sell off collective businesses and charge residents a fixed membership fee—a sort of regressive tax—to remain on their land. Those who worked on collective Farm projects like road maintenance found themselves with fixed expenses but no source of income. Besides having to pay membership fees, they had to pay for items that used to be available free at the community's collective store. The Farm privatized its motor pool, leaving many residents without transportation to go out and find work. Unprepared to cope with the rapid changes, about seven hundred people left the Farm in 1983 alone. By the late 1980s, fewer than three hundred people remained.

Today's Farm has wandered considerably from its egalitarian roots. A class schism has developed. Some people drive around in new Toyota pickups and Volvos; others bike, hitch, or walk. Ramshackle homes, originally built up from tent platforms, stand just up the road from state-of-the-art new-builds. The privatization of businesses has created entrepreneurs and workers, albeit working side by side in a relatively democratic environment.

Farm history, as told today, no matter who the narrator, falls into two eras—before "the changes" and after. "Before" is a nostalgic amalgam of romanticized chaos, idealism, power, and triumph. "After" is a story of pragmatism, survival, and balance sheets, peppered with a litany of business successes. The Farm, like the Rainbow Family, grew out of an idea incubated in the 1960s, was established in the early 1970s, and is surviving today in the 1990s. However, economic necessity forced the Farm, unlike the Family, to undergo major changes and abandon its central tenet of collectivity. The Family, by comparison, has changed remarkably little over the years. Far from being trapped in a time warp, the Family has evolved culturally, assimilating new forms of culture,[9] music, dress, and food. Yet ideologically, the Family has remained committed to its original goals of maintaining a nonhierarchical, noncommercial, egalitarian, nonviolent demonstration society.

To survive as a land-based community, the Farm had no choice but to change. Rainbows, by comparison, have no land base to protect. Since they can't lose assets they don't have, they aren't under the same pressures as the Farm. Rainbows have the luxury of being more insouciant in the face of adversity. Farm residents, and ex-Farm residents, still argue over the changes of 1983. Roan Carratu, a former Farm resident, now a computer consultant in Nashville, questions the merit of restructuring the Farm to save the land. The land, he says, was meaningless in comparison with the Farm's purpose: "The mission of The Farm was to save the planet—the land was just a place where we set down to try to show an example of how people could live—and if everyone lived that way it could save the planet" (interview 1994).

While Carratu's description of the Farm's mission resembles the Family's, it is different: the Rainbow Family prides itself on having neither an "organization" nor a land base. Although Rainbow Gatherings draw up to twenty times the peak population of the Farm, the Family has not been able to provide the global human services that the Farm has. An elderly Rainbow sister, for example, spoke her Heartsong during a Council: as she grew older and more frail, she was counting on the Family to provide for her in her old age. Everyone present muttered "Ho!" in agreement, but they laid no plans, and save for possible individual actions, no mechanism exists within the Family to care for this sister or anyone else over the long term. Farm founder Stephen Gaskin, by comparison, has begun the Rocinante community. Geographically adjacent to the Farm, it is a retirement community, a healing center, and a birthing center, able to meet the needs described by the Rainbow Sister, providing a space to grow old with ease and dignity.

Where Rainbows have fed, housed, and provided medical care to the homeless for a week here or there, the Farm has made its presence known around the world, training medical personnel, establishing ambulance services, building schools and houses, starting soy dairies, and so forth. But to finance such programs, however, the Farm entered into "high-stakes commerce with the outside world," increasing their "vulnerability to macroeconomic trends" (Bates 1993). Such industrial endeavors led the Farm to develop a large hierarchical bureaucracy, replete with incompetence and mismanagement (Bates 1993), eventually leading to bankruptcy. Free from manic business cycles, Rainbows have continued to provide basic services sporadically to needy populations, slowly expanding such services as the Family grows.

Today the Farm is split into two ideological camps—the conservatives, who support the current land-trust model of organization with private homes on communal property, and the liberals, who want to return to a more collective economy. Each group claims roughly half of the Farm's residents. An evolving new Farm economy lets members choose between private ownership of property and wealth, or a limited "cafeteria plan" opting into differing levels of an emerging new limited collectivity.[10]

These two camps divide not only on economic issues, but on many other questions, like recruitment. Currently, not even members' children who have been raised on the Farm are guaranteed membership. Conservatives want to maintain the current system whereby the full membership votes on whether children will be allowed membership upon reaching adulthood; liberals want to grant children automatic membership when they come of age. Both sides, however, oppose the type of open admission Rainbows practice. This opposition is understandable, since Rainbows would stand to risk only a difficult Gathering or two, while Farm residents would be risking their homes if the population was unable to support itself.

A Bargain-Basement Tribal Identity

The difference between the Farm and The Rainbow Family comes down to commitment. The pre-1983 Farm required new recruits to turn over all of their assets to the collective coffers. The current Farm requires the few new members they accept[11] to ante up three thousand dollars and buy equity in a house. The Rainbow Family requires nothing from new members other than an open mind. With no investment, Rainbows can come and go freely. While many Rainbows have been associated with the Family since its inception, there is no commitment mechanism to tie members to the Family. Where successful utopias have often required members to give up individual privileges as a price of membership (Kanter 1972, 57), Rainbows have no such requirements. Put bluntly, The Rainbow Family represents a sort of bargain basement route to tribal affiliation or communal identity, with all the trimmings and none of the obligations.

Both the Rainbow Family and the Farm share the same basic goal: to save the world. They differ, however, when it comes to tactics. The Farm has struggled, often at great cost, both physically and ideologically, to maintain a land base and a bureaucratic network to support a constant stream of new environmental and social projects. Even with its current diminished population, the Farm still maintains a strong role in the fields of sustainable agriculture, alternative energy, midwifery, and land conservation. Their relief organization, Plenty, is again growing, providing ecologically sustainable development projects to the third world. To accomplish these goals and to support themselves, they currently operate over seventy businesses, partnerships, and corporations. Of all utopian communities started in the United States, their service out-reach has been both the most ambitious and the most successful.

Rainbows represent the anarchist front in the same race to save the world. Free of bureaucratic constraints and with no assets to lose, they can take their model community anywhere on the globe, often creating spontaneous cities in many nations simultaneously. Currently there is *always* a Rainbow Gathering somewhere. Unhindered by restrictive admissions standards or requirements for investment or commitment, hundreds of thousands of people have, at one time or another, lived in the Rainbow Family's utopia. After experiencing the Rainbow world, many people go on to commit themselves to projects such as those run by the Farm, Greenpeace, or Sea Shepherd, to name a few. Others find Buddhism, Christianity, or reconstructed Native American spirituality. Others, experiencing less radical changes in their lives, might return home after a Gathering to plant a garden, clean up a vacant lot, organize a block club, or introduce themselves to their neighbors. The Family provides a portal through which people can pass into a new life, a life first tasted at a Gathering.

The struggle to save the planet depends on the success of the Farm and Rainbow Family models in tandem. While the Farm has accumulated the resources to experiment with sustainable development technologies, the Rainbow Family, un-hindered by material assets, has the freedom to conduct radical experiments with social organization, decision making, and the healing of violent or addicted personalities.

Consistency and Change

Despite their accomplishments, it is debatable whether the Farm is a long-lived utopia; because of the radical changes during their history, their current organization bears little resemblance to the pre-1983 entity. Using not just chronological survival, but consistency, as a criterion for longevity (Shenker 1986, 12–13), leaves no doubt, however, that the Rainbow Family is a successful utopia, having resisted ideological change for over a generation.[12]

Basic survival strategies, especially for groups facing persistent persecution, involve adaptation and change, as Anthony Wallace pointed out four decades ago (Wallace 1956, 274). The Rainbows, while remaining steadfast in their ideals, *are* moving closer to mainstream society, not because they are adapting to Babylon, but because Babylon is adapting, ever so slowly, to Rainbow values. Rainbow practices like recycling, vegetarianism and veganism, holistic health, and Indian worship, considered alien when the Family first gathered, have since been adopted by large segments of the mainstream society. Schools are beginning to teach nonviolent conflict resolution, and the general population is becoming more sensitive to threats against civil rights. Even suburban housing developments, once a bastion of alienation, are starting to resemble communal utopias, as developers experiment with self-contained co-dependent communities, albeit at the cost of excluding other elements of society from their walled enclaves.

Aside from embracing and promoting communalism, the Family also supports individual rights and liberty even when individual rights are at odds with collective responsibility. Where other utopias have sacrificed individual concerns to the collective good, the Rainbow Family seeks to balance individual and collective needs. Hence, each singular voice in Council holds as much weight as the total of all other voices. Allowing individuals to block consensus assures, when the system is working, that no individual's rights will be trampled by a majority. Rainbows expect individuals, on the other hand, as a prerequisite for participating, to have reciprocal respect for the group, and not abuse their power to block consensus. The evolving "consensus minus one" policy, however, limits individual power in the interest of maintaining greater group cohesion in the face of a persistent consensus blocker.

Rainbow reverence for individual rights extends to respect for unpopular views and other forms of nonthreatening deviance. Such tolerance has allowed the Family to stay politically diverse, with membership crossing a wide libertarian spectrum from Republican-conservative to anarcho-syndicalist or communist. Rainbows range across a wide spiritual-religious spectrum as well. The only requirement spiritually, or politically, is respect for diversity and a willingness to listen to alternative views. Conversations at Gatherings are enlightening, as members strive for, and find, common ground.

Since Rainbow communitarianism, for example, is on a voluntary level, with no required Magic Hat contributions, there is room for communists and capitalists to coexist. Since there are no persistent expenses, profits, debts, or assets, there is no real need to choose one economic system over another. For all intents and purposes, Rainbow economy is communalistic, encouraging sharing and discouraging profiteering. The transience of the Gatherings allows capitalists to journey into this communal world but limits their economic participation, so they can return to their world of private holdings between Gatherings.

While one can argue that such a system, where the rich need not share their wealth, is not socialistic or communistic, it is undeniable that the temporary Gathering economy succeeds because the wealthy underwrite the poor. The difference between the Rainbow economy and a hierarchical socialist economy is that Rainbow socialism or communism is voluntary. Hence, there is room for noncommunists and noncommunalists in this communal society. Such inclusion both swells the Family's membership and allows socialist Rainbows an opportunity to demonstrate the viability of their system to nonbelievers. The fact that Rainbow communism is pervasive while being completely voluntary demonstrates the Family's commitment both to communalism and to individual liberty.

Endless Summer

Despite a history of being short-lived, utopian movements persist in North America, with new experiments rising up from the ashes of their predecessors (Gide 1930, 10–11). Given this model for perpetual utopian regeneration, the Rainbow Family is an eternal phoenix, incessantly rising up from its own ashes. Where one Gathering ends, the next begins. The Family, while maintaining consistency for a quarter of a century, has endless opportunities for new beginnings, as it gives birth to itself. Hence, the Rainbow Family *cannot* fail. At worst, they can only have a bad Gathering.

The formula for birthing a Gathering is simple. Unlike the intricate social or economic systems involved in, for example, a nineteenth-century Fourierist Phalanx or even a contemporary commune, the Rainbow utopia is easy to assemble. At its simplest, it just involves starting a rumor that it *will* happen and spreading Rap 107 *when* it happens. The fact that Gatherings are easy to start, and as the Forest Service will attest, difficult to stop, ensures the continuing survival of the Family, even in the face of adversity.

The Family, as a nomadic group, is immune to even the natural adversities of changing seasons. "The rural communities often seemed like paradise, at least in the summer, with the cool streams and lush gardens of rural farms. But then the inevitable snows would come, and with them came the hassles of cutting wood to stay warm, the restlessness of cabin fever, and the impassibility of mountain roads" (McLaughlin and Davidson 1985, 99). The Rainbows, on the road following the sun, live in a true utopia, an endless summer. With the exception of a hardy handful of Michigan Rainbows who gather each winter, Rainbow Gatherings are held in the most hospitable seasons; northern Gatherings are in the warm summers while southern Gatherings are in the cool winters. Hence, a minimal infrastructure is required to gather. The only obstacles are human.

The Rainbow example threatens governments. It shows that people can live without rulers, without yielding their voices to representatives. It demonstrates that people can be responsible for themselves and maintain peace without coercion or force, without police. It is a model of a true participatory democracy, "Government by the People." The European Gatherings are bringing people of different ethnic and national backgrounds together to discuss their common future; to dream of a world without armies or wars. The Rainbow Family is the antithesis of a police state. It challenges all entities that govern by fear instead of cooperation. For them, the Rainbow Family provides the "threat of a good example," one others might follow (Chomsky 1987).

Rainbows have, since their beginning, faced opposition both internally, with the "A" Camp being the most obvious persistent problem, and externally, with ubiquitous government harassment wherever they gather. In 1897, a member of the Ruskin community, explaining how their utopia was not a "paradise," wrote, "We

are but human, with 5,000 years of inherited prejudices" (Egerton 1977, 78). A
century later the same holds true for the Rainbow Family as they also struggle to
perfect society. It will remain a struggle, for utopia is never realized. It will, also,
as it grows more successful, become more threatening, and hence, generate more
resistance.

Rainbows are dreamers, hoping for nothing less than utopia. For twenty-five years
the Gatherings have demonstrated that a predominantly nonviolent and
nonhierarchical society can successfully operate on a large scale. They have demonstrated not only the strengths of such a society but also its weaknesses. They are
providing opportunities to test methods of decision making and nonviolent intervention. Rainbows are successfully and unsuccessfully grappling with their problems as
they work to perfect their model society. Their goal is unwavering. Eventually, they
hope, everyone everywhere will always be at a Rainbow Gathering.

Appendix A
Committees Formed at 1990 Thanksgiving Council

Magic Hat/fun(d)raising

Banking Council (to decide how Magic Hat money is spent)

Office (networking and coordination)

Supply Council (purchases/procures food and supplies)

Water System (facilitates hydraulics and/or water procurement and disbursal)

Parking

Peacekeeping (non-violent intervention)

Peace Ceremony (on-site)

Rainbow Peace Projects (coordinates ongoing peace projects)

Peacenet (Rainbow participation in computer network)

Peace Issues

Rainbow Violence (verbal, etc., amongst Rainbows)

Welcome Center

CALM (medical unit)

Site Planning and Mapping

Main Circle Space

Sanitation

Mental Health Issues

Spiritual Focus (of Family and Gathering)

Info Center

Outreach

All Ways Free (Rainbow newspaper)

Scouting (site selection)

Legal Liaison (Rainbow legal defense collective)

Rainbow Historians (information exchange and archives)

Special Needs (disabled people, etc.)

Support for Earth People's Park

Publicity/Media

Save the First Amendment

Council Process

Kids' Village

Sister's Space

Brother's Space

Hemp/Drug War Issues

Proposition One (a pet political cause)

Native Issues (Big Mountain, James Bay II)

Recycling

Twelve-Step Recovery Programs—at Gatherings

On-Site Vegetable Gardening

Cleanup Crew

Political Activist Info Center

Workshops

Drumming

Barter Lane/Trade Circle

Defending Against State Seizure of Children

Sweatlodges

Peace Pageant

Talent Show

Elitism (within Rainbow)

Conspiracy (theories—examine and evaluate)

Appendix B
Rainbow Self-Descriptions

Many people who attend the Gatherings sign up to be listed in the Rainbow Guide, often writing a short self-description or Heartsong. The following excerpts (spelling and punctuation appears as it does in the guide) from Rainbow Guides, provide a sampling of Family members:

Artist, poet, musician, engineer, human willing to communicate, share, focalize; share the Light!

Rhythms of the drum, the soul, the planet, the Universe. May all the ways of our religions and all the paths we walk on rise up to join in unison, as do the poles of a tepee.

My vision is a world where womyn share power equally with men and where there is unity encompassing and respecting all our differences—a world where no form of oppression or power exists—where conflicts are resolved creatively by non-violent means.

Interests: music, I play sitar and tambouras. Electronic music composition/ soundscaping for theater, video, dance, etc. Contact improvision dance. Resources: small recording studio; extensive knowledge of electronics and musical applications there-of. The love and light all of us share. Camped at Sunrise kitchen.

Having done well in the realm of rationality, I stepped forth into the non-rational. With no residence, no job, no support but the universe, I wander after a dream of community. Aspects of myself, once lost, return, and new ones appear. I become a dancer, gardener, craftswoman, singer, writer, shamaness, counselor, telepath, healer of nations. It scares me, and leaves me awed. I remain at the same time a pragmatist and a skeptic, a motormouth, a flawed mortal, cowardly about criticism and anxious over irresponsible use of The Gifts, even though most of them are barely postnaescent [sic]. I proceed. I love you all.

Therapeutic massage, holistic counselor, mind-body-spirit, healing worker, overnight visitors welcome.

I do computers and build recumbent bicycles. Love the Mud!

Bamboo flutemaker (bamboo saxophone, shakuhachi); single parent; poet; musician; healer; scribe; camped in upper kid village... let us seek to live in harmony with one another, our earth, our creator, our source; let our children remain the angelic beings we seek to be; seeking a land-based or caravan community of like-minded artists/spiritualists.

Resources: I am a graphic artist and illustrator presently illustrating children's books, album covers, poster designs, with focus on Celtic knotwork, fantasy & magical themes. DJ. . . . Interests: Celtic interlace, pre-Raphelite art, pagan ritual, earth lore, tribal and folk music. We do alternative dance jams once a month...

Resources: poet, writer; I'll have my teachers' certification by May and I'm interested in alternative Waldorf schools. I'm also a flower essence practitioner and I.H. childbirth educator. Interests: community, networking, dance, poetry, music, birth, herbs, healing, children, flowers, herbs, crystals, wiccan rituals, counseling, meditation, Love, Light, Laughter. I camped behind Miso Magic! The beauty of this Gathering touched me deeply—so much Joy & healing. A truly ecstatic experience. I feel blessed to be a part of this ever growing tribe.

I am a part of the International Conference on Human Rights and Psychological Oppression. We work to free mental patients. Stop and visit...

Historian and carpenter, following the Incarnation, caller of New England contra dances and singer of old songs.

My interests are love, life and fun. [I am] an initiated Wiccan... Studying medicine (traditional/non-traditional and going for Masters in Anthropology. Associated with the Faire Camp....

Clown/Juggler, teacher of both. If in NY area, call.

Real Estate Consultant

We are in Lafayette Park in front of the White House and would love to entertain Rainbow brothers and sisters at our 6 year old 24 hour 7 day a week vigil. We love You!!

As of September, I will be traveling extensively throughout Central America contacting service projects and communities. I would love contacts toward this as well as similar service/communities in New Zealand, India and the surrounding area. I've done work with Rainbow Sprout Gardens.

Conservative scientist & anti-political faerie.

Aboriginal Tao Zen Quaker Faerie seeks friends.

Carpenter, hiker, confused, lookin' for good vibes.

I am vagabonding with my bicycle. Mail will be forwarded. Peace.

Crafts (Advertising, Graphic Art, Illustration) & Holistic Healer (Home Health Care). All free alternative lifestyles.

I want to make movies. I want to spread the vision I see and feel when I'm here / home.

Working toward realizing higher levels of consciousness, my own personal power and a more total awareness of myself, others and the world in and around us. Can offer a short-term place to sleep.

Interested in literature, religion (paganism, animism, gnosticism), sociology. I worked at a women's center counseling women who have been battered or sexually assaulted—I am a survivor of childhood sexual assault myself. Leftist communitarian, anarchist, bisexual, politically active.

I run a place called "The Turning Point," an empty space where people can be & do what is their true nature.

I'm interested in cooking for people. I would enjoy information and ideas about the food service needs across the country. I love you!

Surfing Camp & Alcohol Fuel Project w/ bananas and other alternatives (French intensive gardening, solar stills) in Nicaragua and/or Costa Rica.

Electrical mechanical contractor by trade—very useful at setting up power, water, etc. Married with one child.

My real fantasy is having a baby at Rainbow after I get my head together. I'm not in a hurry for a permanent relationship unless I get talked into it, but having a baby will be by Larry who I met at Moondancer's and Yonder Family Kitchen.

Congo [sic] player & dental assistant.

I am a Green and a NeoPagan. Welcome Rainbow visitors. Looking to help build or join intentional community.

. . . Passive solar design & construction, hospitality, food production & preservation. College professor, environmentalist.

I am a healer of the Earth. My profession is in pollution control. I commune with the spirits of Nature and her cycles and practice Shamanism, Wicca, and other spiritual practice, as well as my mundane skills as a professional Environmental Engineer.

Graphics, music, anarchism, no drugs, not skilled in much, willing to learn.

Minstrel Apothecary mystic fool laborer jongleur sorcerer librarian libra Russian expert farmer builder caver woodsman head astronomer herbalist bibliophile woodcutter composer tree climber scientist—I Love You.

I am a street minister helping the poor of This Country. Worked at Main Circle and spread Help and Love. Licensed spiritual counselor.

I will protest against all things that hurt people.

Mommy poet person.

People at Rainbow taught me, through good example, to care about myself, my planet, and everyone on it. Long live anarchy.

Homeless. The N.C. gathering was my 2nd gathering. If you see me on the road hitchhiking please give me some work & a ride. I would like to buy some land in Tenn. and turn it into a Rainbow camp or farm. Love You.

As noted in chapter 4, the *Rainbow Guide* was used by the U.S. Forest Service to harass Rainbow Family members in 1988 [U.S.F.S. Texas May 11, 1988]. It was also used by the U.S. National Park Service for gathering "intelligence" [Malanka May 4, 1990]. Since then, many people have chosen not to list their names in the Guide. Their reasons include fear of government harassment (present and future), fear of commercial exploitation of the Guide, fear of discrimination on their jobs due to their Rainbow Family affiliations, and not wanting to be annoyed by travelers. Most people listed in the Guide do not provide much information about themselves.

Appendix C
1972 Rainbow Demands

1. Immediate withdrawal of all American troops, advisors, and military aid from Vietnam and all of Southeast Asia.
2. Immediate withdrawal of all American troops, advisors, and military aid from Latin America, Africa, Asia, Europe, all islands, both polar regions—in short, all foreign soil.
3. Resignation of all law enforcement officers not part of the community which they serve to be replaced by community control of all peace officers.
4. Immediate release of all political prisoners.
5. Immediate release of all prisoners being held for crimes without victims.
6. Transformation of the American penal system into a compassionate, educational system.
7. Immediate legalization of all healthful herbs.
8. Equal respect for the rights of all people, minorities as well as majorities—including blacks, whites, reds, yellows, browns, women, minors, longhairs, the elderly, the poor, the sick, the rednecks, mentally disturbed, and those of minority religions.
9. Total respect for the life pattern and understanding that we cannot continue to upset and interfere with the balance of nature.
10. Recognition of the rights of all children and their parents to choose their own means and sources of education.
11. That free and unrestricted travel be allowed without need of "permits" such as identification papers, money, passports—and that all border crossings be made into welcome areas and free medical aid stations.
12. Abolition of the conscriptive system and rechanelling [sic] of all military forces into the Green Guard, to clean up, recycle, replant, and rebuild planet home.
13. United States withdrawal from all economic involvements that are oppressive to the peoples of the world; institute Share the Wealth programs whereby everyone can be fed healthful, wholesome foods, have adequate housing, and receive ample, free medical care. This can be done simply by sharing America's abundance throughout the world. (Stop paying farmers not to grow food.) feed the people heal the sick share the wealth
14. Donate 3,000 acres of unwanted, unused government land to the Rainbow Family of Living Light... to build a healthy, harmonious city—a permanent living example of peace upon the earth [Rainbow Oracle 1972: 119].

This demand for a landbase dates to the year of the first Gathering. The Family has since abandoned a desire for a landbase as it emerged as a successful nomadic society, creating Temporary Autonomous Zones [Bey 1991] or "refuges" [Dentan 1992].

Appendix D
Rap 107

#107

GATHERING CONSCIOUSNESS

PLEASE PROTECT THIS BEAUTIFUL LAND. WALK SOFTLY. ALLOW PLANTS & ANIMALS TO BE HARMONIZED ♫ BLENDIN≋. USE ONLY DOWN, DEAD WOOD. PRESERVE THE MEADOWS... CAMP IN THE WOODS.

EVERYONE SHARING MAKES A STRONG HUMAN TRIBE!

PLEASE PROTECT THE WATER SOURCES, STAY OUT OF DELICATE SPRING AREAS, PLEASE. AVOID CAMPING, PEEING, WASHING ABOVE SPRING AREAS. KEEP ALL SOAP OUT OF STREAMS, SPRINGS OR THE LAKE!

USE THE SLIT TRENCHES OR COVERED LATRINES, COVER YOUR PAPER & WASTE WITH ASHES/LIME... WASH HANDS.

CAMP TOGETHER ~ ESTABLISH NEIGHBORHOODS.

COMMUNITY FIRES ONLY! ~ EACH WITH WATER BUCKET, SHOVEL AND AX OR SAW FOR FIRE PROTECTION. WATCH YOUR GEAR ~ "TEMPT NOT LEST YE BE LIFTED FROM." BE RESPONSIBLE FOR YOUR ANIMALS. KEEP THEM FED AND OUT OF THE KITCHENS & SPRINGS. LOVE THEM. SEPARATE GARBAGE FOR RECYCLING. FIND NEAREST COLLECTION POINT. COMPOST IN PITS ONLY.

USE YOUR OWN BOWL & SPOON! PARTICIPATE IN ALL ACTIVITIES, COUNCILS, WORK CREWS, WORKSHOPS. YOU ARE THE GATHERING! R-E-S-P-E-C-T YOUR SISTERS & BROTHERS ENERGIES. HEALTH PROBLEMS? CONTACT C.A.L.M./M.A.S.H. FOR AID!

NOTICE THE BALANCE: EARTH, SKY, TREES, WATER & PEOPLE!

ALCOHOL IS DISCOURAGED, GUNS ARE INAPPROPRIATE.

DONATIONS TO THE MAGIC HAT FUND OUR NEEDS.

JOIN US FOR JULY 4TH SILENT CONTEMPLATION & PRAYER

TO BE CERTAIN OF DRINKING WATER: BOIL IT!

Appendix E
Rap 701

#701

 Happy Trails

In preparation for leaving... Pack up all your trash & bring to the appropriate recycle areas. Dismantle & disappear your encampment. Vanish ALL traces. Firerocks scattered, ashes cold out & buried, pits filled in. Latrines & compost holes covered over. String & twine get removed from tree limbs. Hardened ground gets areated with tools for future root growth & moisture catch. All litter is picked up. Help with Recycling. Where everyone helps, the effort is easy.

When an area is clear & clean, then Naturalize! Scatter logs, branches, leaves, duff to disappear trails & camps and renew forest habitat. H_2O systems & latrine tops are removed & cleaned for next time. In parking areas help with disabled vehicles and fully dismantle ramps & bridges. Steep places are water-barred to prevent erosion. The final crew reseeds appropriate seed to renew vegetation and complete the process.

Transport as many riders as possible to aid our travels. Treat local folks with great kindness. They have been kind to us.

Drive safely and share this love wherever you go.

Appendix F
Sample *Howdy Folks!*

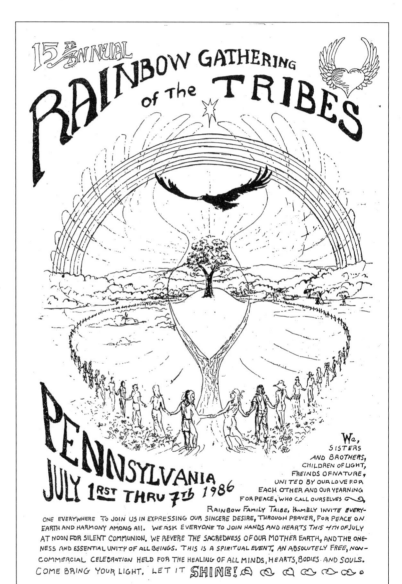

Appendix G
Chronological Listing of Annual North American Gatherings

1972—Colorado

1973—Wyoming

1974—Utah

1975—Arkansas

1976—Montana

1977—New Mexico

1978—Oregon

1979—Arizona

1980—West Virginia

1981—Washington

1982—Idaho

1983—Michigan

1984—California

1985—Missouri

1986—Pennsylvania

1987—North Carolina

1988—Texas

1989—Nevada

1990—Minnesota

1991—Vermont

1992—*Colorado*, South Dakota

1993—*Alabama*, Kentucky

1994—Wyoming

1995—New Mexico

1996—Missouri

1997—Oregon

1998—Arizona

1999—Pennsylvania

For years where simultaneous Gatherings were held, the state with the larger Gathering is italicized.

Appendix H
Chronological Listing of Annual European Continental Gatherings

1983—Italy

1984—Switzerland

1985—Italy

1986—France

1987—Spain

1988—Spain

1989—Norway

1990—Austria

1991—Poland

1992—Poland

1993—Ireland

1994—Slovenia

1995—Czech Republic

1996—Portugal

1997—Scotland/Greece

1998—Russia

1999—Hungary

Notes

Chapter 2. Roots, Rock, Rainbow

1. As an "intentional group," it has an explicit program that rationalizes and justifies perpetuating itself (Chang 1981).
2. The Rainbow Family stands in sharp contrast to most North American utopian communities, which employed rigid criteria in selecting new members. The open membership policy has resulted in a number of problems, which are examined throughout this book. Rainbows are adamant, however, that acceptance of all living beings as Rainbow is central to their commitment to reform the earth.
3. Ting is a Scandinavian traditional gathering, revived from Nordic mythology. Ting activists were instrumental in facilitating the 1989 European Rainbow Gathering in Norway, which followed the Ting gathering on the same site.
4. Systema is an annual Gathering very much like a Rainbow Gathering.
5. Followers of Robert Owen's philosophies established seven colonies between 1825 and 1826. Fourier's followers established twenty-nine "Phalanxes" between 1842 and 1858.
6. To have "toured" with the Grateful Dead meant to travel around the country, taking in all or most band concerts when the band was on tour. Each stop on tour became a spontaneous celebration, embodying many aspects of a Rainbow Gathering. Deadheads often camped and ate communally while touring, but unlike Rainbow Gatherers, deadheads engaged in commerce and drank alcohol while usually camping in parking lots instead of forests. To many Deadheads, the tour itself and the community it provided, and not the band or the actual concerts, were the main attraction. The death of band member Jerry Garcia effectively derailed the Dead tour phenomenon—at least for a while.

Chapter 3. "The Way We Make Decisions Is More Important Than the Decisions We Make"

1. This conservative estimate rests on U.S. Forest Service attendance figures and estimates from longtime participants.
2. There are exceptions to this "rule." The occasional *small* regional Rainbow Gathering, as well as many Rainbow Family picnics and potluck dinners, occur on private property.
3. The passing of a focal object is not unique to the Rainbow Family. The Movement for a New Society, for example, also recommends passing a focal object around the circle.

4. The Forest Service called the meeting on July 9, 1990, to discuss the impact of the Gathering on the community.

5. For a comparison of Alcoholics Anonymous and the Rainbow Family, see Dentan 1994.

6. Bus Village is where live-in vehicles (like converted school buses, vans and campers) are parked. Bus Village should be as close as is practical to the main Gathering area, to allow easy access to and from the main Gathering.

7. The actual recommendation, as put forth in 1980, based on Forest Service reports from 1976, 1977, and 1978, states that Bus Village should be located "so as to require a long hike from the Gathering area to the Bus Village—the longer the better."

8. Volunteer scouts arrive in the region where the Gathering is scheduled to occur during the spring thaw. They fan out over the region exploring potential sites, which they then discuss at Scouting Council, eventually consensing on which site the Gathering will occur.

9. This is the time period of the National Gathering. It usually remains constant from year to year. The period before July 1 is considered Seed Camp, and the period after July 7, Cleanup Camp. There is no Council on the Fourth of July, as this is officially a time for silent meditation and prayer.

10. This is in and of itself a notable occurrence, as it is rare that any subject ever escapes debate when put before Council.

11. The original vision was for people to be shuttled to the end of the road, and then hike two miles in to the Main Circle area, which was to be the center of the Gathering. The gate was about two miles before the end of the road. The result was that people would walk the last two miles on the road, be tired, and set up their camps at the end of the road instead of deeper in the woods.

12. This problem afflicts most hierarchical states as they seek to extend their control over egalitarian "acephalous" (leaderless) peoples. (See, e.g., Benjamin 1968; Idris 1983).

13. Scuzzy Womp was a small kitchen/camp consisting primarily of people from the New England region.

14. Although seven years have passed since this Council, there is still no "Rainbow Peace Village" for Rainbow elders to retire to. There are other utopian communities, however, such as Rocinante in Summertown, Tennessee, which provide eldercare. Rocinante, started by Stephen Gaskin, is an outgrowth of the Farm community.

15. Rainbows expect facilitators to serve, not direct, the Council. Council participants choose facilitator(s) before the Council opens. Sometimes more than one facilitator will be selected, so that one can relieve the other.

16. In this regard, a "process point" is similar to a "point of order" from Robert's *Rules of Order*.

17. Hayden studied Shakers, Mormons, Fourierists, Perfectionists, Inspirationists,

Union Colonists, and Llano Colonists in the communities of Hancock (Massachusetts), Nauvoo (Illinois), the New Jersey Phalanx, Oneida (New York), Amana (New York and Iowa), Greeley (Colorado), and Llano del Rio (California and Louisiana).

18. The Icarian community founded by French expatriates in 1848 provides a good example of the continued disenfranchisement of women during supposed democratic communal reforms. (Founded in Texas, the group moved to the former Mormon site at Nauvoo, Illinois, in 1849.)

19. McLaughlin and Davidson are also former members of the Findhorn Community in Scotland. Both have taught courses and lectured about alternative communities at the American University and Boston College.

20. Ward Churchill, professor of American Indian Studies and Communications at the University of Colorado and vice chairperson of the American Indian Anti-Defamation Council, in his Book *Indians Are Us? Culture and Genocide in Native North America,* refers to Sun Bear (Vincent LaDuke) as "an erstwhile Chippewa 'holy man' and founder of something called the 'Bear Tribe,' who has made a lucrative career penning New Age texts and peddling ersatz 'Indian ceremonies' to an endless gaggle of white groupies" (Churchill 1994, 287). Churchill has also coined the term "Spiritual Hucksterism" to describe Sun Bear and his ilk (Churchill 1992, 4).

Chapter 4. The Nuts and Bolts of Making a Rainbow: Rainbow Infrastructure

1. Rainbows prefer to Gather away from roads. However the U.S. National Forest Service has been very active during the Reagan/Bush/Clinton era, building access roads for commercial logging in National Forests. Hence, remote sites away from all roads are becoming more and more elusive.

2. Rainbows refer to their latrines as "shitters." They are primarily used for defecation. Urine, which is easily and safely absorbed by the forest, disrupts the fecal decomposition process. Hence the term "shitter" is direct and to the point. Babylon terms such as "powder room," "ladies'/men's room," "rest room," "washroom," "head," "john," "can," "pot," "toilet," "little boy's/girl's room," and "throne" (Kira 1967, 102) all fail to adequately describe Rainbow latrines. Even the term "latrine" fails to distinguish between the acts of defecation and urination.

3. For a detailed description of proper posture for defecation, see Kira, 1967, 119–21.

4. Many Rainbows value crystals for their supposed healing powers which are popularized by New Age publications.

5. Rainbows usually make ovens from used fifty-five-gallon oil drums that are cooked in a fire for a day to burn out any residual impurities.

6. Rumors abound at Gatherings. The Information Area, also called "Rumor Control," is a place where Rainbows can attempt to verify a rumor's accuracy. Rainbows attribute the proliferation of rumors to the lack of Rainbow mass media at Gatherings. If present, they assert, the media would create "official rumors," and "factoids."

7. Taco Mike's kitchen has operated in tandem with the Hobo Hilton, a rough-and-ready coffee kitchen that set the Gathering record for reusing coffee grounds.

8. Such struggles within the Rainbow Family are described briefly in both chapter 1 ("Sunflower's Day") and chapter 3 ("How We Make Decisions . . .") of this book.

9. The city of Buffalo, New York, for example, holds an annual "Drug and Alcohol Free" New Year's Eve celebration, yet Folger's Coffee cosponsors the event.

10. They do, however, serve tea, which contains the addictive alkaloid theobromine. They also serve sugar and hot chocolate, both drugs.

11. Brew-Ha-Ha, not able to get the five hundred gallons a day needed, often ran out of tea.

12. Many CALM practitioners don't view diseases as "chronic" or "terminal," feeling that all diseases are curable.

13. For unsympathetic summaries of the nineteenth-century precursors of CALM, see Gardner 1957, 98–115.

14. They did not, however, leave the Family. In ensuing years, the Sage Hollow kitchen developed into one of the Family's most reliable kitchens.

15. Many city dwellers have acclimated to sterilized chlorinated municipal water and therefore lack resistance to waterborne bacteria.

16. At the 1990 North American Gathering, someone made tie-dyed T-shirts bearing the screened imprint "Rainbow Shitter Digger" and gave them out to latrine diggers.

17. The North American Phalanx (New Jersey, 1843–55), however, employed farm hands who, unlike their utopian overlords, did not enjoy such privileges as job rotation.

18. Yacoov Oved writes: "The imperative of rotation was ingrained in the communal experience and was meant to make the equal and just division of difficult and unpleasant service jobs feasible. Furthermore, this enabled members to develop a many-sided affinity with various branches and also prevented the forming of exclusive and elitist groups and professions" (Oved 1988, 439).

19. Changing locations and collectives annually is the ideal, but lack of volunteers forced *All Ways Free* to publish, for example, from Tucson, Arizona, in both 1990 and 1991.

20. Half-tabloid refers to the size of the pages. For comparison, the *Village Voice*,

the *National Enquirer*, and the *New York Daily News* are half-tabloid publications.

21. Government documents released to this author confirm that Forest Service agents used the *Rainbow Guide* in 1988 to compile a list of Rainbow Family members, who were then contacted by Forest Service agents spreading false rumors that the 1988 North American Gathering in Texas was canceled. In fact, a federal judge reaffirmed the right of Rainbows to gather in Texas (see chapter 10).

22. At presstime, Savoye's Rainbow page World Wide Web address is www.welcomehome.org/rainbow.html. Savoye and associates also maintain an E-mail subscription version of the alt.gathering.rainbow newsgroup.

23. I use the term "gypsies," as Rainbows do, in referring to wanderers and vagabonds—people on the road. I am not referring to the European Romany (Roma) who are often called "Gypsies" despite their preference for the accurate descriptive "Roma" or "Romany."

Chapter 5. People of the Rainbow

1. Police actions to monitor, disrupt, or attempt to control Gatherings are documented in chapter 10 of this book.

2. This figure does not take into account the Bruderhof movement, which is loosely affiliated with the Hutterites. The American Bruderhofs, located in Rifton, New York (originally from Germany, via Paraguay, moved to New York in 1954), Deer Springs, Connecticut, and New Meadow Run, Pennsylvania, are, like the Hutterites, members of the Hutterian Society of Brothers (Oved 1988: 362).

3. While many Rainbows describe themselves as Rastafarian, without fully understanding or practicing the religion, Remi *is* a Rastafarian.

4. Many names in the Guide are not gender-specific, making an exact count impossible.

5. In the 1990s Rush Limbaugh was a ubiquitously syndicated radio talk-show host in the United States. He both appealed to and fed the insecurities of a white male audience—using misogyny, racism, xenophobia, nationalism, and hatred of the poor to stir up his listeners, whom he called "Dittoheads." I hope that this note will be necessary to identify a man and a phenomenon that history has forgotten.

6. Earth First!ers claim Earth First! is a "movement" and not an "organization," since, like the Rainbow Family, there is no central hierarchy.

7. Currently the sole criterion for AA membership is a desire to stop drinking (Dentan 1994).

Chapter 6. Violence and Peace

1. Om circles are not exclusive to peacekeeping. They are also common before meals and at the opening of meetings and Councils.
2. "Yippie" is an acronym for the Youth International Party, a remnant of a 1960s-era political organization that waned as its members aged.
3. These orders are usually reasonable and are intended to ease congestion and chaos in the parking lots, ease traffic on eroding trails, preserve environmentally sensitive areas, etc.
4. Police are welcome at the Gatherings. Their guns are not.
5. On one occasion the Forest Service interceded to help a water delivery pass through the Shanti Sena's roadblock (Joens 1990a).
6. Almost everybody who self-identifies as a member of the "Shanti Sena" is male.
7. The Rainbow Family refers to child molesters, people who expose themselves to children in a lewd way, and otherwise abuse children, as "child predators."
8. One Forest Ranger, concerned about the arrest of his "Shanti Sena" friend, contributed money to the bail fund.
9. The A-Camp scene is overwhelmingly and sometimes exclusively male.

Chapter 7. Fakelore

1. "Medicine Wheels," while central to many New Age "Indian" spiritual gatherings, have never played a central role in authentic Native American spiritual ceremonies (Kehoe 1990, 200).
2. McGaa also regrets "that traditional Native Americans have to suffer their undeserved association with those Native Americans who use peyote in their ceremonies" (McGaa 1992, 8–9).
3. Plockhoy, a Dutch Mennonite, had his plans cut short by the outbreak of war between Holland and England.
4. Many locals living near the 1990 North American Gathering site in Minnesota became irritated with law enforcement officials after being caught repeatedly in roadblocks designed to harass Rainbows en route to the Gathering.
5. The Declaration of War is reprinted in its entirety in *Indians Are Us: Culture and Genocide in Native North America* by Ward Churchill (1994), available from Common Courage Books.
6. SPIRIT is an acronym for Support and Protection of Indian Religions and Indigenous Traditions.

Chapter 8. The Mediated Rainbow

1. A forty-eight-year-old St. Louis woman shot her teenage son because she was supposedly upset about his plans to travel with a group of Rainbows.
2. The National Park Service's "intelligence report" on the Rainbow Family repeatedly refers to the Family as "the Rainbow Children" (Malanka 1990b).
3. In the summer of 1995, for instance, there were eleven major week-long Rainbow Gatherings in the United States and Canada, plus another ten in Europe, as well as ongoing regularly scheduled day-long Gatherings in sixteen U.S. and Canadian cities.
4. Mushers race dog sleds.
5. Better late than never: in 1994, the New York Times Magazine used the word "Rainbow" in a headline for a July 3 story about the Family, "Red, White and Blue Rainbow."
6. Here too, the Allegheny Forest Service approach differed from that of local branches in other forests such as Nantahala in North Carolina and Angelina National Forest in Texas. Allegheny officials spoke highly of the Rainbow Family, pointing out the Family's record for site rehabilitation and a general lack of problems with past Gatherings. Forest officials were even quoted as being excited about the Gathering and looking forward to it.
7. The Forest Service rented a number of rooms in the Lutsen Village Inn, in Lutsen, Minnesota, where they set up an Incident Command Post.
8. It was particularly damaging that these allegations were given validity by the Associated Press, which is the United States' largest news dissemination service, serving 85 percent of the nation's newspapers and over six thousand television stations (Lee and Solomon 1990, 23).
9. Todd Gitlin writes, "From the media point of view, news consists of events which can be recognized and interpreted as drama; and for the most part, news is what is made by individuals who are certified as newsworthy. Once an individual has been certified as newsworthy, he or she has been empowered, within limits, to make news" (Gitlin 1980, 146).

Chapter 9. Leave Only Smiles

1. The Forest Service, however, supervised the destruction of much of the site a few years later during an intensive logging operation.
2. Construction contractors dumped debris, including asbestos, around the site. A burn pit on the site contained the ashes from various plastics.
3. Following the 1971 raid, the Farm enacted a policy prohibiting marijuana growing and selling in their community. Members still adhere to the policy. There has not been a marijuana or drug bust at the Farm since 1971.

4. The Indians never actually complained about the nudity. The Quebec Rainbows, in fantasizing that their Gathering site was sacred Indian land, imagined a scenario in which the Indians would be offended by their nudity. They never imagined, however, a scenario in which local Indians would be offended by a bunch of white folks practicing an ersatz Indianism.

Chapter 10. The Rainbow and the U.S. Government

1. The officers were more successful in finding cars than people, locating twenty autos and trucks, but only twelve Rainbows.
2. This figure is based on a small sample group who responded to a Centers for Disease Control survey sent to people listed in the Rainbow Guide (Wharton and Spiegel 1987). Since those who contracted illness were more likely to respond, the resultant statistics may exaggerate the disease morbidity.
3. Dr. Richard Allen Spiegel of the Centers for Disease Control testified (*U.S.A. v. Rainbow Family* 1-88-68-CA, 141–44) that a statistical association existed between illness and eating at Krishna Kitchen. Diarrheal illness was documented at Krishna Headquarters in West Virginia before the Gathering. A secondary outbreak of "shigellosis" diarrhea occurred at the Krishna Headquarters after the Gathering (Nelson 1987).
4. The proposed amended regulations provide that a permit may be denied if no one from the group seeking the permit signs the permit application on behalf of the group and agrees to be responsible for meeting the terms of the permit (Justice 1989, 28).
5. Ball's venom is not reserved exclusively for the Rainbow Family. Six weeks after the 1987 North American Gathering, he was accused of assaulting an Earth First! demonstrator (Russell 1987).
6. The law, filed under 7 CFR Subtitle A, Subpart B, "Conduct and Responsibility of Employee" (U.S.D.A. manual, Jan. 1, 1987) reads: "(b) Employees are specifically prohibited from: . . . (7) Except as authorized by the Inspector General with the consent of a party to the conversation when necessary in criminal investigations, utilizing a mechanical or electronic device to monitor or record non-telephone conversations, unless such monitoring or recording is agreed to in advance by all participants in the conversation."
7. "The World" is Vietnam veterans' slang for America. Given this usage, the implicit analogy could be between Rainbows and Viet Cong, "the enemy," folks to be disabled whenever possible, not U.S. citizens camping out in a park. Another ranger at the same Gathering signed his report to his superior, "Your Devoted Soldier" (Bedlow 1989).
8. "The purpose of such activities was never intelligence gathering per se, but rather the inducement of "paranoia" among those targeted by making them

aware they'd been selected for special treatment" (Churchill and Vander Wall 1988, 39).

9. At a town meeting in Tofte, Minnesota, for instance, officials showed an aerial video of the Gathering, but denied knowing where it came from.

10. Lyght hit an unexpected snag when county commissioners informed him of a state law prohibiting elected officials from collecting overtime, even though the money had already been paid to the county earmarked for Lyght.

Conclusion

1. In 1995, for example, there were ten major regional Rainbow Gatherings in Europe alone.

2. Indeed, a famous utopia is described in a novel by Samuel Butler called *Erewhon,* an anagram for "nowhere."

3. Those communities that have escaped such strain often fall apart when a charismatic leader dies or leaves (Wallace 1956, 274).

4. Rainbows do, however, ask that members refrain from drinking alcohol or using hard drugs or money at Gatherings.

5. By "hungry" I mean, not well fed or lacking a tasty menu. Even under the worst conditions, Rainbows have managed to dumpster dive or purchase some sort of food for a subsistence diet.

6. Alcoholics Anonymous shares this freedom.

7. For a more complete description of the Farm, see "Out to Save the World; Life at The Farm," by Michael I. Niman, *High Times,* Feb. 1995 (pp. 44–46, 62–63), portions of which are excerpted here. Also see *A Short History of the Farm,* by Michael Traugot, available from the author at Box 84, The Farm, Summertown, Tennessee 38483. Also see Popenoe and Popenoe 1984.

8. Although Hutterite membership outnumbers peak Farm membership by a factor of at least 25 (Oved 1988, 357), the Hutterites are dispersed in over three hundred settlements with no single settlement exceeding a population of 150 people (Oved 1988, 351, 357). The Farm, with a peak membership of 1,200 and a peak population of 1,500 (including "guests") was larger than the Llano del Rio socialist commune (which started in California in 1914, moved to Louisiana in 1917, and ended in 1937), although scholars sometimes identify it as the twentieth century's largest communitarian experiment.

9. For example, New Age, twelve-step spinoffs of AA, holistic medicine, Internet culture, etc.

10. A limited number of Farm residents and business concerns have joined together to form the Second Foundation (named after Isaac Asimov's literary invention of the same name) in 1988, continuing the original collective Farm vision on a smaller-scale voluntary basis. The Second Foundation has about

thirty members, with organizers seeing thirty to fifty as the optimal member-ship limit for cohesive governance. The resulting hybrid economy allows members to choose to what degree they want to commit themselves to the collective. For more information about the Second Foundation and other Farm economic experiments, see Bates 1993–94.

11. The Farm does not recruit new members and discourages applications from strangers. They do, however, entertain applications for readmission from previous residents who would like to return.

12. Figuring a generation as demographers do, as twenty years.

Glossary

"A" Camp	Alcohol Camp. A place where chronic alcohol drinkers congregate and drink, usually on the perimeter of a Gathering.
Alcohol Hat	"A" Camp money collection. Used to buy alcoholic beverages.
All Ways Free	Rainbow Family newspaper.
Ally-O Council	Meeting with Forest Service officials.
Aum	See Om.
Babylon	The world outside of the Gathering. "Mainstream" or "mainline" society; the "straight" world (from the Book of Revelation, via Rastafari).
Banking Council	A Council convened to decide how to spend Magic Hat money.
Barter Lane	A place at a Gathering where people congregate to trade crafts, camping supplies, books, etc. Same as "Trade Circle" in function, but linear instead of circular in topography.
Beanbow	Boston Rainbow Family Picnic.
Blissninny	A person at a Rainbow Gathering who does not contribute much work; overly spiritual and out of touch with the physical realities and demands of the environment (derogatory).
Blissing out	Sitting around or wandering around, enjoying the Gathering, in a carefree state.
Bus Village	A large camp of live-in vehicles. Usually located a good distance from the central Gathering area, as Bus Village must be accessible to vehicles.
Business Council	A Council convened to deal with Gathering logistics, Family policy and other organizational concerns.
C.A.L.M.	Center(s) for Alternative Living Medicine. The Rainbow Healing unit. Formerly M.A.S.H. Transformed into C.A.L.M. as it grew from a first aid station to a comprehensive medical unit.
Consense	To agree by consensus.
Conch	A univalve shell, usually of the *Cassia* species, with a hole cut in the tip. Blowing through the hole makes a mellow sound to call people together for Councils, meals, workshops, meetings, etc. The practice is part of the Family's self-conscious primitivism.

Cooperations Council	A Council convened at a Gathering to foster communication between the diverse sub-Councils involved in coordinating the Gathering.
Council (verb)	To meet as a group with the aim of reaching consensus on a given topic.
Council (noun)	Any group of Rainbows meeting to make a decision. Usually refers to the Council that meets between July 1–7 at North American Gatherings.
'Dog	Short for Road Dog.
Dogging It	Living the life of a Road Dog.
Dived (adj.)	Pertaining to an item retrieved from a garbage dumpster.
Drainbow	A person who demands a lot from the Gathering and does not return anything.
Drugs	Unhealthy habit-forming substances ranging from sugar to crack.
Dumpster (verb)	To retrieve food or other goods from a garbage dumpster.
Dumpster Dipping	Neologism coined by U.S. National Park Service Ranger Chris Malanka (1990a). An activity like Dumpster Diving involving the retrieval of "contaminated" food. Malanka does not explain why anyone would want contaminated food.
Dumpster Diving	Same as Dumpster (v).
Dumpster Score	An item or group of items retrieved from a dumpster.
Early	Politically correct alternative to the word "elder," which people often interpret as meaning leader or authority figure.
Elder	Someone who has been to many Gatherings and is supposedly knowledgeable about the Family. Rainbow ideology states that elders, while wise, are not leaders, as the Family admits to no leadership.
Facilitate	To take responsibility for making sure a given task is accomplished.
Facilitator	A person who has taken responsibility to make sure that a given task is accomplished.
Faerie	A homosexual male Rainbow.
Faire	*See* Faerie
The Feather	A feather or other focal object passed around a council circle to identify the person who is speaking.
Focalize	To organize a project

Focalizer	A volunteer responsible for serving as a conduit for Rainbow Family information to both Family members away from the Gatherings and to the public; also responsible for overseeing the organization and publicity for local area Rainbow Family events.
Focus (verb)	To pay attention to, or respect, the speaker or council procedures.
Free Box	A box where Rainbows leave unwanted or surplus possessions so that those who need them can pick them up gratis.
Front Gate	The main entrance to the Gathering.
Fuck You	An "A" Camp greeting used like "Hello."
Full Ride	Staying at the Gathering from the start of Seed Camp through the end of cleanup.
Gate	Same as "Front Gate."
Gate Crew	The people who work at the Front Gate, welcoming people and delivering the "Rap 107" spiel.
Gatekeeper	A person who stands on the perimeter of the Council circle, advising late arrivals as to what has been discussed and what is currently being discussed, what consensus decisions have already been made, and so on.
Green Energy	Money.
Ground Score	An item that is found on the ground.
The Guide	A printed directory of Rainbow Family members. Also known as the Rainbow Guide.
Gypsy	A Rainbow who lives on the road, constantly traveling.
Habit Hat	A money collection for purchasing coffee, tobacco, sugar, and so on, to satisfy addictions.
Happy Trails	A common good-bye to people leaving the Gathering. From the signature sign-off song of the Roy Rogers/Dale Evans television western of the 1950s.
Harmonize	To enter into peaceful harmony with people or the environment.
Harrassle	Harassment and hassles of Rainbows by government agencies and the police.
Heartsong	Personal feelings, emotions, observations and visions as articulated at Gatherings.
Heartsong Council	A meeting to share heartsongs as a group therapy, and often as an introduction to Business Councils.
Heil Holys	A derogatory description of self-righteous Rainbows.

Herkimer	Type of light-refracting quartz crystal generally found near Herkimer, New York; popular trade item.
Hey Now	Greeting, used like "Howdy."
Hipstory	Collectively told oral history of the Rainbow Family. The Rainbow Hipstory is recited each year at the North American Gathering. Anyone is free to join in the telling of the Hipstory.
Hipstorian	One who participates in the telling of the Hipstory.
High Holy Hippie	A derogatory description of Rainbows who feel they are part of a power group, entrenched hierarchy or "old guard" of the countercultural movement.
High Holy Rainbow	Same as High Holy Hippie but is specific to Rainbow Family.
Hippie	Descriptive term referring to 1960s countercultural lifestyle, derogatory when used by non-Rainbows, often to anachronize Rainbows. Also used among Rainbows as familiar greeting or self-descriptive.
Ho!	Used in Council to express agreement with the speaker. Also name of a southeastern United States Rainbow Family publication.
Hobo	Someone who lives on the road (see On the Road), has lived on the road for a while, likes living on the road, and intends to keep living on the road.
Hohner	An authentic unpretentious down-to-earth person. Someone who lives a honed-down lifestyle.
Home	At the Gathering.
Howdy Folks!	The written announcement of a Rainbow Family Gathering or event.
Hug Patrol	A group of people who wander around Gatherings hugging people.
Info Center	An area where information is exchanged. Consists of an information booth and at least one bulletin board. Information ranges from news of the outside world, times and places for workshops, and maps of the Gathering site, to suggestions for dealing with insects.
Kiddie City	A camp for parents, children, and expectant parents. Provides childcare, special activities, and special meals for children.
Kiddie Village	See Kiddie City.
Kids' Village	See Kiddie City.
Katuah	Southeastern United States mountain bioregion.

Kind	Free or nice.
Kind Bud	Free marijuana.
Magic Bedpan	Money collection for the CALM medical facility.
Magic Hat	Money collection for the common coffers. Usually used to fund Main Supply.
Main Circle	Usually a central area where the Council meets and where the July 4 (for North American Gatherings, dates differ for regionals) meditation and prayer celebration occurs. A dinner, prepared by many different kitchens and carried over in five- or six-gallon buckets, is also usually served here.
Mainebow	Maine Regional Rainbow Gathering.
Main Trail	The central, most heavily traveled trail at a Gathering.
Main Supply	Distribution center for kitchen supplies.
M.A.S.H.	Sometimes used interchangeably with C.A.L.M. to refer to the medical unit.
Meat	Specialty at Taco Mike's kitchen. Formerly a living animal—not necessarily a cow, pig, or chicken—now food.
Movie	The spectacle transpiring in front of you at any given time. Often refers to ridiculous antics. Most popular movies: "The Gate Movie," "The 'A' Camp Movie," and "The Cop Movie."
Mud	Rainbow Coffee. Often made 'Field Style' with grounds in the bottom of the pot. A splash of cold water before serving helps sink any floating grounds. Grounds often get reincarnated for future pots.
National Gathering	Refers to the annual North American Gathering.
NERF	North East (North America) Rainbow Family; formerly, New England Rainbow Family.
Newage	Rhymes with "sewage." Derogatory description of a New Ager.
Om	(1) The sacred syllable A+U+M, pronounced "ome" as in "home" or "holy" in the Rig Veda (e.g., the hymn to Siva [Chan, Ismail Ragi and Raju 1969: 25, 29n79; see also ibid., 35]).
	(2) One of the most important mantras in Tantric (Tibetan) Buddhism (e.g., Evans-Wentz 1960; 1967: 127, 301, 312, 320n2, 340), in which "when the disciple's mind is properly attuned, the inner vibrations of this word symbol together with its associa-

tions in the consciousness of the initiate . . . open his mind to higher dimensions" (Kapleau 1966: 346). (3) This Tantric sense, perhaps via the translations of Evans-Wendt's work which occurred in the 1960's, seems to inform Rainbow usage, in which it becomes a somewhat desacralized pacifying syllable that people chant, typically, before meals, after Councils, during meditations and prayers, in order to "harmonize" vibrations." The exact route from Tibet to Rainbow is obscure, however, since North Americans tend to lump all "Eastern religions" together in practice (e.g., D. 1966: 261).

Om Circle   A circle of people chanting "Om," usually to harmonize an uptight situation, sometimes used for coercive purposes.

Omming   Chanting "Om."

On the land   At the site of the Gathering.

On the road   Pertaining to a lifestyle whose adherents are on an extended trip or have no permanent home.

Pothibition   Refers to antimarijuana laws.

Process   Any social-political activity with a goal; e.g., with the word "Council," to describe the mechanism by which the Council reaches decisions.

Rail Tramp   See Tramp.

Rainbow Dark   Sundown or thereabouts. Vision Council rules require proceedings to cease at Rainbow Dark.

Rainbow Noon   Roughly, when the sun is high in the sky, usually between 11 A.M. and 2 P.M., depending on the season, location, and mood of those who need to know when it's Rainbow Noon.

Rainbow Time   A system of keeping time without watches. Rainbow Time is whenever enough people think it is whatever time it is supposed to be. Rainbow Time usually runs about an hour behind clock time, but may be as much as an hour early.

Rainbow Trail   An extended trip, taking in numerous Gatherings.

Rainbow Runs   Diarrhea contracted at Gatherings, usually attributed to change in diet or water as well as soapy dishes.

Rainbozo   A cross between a Blissninny and a High Holy Rainbow, usually loud and obnoxious. Often used by "political" Rainbows to describe "spiritual" ones.

Rap 107   A written or oral introduction to the infrastructure of the Rainbow Gathering.

Rap 107 Below	A written or oral introduction to the infrastructure of a Winter Rainbow Gathering. Developed by the Great Lakes regional Rainbow Family
Rap 115	A written or oral request asking people to treat bothersome drunks at Gatherings with love, not anger. Often described as the "flip side" to Rap 151 (see below).
Rap 151	A written or oral diatribe explaining why alcohol is discouraged at Gatherings; promotes benefits of an alcohol-free space.
Rap 420	Legal information primer explaining individual rights when faced with police harassment.
Rap 701	A written or oral guide to the etiquette of cleaning up after a Rainbow Gathering.
Rap 911	A written or oral reminder to travelers coming to or leaving U.S. Gatherings about their rights in regards to searches of vehicles by the police. Also advises travelers to caravan as protection against police harassment and to document all instances of police harassment.
Road/the Road	See On the road.
Road Burn	A state of mind one slips into after being "on the road" too long; in other words, exhausted and wanting to settle down for a spell.
Road Dog	Someone who calls the Road home; cf. Hobo, 'Dog.
Road Kill	A dead animal found on the road; dead animals in general. See Meat.
Rumor Control	The act of containing runaway rumors within the Rainbow Family; "Info Center."
Runner	Someone who delivers messages, supplies, or food between two points at a Gathering.
Scam	A plan, sometimes dishonest, for getting something for less than its value.
Scattering	Time when most people are leaving the Gathering and dispersing.
Score	To obtain something by purchase, trade, or chance.
Shanti Sena	Peacekeeper. Also a group that considers themselves "leaders."
Shanti Sena Council	A Council convened at a Gathering to discuss peacekeeping and to collectively train people in nonviolent crisis intervention.
Sherpa Patrol	Group or individual who helps people carry supplies to camps and kitchens.

Shitter	A Rainbow latrine.
Shitter Patrol	Group or individual who builds and/or maintains latrines.
Shuttle	A vehicle used to move Rainbows back and forth from the parking area to the trailhead into the Gathering.
Sisters' Space	An area reserved exclusively for women.
Sisters' Meadow	A meadow reserved exclusively for women.
Sisters' Circle	A place where women council together.
Six Up	Slang for gun or armed police officer.
Snifter	See Snifting.
Snifting	Looking to meet someone, primarily for sex. Most snifters are men looking for women.
Styling	Nice.
Supply Council	A Council convened at a Gathering to coordinate collective supply purchases and to distribute supply donations to camps and kitchens.
Tour	Grateful Dead band tour.
Trade Circle	Same as "Barter Lane," only a circle.
Trader's Row	Same as "Barter Lane."
Tramp	Hobo or Road Dog, who hops trains.
Uptight	Frustrated, neurotic.
Vibe (v)	To emit a nonverbal or feeling signal to someone else (from yoga; e.g., [Evans-Wendt 1967]).
Vibe (n)	A nonverbal signal or feeling. Also can be used to describe a mood.
Vibeswatcher	A person who has been chosen by the Council to monitor the Council mood. If the mood is becoming argumentative or in any other way nonconducive to a healthy Council, the vibeswatcher momentarily interrupts council for a breather, an Om, a stretch, jumping jacks or the like.
Vision	A picture of how things should, could or will be.
Vision Council	The Council which chooses the general area (state, country, or region) for the following year's Gathering. Also discusses direction and goals of Rainbow Family.
Wahwah	A tasty morsel of food, easy to eat but not a meal; also not too sweet (From prison slang)
Weekend Rainbow	Someone who only participates in Rainbow activities when on vacation from a job and "mainstream" lifestyle. See Yuppie.

Weekend Hippie	Someone who participates in countercultural activities only when on vacation from a job and "mainstream" lifestyle. *See* Yuppie.
We Love You	Greeting, usually shouted in unison by a group of people. An unseen group elsewhere in the Gathering usually answers with another chorus of "we love you," which might be answered by yet another group.
Welcome Fire	A fire kept burning at the Front Gate to welcome late-night arrivals, heat coffee for new arrivals, etc.
Welcome Home!	Standard Rainbow greeting for someone who is entering the Gathering from Babylon.
Welcome Soup	A pot of soup that is always warm at the Front Gate for new arrivals (Quebec Rainbow tradition).
Yuppie	Someone with a job.
Zuzu	Like a wahwah, but very sweet. Usually candy or doughnuts (from prison slang).

References

Books, Articles, and Other Publications

Adams, Barry. 1988. "One More Broken Treaty." *All Ways Free,* winter.

———. 1991. "Sisters and Brothers, Men, Women, Children, Family." *All Ways Free.*

Albanese, Catherine. 1990. *Nature Religion in America: From the Algonkian Indians to the New Age.* Chicago: Univ. of Chicago Press.

All Ways Free (Rainbow Family newspaper). 1986. "That's not my job," Feb.

———. 1989. "Participation is the key," summer.

———. 1991. "Rap 151," summer.

Anderson, Patrick. 1981. *High in America. The True Story Behind NORML and the Politics of Marijuana.* New York: Viking.

Anonymous

———. No Date(a). Rap 107.

———. No Date(b). Rap 701.

———. No Date(c). The Complete Gatherer.

———. 1995. Rainbow Usenet Internet Post (Identity withheld for this publication).

———. 1995(a). Rainbow Usenet Internet Post (Identity withheld for this publication).

Armstrong, David. 1981. *A Trumpet to Arms: Alternative Media in America.* Boston: South End Press.

Aslam, Abid. 1990. "Marching for Peace." *Lies of our Times,* Feb.

Associated Press. 1987a. "Ousted Rainbow Family Member Says Gatherings No Longer Peaceful." *Franklin Press,* June 24.

———. 1987b. "Rainbow Gatherings Have Changed." *Hendersonville* (N.C.) *Times-News,* June 26.

———. 1987c. "Clouds Darken Rainbow Family Gathering." *Greensboro* (N.C.) *News and Record,* June 30.

———. 1987d. "Rainbow Family Reunion Expects 10,000 at Nantahala National Forest Gathering." *Hendersonville* (N.C.) *Times-News,* June 3.

———. 1990. "Some Rainbows Reappear at North Carolina Camp." *Duluth News-Tribune,* June 24.

———. 1994. "Rainbows, Ranchers Get Along Fine." *Rocky Mountain News* (Denver), June 23.

Bagdikian, Ben H. 1983. *The Media Monopoly.* Boston: Beacon.

Baker, James N., and Lisa Drew. 1988. "A Fracas over the Rainbows." *Newsweek.* June 27, 31.

Barkun, Michael. 1986. *Crucible of the Millennium: The Burned-Over District of New York in the 1840s.* Syracuse: Syracuse Univ. Press.

Bates, Albert. 1993–94. "The Changing Economy of the Farm." *Green Revolution* 50 (winter): 4.

Bay Area Rainbow News (B.A.R.N.). 1991. "Rap 151."

Beck, Garrick. 1986. Basic Rainbow Pamphlet. New York: self-published.

———. 1987. "Keeping the Peace." *All Most Broke*. Chicago: *All Ways Free*.

———. 1991. "A Gathering for All People: 20 Years of Rainbow." *High Times*.

Becklund, Jack. 1990a. "Uffda." *Cook County* (Minn.) *News-Herald*, May 28.

———. 1990b. "Uffda." *Cook County* (Minn.) *News-Herald*, July 2.

Behrens, Gordy. 1990. "Rainbows Boost Co-Op Grocery Sales By Gobbling Organic Fruits." *Duluth News-Tribune*, July 4.

Belasco, Warren James. 1979. *Americans on the Road: From Autocamp to Motel, 1910–1945*. Cambridge: MIT Press.

Belkin, Lisa. 1988a. "Hippies Find a Way in a Texas Court." *New York Times*, June 17.

———. 1988b. "2-way Shock as Hippie Meets Texan." *New York Times*, July 5.

Benedict Ruth. [1934] 1959. *Patterns of Culture*. Cambridge: Riverside Press.

Benjamin, Geoffrey. 1968. "Headmanship and Leadership in Temiar Society." *Federation Museums Journal* 13: 1–43.

Berger, John. 1979. *Pig Earth*. New York: Pantheon.

Berliner, Uri. 1994. "The Real Woodstock? Spirit of '69 Lives on in Rainbow Festival." *San Diego Union-Tribune*, Aug. 7.

Bey, Hakim. 1991. *T.A.Z.: The Temporary Autonomous Zone, Ontological Anarchy, Poetic Terrorism*. Brooklyn: Autonomedia.

Bishop, Steve. 1985. "Flower Children May Bloom on ANF." *Ridgeway* (Pa.) *Record*, Oct. 30.

———. 1986. "'Rainbow' Lifestyle Often Unique." *Ridgeway* (Pa.) *Record*, Apr. 18.

Black, Sam. 1993. "Doing Business at The Farm." *Columbia* (Tenn.) *Daily Herald*, May 30.

Blickle, Peter. 1981. *The Revolution of 1525. The German Peasant's War from a New Perspective*. Trans. T. A. Brady Jr. and H. C. E. Middlefort. Baltimore: Johns Hopkins Univ. Press.

Blank, Beth. 1990. "Historic Gathering of the Tofte Clan." *Cook County* (Minn.) *News-Herald*, July 9.

Brison, Karen J. 1989. "All talk and No Action? Saying and Doing in Kwanda meetings." *Ethnology* 28: 97–116

Bushwah, P. M. 1991. "The North American Gathering!" *B.A.R.N.*

Byers, Robert J. 1994. "Dyer Situation: Remote Webster Town Is Off Map." *Charleston* (W.V.) *Gazette*, Aug. 29.

Bynum, W. F. 1981. "Healing Power of Nature." In *Dictionary of the History of Science*. Ed. W. F. Bynum, E. J. Browne, and Roy Porter, eds. Princeton: Princeton Univ. Press, 175–76.

Campbell, Ramsey. 1992. "Hippies of the '60s Take Time for Peace and Love in the '90s." *Orlando Sentinel Tribune*, Mar. 1.

Campbell, Ramsey, and Mary Murphy. 1995. "Fading Freaks Finding Funk in Forest." *Tampa Tribune,* Feb. 19.

Casper (Wyo.) *Star-Tribune.* 1994. "Big Piney Criticizes Law Enforcement," July 10.

Coats, James. 1987. *Armed and Dangerous. The Rise of the Survivalist Right.* New York: Hill and Wang.

Chan, Wing-Tsit, Isma'il Ragi al Faruqi, and P. T. Rau, eds. 1969. *The Great Asian Religions. An Anthology.* London: Macmillan.

Chomsky, Noam. 1987. *On Power and Ideology. The Managua Lectures.* Boston: South End Press.

Churchill, Ward. 1992. *Fantasies of the Master Race; Literature, Cinema and the Colonization of American Indians.* Monroe, Me.: Common Courage Press.

———. 1994. *Indians Are Us?: Culture and Genocide in Native North America.* Monroe, Me.: Common Courage Press.

Churchill, Ward, and Jim Vander Wall. 1988. *Agents of Repression. The FBI's Secret Wars Against the Black Panther Party and the American Indian Movement.* Boston: South End Press.

Cirino, Robert. 1974. *Power to Persuade.* New York: Bantam

Clastres, Pierre. 1994. *The Archeology of Violence.* New York: Semiotext(e).

Cleary, Thomas. 1987. Foreword. In *Chang Po-tuan, Understanding Reality. A Taoist Alchemical Classic. With a Concise Commentary by Lin I-ming.* Trans. Thomas Cleary. Honolulu: Univ. of Hawaii Press, xi–xiv.

Clever, Bob. 1986a. "Land of the Rainbows." *Tionesta* (Pa.) *Forest Press,* July 2.

———. 1986b. "Only Footsteps and Money." *Tionesta* (Pa.) *Forest Press,* July 9.

Cohn, Norman. 1970. *The Pursuit of the Millennium.* Rev. ed. New York: Oxford Univ. Press.

Collins, Neil. 1990, Personal correspondence, Sept.

Colorado Rainbow Family. 1990. *Howdy Folks!* Sept.

Conway, Flo, and Jim Siegelman. 1978. *Snapping: America's Epidemic of Sudden Personality Change.* Philadelphia: J. B. Lippincott.

Cook County (Minn.) *News-Herald.* 1990a. "Officials Ready for Rainbow Gathering," May 28.

———. 1990b. "CALM Cares for Campers," July 2.

———. 1990c. "The Fourth at Tofte; An All-Day Festival," July 9.

———. 1990d. "Trooper Injured as Moose Takes Out Two Cars," July 9.

———. 1990e. "Government Spends $300,000 on Gathering," July 16.

———. 1991. "Board Denies Sheriff Overtime," Jan. 14.

Cultural Survival Quarterly (Canada). 1991a. Update. Vol. 15, no. 1: 53.

———. 1991b. Update. Vol. 15, no. 2: 79.

Curtin, Tom. 1988. "Rainbow Family Returns." *Sheffield* (Pa.) *Valley Voice,* Aug. 26.

Davis, Mark. 1990. "Rainbow Member Leaves Family Camp with Bad Memories." *Asheville* (N.C.) *Citizen,* June 25.

Deloria, Vine Jr. 1970a. *Custer Died for Your Sins.* New York: Avon.

———. 1970b. *We Talk, You Listen*. New York: Dell.

———. 1983. *God Is Red*. New York: Dell.

de Mille, Richard. 1976. *Castaneda's Journey: The Power and the Allegory*. Santa Barbara: Capra Press.

———. 1990a. "Distinguishing Two Components of Truth." In James A. Clifton, *The Invented Indian; Cultural Fictions and Government Policies*. New Brunswick, N.J.: Transaction.

———. 1990b. *The Don Juan Papers: Further Casteneda Controversies*. Belmont, Calif.: Wadsworth.

Dentan, Robert K. 1979. *The Semai, A Nonviolent People of Malaya*. New York: Holt, Rinehart and Winston.

———. 1983. *A Dream of Senoi*. Council on International Studies, State Univ. of New York at Buffalo, Special Study 150.

———. 1992. "The Rise, Maintenance and Destruction of Peaceful Polity; A Preliminary Essay in Political Ecology." In *Aggression and Peacefulness in Humans and Other Primates*. Ed. James Silverberg and J. Patrick Gray. New York: Oxford Univ. Press.

———. 1994. "Surrendered Men": Peaceable Enclaves in the Post-Enlightenment West. In *The Anthropology of Peace and Nonviolence*. Ed. Leslie Sponsel and Thomas Gregor. Boulder, Colo.: Lynne Rienner.

Dentan, Robert K., Kirk Endicott, Alberto Gomez, and M. B. Hooker. 1997. *Development and the Orang Asli of Malaysia*. Boston: Allyn and Bacon/Simon and Schuster.

Dorson, Richard. 1976. *Folklore and Fakelore*. Cambridge, Mass.: Harvard Univ. Press.

Douglas, Mary. 1973. *Natural Symbols. Explorations in Cosmology*. New York: Vintage.

Duluth (Minn.) *News-Tribune*. 1990a. "Rainbow Campers 'Filtering In,'" May 26.

———. 1990b. "Rainbows' 1st Wave Arrives at Campsite," June 4.

———. 1990c. "Officer Fights Rainbow Family Fears," June 5.

———. 1990d. "Colorful Rainbows Try to Calm Community Fears," June 20.

———.1990e. "Dumpster Divers Delve for Goodies in Duluth," June 24.

———. 1990f. "The People," June 24.

———. 1990g. "Time Becomes Lost in the Shuffle at Gathering," July 1.

———. 1990h. "Road Stop Ends in Drug Arrests," July 4.

———. 1990i. "Rainbow's Death Remains a Mystery," July 12.

———. 1990j. "Rainbow Body Mystery Could Be Solved Soon," July 18.

———. 1990k. "Rainbows Suspected in Stabbing," July 24.

Dwork, Deborah. 1981. "Homeopathy." In *Dictionary of the History of Science*. Ed. W. F. Bynum, E. J. Browne, and Roy Porter. Princeton: Princeton Univ. Press, 189–90.

Egerton, John. 1977. *Visions of Utopia: Nashoba, Rugby, Ruskin, and the "New Communities" in Tennessee's Past*. Knoxville: Univ. of Tennessee Press.

Endicott, Marcus. 1990. "Eurotopia." *All Ways Free,* summer.

Erasmus, Charles J. 1981. "Anarchy, Enclavement, and Syntropy in Intentional and Traditional Communities." In *Persistent Peoples: Cultural Enclaves in Perspective.* Ed. George Pierre Castile and Gilbert Kushner. Tucson: Univ. of Arizona Press, 192–211.

Evans-Wentz, W. Y., ed. 1960. *The Tibetan Book of the Dead or The After-Death Experiences on the Bardo Plane, According to Lama Kazi Dawa—Samdup's English Rendering.* 2nd. ed. Oxford: Oxford Univ. Press.

————. 1967. *Tibetan Yoga and Secret Doctrines or Seven Books of Wisdom of the Great Path, According to the late Lama Kazi Dawa—Samdup's English Rendering.* Oxford: Oxford Univ. Press.

Farm Oral History. 1994. Public Oral History Presentation by members of The Farm presented at The Farm, Summertown Tennessee. Accompanied by slide show, Sept. 18.

Ferguson, Sarah. 1995. "Raving at the Edge of the World." *High Times,* Feb.

Fischer, Michael L. 1991 Sierra Club. Solicitation.

Fitterman, Lisa. 1994. "Peace, Love and Nudity Startle the Locals in Gaspe." *Montreal Gazette,* Aug. 1.

Fix, Alan G. 1975. "Fission-Fusion and Lineal Effect: Aspects of the Population Structure of the Semai Senoi of Malaysia." *American Journal of Physical Anthropology* 43: 295–302.

Fogarty, Robert S. 1980. *Dictionary of American Communal and Utopian History.* Westport, Conn.: Greenwood Press.

————. 1990. *All Things New: American Communities and Utopian Movements 1860–1914.* Chicago: Univ. of Chicago Press.

Forrester, Jim. 1991. "Europa Rainbow Poland 1991." *L.I.G.H.T.,* no. 4. (Stony Brook, N.Y.).

Foster, Dick. 1994. "Hippies Color Colorado Again." *Rocky Mountain News,* May 11.

Frazier, Deborah. 1994. "Rainbows Gathering; 500 Hippies Expected for Hunting Season." *Rocky Mountain News,* Sept. 8.

Frederick, Chuck. 1990a. "Officials Afraid Rainbow Gathering May Leave Them Seeing Mostly Red." *Duluth News-Tribune,* May 2.

————. 1990b. "Colorful Call for Peace." *Duluth News-Tribune,* July 1.

————. 1990c. "Family Atmosphere Abounds at Camp." *Duluth News-Tribune,* July 1.

————. 1990d. "Crunch Time." *Duluth News-Tribune,* July 4.

————. 1990e. "Firefighters Help Ease Water Shortage." *Duluth News-Tribune,* July 4.

————. 1990f. "Group May Go to Court Over Police Searches." *Duluth News-Tribune,* July 4.

————. 1990g. "Rainbows Join Hands for Peace, Love." *Duluth News-Tribune,* July 5.

————. 1990h. "Police Identify Body Found at Rainbow Gathering." *Duluth News-Tribune,* July 21.

Gardner, Martin. 1957. *Fads & Fallacies in the Name of Science.* Abridged ed. New York: Ballantine.

Geoffrey, Benjamin. 1968. "Headmanship and Leadership in Temiar Society," *Federation Museums Journal,* new series 13: 1–43.

George, Mary. 1994. "Nomads, Boulder Face Off, Rainbows Protest Crackdown on Mall." *Denver Post.* July 26.

Gibson, David. 1994. "Spreading the Word about the Koran." *Bergen* (N.J.) *Record,* July 1.

Gide, Charles. 1930. (1974 edition) *Communist and Cooperative Colonies.* New York: AMS Press.

Gilbert, Matthew. 1992. "The Rainbow Gathering Puts the '60s in the Present." *Boston Globe,* Aug. 12.

Gitlin, Todd. 1980. *The Whole World Is Watching.* Berkeley, Calif.: Univ. of California Press.

Gold, Herbert. 1993. *Bohemia: Where Art, Angst, Love, and Strong Coffee Meet.* New York: Simon and Schuster.

Goldenberg, Zena. 1993. "The Power of Feminism at Twin Oaks Community." In *Women in Spiritual and Communitarian Societies in the United States.* Ed. Wendy E. Chmielewski, Louis J. Kern, and Marlyn Klee-Hartzell. Syracuse: Syracuse Univ. Press.

Gravelle, Julie. 1990a. "Arrests Made Near Rainbow Gathering." *Duluth News-Tribune,* July 2.

————. 1990b. "Body Discovered at Rainbow Camp." *Duluth News-Tribune,* July 10.

————. 1990c. "Last Rainbows Still Cleaning at Encampment." *Duluth News-Tribune,* Aug. 4.

Great Falls (Mont.) *Tribune.* 1976. Editorial—Rainbow's Promises Kept.

Greenfeather, Joseff, and Water Singing-on-the-Rocks. 1988. CALM report on CDC conference. Jan.

Guide Crew (Rainbow Family). 1993. *1993 Rainbow Guide.* Madison Wis.: Guide Crew.

Gwaltney, John. 1976a. "A Native Replies." *Natural History* 85, no. 12: 8–14.

————. 1976b. "On Going Home Again—Some Reflections of a Native Anthropologist." *Phylon* 30: 236–42.

Hager, Steven. 1990. "Paradise now." *High Times,* Oct., 34–43, 51, 52, 56, 57, 60, 69.

Hallinan, Michael. 1978. "Family Members 'Healing' Umpqua Forest." *Roseburg* (Oreg.) *News-Review,* July 13.

Harmony, Learner. 1989. "Rainbow Consensus." *All Ways Free,* Summer, 28

Haukebo, Kirsten. 1993. "Legal Troubles May Dim Memories of Rainbow Family's Gathering." (Ky.) *Courier-Journal,* July 8.

Hayden, Dolores. 1976. *Seven American Utopias: The Architecture of Communitarian Socialism, 1790–1975.* Cambridge: MIT Press.

Hayes, Chuck. 1986. "Missouri Sheriff Remembers 'Leftover Hippies.'" *Warren* (Pa.) *Times Observer,* June 20.

Heimel, Paul W. 1988. Letter from the Editor. *The Olean* (N.Y.) *Times-Herald,* Aug. 17.

Holloway, Mark. 1951. *Heavens on Earth: Utopian Communities in America 1680–1880.* London: Turnstile Press.

Holloway, Rick. 1984. "The Rainbow Fades . . ." *Modoc* (Calif.) *Record,* July 12.

Hunter, Robert. 1979. *Warriors of the Rainbow. A Chronicle of the Greenpeace Movement.* New York: Holt, Rinehart and Winston.

Idris, Jimin bin, and Mohd Tap Salleh, Jailani M. Dom, Abd. Halim Hj. Jawi, Mohd Razim Shafie. 1983. Planning and Administration of Development Programmes for Tribal Peoples (the Malaysian Setting). Kuala Lumpur: Rural Development for Asia and the Pacific. Photocopy.

Idries, Shah. 1970. *The Way of Sufi.* New York: Dutton.

Jeri, Dr. 1990. Report on Minnesota Gathering Main Council re: RPP and AWF. *Rainbow Peace Projects Newsletter,* Nov.

Jodey. 1988. "Wherever Two Are Gathered." *All Ways Free,* winter.

John, Michael. 1980. "Introduction." Tacoma, Wash.: The Rainbow Nation 1980 Cooperative Community Guide, a People's Guide to the Liberation of the Earth.

K., D. 1966. "Mrs. D. K., a Canadian Housewife." In *The Three Pillars of Zen: Teaching, Practice, and Enlightenment.* Ed. and trans. Philip Kapleau. New York: Harper and Row, 254–67.

Kanter, Rosabeth Moss. 1972. *Commitment and Community: Communes and Utopias in Sociological Perspective.* Cambridge: Harvard Univ. Press.

———. 1973. *Communes: Creating and Managing the Collective Life.* New York: Harper and Row.

Kapleau, Philip. 1966. "Notes on Zen Vocabulary and Buddhist Doctrine." In *The Three Pillars of Zen: Teaching, Practice, and Enlightenment.* Ed. and trans. Philip Kapleau. New York: Harper and Row, 321–50.

Kehoe, Alice B. 1990. "Primal Gaia: Primitivists and Plastic Medicine Men." In *The Invented Indian.* Ed. James A. Clifton. New Brunswick, N.J.: Transaction Publishers.

Kern, Louis J. 1993. "Pronatalism, Midwifery, and Synergistic Marriage; Spiritual Enlightenment and Sexual Ideology on The Farm (Tennessee)". In *Women in Spiritual and Communitarian Societies in the United States.* Ed. Wendy E. Chmielewski, Louis J. Kern, and Marlyn Klee-Hartzell. Syracuse: Syracuse Univ. Press.

Kira, Alexander. 1967. *The Bathroom: Criteria for Design.* New York: Bantam.

Klee-Hartzell, Marlyn. 1993. "Family Love, True Womanliness, Motherhood, and the Socialization of Girls in the Oneida Community, 1848–1880." In

Women in Spiritual and Communitarian Societies in the United States. Ed. Wendy E. Chmielewski, Louis J. Kern, and Marlyn Klee-Hartzell. Syracuse: Syracuse Univ. Press.

Kolmerten, Carol A. 1993. "Women's Experiences in the American Owenite Communities." In *Women in Spiritual and Communitarian Societies in the United States.* Ed. Wendy E. Chmielewski, Louis J. Kern, and Marlyn Klee-Hartzell. Syracuse: Syracuse Univ. Press.

Kuper, Hilda. 1960 [1947]. "The Uniform of Color in Swaziland." In *Cultures and Societies of Africa.* Ed. Simon and Phoebe Ottenburg. New York: Random House, 536–45.

Kyla. 1989. "A Melange of Heartsong Contribution." *Journal de L'Arc-en-Ciel* 90.

LaDuke, Winona. 1990. "James Bay." *Z Magazine,* June.

Leaming, Hugo P. 1993. "The Ben Ishmael Tribe; A Fugitive "Nation" of the Old Northwest." In *Gone to Croatan: Origins of North American Dropout Culture.* Ed. Ron Sakolsky and James Koehnline. Brooklyn: Autonomedia. Reprinted from *The Ethnic Frontier: Essays in the History of Group Survival in Chicago and the Midwest.* Ed. Melvin G. Holli, 1977.

Lee, Martin A., and Norman Solomon. 1990. *Unreliable Sources.* New York: Lyle Stuart.

Legaliaison Network. 1990. "Why We Don't Sign Permits." *All Ways Free and Ho!,* summer.

———. 1991. Legaliaison/DC Crew Update—May 31, 1991. *All Ways Free.*

Leiby, Richard. 1994. "The Hottest Band The World Has Never Heard." *Washington Post,* Oct. 16.

Linden, Eugene. 1991. "Bury My Heart at James Bay." *Time,* July 15.

Lofland, John. 1978. "'Becoming a World-Saver' Revisited." In *Conversion Careers: In and Out of the New Religions.* Ed. James T. Richardson. Beverly Hills: Sage, 10–23.

Lofland, John, and R. Stark. 1965. "Becoming a World-Saver: A Theory of Conversion to a Deviant Perspective." *American Sociological Review* 30: 862–74.

Lovejoy, Arthur O., and George Boas. [1935] 1965. *Primitivism and Related Ideas in Antiquity.* New York: Octagon Books.

Lowe, Warren. 1986. *Indian Giver: A Legacy of North American Native Peoples.* Penticton, B.C., Canada: Theytus.

McClure, Timothy. 1994. *The Belize Project Newsletter.* Glen Ellen, Calif.: Timothy McClure.

McCullen, Kevin. 1995. "Protesters Drown Out the Klan." *Rocky Mountain News,* Jan. 15.

McCutcheon, Sean. 1991. *Electric Rivers: The Story of the James Bay Project.* Montreal: Black Rose Books.

McFadden, Steven. 1992. *Ancient Voices, Current Affairs: The Legend of the Rainbow Warriors.* Santa Fe: Bear and Company.

McGaa, Ed. 1992. *Rainbow Tribe: Ordinary People Journeying on the Red Road.* HarperCollins: New York.

McLaughlin, Corinne, and Gordon Davidson. 1985. *Builders of the Dawn; Community Lifestyles in a Changing World.* Summertown, Tenn.: Book Publishing Company.

Madore, James T. 1988a. "'Rainbows' Return to Nature, 60s Ideals." *Buffalo News,* Aug. 21.

———. 1988b. "Back-to-Nature Hippie Campout in Forest Is Relatively Peaceful." *Buffalo News,* Aug. 28.

Mehta, Gita. 1979. *Karma Cola: Marketing the Mystic East.* New York: Touchstone.

Merton, Robert K. 1972. "Insiders and Outsiders: A Chapter in the Sociology of Knowledge." *American Journal of Sociology* 78, no. 1: 9–47.

Miller, Perry, ed. 1956. *The American Puritans: Their Prose and Poetry.* Garden City, N.Y.: Anchor.

Miller, Timothy. 1991. *The Hippies and American Values.* Knoxville: Univ. of Tennessee Press.

———. 1993. "Peter Cornelius Plockhoy and the Beginnings of the American Communal Tradition." In *Gone to Croatan: Origins of North American Dropout Culture.* Ed. Ron Sakolsky and James Koehnline. Brooklyn: Autonomedia.

Minnesota Rainbow Family. 1990. *Howdy Folks!*

Modoc County Record. 1984. "On the Rainbow Family . . . ," June 21.

Morgan, Andrew. 1987. "Wigwam Hippies Told to Go." (London) *Times,* Aug. 13.

Morrison, Jim. June 12, 1986. Everyone Belongs. *Warren* (Pa.) *Times Observer.*

Mrozowski, Chrisl. 1992. "Caring, Sharing and Doing." *Warsaw Voice.* Warsaw, Poland, Aug. 9.

Mullins, Steve. 1980. "Two Women Found Slain in Pocahontas." *Charleston* (W.V.) *Daily Mail,* June 26.

Myers, John. 1990a. "Rainbow Family Pitches Tents at Pine Mountain." *Duluth News-Tribune,* May 22.

———. 1990b. "Bike-Bus Man into Re-Cycling." *Duluth News-Tribune,* July 2.

———. 1990c. "Pair Weds at Rainbow Gathering." *Duluth News-Tribune,* July 2.

———. 1990d. "Rainbow Family Gathering Growing." *Duluth News-Tribune,* July 2.

———. 1990e. "Store Booms with Rainbow Business." *Duluth News-Tribune,* July 2.

———. 1990f. "Peace Pole Symbolizes Rainbows." *Duluth News-Tribune,* July 3.

———. 1990g. "Store Booms with Rainbow Business." *Duluth News Tribune,* July 3.

———. 1990h. "Water Shortage Hits Rainbows as Campers, Temperatures Increase." *Duluth News-Tribune,* July 3.

Naedele, Walter, F. 1986. "A Communal Gathering." *Philadelphia Inquirer,* June 30.

Nather, David. 1988. "Rainbow Conclave Begins to Break Up." *Dallas Morning News,* July 6.

Neel, J. V., F. M. Salzano, P. C. Junquerira, F. Keiter, and D. Maybury Lewis. 1964. "Studies on the Xavante Indians of the Brazilian Mato Grosso." *American Journal of Human Genetics* 16: 52–140.

Nelson, Holly. 1990. Work in Progress. Video of 1990 Gathering and Various Cook County Meetings. Unedited.

Nelson, Janet, and Holly. 1990. Letter to author, Nov. 7.

NERF (North East Rainbow Family). 1989a. Rap 107, June.

———. 1989b. Rap 701, June.

———. 1991. *Howdy Folks!* Hancock, Vt.: NERF.

New York Times. 1980. Hippie Family Takes to West Virginia Hills for a Reunion. *New York Times,* July 7.

———. 1982. "Holdover Hippies Meet for Their Annual Fling." *New York Times,* July 9.

Nickless, Karen K., and Pamela J. Nickless. 1993. "Sexual Equality and Economic Authority; The Shaker Experience, 1784–1900." In *Woman in Spiritual and Communitarian Societies in the United States.* Edited Wendy E. Chmielewski, Louis J. Kern, and Marlyn Klee-Hartzell.

Nixon, Edgar B. 1973. "Applications for Membership in Zoar." In *Communes: Creating and Managing the Collective Life.* Ed. Rosabeth Moss Kanter. New York: Harper and Row.

Norway Rainbow. 1989. Rainbow Gathering 1989.

Novel, Andrea. 1990a. "Who Needs Money at Rainbow Camp." *Duluth News-Tribune,* July 1.

———. 1990b. "Rainbow Gathering Peaks With a Vigil for World Peace." *Duluth News-Tribune,* July 4.

———. July 5, 1990c. Peaceful Gathering Turns 'Wild.' *Duluth News-Tribune.*

O'Halloran, Marie. 1993. "Somewhere Under the Rainbow." *Irish Times* (Ireland).

O'Hara, Robert C. 1961. *Media for the Millions.* New York: Random House.

Omega Institute. 1995. Summer 1995 Catalog. Rhinebeck, N.Y.: Omega Institute.

Orwell, George. 1964. *Animal Farm.* New York: Signet.

Osgood, Richard L. 1990. Letter to the Editor. "Searches Are a Farce." *Cook County* (Minn.) *News-Herald,* July 16.

Oved, Yaacov. 1988. *Two Hundred Years of American Communes.* New Brunswick, N.J.: Transaction.

Parenti, Michael. 1986. *Inventing Reality.* New York: St. Martin's.

Peaceray. 1991. Thanksgiving 1990 Council for the Northeastern Gathering, Jan.

Pennsylvania Rainbow Family. 1986. *Howdy Folks!.*

Perich, Shawn. 1990a. "Hippie Happening May Happen Here." *Cook County* (Minn.) *News-Herald,* Jan. 8.

———. 1990b. "Publication Depicts Rainbows in Different Light." *Cook County* (Minn.) *News-Herald,* Jan. 8.

———. 1990c. "A Weird Fourth." *Cook County* (Minn.) *News-Herald,* July 9.

————. 1990d. "Rainbows Gone, Garbage Stays Behind." *Cook County* (Minn.) *News Herald*, Nov. 12.

Perkins, William Rufus, and Barthinius L. Wick. [1891] 1975. *History of the Amana Society or Community of True Inspiration*. New York: Arno Press.

Perkinson, Sharon. 1987a. Story tag: rainbow. UPI wire, July 1.

————. 1987b. Story tag: rainbow. UPI wire, July 2.

————. 1987c. Story tag: rainbow. UPI wire, July 2.

————. 1987d. Story tag: rainbow. UPI wire, July 3.

Pitt River Tribal Council. 1984. Resolution 84-06-02, June 15.

Popenoe, Chris and Oliver. 1984. *Seeds of Tomorrow; New Age Communities That Work*. San Francisco: Harper and Row.

Pospisil, Leopold. 1964. "Law and Societal Structure among the Nunamint Eskimo." In *Explorations in Cultural Anthropology*. Ed. Ward H. Goodenough. New York: McGraw Hill, 395–432.

Rainbow Family Net. 1988. *The Rainbow Guide*. Lansing, Mich.: Rainbow Family Net.

Rainbow Family Tribal Council. No Date. The mini-manual for new Gatherers.

Rainbow Hawk. 1985. "Spiritual Rights. An Aspect of Rainbow Spiritual Rights." *All Ways Free*.

————. 1990. Letter to author, Sept. 26.

Rainbow Oracle. 1972. "Squatter's rights." In *Rainbow Oracle*, 100. Eugene, Oreg.: Rainbow Family of Living Light.

Reiss, Tom. 1995. "An 'Aryan Homeland' sought by hate groups in Pacific Northwest." *Buffalo News*, June 11.

Richardson, Valerie. 1994. "Rainbow Family Goes On The Road Again; Neo-Hippies to Gather in Wyoming." *Washington Times*, June 26.

Ridgeway, James. 1989. *Village Voice*, Sept. 12.

Rifkin, Jeremy. 1979. *The Emerging Order: God in an Age of Scarcity*. New York: G. P. Putnam's Sons.

Robie, Harry. 1986. "Red Jacket's reply: Problems in the Verification of a Native American Speech Text." *New York Folklore* 12, nos. 3–4.

Rowe, Jonathan. 1990. ". . . in Eastern Europe. *Washington Monthly*, Nov., 20–26.

Russell, George. 1987. "Freddie Gestapo in Texas." *Earth First!* Nov. 1.

Ruz Buenfil, Alberto. 1991. *Rainbow Nation Without Borders: Toward an Ecotopian Millennium*. Santa Fe: Bear and Company.

Ryan, Paul. 1993. "Indian Heritage; William 'Pooch' Van Dunk (as told to Paul Ryan)". In *Gone to Croatan; Origins of North American Dropout Culture*. Ed. Ron Sakolsky and James Koehnline. Brooklyn: Autonomedia.

Sager, Mike. 1980. "Peaceful Glow Graces Rainbow Demonstration at the Pentagon." *Washington Post*, July 7.

Sanchez, Victor. 1995. *The Teachings of Don Carlos; Practical Applications of the Works of Carlos Castaneda*. Santa Fe: Bear and Company.

Saunders, Michael. 1994a. "Chaos Reigns in Bethel." *Boston Globe*, Aug. 13.

————. 1994b. "A Double Dose of Woodstock." *Boston Globe,* Aug. 15.

Schiller, Herbert I. 1973. *The Mind Managers.* Boston: Beacon.

Schmidt, William E. 1982. "Holdover Hippies Meet for Their Annual Fling." *New York Times.*

Scott, Bob. 1987. "Rainbow Family; It's Tempting to Join Them." *Asheville* (N.C.) *Citizen-Times,* June 7.

Seals, David. 1991. "The New Custerism." *The Nation* 252, no. 18.

Secret Rainbow Press. No Date. Rainbow Revenge.

Seipel, Tracy. 1994. "Bongo Jam in Boulder Turns Ugly; 13 Arrested." *Denver Post,* Sept. 8.

Semmes, Clovis E. 1991. "Developing Trust: Patient-Practitioner Encounters in Natural Health Care." *Journal of Contemporary Ethnography* 19: 450–70.

Seton, Ernest Thompson, and Julia Seton. [1937] 1966. *The Gospel of the Redman. A Way of Life.* Santa Fe: Seton Village.

Shenker, Barry. 1986. *Intentional Communities: Ideology and Alienation in Communal Societies.* London: Routledge & Kegan Paul.

Silkworm, Paolo. 1991. "The Gatherings Expand." In Buenfil, *Rainbow Nation Without Borders. Toward an Ecotopian Millennium.* Santa Fe: Bear & Co.

Skow, John. 1991. "Over the Rainbow. Where Peaceable Wanderers Gather to Hug Each Other, Wear Feathers, Dance All Night and Sooth the Soul." *Time,* July 15, 74–75.

Sky Bear. Jan. 1991. Councils and Consensus. Tionesta, Pa.: self-published.

Smith, Andrea. 1994. "For All Those Who Were Indian in a Former Life." In *Cultural Survival Quarterly,* Winter.

Snyder, Gary. 1969. *Earth House Hold: Technical Notes & Queries to Fellow Dharma Revolutionaries.* New York: New Directions.

South Dakota Rainbow. 1992. Update From the Focalizers Thanksgiving Council Report. Oglala, S.D.: Rainbow Family.

Spicer, Edward H. 1971. "Persistent Cultural Systems: A Comparative Study of Identity Systems That Can Adapt to Contrasting Environments." *Science* 174: 797. Qtd. in George P. Castile and Gilbert Kusher, 1981. *Persistent Peoples.* Tucson: Univ. of Arizona Press, xix.

Stanich, Susan, and Julie Gravelle. 1990. Rainbow Feature Series. *Duluth News-Tribune,* June 24.

Stauber, John, and Sheldon Rampton. 1995. *Toxic Sludge Is Good For You! Lies, Damn Lies and the Public Relations Industry.* Monroe, Me.: Common Courage Press.

Stodghill, Mark. 1990a. "Rainbows Bring Peace, Possible Headaches." *Duluth News-Tribune,* Mar. 17.

————. 1990b. "Rainbows to Narrow Site List." *Duluth News-Tribune,* May 17.

————. 1990c. "Rainbow Family to Start 'Seed Camp' Near Grand Marais." *Duluth News-Tribune,* May 21.

————. 1990d. "Rainbow family Coming 'Home.'" *Duluth News-Tribune.* June 9.

————. 1990e. "Taco Hilton Going Up in the Woods." *Duluth News-Tribune,* June 9.

————. 1990f. "'The Pieman' Tosses His Views Around." *Duluth News-Tribune,* July 1.

————. 1990g. "Pot Has Its Advocates, Critics at Rainbow Camp." *Duluth News-Tribune,* July 1.

Strickland, Rose. 1984. Letter to Glenn Bradley, Forest Supervisor. Toiyabe Chapter, Sierra Club, June 13.

Swanson, Craig D. 1988. "On Rainbows." *Warren* (Pa.) *Times Observer,* Aug. 24.

Swanson, Nancy. 1986. "A Short Visit with Caring Folks." *Sheffield* (Pa.) *Valley Voice,* July 4.

Teter, Don. 1980. "Two Days of Rainbows." *Tygart Valley* (W.V.) *Press,* July 9.

Thumper. 1990. Letter to Focalizers, Dec. 12.

Tionesta (Pa.) *Forest Press.* 1986a. "Peace, Healing Rainbow Theme," June.

————. 1986b. Editorial, June 25.

Tofte, Town of. 1990 Town Meeting (Recording of), July 9.

Toussaint, Danielle. 1984. "In the Aftermath of the Rainbow Gathering." *Chico* (Calif.) *News and Review,* July 26.

Traugot, Michael. 1994. *A Short History of the Farm.* Summertown, Tenn.: Michael Traugot.

Truthhawk. 1989. "To the Folks at All Ways Free." *All Ways Free,* 28

Turnbull, Colin M. 1962. *The Forest People. A Study of the Pygmies of the Congo.* New York: Simon and Schuster.

United Press International. 1984–88. Story tag: hippies. UPI wire stories, June 30, 1984–July 3, 1988.

Varkonyi, Tina. 1990. "What's a Focalizer." Leaflet.

Wagner, Jon. 1982. *Sex Roles in Contemporary American Communes.* Bloomington: Indiana Univ. Press.

Wagster, Emily. 1993. "Convergence of Hippies in Mississippi Leads to Arrests." Gannett News Service, Jan. 12.

Wallace, Anthony. 1956. *Revitalization Movements.* Indianapolis: Bobbs-Merrill.

Warner, J. H. 1977–78. "The Nature-Trusting Heresy": American Physicians and the Concept of the Healing Power of Nature in the 1850's and 1860's. *Perspectives in American History* 9: 291–324.

Wasik, Paul. 1990. "Searches on Shaky Ground." Letter to the Editor. *Cook County* (Minn.) *News-Herald,* June 23.

Webber, Everett. 1959. *Escape to Utopia: The Communal Movement in America.* New York: Hastings House.

Weidert, Carl L. 1984. Letter to Rainbow Family. Mother Lode Chapter, Sierra Club.

Weinberg, Bill. 1989a. "Rainbow Lore. An Interview with Garrick Beck." *Downtown,* Oct. 25.

————. 1989b. "Rainbow Lore. An Interview with Garrick Beck. Part Two." *Downtown,* Nov. 1.

————. 1989c. "Rainbow Lore. An Interview with Garrick Beck. Part Three." *Downtown*, Nov. 8.

————. 1990a. "Rainbow Warriors and the Ecotopian Millennium: An Interview with Alberto Ruz." *Downtown*, Sept. 19.

————. 1990b. "For One of The Biggest Environmental Disasters Ever, Try James Bay II!" *Downtown*, Nov. 21.

Weiner, Michael. 1989. *The Complete Book of Homeopathy*. Garden City Park, New York: Avery.

West Virginia Rainbow. 1990. Rap 107.

Wetmore, Joseph, P. C. 1990a. Letter to Heartsong, Sept. 17.

————. 1990b. MS Rainbow 1990 Journal. Personal unpublished notes.

Willoya, William, and Vinson Brown. 1962. *Warriors of the Rainbow: Strange and Prophetic Dreams of the Indian Peoples*. Healdsburg, Calif.: Naturegraph.

Wing, Steven. 1987. "All Ways Free!" *All Most Broke*. Chicago: *All Ways Free*, fall.

————. 1990. "Passing the feather for Sam." *Ho!*, Summer.

Wirtshafter, Don. 1989. Letter to Regional Focalizers, Aug. 31.

Wittfogel, K. A. 1957. *Oriental Despotism: A Study in Total Power*. New Haven, Conn.: Yale Univ. Press.

Wolfe, Tom. 1968. *The Electric Kool-Aid Acid Test*. New York: Farrar, Straus and Giroux.

Wong, Eva, trans. 1990. *Seven Taoist Masters: A Folk Novel of China*. Boston: Shambala.

Wood. 1989. "Sneaky Shitter Person Coaxes Ancient Secrets of Dysentery Prevention from an Unsuspecting Insect." *All Ways Free*, winter.

Worster, Donald. 1985. *Rivers of Empire*. New York: Pantheon

Yes Educational Society. 1990. 1990 East Coast Medicine Wheel Gathering. Takoma Park, Md.: Yes Educational Society.

Zeitlin, Dawn Aura. 1990. Katua Blueberry '89 Rumor Control. *Ho!*, summer.

Zimmerman, Jack, and Virginia Coyle. 1991. Council. *Utne Reader*, Mar.–Apr., 79–85.

Interviews

Alita. 1990. Interview by author, June 28.

Bahana Followers. 1990. Interview by author, July 7.

Banyaca, Thomas. 1991. Interview by author, May 4.

Bear, Snake Mountain. 1990. Interview by author, July 7.

Beck, Garrick. 1990. Interview by author, May 21.

Bhakti Steve. 1990. Interview by author, July 1.

Boulder Bob. 1990. Interview by author, July 28.

Bubbleman. 1990. Interview by author, July 27.

Carratu, Roan. 1994. Interview by author, Sept. 17.

Chosa, Heart Warrior. 1990. Interview by author, July 8.

Collector. 1990. Interview by author, July 9.

Crow. 1990. Interview by author, June 28.

Dream Peace, Marilyn. 1990. Interview by author, July 2.

Ed. 1990. Interview by author, June 27.

Felipe. 1990 Interview by author, July 8.

Gaskin, Stephen. 1994a. Interview by author, Sept. 17.

———. 1994b. Interview by author, Sept. 19.

Grey Bear. 1990a. Interview by author, June 10.

———. 1990b. Interview by author, July 17.

Harmony, Learner. 1990. Interview by author, July 11.

Hoffman, Barry. 1990. Interview by author, July 22.

Holly. 1991a. Interview by author, June 27.

———. 1991b. Interview by author, Aug. 1.

Jimbo. 1990. Interview by author, June 28.

Joanne. 1990. Interview by author, July 27.

John (mall manager). 1990. Interview by author, July 24.

John, Michael. 1990. Interview by author, June 25.

Latz, Jeff. 1990. Interview by author, July 13.

Louie. 1990. Interview by author, Aug. 17.

Lyght, John, 1990. Interview by author, July 11.

Lyons, Oren. 1991. Interview by author, June 30.

Many Paths, José. 1990. Interview by author, July 26.

Mariann. 1990. Interview by author, July 17.

Marianna. 1990. Interview by author, June 23.

Medicine Tools. 1990. Interview by author, June 23.

Mother Nature. 1990. Interview by author, July 6.

No Myths. 1990. Interview by author, July 24.

Perich, Shawn. 1990. Interview by author, July 10.

Remi. 1990. Interview by author, July 7.

Rock Soup staff. 1990. Interview by author, July 2.

Schwartzbaum, Joseph. 1990. Interview by author, July 6.

Starwatcher, Mark. 1990. Interview by author, June 27.

Taco Mike. 1990. Interview by author, June 21.

Water Singing on the Rocks. 1990. Interview by author, July 28.

Wetmore, Joseph P. C. 1990. Interview by author, Nov. 11.

———. 1991. Interview by author, Apr. 22.

White Raven. 1990. Interview by author, June 26.

Wingel, Gillette K. B. 1990. Interview by author, July 8.

Zimmerman, Diane. 1990. Interview by author, Nov. 23.

Government Documents

Allegheny National Forest. 1986. Operating Procedures [for Rainbow Gathering].

Ballantyne, John. 1980. Letter to Henry Fiddler. Monogahela National Forest, Apr. 23.

Bedlow, T. Wayne. 1989. The Rainbow Family Gathering. Jarbidge Ranger District. Humboldt National Forest, July 1.

Benjamin, Richard O. 1984. Inter-Office Memo—Planning Future Decision Making.

Bergerson, Jean. 1990. Critique.

Big South Fork National River and Recreation Area. 1990. Action Plan (Case Incident # 900031). U.S. National Park Service. S.E. Regional Office.

Bilby, Richard M. 1986. *United States of America v. Gideon Israel.* U.S. District Court for the District of Arizona. May 15.

Burton, Bob. 1990. Rainbow Family Tribal Gathering—1990. Report. Superior National Forest.

———. 1990. Letter to Media Personnel. Superior National Forest, June 22.

Carpenter, R. Forrest. 1986. Cooperative Law Enforcement Agreement. Allegheny National Forest, June 20.

Christiansen, Marty. 1990. Unit Log. Superior National Forest, June 27.

Colaninno, Andrew, and Dale Dunshie. 1988. Report of Regional Rainbow Gathering— Allegheny National Forest August 20–28, 1988. Sept.

Colville National Forest reports 1981.

Federal Bureau of Investigation. 1983. DE BQ 0115 UNCLAS. Inter-office memo.

Filius, David A. 1990. Letter to Honorable James L. Oberstar, Mar. 23.

Hawkins, Charles E. 1989. Reply to: 5300. Payette N.F. 1989. Law Enforcement Report. Humboldt N.F., July 12.

Howard, Roderick. 1989a. Unit Log, July 1–18.

———. 1989b. Speed memo—Rainbow Family, July 27.

Huff, Richard L. 1990. Response to F.O.I.A. appeal. DEA. Mar. 4.

Humboldt National Forest. 1989. Critique.

Inman. 1989. Amendment Operating and Financial Plan. Rainbow Family Gathering Event. Reimbursable Services Requested by the Forest Service. Humboldt National Forest, June 16.

Jarbidge Ranger District. 1989. Reports and publications.

Joens, Robert. 1990a. Unit log. June 30.

———. 1990b. Notes for public meeting held at Birch Grove School in Tofte, Minnesota, July 9.

Justice, William Wayne. 1988a. Order. L-88-68-CA. U.S. District Court for the Eastern District of Texas, June 1.

———. 1988b. Memorandum opinion. L-88-68-CA. U.S. District Court for the Eastern District of Texas, June 23.

———. 1989. Final Judgment. L-88-68-CA. U.S. District Court for the Eastern District of Texas, Apr. 14.

Laflam, Candy. 1989a. Message Scan. June 16.

———. 1989b. Rainbow Gathering on the Manchester District in Retrospect. *Maple Leaves,* Sept.

Langer, John H. 1990. Response to F.O.I.A. request. DEA, Nov. 2.

LaNier, Tommy C. 1989. Reply to 5300. Cleveland National Forest, July 12.

Lee, Michael, P. 1984. Rainbow Family Gathering 1984. Modoc National Forest.

Lotspeich, Sergeant. 1989. Incident Report/Narrative.

Lundberg, Paul A. 1988. Reply to 2720. Green Mountain National Forest, July 11.

Lyght, John R. 1990. Letter to Representative James Oberstar, Mar. 9.

Malanka, Christian, J. 1990a. Confidential. Regional Rainbow Children Gatherings at Big South Fork NRRA. Atlanta: U.S. National Park Service, Mar. 15.

———. 1990b. Confidential Intelligence Update. Atlanta: U.S. National Park Service, Mar. 23.

———. 1990c. Case Incident # 900031. Report. U.S.N.P.S. Southeast Regional Office, May 4.

Marshall, Gordon, W. 1980. Reply to Action and Procedures. Forest Service Region 9, May 15.

Marteney, Scott. 1989 . Evaluation of the 1989 Rainbow Incident. Nevada Dept. of Human Resources, July 20.

Martin, Dennis W. 1978. Final report. 1978 Rainbow Family Healing Gathering. U.S.F.S. Region 6, Oct. 30.

Modoc National Forest. 1984. Reports.

Monongahela National Forest. 1980. Report on the 1980 Rainbow Family World Peace Gathering. USDA F.S. Region 9.

Nelson, Ann. 1987. Letter and test results sent to Joy Wells, Center for Disease Control. State of West Virginia, Aug. 12.

Okanogan National Forest. 1981. Report on Perspectives Gained During Negotiations with Rainbow Family During Winter and Spring of 1981.

Olson, George A. 1989. R-4 2330. Report. U.S.N.F.S. Region Four.

Quintanar, Ray. 1981. Rainbow Report. Colville National Forest, Aug.

Rickerson, Steve, and Peg Boland, Sally Browning, Karen Hughes, Terry Pierce, and Donnie Richardson. 1987. 1987 Annual Rainbow Family Gathering Report. Cheoah Ranger District. Nantahala National Forest.

Schuler, James L. 1987. Rainbows—Final report. Allegheny National Forest, Feb. 27.

Shenk, William D. 1981. 1300 Management, June 18.

Smith, Zane A. 1984. Letter to John K. Van de Kamp, Apr. 20.

Superior National Forest publications and meeting notes, 1990.

Umpqua National Forest. 1978. 1978 Rainbow Family Gathering Environmental Analysis Report.

United States of America v. The Rainbow Family et al. 1988. Oral Hearing of plaintiff's motion for Permanent Injunction. Transcript of Civil Action no. L-88-68-CA. U.S. District Court for the Eastern District of Texas, June 13–16.

U.S. National Forest Service, North Carolina. 1987. In-Service Video of 1987 Rainbow Gathering.

U.S. National Forest Service, Texas, 1988. Notes and publications.

U.S. National Forest Service, Washington, D.C. 1978. Rainbow Family Healing Gatherings.

Watson, Detective Curtis. 1989. Critique. Rainbow Family Gathering 1989.

Wharton, Melinda, and Richard Spiegel. 1987. Report of Findings to J. N. MaCormack. Centers for Disease Control. Dec. 10.

Wortham, Bob. 1988. Letter to Mike Lannon, forest supervisor, June 23.

Wright, David J. 1988a. Letter to Richard Hernan, district attorney, Aug. 15.

———. 1988b. Regional Rainbow Report. Warren, Pa.: Allegheny National Forest, Sept. 30.

Ziegler, Bob. 1980. Speed Memo. U.S.F.S. Eastern Section, June 10.

Index

A Camp, 125–30, 172, 199, 204, 207, 234n9; misogyny, 106
Abenaki, 142, 143
Acupuncture, 19, 82, 83, 84
Adams, Barry, 125, 134
Airplane flights over Gatherings, 194
Alabama, 57, 97, 183
Albanese, Catherine, 140
Alcohol, 17, 53, 63, 66, 80, 124, 127–28, 129, 229n6, 237n4; drunkenness, 4, 80, 101, 122, 126–27, 128, 169, 189, 207
Alcohol Camp. See A Camp
Alcohol Hat, 126
Alcoholics Anonymous, 44, 56, 112, 113, 205, 206, 230n5
Alcoholism. See A Camp, alcohol
Alita, 102, 107
All Most Broke, 93, 115
All Ways Free, 35, 38, 67, 69, 72, 85, 93–94, 124, 135, 141, 156, 232n19
Allegheny National Forest, 160, 162, 173–74, 235n6
Alpha Farm, 40
Amana Colony, 55, 56, 63, 72, 100, 107, 143
American flag, 13
American Indian Movement (AIM), 111
American Medical Association, 84
Anarchism, 25, 69, 70, 95, 121, 122, 193, 194, 200, 204, 212, 213, 214; see also egalitarianism; nonhierarchical
Ancient Voices, Current Affairs: The Legend of the Rainbow Warriors, 137–38
Animals: Rainbow rapport with, 4, 9
Apathy, 40
Architecture, 75
Arizona, 188, 200
Arkansas, 126
Asheville Citizen, 166
Associated Press, 166, 235n8
Audubon Society, 35
Aurora Borealis, 12, 63
Austria, 92
Authoritarianism, 55–56, 58

Babylon, 17, 28, 32, 33–34, 37, 41, 56, 63, 69, 89, 97, 100, 106–7, 108, 110, 111, 115, 122, 125, 128, 181, 212
Ball, Special Agent Billy S., 95–96, 189, 236n5

Banking Council, 46, 53, 171
Banyaca, Thomas, 134
Be-In (San Francisco), 32
Bear, Snake Mountain, 101–2, 122–24
Bear Tribe, 138; see also Sun Bear
Beatniks, 35
Beck, Garrick, 32, 35–36, 41, 60, 65, 86–87, 90, 97, 109, 142–43, 189
Beck, Julian, 36
Becklund, Jack, 154–55, 157
Belize, 143
Belkin, Lisa, 151–52
Ben Ismael Tribe, 141
Benedict, Ruth, 134
Bergen Record, 154
Bergerson, Jean, 164
Bey, Hakim, 97
Bhakti Steve, 76
Bishop Hill Community, 179, 205
Bishop, Steve, 160
Bliss ninnies, 88
Bohemian, 37
Boston Globe, 154, 161, 168
Boulder Bob, 80–81
Boy Scouts of America, 132, 173
Brison, Karan, 44
Brook Farm, 77
Brown, Vinson, 133, 135, 137, 139
Bubbleman. See Thomas, Gary
Buddhism, 34, 35, 36, 147, 212
Buenfil, Alberto Ruz, 135, 137
Buffalo, John, 120–21
Buffalo Camp, 158
Buffalo News, The, 162, 168
Bureau of Land Management, 191
Burton, Ranger Bob, 48, 121, 158, 163
Business owners' reactions to Gatherings, 176–77
Bus Village, 46, 47, 102, 110, 126, 197, 230n6

California, 71, 97, 111, 121, 142, 164, 173, 175; Bureau of Organized Crime and Criminal Intelligence, 192–93
Caliph, 119
CALM, 18–20, 21, 22, 24, 34, 66, 80–85, 88, 110, 121, 123, 126, 171, 232n12; philosophy, 80–81
Captain Crunch, 81

Carratu, Roan, 210
Castaneda, Carlos, 140
Cattle ranchers, 181
Cayuga Nation, 144
Center for the Spirit, 146–47, 234n6
Centers for Disease Control, 185–86
Charleston Gazette, 155
Child predators, 7, 124, 234n7
Chiropractic, 19, 81, 82, 83
Chosa, Heart Warrior, 145–46
Christiana, 33
Christianity, 34, 35, 68, 69, 95, 108, 136, 147, 212
Churchill, Ward, 137, 139, 231n20
CIA, 36
Citronella, 12
City-planning, 64
Civil disobedience, 32, 182, 201
Class issues, 35, 41, 51, 53, 57, 65, 76, 89, 96, 100, 102, 107, 109, 111, 112–13, 128, 129, 184
Cleanup, 171–75; Camp, 230n9; Council, 171
Clever, Bob, 119
Cocaine, 78
Coffee, 2, 12, 21, 24, 53, 68, 74, 76, 77, 78, 198, 232n7
Colaninno, Andrew, 173–74
Collector, 3,4, 30, 74–75, 86
Collins, Neil, 92
Colorado, 57, 92, 161
Colville National Forest, 199
Coming Nation, The, 95
Commitment, 69, 100, 204–6, 211, 212
Communism, 68–69, 70, 203, 213
Community relations, 62, 170, 175–83
Compost, 20
Compost, Shalom, 78
Conch, 21, 47
Conflict resolution, 64, 115; see also nonviolence; pacifism
Consensus, 38, 39–41, 44, 48, 50, 54–59; blocking of, 45, 57, 119, 213; by attrition, 45, 57; consensus minus one, 58, 213; Native American roots of consensus government, 40; spontaneous consensus, 125
Conservative values, 180–81
Cook County News Herald, 121, 154–58, 191
Council, 21–26, 38–59, 91, 213; gender balance, 42, 50–51, 56; how to convene, 46–47; long inconclusive meetings, 44, 59;

male domination of, 56–57, 106; N.E.R.F. council guideline, 54
Coyle, Virginia, 42
Crime at Gatherings, 190
Crow, 102
Crystals, 71
Cultural Primitivism, 146
Cumberland Plateau, 94
Curtin, Tom, 160

Dallas Morning News, 165
Davidson, Gordon, 56, 58, 77, 214, 231n19
Dawson, Larry, 172
Declaration of War Against Exploiters of Lakota Spirituality, 146
Deloria, Vine, 133, 140–41
Dentan, Robert Knox, 98, 129, 141, 195, 204
Denver Post, 154, 166
Department of Defense, 191
Detoxification, 167, 212; see also drug-free
Diarrhea, 185–86
Dogs, drug sniffing, 190, 191
Downtown, 168
Drainbows, 90
Dream Peace, Marilyn, 77–79, 86
Drew, Lisa, 153, 166
Drug Enforcement Administration, 192
Drug-free, 21, 27, 78
Drug hype, 166–69
Drugs (illicit), 21, 77–78, 84, 156, 190; allegations of abuse, 189–92
Drumming, 1, 17, 27, 28, 29
Duluth News-Tribune, 158–59
Dumpster Diving, 6, 65, 74
Dunshie, Dale, 173–74

Earth People's Park, 101–2, 207
Economics, 68–72, 213; see also Magic Hat
Ed, 117
Egalitarianism, 35, 37, 55, 59, 80, 87, 106, 108, 122, 171, 185, 195, 202, 210
Egerton, John, 203
Elders, 22, 25, 40, 57, 168
Endicott, Marcus, 55
Environmental impact, 61; see also cleanup; recycling
Equity Store, 69
Ethnocide, 140, 146
European Rainbow Family, 33, 55, 70, 71, 87, 92, 128, 141, 169, 177, 203, 214, 229n3, 237n1

Facilitators, 54, 230n15
Faeries, 108–9
Fairhope Colony, 110
Fakelore, 37, 109–10, 131–47, 212
Fall Council, 50
Farm, The, 69, 72, 77, 78, 100, 108, 180–81, 208–12, 235n3, 237n7, 238n11
FBI, 192
Feather, the, 22, 42–43, 54, 61
Federal Emergency Management Agency, 200
Felipé, 101
Finger Lakes National Forest, 144
Fission-fusion, 98, 113, 130, 183, 201, 204, 214
Flood, Paul, 171–72
Florida, 94
Focalizers, 60, 63, 90–92
Food: descriptions of, 2–3, 11
Forest Press, The, 160
Forest Service. See United States National Forest Service
Fourierists, 33, 90, 112, 229n5, 232n17
Foxfire, 12
France, 141

Gannett News Service, 154
Garlic, 7, 12, 82
Gaskin, Stephen, 208–10
Gatekeepers, 51, 54
Gender, 107–9; imbalance, 105–6
Genesis, 136
Gilbert, Matthew, 161, 168
Gitlin, Todd, 235n9
Gold, Herbert, 92
Grateful Dead, 37, 229n6
Gravelle, Julie, 158–59
Great Falls Tribune, 172
Greece, 92
Green Mountain National Forest, 49
Greenpeace, 135
Greens, the, 33
Grey Bear, 120, 122
Gypsies, 97, 102, 233n23

Habit-free. See Drug-free
Hager, Steven, 167–68
Handicapped accessibility, 110
Harmony, Learner, 44–45, 61
Hasidic, 35
Haudenosaunee, 137, 139, 143–44
Hawk, 101
Hawkins, Special Agent Charles E., 194

Hayden, Dolores, 55, 230n17
Hayes, Chuck, 177
Heartsong, 23, 43, 46, 47, 51–52, 54, 82, 91, 95, 111
Hendersonville Times-News, 166
Hierarchical, 48, 124, 129, 185, 204; see also nonhierarchical
High Times, 167–68
Hindus, 34, 147
Hipstory, 33, 34–35, 106, 133, 179
Hitchhiking, 75, 176
Ho!, 94
Hobos, 35, 65, 75, 76, 100, 102, 105–6, 108, 109
Holloway, Mark, 203, 206
Holloway, Rick, 169
Homelessness, 18, 24, 35, 65, 95, 101
Homeopathy, 19, 81
Homophobia, 108
Homosexuality, 108–9
Hopedale Community, 112
Hopi, 134, 137, 141, 144
Howard, Ranger Roderick, 174, 198–99
Howdy Folks!, 22, 63, 64, 70, 96, 127, 132, 142, 170, 196
Humboldt National Forest, 164
Hunter, Robert, 135
Hutterites, 36–37, 63, 108, 129, 182, 233n2, 237n8

Icarian Community, 231n18
Iconography, 132
Idaho, 102, 191
Impact on neighboring communities. See community relations
Intentional groups, 31, 115, 229n1
Internet, 90–91, 96, 128
Ireland, 87, 97, 177
Irish Times, 177
Iroquois. See Haudenosaunee
Irwin, Supervisor Doug, 178
Island Pond Community, 108
Italy, 33
Ithaca, New York, 49, 53–54, 56, 69, 70, 90, 199

Jimbo, 80, 82–84, 127
Joanne, 111
John, Michael, 37, 95
John the mall manager, 88–89
Joke toll booth, 22

Journal de L'Arc-en-Ciel, 94
Joven, Jonathan, 117
Judaism, 34, 35, 147; anti-Semitism, 137
Justice, Judge William Wayne, 186–87, 188, 193

Kansas Emigration Society, 77
Kanter, Rosabeth Moss, 56, 58–59, 69, 86, 87, 113, 181, 201, 202, 205
Katuah, 94
Kentucky, 57, 192
Kids' Parade, 33
Kids' Village, 9–10, 51, 70, 76, 101, 204
Kira, Alexander, 66
Kitchen Council, 46
Kitchen maintenance, 78
Kitchens, 72–78
—Brew-Ha-Ha, 27, 77–78, 79, 232n11
—Common Loaf Bakery, 108
—Doughnut Kitchen, 3, 29, 74–75, 86
—Hobo Hilton, 88, 232n7
—J.E.S.U.S., 20–21, 89, 124
—Joy of Soy, 74
—Kids' Village kitchen. *See* Kids' Village
—Krishna, 26–27, 76, 77, 186; sanitation, 236n3
—Popcorn Palace, 11
—Quebec Kitchen, 74
—Rock Soup, 73–74, 79, 89
—Sage Hollow, 74, 85
—Sprout Kitchen, 74
—Sunrise, 74
—Taco Hilton, 3, 75–76, 77, 232n7
—Taco Mike's. *See* Taco Hilton
—Tea Time, 13
Kwanda, 44
Kyla, 92

Labadist colony at Bohemia Manor, 206
Labor credits, 69
LaFlam, Cindy, 199
Lama Community, 40
Land stewardship. *See* cleanup
Latrines, 5, 8, 34, 47, 66–68, 85, 86, 89, 159, 172, 174, 185, 194, 231n2, 232n16
Latz, Jeff, 177
Leaders, government demands to meet, 185
Lee, Martin A., 148
Lee, Michael, 176, 193, 196
Legaliason, 23, 35, 36, 187
Lesbianism, 109
Liaisons, between Family and government, 185

Libertarianism, 60, 213
Limbaugh, Rush, 107, 233n5
Listening skills, 42
Living Theater, The, 36
London Times, 151
Longfellow, Henry Wadsworth, 140
Los Angeles Times, 163
Love, Governor John, 32
LSD, 21, 23, 167, 169
Lundberg, Paul, 199
Lyght, Sheriff John, 155–56, 158, 167, 174, 178, 194–95, 237n10
Lyons, Oren, 144

Magic Hat, 47, 53, 68, 69–70, 78, 100, 126, 175, 176, 207–8, 213
Malanka, Christian, 117
Male domination, 105–16; of Shanti Sena, 122, 234n6; *see also* council, male domination of
Malina, Judith, 36
Many Paths, José, 46
Map (of Gathering), 16
Marianna, 83
Marijuana, 21, 23, 78, 167
Mark Twain National Forest, 173
Marten, Dennis, 197–98
Marteney, Scott, 194
Martinique, 92
Maya, 143
McClure, Timothy, 143–44
McFadden, Steven, 137–38
McGaa, Eagle Man Ed, 137, 138–39
McGee, John, 120
McLaughlin, Corinne, 56, 58, 77, 214, 231n19
Meat, 53, 75–76, 77; *see also* vegetarianism
Media: anachronisms, 17, 101, 149–54; Council, 169; portrayal, 86, 110, 148–69, 206; reliance on offical sources, 161–62, 165; spokespersons, 169; staged events, 165; *see also* drug hype; misinformation; United States National Forest Service: media management
Medicine Tools, 81, 83
Medicine Wheel Gatherings, 138
Membership, 99–113, 128; criteria, 32, 99–100, 108, 112–13, 119, 229n2; *see also* recruitment
Mental health system, 123–25
Michigan, 103, 214
Militia movement, 182–83
Mini Manual for New Gatherers, 118

Minnesota, 45–49, 60–61, 63, 67, 70, 73, 75–76, 84, 88, 92, 120, 126, 140, 145, 154–59, 164, 167, 171–72, 173, 174, 180, 191, 194
Misinformation, FBA, 192; see also United States National Forest Service: misinformation
Missouri, 103, 111, 173, 176
Modern Times Community, 121, 168–69
Modoc National Forest, 142
Montagnais, 144
Montana, 97
Mormons, 132, 136, 143, 182
Mosquitoes, 12–13, 26, 63, 78
Mother Nature, 89, 101, 124
Movement for a New Society, 40, 51, 229n3
Multiculturalism, 110
Music: descriptions of, 28
Myers, John, 177

Names, 101
Narcotics Anonymous, 27, 78
Nashoba Community, 107, 110, 205
Nather, David, 165
National Rifle Association, 181
Native American Church, 134
Nelson, Holly, 157–58
Nelson, Janet, 157–58
Nevada, 44, 45, 61, 164, 174, 185, 191, 198
New Age, 86–87, 131, 133, 135, 137–38, 139, 140, 146, 231n20, 234n1; myths, 109–10; racism, 110
New Harmony Community, 205
New Jersey, 49
New Mexico, 14, 101, 126
New York, 49, 174; see also Ithaca
New York Times, 151–53, 158, 159, 161, 179, 198, 235n5
Newsweek, 153, 166
Night vision, 27–29
Noguns, 189
Nonhierarchical, 38, 112, 114, 129, 205, 206, 210, 215; see also anarchism; hierarchical
Nonsectarian, 206–7
Nonviolence, 34, 112, 114–30, 150, 204, 206, 210, 215; see also conflict resolution; pacifism
North Carolina, 44, 49, 50, 84, 115–17, 163–64, 174, 186–87, 189, 193
North East Rainbow Family (N.E.R.F.), 38, 49–55, 64, 66, 70, 86, 88, 96, 102, 125, 144, 174, 199
Norway, 70, 229n3

Nudity, 13–14, 150, 162, 177–79, 182, 185, 198, 236n4
Nyabinghe, 28, 104–5

O'Halloran, Marie, 87, 177
O'Hara, Robert C., 149
Okanogan National Forest, 43
Olean Times Herald, The, 160
Oliver, Leroy, 67
Om, 26, 47, 50, 51, 52, 54, 85, 117–18, 234n1
Omega Institute, 139
Oneida Community, 72, 87, 107, 179, 182
Onondaga Nation, 144
Oregon, 172
Orlando Sentinel Tribune, 154
Oved, Yacoov, 55, 58, 232n18
Owen, Robert, 107, 203
Owenites, 33, 107–8, 112; see also Owen, Robert

Pacifism, 35, 36, 37, 115, 129, 182; see also conflict resolution; nonviolence
Paganism, 34, 37, 95, 147
Paranoia, 193, 236n8
Patterns of Culture, 134
Paulseth, Undersheriff Harold, 173
Peace Pagent, 33
Peace Village, 51, 230n14
Pennsylvania, 97, 160–61, 178, 197
Pentagon, 117, 192
Perich, Shawn, 156–57
Perkins, William Rufus, 55
Perkinson, Sharon, 151
Permits, 43, 187–88
Peyote, 134
Philadelphia Inquirer, The, 160, 163
Philadelphia Life Center, 40
Piedmont, 94
Pitt River Tribal Council, 142, 144
Platt, Bruce, 173
Plockhoy, Peter Cornelius, 143, 207
Poland, 33, 70–71, 97, 141, 169
Police, 99, 113, 121–22, 123, 126, 128, 156, 234n4; boredom, 200; contracts with Forest Service, 190; good relations with Rainbow Family, 198–99; harassment of Rainbows, 23, 116, 190, 191, 192, 199, 200; road-blocks, 145, 190, 234n4
Pond duck, 76
Popeye the Sailor Man, 99

Prasadam, 76
Prayer, 26, 31, 32
Presti, Mike, 194
Primitivism, 37
Process points, 54, 230n16
Prophesy, 134–35, 137, 141, 143
Publications, 93–95
Public Lands, why Rainbows gather on, 184

Quaker, 40
Quebec, 40, 49, 52, 61, 70, 71, 84, 92, 94, 97,
    128, 144, 174–75, 182
Quintanar, Ray, 43

Racism, 109–10, 137
Rail Tramps, 100, 105–6, 109
Rainbow Guide, 57, 95–96, 101, 105, 233n21
Rainbow Hawk, 134
Rainbow names. *See* names
Rainbow Nation Without Borders, 137
Rainbow Oracle, 32, 68, 132, 133, 135, 137
Rainbow Peace Projects International Newsletter,
    94, 134
*Rainbow Tribe: Ordinary People Journying on the
    Red Road*, 138
Rainbow Warriors, Legend of, 109–10, 135; *see
    also* Warriors of the Rainbow
Rainbows (in the sky), 12, 63, 136
Rap 107, 22, 25, 66, 96, 114, 206, 214
Rap 151, 127
Rap 151: The Flip Side, 127
Rap 701, 114, 171–72
Rastafarianism, 35, 104, 233n3
Raves, 153
Reagan-Bush-Clinton era, 33
Recruitment, 113, 125, 127, 129, 183, 205, 211,
    212; of minorities, 109; *see also* membership
Recycling, 20, 66, 86, 175, 212
Remi, 104
Renunciation, 113
Revitalization movements, 31
Ridgeway, James, 189–90
Ridgeway Record, 160
Rifkin, Jeremy, 97
Road Dogs, 100, 102, 105–6, 109
Roanoke, 146
Robert's *Rules of Order*, 54
Robie, Harry, 139
Rocinante, 210, 230n14
Rocky Mountain News, 154, 166

Roots, 34–37
Rowe, Jonathan, 71
Rumor Control, 66
Rumors, 75, 232n6
Ruskin Cooperative, 95, 181, 214
Russia, 33, 97

Sanchez, Victor, 140
San Diego Union-Tribune, 154
Savoye, Rob, 96, 233n22
Scouting, 46, 61, 63, 230n8
Scribe, 54
Schuler, James, 173, 199
Schwartzbaum, Joseph, 103, 115
Scott, Bob, 180
Seals, David, 141
Seed Camp, 18, 22, 45–48, 53, 64–65, 75–76,
    92, 105, 109, 171, 179, 185, 208, 230n9
Seton, Ernest and Julia, 132, 136
Sexism, 105–8
Sexual relations, 205
Shakers, 44, 90, 107, 109, 112
Shanti Sena, 17, 26, 118–25, 126–27, 128,
    234n5; Council, 119
Sherrill, Greg, 114, 120
Sierra Club, 35, 196
Sirius Community, 56
Sister's Circle, 106
Sister's Space, 106
Site selection and layout, 52–53, 61–62
Sitting Bull, 133
Size, Rainbow Family, 40, 97
Skaneateles Community, 112, 205
Skow, John, 33, 204
Sky Bear, 39, 54
Smith, Andrea, 131, 140
Snickers, 71–72
Snyder, Gary, 31
Social Class. *See* Class issues
The Society of Separatists of Zoar, Ohio, 100
Solomon, Norman, 148
South Dakota, 57, 133
Spain, 97
Spirituality vs. Politics, 111–12, 117
Spring Council, 50, 52, 53
Squatters: Europe, 33; New York City, 4
Stanich, 158–59
Starwatcher, Mark, 88, 101
Stonehenge festival, 33
Sufi beliefs, 32, 34, 36

Sugar, 76, 77
Sun Bear, 56, 140, 231n20; *see also* Bear Tribe
Superior National Forest, 67, 164
Supply Council, 22, 70, 85
Swager, Lloyd, 172
Swami Mommy, 175
Swanson, Nancy, 131
Sweat lodges, 131, 138
Sweet, Sheriff Ray, 162–63
Systema, 33, 229n4

Taco Mike, 64, 73, 75, 79, 86, 88; *see also*
    kitchens: Taco Hilton
Tampa Tribune, 154
Taoism, 32, 34, 36
Teachings of Don Carlos, The, 140
Television, 17
Temporary Autonomous Zone (TAZ), 97–98,
    204
Tennessee, 57
Teter, Don, 172, 178–79
Texas, 44, 45, 50, 96, 97, 134, 151, 156, 165,
    174, 179, 183, 188, 189, 193, 200
Thanksgiving Council, 50–55, 109, 144
Theater, 28, 68
Thomas, Gary, 103–4
Thumper, 172
Time magazine, 33, 204
Timekeeper, 54
Ting, 33, 229n3
Tobacco, 76
Trade Circle, 71–72
Traugot, Michael, 77
True Story, 159
Truthhawk, 45
Twin Oaks Community, 69, 72, 107, 108
Tygart Valley Press, 178–79

Umpqua National Forest, 172
Union Colony, 87
United Press International, 149–51, 161–63
United States Border Patrol, 191
United States Customs Service, 156, 191
United States Fish and Wildlife Service, 191
United States National Forest Service, 14, 43,
    46, 48, 62, 111, 119, 121, 122, 125, 152,
    153, 156, 179, 183, 184–201; collaborative
    projects with Rainbow Family, 173–74;
    confusion in dealing with non-hierarchical
    people, 185; decentralized organization,
185; disruption of cleanup, 186, 174;
    expenditures, 70, 185, 190, 191, 193–95;
    Good Host approach, 186, 190; harassment
    of medical personnel, 186; harassment of
    Rainbow Family, 115–17, 174, 190; illegality
    of video surveillance, 189, 236n6; Incident
    Command, 162, 164, 196; intelligence
    reports, 185, 192; judicial condemnation of
    permit system, 188; judicial condemnation
    of selective enforcement, 187–88; Law
    Enforcement Ground Rules, 120; media
    management, 160, 161–65; misinformation,
    95–96, 155, 163, 167, 174, 182, 233n21;
    new regulations, 200; operating plan, 22;
    paternalism, 150, 195–96; poetry, 195;
    Rainbow Family judgment against, 189;
    rangers going native, 198–99; Rehabilitation
    Plan, 171; survey of local business owners,
    176; threats against Rainbow Family, 189
United States National Park Service, 165, 192;
    intelligence reports, 117, 119, 120, 196,
    235n2
Utah, 33
Utopian publications, 19th century, 95

Vagabonds, 37, 97
Valley Voice, The, 160
Varkonyi, Tina, 91
Vegetarianism, 53, 75–77, 86, 212; *see also* meat
Vermont, 49, 79, 84, 97, 101, 126, 142, 174,
    192, 199
Vibeswatchers, 51, 52, 54
Vietnam veterans, 4, 34, 80, 122, 159
Violence, 120, 123, 125–30, 204, 207
Vision Council, 44–45, 49, 50, 57, 60–61, 140
Vortex Festival, 32

Wagner, John, 107
Wallace, Anthony, 212
Warren, Josiah, 69
Warren Times Observer, The, 160
Warriors of the Rainbow, 133, 135–36, 137
Warriors of the Rainbow, 134, 135, 143–44
Wash station (dish): description of, 5
Wash station (foot): description of, 8–9
Washington, 199
Washington Post, 117, 154, 161
Washington Times, 154
Water: potable, 24, 47, 61, 63, 75, 78–80, 85,
    88, 116, 122, 126, 185, 208, 232n15

Water Singing on the Rocks, 81, 82, 88, 179, 185, 189
Watermelons, 14–15
Watson, Detective Curtis, 194
Wavy Gravy, 33
Wayland, Julius, 95
Weapons, 191
Webber, Everett, 77
Weed, Ron, 121
Weinberg, Bill, 168
Well Being Center, 123, 125
Wendell, Massachusetts, 49–50
West Virginia, 84, 117, 162, 172, 178–79
Wetmore, Joseph, 40, 48, 71, 99, 121
White Raven, 60–61, 140
Wick, Barthinius, 55
Williams, William Carlos, 133
Willoya, William, 133, 135, 137, 139
Wing, Stephen, 93
Wingel, Gillette, 145–46

Winter Council, 50, 53
Winthrop, John, 37
Wirtshafter, Don, 91
Women, disenfranchisement in nineteenth-century utopian communities, 55–56
Woodstock Festival, 68, 97
Work, 15, 41, 69, 85–90, 108, 126; job rotation, 90, 97, 232n18
Worster, Donald, 80
Wright, David, 173
Wright, Francis, 107
Wu, Clara, 158
Wyoming, 32, 57, 90, 97

Yes Educational Society, 138
Yippies, 118

Zeus, 57
Zimmerman, Diane, 64, 86
Zimmerman, Jack, 42

People of the Rainbow was designed and typeset on a Macintosh computer system using PageMaker software. The text is set in Gill Sans Regular, titles and headings are set in Gill Sans Ultra Bold, and chapter numerals are set in Wildstyle. This book was designed and composed by Todd Duren and was printed and bound by Thomson-Shore, Inc. The recycled paper used in this book is designed for an effective life of at least three hundred years.